Thomas G. Jackson

Dalmatia, the Quarnero and Istria

With Cettigne in Montenegro and the island of Grado. Vol. 1

Thomas G. Jackson

Dalmatia, the Quarnero and Istria
With Cettigne in Montenegro and the island of Grado. Vol. 1

ISBN/EAN: 9783337244606

Printed in Europe, USA, Canada, Australia, Japan

Cover: Foto ©Andreas Hilbeck / pixelio.de

More available books at **www.hansebooks.com**

DALMATIA

THE QUARNERO AND ISTRIA

WITH

CETTIGNE IN MONTENEGRO AND THE ISLAND OF GRADO

BY

T. G. JACKSON, M.A., F.S.A.

HONORARY FELLOW OF WADHAM COLLEGE, OXFORD
ARCHITECT
AUTHOR OF 'MODERN GOTHIC ARCHITECTURE'

IN THREE VOLUMES

VOLUME I

Oxford
AT THE CLARENDON PRESS
1887

[*All rights reserved*]

TO

MY WIFE

THRICE MY COMPANION

ON THE FARTHER SHORES OF ADRIA

I DEDICATE

THIS RESULT OF OUR TRAVELS

PREFACE.

It is not only now when Europe waits to know whether the war-cloud that threatens her will first burst in thunder on the Rhine or on the Danube, nor only in modern times since the Eastern question has arisen to vex politicians, that the attention of Englishmen has been engaged by the Balkan peninsula and the eastern sea-board of the Adriatic. English travellers were the first to make these countries and the monuments of art which they contain known to western Europeans. George Wheler visited Spalato in 1675, and has left us the earliest description of the ruins of Diocletian's palace; Robert Adam's account of that building, published in 1764, is still the best; the antiquities of Pola were explored by Stuart in 1750, and splendidly illustrated in the fourth volume of the great work that goes by his name; Sir Gardner Wilkinson in 1848 published an excellent general account of Dalmatia Montenegro and part of Herzegovina; Mr. Paton's book followed; more recently Professor

Freeman has published some brief sketches of the earlier architecture of some of the maritime towns; while the well-known researches of Mr. Arthur Evans in the interior of Bosnia and Herzegovina have introduced us to a part of Europe till then unknown. Even foreigners who have written on these lands have found more readers in our country than their own, and Professor Eitelberger of Vienna tells us that the first edition of his book on the mediæval art of Dalmatia was almost entirely bought up in England[1].

Of all these South Slavonic countries none in the estimation of the artist and the historian can compare with Dalmatia, the narrow strip of rock and moorland between the mountains and the sea which fenced out the Turk from the Adriatic, and stayed the tide of Moslem conquest in the south. In Dalmatia arts and letters flourished and commerce sprang up with all her civilizing influences, while the Slavonic kingdoms of the interior remained in semi-barbarism, wasting their strength in internecine struggles, and paving the way for the westward progress of the Turkish hordes. This superiority of Dalmatia is due partly to her maritime position

---

[1] He says, '*Dalmatien war den Engländern seit jeher ein interessantes Land, den meisten Oesterreichern blieb es eine " Terra incognita."*' Kunstdenkmale Dalmatiens, Preface to 2nd edition, 1884.

which brought her into contact with Italy and the West, but still more to the survival along her coast of certain ancient Roman municipalities, which in the midst of a flood of barbarian colonization kept alive the traditions of civil order, settled law, and an ancient culture. Throughout the middle ages they jealously maintained the civic liberties they inherited from the Roman empire; and while outside their boundaries all the world spoke Illyric, the citizens still used the language of their Roman forefathers till it passed into its modern form of Italian. To this day they cling to their '*coltura Latina*' with passionate affection; and though the Croats, backed by the Austrian government, are fighting hard to Slavonize the cities and reduce them to the same rule as the rural districts, the issue of the struggle is still doubtful. The survival of these waifs and strays of the Roman empire is unique; it is an historical phenomenon of almost unparalleled interest; and one cannot contemplate without regret the possibility of its disappearance.

The Roman antiquities of Dalmatia and Istria have been well described and illustrated, but the rich stores of mediæval art in which those countries abound have hitherto been but little noticed and have remained generally unknown. The only work of importance on this subject is that of Professor

Eitelberger, who describes with considerable minuteness the Romanesque and Gothic architecture at Arbe Zara Traü Spalato and Ragusa, and in his second edition has added some brief notes on Sebenico and the valley of the Kerka. In another work he has described the churches of Parenzo and Grado. His premature death in 1885 prevented the visit he had proposed making to Cattaro in the company of Professor Gelcich of Ragusa. His work stops short of the renaissance, and leaves untouched not only Cattaro but all the islands, which are scarcely inferior in interest to the mainland.

In the following pages I have endeavoured to give a tolerably complete description of all the architectural monuments of importance on the mainland of Dalmatia, the islands, the Croatian shore of the Quarnero, and the Litorale of Istria from Pola to Aquileja. To this I have added an account of the island of Grado, which though never like Aquileja part of Istria, is so intimately connected with Dalmatia as the metropolitan see of the Venetian dominion that it naturally belongs to my subject. Grado is I believe unknown to English art students except by report, and many of the places I shall describe will be I am sure unknown to them even by report. Few persons have any idea of the beauty and extent of the art-treasures of these countries, which indeed so far as I know have never before been explored from end to end by a professional student of architecture.

The book is fully illustrated with plates and cuts. The illustrations are not confined to architectural subjects, but include several examples of church plate and silversmiths' work, in which Dalmatia is unusually rich, and also several general views of the towns which will give an idea of Dalmatian scenery. A few illustrations, chiefly plans of buildings, are taken from other works, and these are in all cases acknowledged; the rest are from original drawings of my own.

The brief sketches of the history of Dalmatia and that of Istria which will be found in the first and last volumes are gathered from a variety of sources, some of which are not easily accessible, and they will therefore it is hoped have a certain value. I have also prefixed to each place a short sketch of the local history, derived in many cases from unpublished records. The materials for Dalmatian history can be collected only in the country; the works of the local historians, of whom there are many, often exist only in MS., and even when printed are seldom found beyond the province. Many of them have been prepared with great care, and most of them contain valuable extracts from original documents; but the reader has to be on his guard how he accepts the conclusions of a Latin or a Croat writer in a country where politics of creed and race run so high.

Travelling in Dalmatia is simple enough for those who are satisfied with the glimpse at the four or five principal towns which may be had by travelling down the coast in the Austrian Lloyd's steamers. To do more than this is not so easy, as may be gathered from several incidents of our travels recorded in the following pages, and ordinary tourists would do well to keep to the beaten track. But there are no difficulties to deter those who are strong and well, and enjoy exposure and exercise, and can put up with rustic fare and homely quarters, and speak the Italian language. In all my three visits to Dalmatia, in 1882, 1884, and 1885, my wife was with me, and we agreed that we had often fared worse nearer home. The trifling discomforts we encountered were more than compensated by the pleasure of exploration; the keen delight of sailing away perhaps in early morning from some little mainland port to the unknown wonders of some island, ignorant what there might be to see there, no guide-book having robbed us of our discovery, but never except once failing to find beauties of art and nature exceeding our expectations.

My task has been a laborious one, and has occupied more time than I could well spare from my art: it would have been impossible but for the ready help afforded me on all occasions by the local authorities, and the antiquaries and others in the country interested in my work. To name all to whom I am indebted would be difficult; but I must in particular express my obligations to the archbishop of Zara for leave to enter the Benedictine nunnery; to Monsignor Bianchi, Professors Brunelli and Smirich, and Signor Artale, of Zara; to Monsignor Fosco, bishop of Sebenico, and Dr. Galvani of the same city; to Professor Bulić of Spalato; to Conte Fanfogna-Garagnin, podestà of Traù, and his sons Conte Gian Domenico and Conte Gian Luca; to Canonico Don Andrea Alibranti and Professor Vid Vuletić Vukasović of Curzola; to the bishop of Ragusa for access to the treasury and the statuette of S. Biagio; to Professor Giuseppe Gelcich of Ragusa, who accompanied me to Cattaro, his native place; to Signor Hortis, the civic librarian of Trieste; to Dr. Carlo Gregorutti of Fiumicello near Aquileja; and to many others, from whom I have not only received much valuable information and help, but in many cases copies of their own publications, from which I have derived material assistance. I have also been indebted to Mr. Richard

Greenham and the late Mr. Grant Greenham of Trieste, and to Signor Simeone Salghetti-Drioli of Zara, for much hospitable attention and many useful introductions. I cannot say enough of the kindness and hospitality with which we were received everywhere on our travels by those to whom we brought introductions, and not unfrequently by others to whom our only introduction was that we were strangers. The modern Dalmatians deserve to inherit the character given by an ancient geographer to their predecessors the Illyrians of old :—

θεοσεβεῖς δ' αὐτοὺς ἄγαν
καὶ σφόδρα δικαίους, φασὶ, καὶ φιλοξένους.

T. G. J.

11, NOTTINGHAM PLACE:
March 4, 1887.

INDEX TO THE ILLUSTRATIONS.

Map of Dalmatia, Istria and Croatia at beginning of Vol. I.

	Volume and page.	Plate.	Cut.
ALMISSA.			
View of town and castle Mirabella	ii. 168		52
AQUILEJA.			
Duomo. Interior view	iii. 396	LXIV.	
Do. Capital in crypt	iii. 397		122
Do. Patriarchal throne	iii. 400	...	123
Do. Ascent to choir	iii. 402	LXV	
ARBE.			
Palazzo Nimira	iii. 208	...	94
Seal of Marc' Antonio de Dominis	iii. 210	...	95
Campanile	iii. 210	LVII.	
Do. Inscription on spire	iii. 212		96
Duomo. Inscription in south wall	iii. 216	...	97
Do. Capital in nave	i. 214	i. Fig. 5.	
Do. Ciborio	iii. 218	LVIII.	
Do. Reliquary of S. Cristoforo	iii. 221	...	98
S. Giovanni Battista. Plan.	iii. 226	...	99
Do. View of the apse	iii. 226	LIX.	
Do. Inscription belonging to, now in S. Giustina	iii. 233		100
View of the city	iii. 237		101
BURNUM.			
Roman arches. Šuplja Crkva	ii. 194		55
CASTELNUOVO.			
General view	iii. 19		73
Convent of Savina. Crosses in treasury	iii. 24	LI.	
Do. Silver plate in do.	iii. 28	LII.	

	Volume and page.	Plate.	Cut.
CATTARO.			
Details of the duomo and other buildings	iii. 38	LIII.	
The Duomo. Sacristy doorway	iii. 43	...	74
Do. Inscription over sacristy doorway	iii. 43		75
Do. Epitaph of Andreascio and Maria Saracenis	iii. 44		76
Do. Ciborio	iii. 45		77
Do. Inscription to Bishop Deodati	iii. 47		78
Plans of La Collegiata and S. Luca	iii. 50		79
CETTIGNE.			
View of convent and old tower	iii. 60		80
CHERSO.			
Street view	iii. 115		85
CURZOLA.			
Seal of the Comune	ii. 237	...	56
General view of town	ii. 248	XXXIII.	
Duomo. West front	ii. 250	XXXIV.	
Do. Interior view	ii. 252	XXXV.	
Do. Capital in south nave arcade	ii. 254	XXXVI.	
Do. Sacristy doorway in north aisle	ii. 256	...	58
Do. Mason's marks on the apses	ii. 265	...	59
Knocker on door of Palazzo Arneri	ii. 268	...	60
Cloister of the Badia	ii. 274	XXXVII.	
Epitaph in church of the Badia	ii. 276	...	61
DERNIS.			
Turkish minaret	ii. 180		53
Capital of Turkish workmanship	ii. 181		54
FIUME.			
Roman arch	iii. 165		91
Epitaph in church of Tersatto	iii. 170		92
GRADO.			
View of the city from the lagune	iii. 409		124
Duomo. Ground-plan	iii. 413		125
Do. Inscription in mosaic floor	iii. 415		126
Do. Capital in nave	iii. 417		127

Index to the Illustrations.

		Volume and page.	Plate.	Cut.
Duomo.	Pierced window slab	iii. 420	...	128
Do.	Part of mosaic pavement, in colour	iii. 422	LXVI.	
Do.	Patriarchal throne...	iii. 427	...	129
Do.	Details of do.	iii. 428	...	130
Do.	Pulpit	iii. 430	...	131

ISTRIA.
    Group of Istrian peasants ... iii. 249   102

JÁK (*in Hungary*).
    East end of church and various details of its architecture ... ii. 154   XXV.
    West doorway of do. ... ii. 156   XXVI.

LESINA.
	Vol./page	Plate	Cut
View of the city with the tower of S. Marco	ii. 218	XXVII.	
Porta Maggiore and Palazzo Raimondi	ii. 220	XXVIII.	
The Loggia and Forte Spagnuolo	ii. 222	XXIX.	
The Duomo. Ambo and choir stalls...	ii. 224	XXX.	
Do. Pastorale of Bp. Patrizio	ii. 226	XXXI.	
S. Francesco. Nave window...	ii. 229	...	56
Do. West doorway	ii. 230	XXXII.	

MEZZO.
	Vol./page	Plate	Cut
Chalice	ii. 388	L.	
Window in chiesa matrice	ii. 390	...	71
Tower of S. Domenico	ii. 394	...	72
Diagram of paintings in reredos of Franciscan church	ii. 396		72*a*

MUGGIA VECCHIA.
	Vol./page	Plate	Cut
Ground-plan of church	iii. 372		120
Interior view ...	iii. 373		121

NONA.
	Vol./page	Plate	Cut
Views and plans of S. Croce and S. Nicolò...	i. 342	XI.	
Doorhead from S. Croce	i. 214	I. Fig. 2.	
S. Marcella. Capital from ...	i. 214	I. Fig. 4.	
S. Ambrogio. Exterior view	i. 349	...	18
Do. Detail of window in do....	i. 349	...	19

xviii   *Index to the Illustrations.*

		Volume and page.	Plate.	Cut.
NOVIGRAD.				
View of the castle		i. 327	...	16
Sculptured panel		i. 214	I. Fig. 3.	
OSSERO.				
General view		iii. 100	...	81
Nave capital		iii. 101	...	82
Ostensorio in treasury of duomo		iii. 102	LIV.	
Episcopal throne		iii. 104	...	83
Sketch-plan of ancient basilica		iii. 106	...	84
PARENZO.				
Duomo. Ground-plan		iii. 311		106
Do. Inscription of Euphrasius on mosaics of apse		iii. 312	...	Fig. 106ᵃ.
Do. Do. Do. on ciborio		iii. 313	...	Fig. 106ᵇ.
Do. The Atrium		iii. 316	LX.	
Do. Monogram of Bishop Euphrasius		iii. 317	...	107
Do. Nave capitals, &c.		iii. 318	LXI.	
Do. Interior of the apse		iii. 320	LXII.	
Do. Mosaic floor in chapel B		iii. 326	...	108
Do. Do. do. C		iii. 326	...	109
Do. Stalls in a side chapel		iii. 328	LXIII.	
Canonica. View of front		iii. 330	...	110
Do. Window		iii. 331	...	111
Do. Inscription		iii. 332	...	112
POLA.				
Inscription of Bp. Handegis on the duomo		iii. 295	...	103
S. Michele in Monte. Ground-plan		iii. 298	...	104
S. Maria di Canneto. Fragment		iii. 301	...	105
RAGUSA.				
Old doorway on hill near the duomo		ii. 327	...	62
Panel from S. Stefano		i. 214	I. Fig. 1.	
Palace. View of the Piazza, with the Rector's palace, Dogana and Torre dell' Orologio		ii. 332	XXXVIII.	
Do. Geometrical details of the palace		ii. 333	XXXIX.	
Do. Æsculapius capital		ii. 334	XL.	

Index to the Illustrations. xix

		Volume and page.	Plate.	Cut.
RAGUSA (*continued*).				
Palace. Capital with amorini		ii. 335	...	63
Do. Capital (B) and capital with judgment of Solomon		ii. 336	XLI.	
Do. Cortile of Palace and that of the Sponza		ii. 342	XLII.	
Do. Console with the figure of Justice		ii. 344		64
Do. Capital with the Rector administering justice		ii. 344	XLIII.	
The reliquary of S. Biagio in the duomo		ii. 350	XLIV.	
The Sponza		ii. 358	XLV.	
Dominican convent. The cloister		ii. 364	XLVI.	
Do. Triple arch at west end of church		ii. 366	XLVII.	
Franciscan convent. The cloister		ii. 370	XLVIII.	
Do. do. Capitals in cloister		ii. 370	...	65
Do. do. do.		ii. 371	...	66
Do. do. do.		ii. 372	...	67
Do. Epitaph of Mag. Mycha		ii. 373	...	68
Do. Do. of Gino di Alexio		ii. 373	...	69
Do. Do. of Mag. Radun		ii. 373	...	70
S. Biagio. Silver statuette of the Saint		ii. 374	XLIX.	
SALONA.				
Map of the city		ii. 87	...	42
Basilica. Ground-plan		ii. 89	...	43
Amphitheatre		ii. 98	...	44
S. LORENZO IN PASENATICO.				
Duomo. Ground-plan and section		iii. 336	...	113
Do. Details of columns of do.		iii. 337	...	114
Do. Pierced stone window in do.		iii. 338	...	115
SEBENICO.				
View of town from the landing-place		i. 376	...	21
Duomo. Exterior, from the piazza		i. 378	XII.	
Do. Ground-plan		i. 382	...	22
Do. The Lion doorway		i. 384	XIII.	
Do. Interior		i. 386	...	22*a*
Do. Capital of north-west pier of lantern		i. 388	XIV.	

	Volume and page.	Plate.	Cut.
SEBENICO (continued).			
Duomo. Stringcourse over nave arcades	i. 390		23
Do. View of west end and campanile	i. 392	XV.	
Do. Apse window	i. 399		24
Doorway of house belonging to Giorgio Orsini	i. 406		25
Costume of peasants	i. 408		26
SEGNA.			
Castle of Nehaj	iii. 193		93
SPALATO.			
Plan of Diocletian's palace	ii. 22		27
Porta Aurea. Elevation and plan	ii. 28		28
Temple of Jupiter (*the duomo*). Ground-plan	ii. 33	...	29
Do. Do. Section	ii. 33	...	30
The Duomo. Interior	ii. 34	XVI.	
Do. Finial on roof	ii. 39	...	31
Do. The pulpit	ii. 44	XVII.	
Do. Capital of pulpit	ii. 45	...	32
Do. Panels of great doors	ii. 48	XVIII.	
Do. The choir stalls	ii. 50	XIX.	
The Campanile. Elevation, plans and details	ii. 54	XX.	
Do. Escutcheon on do.	ii. 56	...	33
Treasury. Cypher on a chalice	ii. 60	...	34
The Baptistery (*Temple of Æsculapius*). Plan and section	ii. 65		35
Do. Figure sculpture on font	ii. 69		36
Epitaph of archbishop John of Ravenna	ii. 70		37
Epitaph of archbishop Laurentius	ii. 70		38
Epitaph of princesses Catharine and Margaret	ii. 71	...	39
SS. Trinità. Plan, section and elevation	ii. 73		40
Staircase in cortile of a private house	ii. 82		41
TRAÜ			
General view from the sea	ii. 106		45

Index to the Illustrations. xxi

		Volume and page.	Plate.	Cut.
TRAÜ (continued).				
Duomo.	Ground-plan	ii. 110	...	46
Do.	West doorway	ii. 112	XXI.	
Do.	Inscription on lintel of do.	ii. 113	...	47
Do.	Detail of sculpture on do.	ii. 118	XXII.	
Do.	East end, exterior view	ii. 120	XXIII.	
Do.	Nave capital	ii. 123		48
Do.	Silver brocca in treasury	ii. 126	...	49
Do.	Inscription on campanile	ii. 138	...	50
The Loggia.	Capital of	ii. 141	...	51
Do.	View	ii. 142	XXIV.	
TRIESTE.				
Duomo.	Ground-plan	iii. 354		116
Do.	Capital of northern nave	iii. 358		117
Do.	do. of southern apse	iii. 359		118
Do.	Monogram of Cireneus	iii. 361		119
UGLIANO.				
Ploughs used by Dalmatian peasantry		i. 337		17
VEGLIA.				
Duomo.	Capital in nave	iii. 141	...	86
Do.	Capital in nave	i. 214	I. Fig. 9.	
Do.	Inscription on a column of nave	iii. 143	...	87
Do.	Interior. Nave column and ambo	iii. 144	...	87a
Do.	Pala of silver gilt	iii. 148	LV.	
Do.	Do. one of the figures in do.	iii. 148	...	88
S. Quirino. East end		iii. 152	LVI.	
S. Maria. Capital from		i. 214	I. Fig. 7.	
Inscription on Torre dei Frangipani		iii. 153	...	89
View from the sea		iii. 154	...	90
VRANA.				
View of castle		i. 360		20
ZARA.				
Duomo and S. Donato. Plans of		i. 251	...	1
S. Donato. Doorway of		i. 253	...	2
Do. Interior of		i. 256	II.	
S. Pietro Vecchio. Plan of		i. 262	...	3
S. Lorenzo. Interior and plan of		i. 264	III.	

ZARA (continued).

		Volume and page.	Plate.	Cut.
S. Lorenzo. Capital		i. 214	I. Fig. 6.	
S. Orsola. Plan of		i. 266	...	4
Duomo. Stringcourse over nave arcades		i. 271	...	5
Do. Interior of choir		i. 272	IV.	
Do. Inscription on ciborio		i. 274	...	6
Do. Choir stalls		i. 275	...	7
Do. West front		i. 278	V.	
Do. Pastorale of archbishop Valaresso		i. 282	VI.	
S. Grisogono. Ground-plan		i. 289	...	8
Do. Eastern apses. Exterior		i. 290	VII.	
S. Maria. Campanile		i. 300	VIII.	
Do. Plans and sections of Sala Capitolare		i. 302	...	9
Do. Stringcourse in do.		i. 303	...	10
Do. Tomb of the abbess Vekenega		i. 304		11
Do. Inscription on do.		i. 305		12
Do. Capitals in chapel under tower		i. 307	...	13
S. Francesco. Choir stalls		i. 311	...	14
Do. Chalices		i. 312	IX.	
Do. Old capital lying at		i. 214	I. Fig. 8.	
S. Simeone. One end of the silver ark		i. 318	X.	
Window and balcony		i. 320	...	15

CHRONOLOGICAL LIST OF THOSE INSCRIPTIONS WHICH ARE GIVEN IN FACSIMILE[1].

A.D.			Vol.	Page.
c. 530–540.	Parenzo.	Roman characters... ...	III.	312.
571–580.	Grado.	Do. do.	III.	415, Plate LXVI, 422.
680.	Spalato.	Irregular Roman. Square Os	II.	70, Fig. 37.
c. 800–820.	Cattaro.	Fanciful Roman. Square Os	III.	43, 44.
857.	Pola.	Do. do. Square Cs	III.	295.
1099.	Spalato.	Roman approaching Lombardics	II.	70, Fig. 38.
1111.	Zara.	Do. do. do. much abbreviated ...	I.	305.
1190.	Veglia.	Do. do. do.	III.	143–153.
c. 1200 ?	Arbe.	Do. do. do.	III.	212.
1240.	Traù.	Lombardics	II.	113.
1242.	Spalato.	Do.	II.	71.
1251.	Parenzo.	Do.	III.	332.
1254.	Cattaro.	Do.	III.	47.
1287.	Arbe.	Do.	III.	216.
c. 1317 ?	Ragusa.	Do.	II.	373, Fig. 68.
1332.	Zara.	Do. ...	I.	274.
1363.	Ragusa.	Do.	II.	373, Fig. 69.
1422.	Traù.	Do.	II.	138.
1428.	Ragusa.	Do.	II.	373, Fig. 70.
1430.	Curzola.	Do.	II.	276.
c. 1439 ?	Tersatto.	Roman fancifully abbreviated	III.	170.
1454.	Arbe.	Roman	III.	233.

[1] This series gives the history of the character used from the sixth century to the renaissance. It will be observed that the Gothic or 'black letter' is absent. I can recall no instances of it in Dalmatia except those noted in vol. i. pp. 318, 393, 397, and even in those cases it is mixed with Lombardic or Roman lettering.

CONTENTS OF VOLUME I.

CHAPTER I.
PAGE

THE HISTORY OF DALMATIA 1
First Period, Dalmatia under the Romans, pp. 1–10. *Second Period*, Dalmatia under the Byzantine empire, down to the arrival of the Hungarians, pp. 10–35. *Third Period*, Dalmatia contested by Venice and Hungary, pp. 36–141. *Fourth Period*, Dalmatia under Venice, pp. 141–164. Social condition under Venice, pp. 168–181. Modern condition of Dalmatia, pp. 181–192. Table of Kings of Hungary, p. 193.

CHAPTER II.

DALMATIA 195
The country and the people, pp. 195–203. Sketch of the history of architecture in Dalmatia, pp. 203–226. List of principal buildings, with their dates, p. 226.

CHAPTER III.

ZARA 230
Description of the city, p. 230. History, p. 243. Roman remains, p. 246.

CHAPTER IV.

ZARA 249
S. Donato, p. 249. Other churches, pp. 261–267. The duomo, p. 267. Grisogono, p. 288. S. Maria, p. 296. S. Francesco, p. 309. S. Simeone, p. 312. Domestic architecture, p. 321.

CHAPTER V.
NOVIGRAD 322

CHAPTER VI.
S. MICHELE D' UGLIANO 332

CHAPTER VII.
NONA 338

CHAPTER VIII.
VRANA 353

CHAPTER IX.
SEBENICO 368
History, p. 368. The city, p. 376. The duomo, p. 378. Other churches, p. 405. House of Giorgio Orsini, p. 406. Costume, p. 407. The river Kerka, p. 409. Scardona, 411. The falls of the Kerka, p. 414.

APPENDIX.
Contract of Giorgio Orsini, Architect of the duomo of Sebenico 416

ERRATA TO VOLUME I.

P. 27, line 2, *for* them *read* the Narentines.
P. 29, line 19, *for* Belgrade *read* Belgrad.
P. 33, line 9, and p. 153, line 25, *for* Illyrian *read* Illyric.
P. 39, line 27, *for* or Vranjica *read* of Vranjica.
P. 41, line 2, *for* Tartar *read* Scythian.
Pp. 43, 77, 229, 297, *for* Ursini *read* Orsini.
P. 61, line 2, *for* Mega Juppanus *read* Megajupanus.
P. 178, line 9, *for* Titian *read* Tintoret.
P. 195, *for* Diolcea *read* Dioclea.
P. 196, note, line 1, *for* Primorje *read* Primorie.
P. 274, line 19, *for* Littorale *read* Litorale.
P. 281, line 25, *for* Cassione *read* S. Cassiano.
P. 325, add references to notes.
P. 416, heading to Appendix, *for* p. 98 *read* p. 389.

I. PEL

NOSA

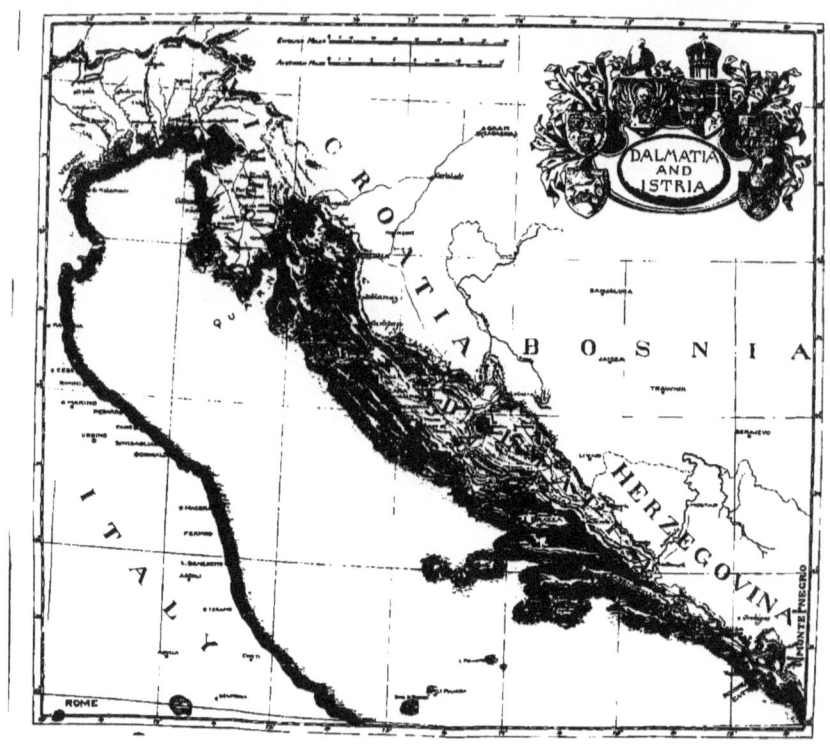

CHAPTER I.

History of Dalmatia.

First Period.—Dalmatia under the Romans, and down to the fall of the Western empire, A.D. 476.

Second Period.—Dalmatia under the Byzantine empire, down to the arrival of the Hungarians, A.D. 1102.

Third Period.—Dalmatia contested by Hungary and Venice, down to the final Venetian occupation, A.D. 1409–1420.

Fourth Period.—Dalmatia under the Venetians, down to the fall of the Republic, A.D. 1797.

Review of the social condition of Dalmatia under Venetian rule from A.D. 1409–1797.

Present condition of the province.

Chronological table of the Kings of Hungary down to 1526.

FIRST PERIOD.

Dalmatia under the Romans.

THE early history of Illyria, like that of other countries, is lost in myths and legends. Its name is variously derived from Illyrius a son of the Cyclops Polyphemus and Galatea[1], or from Hyllus a son of Hercules who conquered it and founded a kingdom there; the Argonauts find their way thither by ascending the Ister from the Euxine sea, and descending a mythical branch into the Adriatic near the peninsula which they name Istria in memory of their route; and the Briseides insulae in the Quarnero are renamed after Ab-

Early inhabitants.

[1] Appian.

syrtus, the brother of Medea, who there met his unhappy fate. After the Trojan war Idomeneus and Diomede and other roving Homeric heroes wander to the shores of Dalmatia, and the Liburni, expelled from Asia, conquer the country, and settle there.

Celtic inmigration. B.C. c. 600.

When the page of veritable history opens we find the Liburni occupying the country as far south as the Titius or Kerka, a race of hardy mariners who afterwards played their part in the triumphs of the Roman navy. But in the seventh century before Christ a Celtic element was infused into the population by the irruption of the Galli Senones who founded Senogallia in Italy, Tedastum (Modrussa) and Senia (Segna) in what is now Croatia, and established a kingdom of Illyria, extending over Istria, Carnia and the northern part of Macedonia, with Scodra or Scutari in Albania as its capital [1]. The Greeks, ever seeking to plant fresh colonies on the shores of the Mediterranean, did not overlook the natural advantages of a coast so sheltered by islands and indented by natural havens. A colony of Sicilian Greeks from Syracuse was settled by Dionysius

Greek colonies. B.C. 406.

---

[1] Dr. Cubich traces some peculiarities of the dialect of the island of Veglia to a Celtic source (Notizie storiche sull' isola di Veglia). Franceschi (L'Istria, ch. 4) gives a list of proper names of places and families in Istria which have a Celtic origin. Mr. Evans (Bosnia and Herzegovina) compares Arauso (Vrana) with Arausio (Orange), Andetrium (Clissa) with Anderida (Pevensey), Narbona or Narona with Narbonne. Corinium (Karin) is our English Cirencester.

on the island of Issa (Lissa), and one from the B.C. 385.
island of Paros in the Aegean built a new Paros
or Pharos on the island of Lesina ; Dyrrhachium or
Epidamnus, Epidaurus, where Ragusa Vecchia now
stands, and Tragurium (Traü) were Greek colonies
on the mainland, the last named being peopled
by Syracusans from Issa, and inscriptions found
on the island of Curzola prove that there were
Greek settlements there also.

In the third century before Christ Illyria was Illyrian kingdom of Agron.
united under the powerful rule of Agron son of
Pleuratus, and his widow Teuta, regent during
the minority of her stepson Pineus, came into
collision with the Romans, who now for the first
time carried their arms across the Adriatic. The
islanders of Lissa, unable to protect themselves
against the attempts of the Illyrians on their
liberties, appealed to the Romans for protection. B.C. 232.
It was the interval of twenty-two years between
the first and second Punic wars; the Romans
had leisure to listen to the appeal, and they had
already received other complaints from Italian
merchantmen of the frequent piracies of the
Illyrians. Three ambassadors were sent to Queen
Teuta to command her to desist from injuring the
friends of the Republic, but the queen put two of
the envoys to death and imprisoned the third[1].

[1] The murdered ambassadors were honoured with statues at Rome. 'Hoc a Romano populo tribui solebat injuria caesis, sicut et P. Junio, et Tito Coruncano qui ab Teuca Illyriorum regina interfecti erant.' Plin. Nat. Hist. xxxiv. 6.

First Illyrian war.
B.C. 229.

The Romans at once sent into Illyria both consuls Cn. Fulvius Centumalus and L. Postumius Albinus with 20,000 infantry and 2000 cavalry. As usual they found allies in the enemies' ranks. Demetrius, a Greek who held Corcyra (Corfù) for Queen Teuta together with Pharos (Lesina) his native place, surrendered them both to Fulvius, and the queen was driven from one stronghold to another and finally shut up in Rhizon (Risano) in the Bocche di Cattaro, and compelled to sue for peace. Demetrius was rewarded with his native island Pharos and a share of the queen's dominions, and Teuta was compelled to pay tribute to Rome for the fourth part of her territory, which was all that was left to her.

Second Illyrian war.
B.C. 219.

Demetrius however was faithless to his new masters; on the death of Teuta he married Triteuta the mother of Pineus and repudiated wife of Agron, and making himself guardian of Pineus, who was still a minor, took advantage of the second Punic war to throw off his allegiance to the Romans. L. Aemilius Paullus was sent to chastise him, his stronghold Pharos was razed to the ground, and he himself driven to take refuge at the court of Macedon, where he continued for some time his intrigues against the Romans.

Istria revolts from Illyria.

The Illyrian kingdom began to fall to pieces after this time. The Istrians revolted and formed themselves into an independent state which maintained its liberties till B.C. 178, when it fell under the power of Rome. The Dalmatians who first begin to be heard of in the second century B.C. are said to have been Illyrians of the country between the Narenta and the Cettina (Narona and Tilurus) who revolted against Gentius the last king of Illyria, and following the example of the Istrians, established an independent republic around the city of Dalmium or Delminium, in the interior, which though sometimes tributary to Rome continued to exist for 200 years till finally absorbed into the Empire. Their territory was afterwards extended to the river Titius (Kerka) which thenceforward divided Dalmatia and Liburnia. *The Dalmatians become independent. B.C. 180.*

The Illyrian kingdom itself came to an end in B.C. 168 when Gentius was involved in the ruin of Perseus, and Macedonia and Illyria were made provinces of Rome. The interference of the Dalmatians with Roman allies brought upon them the chastisement of the Republic, and in the second Dalmatian war Delminium was destroyed by Publ. Scipio Nasica, after which the Dalmatians fixed their capital at Salona[1]. Salona was taken by L. *End of Illyrian kingdom. B.C. 168. First Dalmatian war. B.C. 156. Second do. B.C. 138.*

[1] Appian describes Delminium as 'egregie munitum, et operum machinarumque labor propter altitudinem moenium inutilis videbatur,' de bell. Illyr. The site of Delminium has been much disputed and was long thought undiscoverable. Thomas Archid. (1200–1268) says 'sed ubi haec civitas Delmis in Dalmatiae partibus fuerit non satis patet,' ch. 1, but he elsewhere mentions some old walls 'in superioribus partibus' which were said to represent it. Modern antiquaries believe they have found Delminium at Dumno or Duvno, a village in the interior near Sign, though some with Mommsen place it at Gardun near Trilj in the same district; vid. Bulletino di Storia Dalmata (Spalato, March, 1885).

Roman colonies.

Caecilius Metellus in 117, by surprise it is said, and was made a Roman colony, and in B.C. 78 a colony was planted at Jadera (Zara), a town already in alliance with Rome.

Fifth Dalmatian war.
B.C. 50.
Sixth do.
B.C. 48.

The Dalmatians continually molested the Roman colonies and towns, and taking advantage of the civil wars of Caesar and Pompey, for a time defied the power of Rome. One army sent by Caesar was destroyed, a second was driven back to Salona, and his lieutenant Vatinius, who was sent there in B.C. 45, held his ground with difficulty. Vatinius writes to Cicero from Narona that he had stormed six Dalmatian towns, and among them Narona the largest and strongest of them all, but had been unfairly obliged by the snow, cold and rain of a Dalmatian December to abandon his conquests. Cicero replies 'may the Gods plague the Dalmatians for giving you so much trouble,' and adds that the conquest of so warlike a people would add lustre to his achievements [1]. Vatinius however was not destined to reap any laurels

Seventh do.
B.C. 43.

there, for after the death of Caesar the Dalmatians attacked him and drove him with loss to Epidamnus (Durazzo).

Eighth do.
B.C. 34.

Octavianus in person led an army against the Dalmatians, B.C. 34, and recovered Promona, but he was wounded and did not subdue their resistance till his return in the following spring. In B.C. 29 he celebrated his Dalmatian triumph, and it is

---

[1] Ep. Lib. v. 10. It was Cicero's policy just then to be civil to Vatinius.

said that one of the two figures on the shield of the famous statue of Augustus in the Capitol represents a vanquished Dalmatian.

The final struggle of the Dalmatians for freedom was made A.D. 6, under Bato a Dalmatian general of courage and experience, and another Bato who was a Pannonian. They defeated a Roman army under Caecina and Tiberius, but were conquered by Germanicus, Tiberius, and Postumius; their last stronghold Andetrium (Clissa) surrendered, Bato was carried prisoner to Rome, and Dalmatia became finally part of the province of Illyricum. *Tenth Dalmatian war. A.D. 6.* *Dalmatia finally subdued. A.D. 9.*

Under the Roman Empire the maritime district of Dalmatia seems to have had a propraetor or legate of its own, and the whole province was divided into dioeceses or conventus each with a central city to which the inhabitants of the conventus resorted for public or private business, there being three such conventus in maritime Dalmatia, those of Scardona, Salona and Narona. Salona in time came to be looked upon as the capital of the province of Dalmatia and became a great and populous city, though Constantine Porphyrogenitus exaggerated its dimensions grossly when he described it as having been half as large as Constantinople.

Under the Empire Dalmatia probably flourished as it has never done since, though even then it seems to have met with something of the neglect that has at all times been its portion. Pliny apologises for detaining his readers with any mention of the people, or puzzling them with the uncouth names of their towns. And yet in every part of the province remains of Roman splendour are to be seen, affording evidence of wealth, culture, and considerable population in places that are now miserable villages like Nona Ossero Stobrez and Besca, or barren and uninhabited wildernesses like those where stand the two solitary arches of Burnum or the few shattered walls of vanished Promona[1].

A.D. 305. Diocletian abdicates. In A.D. 305 the Emperor Diocletian, a native of Dioclea, near the lake of Scutari, abdicated and retired to a villa he had built for himself at Aspalathus near Salona, where he lived till 313, one year after the victory of Constantine at the Milvian bridge.

A.D. 454. Dalmatia under Marcellinus. In the fifth century Marcellinus a general attached to Aetius escaped after the murder of his patron by Valentinian III, and on the death of Majorian established himself in Dalmatia as an independent prince. Marcellinus adhered to the religion of ancient Rome in an age when the Empire generally had become Christian. During his reign occurred the great irruption into Illyria of Goths Alans Vandals and Huns, and the Suevi *A.D. 461.* succeeded in penetrating as far as Dalmatia but met with a vigorous resistance and were compelled *A.D. 468.* to retire. Marcellinus bequeathed his sovereignty *Julius Nepos.* to his nephew Julius Nepos who had married a

---

[1] Ἐνδοξότερον τῶν ἄλλων ἑσπερίων θεμάτων τὸ τοιοῦτον θέμα ἐτύγχανεν. Const. Porphyr. de adm. Imp. c. xxx. p. 141, ed. Bonn.

niece of the Empress, and who succeeded his uncle in 468, but was persuaded in 472 to ex-change the security of his hereditary kingdom for the perils of the Imperial throne. Before however he was able to establish himself firmly in his new dignity, his authority was disputed by a rival; Gundobald the Burgundian, who had succeeded to the influence of his uncle the Patrician Ricimer, invested an obscure soldier, Glycerius, with the purple; but Glycerius was unsupported by any considerable party, and was allowed to resign his claims and exchange the Empire for the bishopric of Salona. A.D. 472. Glycerius.

Julius Nepos did not long survive his triumph. The barbarian soldiery at Rome broke out into insurrection and under their leader Orestes marched upon Ravenna. The trembling Emperor did not await their approach, but shamefully abdicating his authority fled to the security of his Dalmatian principality. Here he lived for some five years 'in a very ambiguous state between an Emperor and an exile,' until he was murdered at Salona in 480 by his former rival Glycerius, who according to one account was rewarded for his crime by translation to the Archbishopric of Milan. There seems, however, to be some doubt about the identity of the ex-Emperor and the Archbishop[1]. A.D. 475. Murder of Julius Nepos. A.D. 480.

The Patrician Orestes, a Pannonian by birth, declined the Empire for himself, and conferred it on his son Augustulus in whom the line of

[1] Vid. Gibbon, ch. xxxvi.

Emperors of the western part of the Roman world was extinguished by the victory of Odoacer.

After the murder of Julius Nepos Dalmatia had remained for a year under the rule of Odiva one of his murderers, but in 481 Odoacer attacked him and put him to death, and added Dalmatia to the kingdom of Italy, with which it passed a few years later to Theodoric.

End of Western Empire. A.D. 476.
A.D. 481. Gothic kingdom of Dalmatia.
A.D. 493.

SECOND PERIOD.

Dalmatia under the Byzantine Empire, A.D. 535–1102.

The province had already begun to feel the effects of barbarian inroads and to sink into poverty and desolation. Dalmatia and Pannonia 'no longer exhibited the rich prospect of populous cities, well cultivated fields and convenient highways; the reign of barbarism and desolation was restored,' and the Latin or provincial subjects of Rome were displaced by hordes of Bulgarians Gepidae Sarmatians and Slavonians.

A.D. 482. Of the latter race, and near the modern Sophia, was born in 482 Justinian, who was destined to recover Italy for the Empire by the genius and valour of another Slav Belisarius, who according to Procopius was born somewhere in Bosnia or Herzegovina [1].

---

[1] "Ὥρμητο δὲ ὁ Βελισάριος ἐκ Γερμανίας, ἣ Θρακῶν τε καὶ Ἰλλυρίων μεταξὺ κεῖται. Procop. Vandal. Lib. i. c. 11, quoted by Gibbon, ch. xli, who declares himself unable to find any mention of a Thracian

Dalmatia and Pannonia were taken from the Goths in 535; but while Theodatus the weak Gothic king was parleying with Justinian about the terms of his surrender, two Roman generals who had advanced into Dalmatia were defeated and slain by Gothic troops. The feeble Theodatus was inspired to fresh resistance; Belisarius led an army to the conquest of Rome, and in 539 Ravenna fell, and Vitiges, whom the Goths had raised to the throne in place of the unmanly Theodatus, was taken prisoner and sent to Constantinople. A.D. 535. Dalmatia recovered by the Empire.

In the same year a dreadful inroad of Huns Bulgarians and Slavonians swept over the whole Balkan peninsula, and other visitations of the same kind in succeeding years, marked with every circumstance of cruelty and rapine, reduced those provinces to the extremity of misery. A.D. 539. Barbarian inroads.

During the Second Gothic war after the revival of the Gothic kingdom by Totila, Salona was the port from which Belisarius sailed for Italy. But he was ill-supported by his government, and finally recalled. Rome was retaken by the Goths, who crossed the Adriatic and carried the war into Dalmatia, where, however, they were defeated, and Narses, the new commander-in-chief, sailed from Salona to the re-conquest of Second Gothic war.

Germania in the civil or ecclesiastical lists of the provinces and cities. The name of Justinian is a Latin translation of Upranda, upright; his father Istock and his mother Biglenzia were classicized into Sebatius and Vigilantia. Belisarius is said to be the Slavonic 'Velicar.' Vid. Gibbon, ch. xl; also Introd. to Evans's 'Through Bosnia,' &c.

A.D. 552. Italy and final overthrow of the Gothic kingdom.

A.D. 554. Dalmatia under the Exarchate.
Dalmatia formed part of the exarchate of Ravenna; but it is supposed that when the exarch Longinus, who succeeded Narses, created the Italian duchies of Rome, Venice, and Naples, he also created one of Dalmatia, subject like the others to the supremacy of the exarch, but possessing a certain measure of administrative independence.

It was about this time that the Avars first came on the scene, a race akin to the Huns, who were driven forward from Central Asia by the growing power of the Turks. Justinian, dissembling his indignation at the arrogant tone assumed by their ambassadors, employed them to attack the Bulgarians and Slavonians in Poland and Germany, whom they reduced to vassalage.

The Avars and Slavs.

A.D. 559. But in the following year a Bulgarian and Slavonian horde under Zabergan crossed the frozen Danube, invaded Macedonia and Thrace, and advanced to within twenty miles of Constantinople, which was saved by the last victory of Belisarius.

A.D. 566. On the accession of Justin another embassy of the Avars approached him, but, daunted by his firmness, returned to their chagan with a report that induced him to turn his arms against the Franks rather than against the Empire. Unsuccessful against this new enemy, the Avars found fresh employment for their arms in an

alliance with Alboin King of the Lombards, with
whom they joined in the overthrow of the Ge- <small>A.D. 566.</small>
pidae, a tribe which since the invasion of Attila
had been settled in Transylvania and was at this
time in the pay of the Empire. The Lombards
advanced to the conquest of Italy by way of
Friuli and Aquileja, leaving the territory of the
Gepidae to be occupied by the Avars.

    The Avars, thus relieved by the departure of <small>A.D. 570.</small>
the Lombards and the ruin of the Gepidae, rapidly
extended their conquests from the Alps to the
Euxine, threatened Constantinople, and overran
the provinces. But the Roman provincials were
not the only sufferers by the cruelties of the
Avars; their vassal subjects were scarcely less oppressed. The Slavonians were not only governed
tyrannically at home, but in battle they were
exposed to the first assault, 'and the swords
of the enemy were blunted before they en-
countered the native valour of the Avars[1].' The <small>A.D. 624. Revolt of</small>
Slavonians resolved to attempt their freedom; their <small>the Slavs</small>
Bohemian brethren seconded their resolution; <small>from the Avars.</small>
Samo, a Frank, put himself at the head of their
insurrection; the Avars were defeated, and the
Slavonians once more became a free people.

    Heraclius at once offered them his support, <small>A.D. 634.</small>
and invited the tribe of the Χρωβάτοι, Chorvati <small>Heraclius settles the</small>
or Chorvates, Croats from Southern Poland and <small>Slavs in Dalmatia,</small>
Gallicia, to drive the Avars out of Illyria and <small>&c.</small>
occupy that province as vassals of the Empire.

    [1] Gibbon, ch. xlvi.

They accepted the invitation, and, advancing into Dalmatia, succeeded after a war of about five years in reducing the Avars to subjection. In the struggle that desolated the province the old Roman towns of the sea-coast did not escape. Driven from the country by the constant irruptions of one barbarian horde after another the old pro-vincials of the Empire had been collected within the walls of the cities; and most, if not all, of these now fell before the separate or united forces of the Slavs or Avars, who were contending for the mastery of Dalmatia[1]. Salona was taken after scarcely any defence and entirely destroyed, the wretched inhabitants flying to the islands, where they lived in huts and wigwams, enduring every privation, and reduced to extremities by scarcity of water. Scardona, Narona, and most probably Jadera (Zara) shared the fate of Salona, as well as Epidaurus, the oldest Greek colony in Illyria, whose site is now occupied by the modern Ragusa Vecchia. About the same time the Serbs, or Servians, another Slavonic tribe, obtained leave from Heraclius to settle to the east of the Croats and in Southern Dalmatia, and the whole province

A.D. 639.
Destruction of Roman towns in Dalmatia by Avars and Slavs.

[1] Salona and Epidaurus are said to have been destroyed by Avars, but the early writers are very careless of ethnological distinctions. Constantine Porphyrogenitus says Epidaurus was destroyed παρὰ τῶν Σκλάβων, but in another place he calls the Avars Slavs, and Attila βασιλεὺς τῶν Ἀβάρων. Thomas Archidiaconus says that the destroyers of Salona were called indifferently Goths or Slavs, and were the same as the Croatians. Most probably the invading hordes were composed of Goths and Slavs as well as Avars.

became thus peopled by Slavonians, the Croats occupying what we know as Hungarian and Turkish Croatia, and Northern Dalmatia as far as the River Cettina which falls into the sea at Almissa, while the Serbs occupied nearly the whole of modern Servia Bosnia Herzegovina and Montenegro, with the northern part of Albania, and the coast from the Cettina to Durazzo.

The old Latin, or Roman, population, however sadly it was crushed and weakened by this irruption, did not disappear, nor did it lose its identity and become merged in the ranks of the conquerors. When the first shock was over, the Romans either returned to their old towns or founded new ones, where they managed to live in a state between independence and vassalage till they became strong enough in time to take care of themselves. Zara soon rose again from its ruin, the fugitives from Epidaurus settled on an isolated rock not far from their ancient home and founded the city of Ragusa, and the unhappy Salonitans, not daring to return as yet to the ruins of their old capital, crept back to the mainland in reduced numbers, and found a refuge within the impregnable walls of the deserted villa of Diocletian, which has grown into the modern Spalato. The fate of Traü on the mainland and of the island towns of Arbe Veglia and Ossero in the Quarnero during this general catastrophe is obscure, but we find them in the tenth century still peopled by Roman citizens and

Recovery of the Roman municipalities.

living under their old Roman institutions; and if they fell at first under the onslaught of the immigrant Slavs, they at all events recovered themselves like Zara and escaped being Slavonized like the rest of the province. It is, however, possible that their insular position saved them from injury by a people who had no maritime resources. These seven towns were the sole survivors of the ancient Roman civilization in Dalmatia. A few old Roman cities like Aenona, Corinium and Scardona were inhabited by the conquering Slavs, but for the most part the ancient sites were abandoned and the buildings either destroyed or allowed to fall into ruin. The islands of Northern Dalmatia, except those above named, were uninhabited and their towns deserted even as late as the tenth century. But the larger islands of Southern Dalmatia—Lesina, Curzola, Méleda—were colonized by the Serbs of the Narenta, and in time Croatian immigrants occupied the rural districts of those in the northern sea, for the Slavs of the sea-coast soon adapted themselves to their maritime position and became as formidable by water as they had been by land[1].

[1] Constantine Porphyrogenitus de administrando Imperio, ch. xxix–xxxi. His account was written in the year 949, as he tells us in ch. xxix : Οἱ δὲ λοιποὶ ʽΡωμᾶνοι εἰς τὰ τῆς παραλίας κάστρα διεσώθησαν, καὶ μέχρι τοῦ νῦν κρατοῦσιν αὐτά· ἅτινά εἰσι τάδε κάστρα, τὸ ʽΡαοῦσιν, τὸ Ἀσπάλαθον, τὸ Τετραγγούριν, τὰ Διάδωρα, ἡ Ἄρβη, ἡ Βέκλα, καὶ τὰ Ὄψαρα· ὧν τινῶν καὶ οἰκήτορες μέχρι τοῦ νῦν οἱ ʽΡωμᾶνοι καλοῦνται. p. 128, ed. Bonn. Τὰ δὲ λοιπὰ κάστρα τὰ ὄντα εἰς τὴν ξηρὰν τοῦ θέματος καὶ κρατηθέντα παρὰ τῶν εἰρημένων Σκλάβων ἀοίκητα καὶ ἔρημα ἵστανται, μηδενὸς κατοικοῦντος ἐν αὐτοῖς. ibid. p. 140.

The communal family organization of the Slavs was not favourable to the formation of a compact and formidable nation. Each tribe or village existed as a separate republic, and in the absence of any tendency to cohere and assert their general and national independence, they settled down readily as vassals or provincials of the Empire. Both Serbs and Croats acknowledged the dominion of the Byzantine Court and at first submitted to a Praetor from Constantinople, who collected tribute from them and sent it to the capital; and it was not till the ninth or tenth century, when the decline of the Empire loosened its hold on the distant provinces, that the Dalmatian Slavs shook off the yoke which had long ceased to be more than nominal.

Organization of the Slavs.

This he to some extent contradicts afterwards, v. infra. Of the islands except Βέκλα (Veglia),"Αρβη, "Οψαρα (Ossero) and Λουμβρικάτον (Vergada), the rest εἰσὶν ἀοίκητα, ἔχοντα ἐρημόκαστρα ὧν τὰ ὀνόματα εἰσὶν οὕτω, Καταυτρεβενὼ (?), Πιζύχ (Sale), Σελβώ (Selve), Σκερδά (Scherda), 'Αλωήπ (Nun), Σκιρδάκισσα (Pago), Πυρότιμα (?), Μελετά (Meláda), Ἑστιουνήξ (Sestrum), καὶ ἕτερα πάμπολλα ὧν τὰ ὀνόματα οὐ νοοῦνται, ibid. p. 140. These are all in the Northern waters. Of the Southern islands he says the Serbs of Pagania (i. e. the valley of the Narenta) κρατοῦσι καὶ ταύτας τὰς νήσους. Νῆσος μεγάλη ἡ Κούρκρα ἤτοι τὸ Κίκερ (Curzola), ἐν ᾗ ἐστὶ καὶ κάστρον. Νῆσος ἑτέρα μεγάλη τὰ Μέλετα (Méleda), ἤτοι τὸ Μαλοζεάται. Νῆσος ἑτέρα μεγάλη τὸ Φάρα (Lesina), νῆσος ἑτέρα μεγάλη ὁ Βράτζης (Brazza), ibid. p. 163, 4. Lagosta, τὸ Λάστοβον, and the islands Χόαρα and "Ιης, though near the Pagani, did not belong to them, ibid. p. 164. He mentions the following towns as inhabited by the βαπτισμένοι Χρωβάτοι: Νόνα (Nona), Βελόγραδον (Belgrad or Zara Vecchia), Βελίτζειν (Belina?), Σκόρδονα (Scardona), Χλεβένα (Chlebna), Στύλπον (Stulba), Τενήν (Knin), Κόρι (Karin), Κλαβώκα (Klapaz?), ibid. p. 151.

VOL. I. C

It is more difficult to say what became of the ancient Dalmatian and Liburnian populations of the province. They probably shared to some extent the fortunes of the Roman colonists, with whom they had doubtless become a good deal intermingled, and it is supposed that their descendants may be found in the cities of the coast and on the islands. Lucio sees in the Morlacchi, who retired from the hill country into the plains as the Turks advanced towards the sea-coast in the sixteenth century, and who now form the peasantry of the northern part of continental Dalmatia, the descendants of the old Roman provincials who fled to the mountains and took to a pastoral life when the Slavs occupied the plains[1]. Of the provincials themselves, many were already Slavs by descent and ready to be merged in the ranks of their conquerors, for a gradual infiltration of a Slavonic element had been going on among the population of the Balkan peninsula long before the irruption of the seventh century and the settlement of the Croats and Serbs by Heraclius. It is only in this way that the population can have become so thoroughly Slavonized, for it is impossible to suppose that the whole district was entirely repeopled at the time of the Slavonic conquest.

A.D. 752. End of the exarchate. Such was the condition of Dalmatia when Ravenna fell before the Lombards, the exarchate

[1] De Regno Dalm. et Croat. lib. vi. c. v. de Vlahis.; vid. also note, page 149 infra.

was extinguished, and the Imperial prefects of the Adriatic removed themselves and their fleet to Zara, which became the capital of the province and the seat of the dukes of Dalmatia. Side by side with their somewhat shadowy authority was the native organization of the Slavs, who were grouped into districts called zupys, each with a Zupan at its head. Over these were grand Zupans, or presidents of the federation, and now and then we read of a Ban, or personage of still more exalted authority. All these 'archons' acknowledged and condescended to accept dignities and titles from the Empire, and, in name at all events, professed obedience to the representative of the Emperor. Side by side again with these organizations were the old Roman municipalities of the maritime towns, speaking the old Roman tongue, governed by the old Roman law, owning allegiance to none but the Roman Emperor and the Prior who represented him in each community, and looking to Constantinople for protection in their ancient municipal liberties against the Slavs, whose rule began beyond the narrow limits of the territory which each city claimed as its own. This was the beginning of that dual element in Dalmatian history which must be thoroughly appreciated before the after history of the country can be understood, which has continued with comparatively little difference to our own days, and which is at this moment the key to the

Byzantine dukes of Dalmatia.

Distinction between Latin and Slavonic Dalmatians.

proper intelligence of Dalmatian politics and the pivot on which they turn.

Conversion of the Slavs to Christianity about A.D. 640.

If Christianity had not made material progress among the Slavs before their descent into Dalmatia[1], their contact with the population of a province that dated its Christianity from apostolic times, and their residence under the sovereignty of a Christian Empire, resulted in the speedy conversion of the greater part of them from paganism. Before 640 it is supposed that most of the Slavs had accepted Christianity, except the Serbs of Southern Dalmatia, in the district of the Narenta, who clung for a much longer time to their ancient faith. In the tenth century their country was known as Pagania, and is described under that name by Constantine Porphyrogenitus[2]. On the deserted site of Roman Narona the Slavonic conquerors had raised

---

[1] If Thomas Archid. ch. vii. may be trusted the conquerors of Salona ' quamvis pravi essent et feroces, tamen Christiani erant sed rudes valde. Ariana etiam erant tabe infecti.' This would have been true of the Goths among them at all events.

The ' Historia Salonitanorum Pontificum atque Spalatensium Thomae Archidiaconi Spalatensis' will be frequently quoted. Thomas was born in 1200 and died in 1268, and his narrative of the events of his own time is of the greatest value. For his own personal history v. inf. chapter xi.

[2] Οἱ δὲ Παγανοί, οἱ καὶ τῇ Ῥωμαίων διαλέκτῳ Ἀρεντανοὶ καλούμενοι, εἰς δυσβάτους τόπους καὶ κρημνώδεις κατελείφθησαν ἀβάπτιστοι· καὶ γὰρ Παγανοὶ κατὰ τὴν τῶν Σκλάβων γλῶσσαν ἀβάπτιστοι ἑρμηνεύονται. Μετὰ δὲ τοῦτο καὶ αὐτοὶ ἀποστείλαντες εἰς τὸν ἀοίδιμον βασιλέα ἐξητήσαντο βαπτισθῆναι καὶ αὐτοί· καὶ ἀποστείλας ἐβάπτισε καὶ αὐτούς. Const. Porphyr. de adm. Imp. ch. xxix.

Basil I. the Macedonian reigned from 867 till 886. Farlati gives 872 as the date of the conversion of the Narentines.

a temple to their national god Viddo, whose name survives in the modern village of Vido, and when in the reign of Basil the Macedonian the Narentines were baptized into the new faith, Viddo himself shared in their conversion and became the S. Vito, the uneasy Saint Vitus, of the new mythology. As lately, however, as the beginning of the nineteenth century, in a visitation that was made of the churches of this district, ancient idols were found still preserved and still receiving the veneration of the people[1], I presume like S. Vito, under names in Christian hagiology most nearly corresponding to their Pagan titles.

After Charlemagne had overthrown the kingdom of the Lombards he extended his conquest without difficulty over Istria, Liburnia, and Dalmatia, and the dominion of ὁ μέγας Κάρουλος was admitted, not only by the Slavonic population, but by the Latins, or as they began to call themselves by distinction, *Dalmatians*, of the maritime cities, who are even said to have voluntarily thrown themselves on the protection of the new Emperor of the West to escape the tyranny of Nicephorus the reigning Emperor of the East. Whether their surrender was voluntary, or whether it is an invention of the vanity of the Dalmatians and they were conquered by force, it is certain that the cities of the coast were for the moment

A.D. 806. Dalmatia conquered by Charlemagne.

[1] Vid. Schatzmayer, La Dalmazia. Trieste, 1877.

actually detached from the Eastern Empire and attached to that of the West[1]. Nicephorus did not submit tamely, but sent a fleet into Dalmatian waters, which, however, effected nothing; and had the dispute come to the arbitration of arms the Byzantines would perhaps have made but a poor defence against the destroyer of the Avars. It was not, however, the policy of Charlemagne to break up the Empire of Eastern Rome, and the maritime cities and islands which seem to have been overawed into submission to Nicephorus by a fresh naval demonstration in 809 were allowed to remain subject to the Eastern Empire, while Istria and Croatia remained part of the new Empire of the West[2]. These terms were embodied in a treaty, and the biographer of Charlemagne is careful to convey the impression that the concession to his Eastern brother was the effect, not of compulsion, but of generosity[3].

Restoration of the maritime cities to the Eastern Empire.

[1] *Annales Regum Francorum*, dcccvi : ' Statim post Natalem domini venerunt Wilharius (*Obelerio*) et Beatus Duces Venetiae nec non et Paulus dux Jaderae atque Donatus ejusdem civitatis episcopus legati Dalmatarum ad praesentiam imperatoris cum magnis donis ; et facta est ibi ordinatio ab imperatore de ducibus et populis tam Venetiae quam Dalmatiae.'

[2] 'De Dalmatia autem sicuti eam partem, quam Croati cum Liburnia occupaverant, simul cum reliqua Croatia Carolum subegisse censendum est, ita illa exceptio Civitatum marinarum de civitatibus continentis Dalmatiae, scilicet Iadra, Tragurio, et Spalato Croatis conterminis quae cum insulis Dalmatiae nomen retinebant intelligenda est.' Lucio, de Regn. Dalm. lib. I. xv. To these he afterwards adds Ragusa and Capodistria, ibid. ch. xvi.

[3] 'Exceptis maritimis civitatibus, quas ob amicitiam et junctum

The Frank dominion in Dalmatia, however, was a mere episode in its history, and lasted too short a time to make any lasting impression. The truth seems to have been that the Byzantines, as masters of the sea, were able to retain their hold on the maritime towns, and that the Franks, being stronger by land, imposed their rule, though perhaps not very firmly, on the Slavs of the rest of Dalmatia, and of Istria and Croatia. This yoke was easily shaken off by the Croatian and Dalmatian Slavs after the death of Charlemagne, and the dukes of Croatia, being practically independent of both Empires, rapidly advanced their authority to a position that wanted nothing of royalty but the name. Even the maritime cities were obliged to yield them a qualified subjection. The cities were too weak to resist their Slavonic neighbours except with the aid of the Byzantine Empire, and as the Empire found it daily more and more difficult to extend its protection over dependencies at such a distance, Basil the Macedonian advised them to purchase immunity by an annual tribute to the barbarians, reserving a nominal sum for the Empire as an acknowledgment of their continued fidelity[1].

End of Frank dominion.

Independence of Croatia.

cum eo foedus Constantinopolitano Imperatori habere permisit.'
Eginhart, Vita Carol. Magn.

[1] Const. Porphyr. de adm. Imp. ch. xxx. p. 147, ed. Bonn. : ὁ οὖν ἀοίδιμος ἐκεῖνος βασιλεὺς Βασίλειος προετρέψατο πάντα τὰ διδόμενα τῷ στρατηγῷ δίδοσθαι παρ' αὐτῶν τοῖς Σκλάβοις καὶ εἰρηνικῶς ζῆν μετ' αὐτῶν, καὶ βραχύ τι δίδοσθαι τῷ στρατηγῷ ἵνα μόνον δείκνυται ἡ πρὸς τοὺς βασιλεῖς τῶν Ῥωμαίων καὶ πρὸς τὸν στρατηγὸν αὐτῶν ὑποταγὴ καὶ δούλωσις.

The homage which the dukes of Croatia still professed to yield to the Empire was only rendered occasionally and was little more than nominal, till finally it was dropped entirely, and in the eleventh century the duchy became the Kingdom of Croatia and Dalmatia.

The Narentines.

The intricate channels among the Dalmatian islands, and the secret harbours and inland seas that indent the coast, have always disposed the people to piracy in barbarous times, and the Slavs had no sooner established themselves on the seaboard and taken to maritime pursuits than they did as their predecessors had done in the days of Queen Teuta. The still Pagan Narentines were powerful enough to impede the commerce of the Adriatic and harass the cities of the Dalmatian coast, and the Venetians were preparing an armament to check their piracies, when a more formidable enemy appeared on the scene. The Saracens from Sicily entered the Adriatic, captured Bari on the Apulian shore, ravaged Cattaro Rosa and Budua on the Dalmatian side, and laid siege to Ragusa, which they invested for fifteen months. A fleet under the Doge Partecipazio was dispatched to co-operate with that of the Emperor Theophilus, but the cowardice of the Greeks involved the Venetians in a severe defeat off Taranto or Crotona. The siege of Ragusa was raised by the Emperor Basil I, the Macedonian, who sent a fleet of one hundred sail, and the Saracens retired to Bari. 'Their impartial de-

Saracen piracies. A.D. 829.

predations provoked the resentment and conciliated the union of the two Emperors. An offensive alliance was concluded between Basil the Macedonian, the first of his race, and Lewis the great-grandson of Charlemagne[1].' Lewis furnished the land forces, and Basil the naval contingent. At his summons the Croats and Serbs and the Latins of the maritime cities, all of whom still formed nominally a part of his Empire, flocked to the rendezvous at Ragusa, whence they were transported in Ragusan vessels to Bari[2]. The siege lasted four years and was conducted by Lewis in person, and the fall of the Saracen citadel and the subsequent death of Lewis were followed by the establishment of the Byzantine theme of Apulia governed by a Catapan, with Bari for his capital, which lasted till subverted by the Norman conquest in 1040–1043. *Siege of Bari, A.D. 867–871.*

Of all the Dalmatians the Narentines alone had not been invited to join in the campaign against the Saracens, and they profited by the absence and occupation of the Venetian fleet at Bari, to strengthen their forces and prosecute their piracies. A fleet which the Venetians sent against them under the Doge Pietro Candiano was utterly defeated off Puntamica near Zara, and the Doge was killed. His body was found after the battle by the Croatians who seem to *Narentine victory at Puntamica. A.D. 887.*

[1] Gibbon, ch. lvi.
[2] Const. Porphyr. ch. xxix. p. 88, ed. Bonn.

have had at that time no sympathy with the Narentines, and was sent to Grado and buried in the atrium of the cathedral[1].

Struggle between Venice and the Narentines for supremacy in the Adriatic.
The time had come when the question of the future supremacy of the Adriatic seemed evenly balanced between the Venetians and the Slavs of Southern Dalmatia. Venice was still in her youth, and only beginning to be formidable, and the Narentines with their allies and dependencies were no unworthy antagonists in point of strength. They occupied the valley of the Narenta, the sea-coast from that river to the Cettina at Almissa, with the towns of Makarska, Berulla, Ostrog, and Labinetza on the shore, other places in the interior, and the large islands of Curzola, Méleda, Lesina, and Brazza[2]. Envy and fear of the growing naval strength of Venice procured them the favour of the neighbouring powers; their attacks on Venetian commerce were secretly or openly supported by the dukes of Croatia and by the Ragusans, some of whom even took service with the Narentine prince Muiis, and they were regarded not unfavourably even by the Byzantine Empire.

In estimating the character of the Narentine pretensions it must be remembered that we have

---

[1] 'Croatos ergo tunc temporis ab infestatione maris se abstinentes cum Venetis et Dalmatis concordes navigasse, et sequuta inter Venetos et Narentanos prope suum promontorium pugna navali, amici occisi Ducis cadaver derelictum inventum Gradum ad sepeliendum tulisse dicendum est.' Luc. de Regn. ii. p. 65.

[2] Const. Porphyr. de adm. Imp. ch. xxx–xxxvi. v. sup. p. 17, note.

only the one-sided account of the Venetian historians, who represent them as simple corsairs levying black mail on the commerce of the Adriatic, and harassing the maritime towns of Dalmatia. It seems likely that they were not merely sea-robbers but had developed a considerable legitimate commerce with Italy, whither we hear that their merchants used to go to transact business. The narrative of a Narentine historian might have given a different aspect to the struggle, and shown it to have been not a mere crushing of a nest of pirates as the Venetian historians describe it, but rather a contest for supremacy between two young and growing naval powers, both of whom aspired to the mastery of the sea.

At first the Narentines had decidedly the best of it; for a hundred and fifty years the Venetians had been compelled to pay them tribute for liberty to navigate the Adriatic; and it was not till the time of their great Doge Pietro Orseolo II that they felt themselves strong enough to refuse it themselves, and to forbid its payment by others. The cities of Dalmatia, afflicted by the constant attacks of both Croatians and Narentines, eagerly welcomed the prospect of a deliverer, and offered their allegiance to the Doge and his successors if he would relieve them from the oppression of the Slavs. As the Croatian dukes or kings had originally received their authority from the Eastern Empire permission was sought from the

Pietro Orseolo II, Doge, A.D. 991-1008.

Emperors Basil II. and Constantine IX. before the Republic acceded to the request of the suppliants, and assumed the dominion of Dalmatia[1]. Permission was granted, and in the eighth year of his dukedom, Pietro Orseolo set sail from Venice with a formidable fleet. At Grado he was met by the Patriarch Vitale at the head of the people and clergy; at Parenzo, at the bishop's request, he visited the Euphrasian basilica, entering the city surrounded with a large military force; at S. Andrea, an island near Pola, he received the homage of the bishop and citizens of that place: sailing thence to Ossero he was welcomed not only by the citizens, but by the people from the neighbouring towns '*both Roman and Slavonic*,' who swore allegiance to him, and at the feast of Pentecost, which occurred during his stay, celebrated him in the public 'lauds[2].' At Zara he

Conquest of the Narentines.
A.D. 998.

A.D. 998.

---

[1] 'Qua de causa Veneti ab illis evocati, cum permissione Basilii et Constantini Imperatorum Constantinopol. a quibus reges illi sceptrum antiquitus recognoverant, dominium Dalmatiae primitùs acceperunt.' Dandolo, lib. ix. c. i. pars 15.

[2] Lucio devotes a chapter (lib. ii. ch. vi. de Laudibus) to an account of the 'Lauds,' sung in Dalmatian churches down even to his day. They were unknown except in the old Roman or 'Dalmatian' cities. 'Hae autem laudes nunc canuntur in his tantum civitatibus quae olim Romanorum vel Dalmatarum nomen retinuere, ut dictum est, quae Imperiales etiam dictae fuere ad differentiam Croaticarum quae Regales, suntque Ragusium, Spalatum, Tragurium, Iadra, Arbum, Viglia. Sola Absarus ex Dalmaticis iis caret, quae cum pene deserta sit civibus et magistratibus nunc Chersum habitantibus ob id forsan omissae fuere. Curzolae et Phari uti Narentanorum, Sibenici et Nonae uti Croatorum neque olim cantatas ulla memoria reperitur neque

was met by the prior, or representative of the Emperor, with the bishop of the city, and also by the priors and bishops of Veglia and Arbe, who all swore allegiance on the gospels and engaged that on festivals the name of the Doge should be celebrated in the public lauds after that of the Byzantine Emperor. An ambassador from the king of Croatia was received coldly, and his overtures were rejected; the resources of the Narentines were carefully ascertained, and measures were taken at once to put them to the proof. A squadron of ten ships was sent to intercept forty Narentine nobles on their way home from Apulia, where they had been on affairs of business, who were captured at the island of Chaza, between Issa and Lagosta, and carried to Traü. The Doge was already moving southwards towards the same place, receiving on his way the submission of Belgrade, and the island Lenigrad which Lucio identifies either with Zuri or Mortér. At Traü he found his victorious vanguard with their prisoners, and received the homage of the bishop and people, and also that of Surigna the brother and unsuccessful rival of Mucimir king or duke of Croatia, to whose son the Doge gave his daughter Hicela in marriage. By this alliance Lucio supposes the Doge ratified a treaty with the Croatians which bound them to abstain from molesting the Dalmatians, and detached

A.D. 998.

nunc canuntur.' Nor at Cattaro which for some time was subject to Servia. They were sung also at Capodistria.

them from the Narentines[1]. The Narentines thus left alone face to face with a superior force were glad enough to come to terms. The Doge had advanced to Spalato, and his fleet augmented by contingents from his new Dalmatian subjects was far more than a match for his opponents. Six of the Narentine captives were retained as hostages, and the rest were restored to liberty, and the Narentine prince in return bound himself to exact no tolls in future on the commerce of the Adriatic, and not to molest any Venetian travellers. The islanders of Curzola and Lagosta[2] alone offered any resistance. The former were easily conquered, but the latter, relying on their impregnable cliffs and walls, made a stubborn fight, and were with difficulty overcome. As the Lagostans had been the worst corsairs in those seas, their city was destroyed. The Doge returned to the church of S. Maximus, which, with no doubt a convent attached to it, was situated on an islet near Curzola, and there received the bishop and clergy of Ragusa who came to tender their submission, after which he returned in triumph to Venice, revisiting on his way the several Dalmatian cities, and assuming with the general consent the title of Duke of Dalmatia.

Submission of the Narentines.
Venetian Dukedom of Dalmatia.

[1] Luc. de Regn. lib. ii. ch. iv.
[2] Dandolo calls the island Ladestina, and it has sometimes been mistaken for Lesina. Lucio, with more probability, identifies it with Lagosta. Yet Constantine Porphyrog. says that Lastobon (Lagosta) did not belong to the Narentines or Pagani. Vid. sup. note, p. 17.

Cresimir II, king of Croatia, who harassed Zara A.D. 1018. and the maritime cities, was defeated by Doge Ottone Orseolo, to whom afterwards the priors and bishops of Veglia, Arbe, Albona, and Ossero renewed their oaths of fidelity, agreeing to pay an annual acknowledgment. That paid by the island of Arbe was ten pounds of silk, an interesting fact in connection with the introduction of silk into western Europe[1].

Once more in this century the power of the Byzantine Empire was revived in Dalmatia. Basil II, 'Bulgaroktonos,' the destroyer of the Bulgarians, after crushing Samuel the successor of their great Czar Simeon in 1014, is said to have subdued all Bosnia, Rascia, and Dalmatia, and to have established Governors, Protospathars and generals throughout these provinces[2]; and till 1076 the Croatian king held his crown as a dependent of the Empire. The Venetians had always nominally respected the sovereignty of the Empire, and at this time were too much occupied by intestine disturbances to interfere, and the title of Duke of Dalmatia seems to have been dropped after the time of Orseolo till it was resumed by Vitale Faliero in 1084. The history

A.D. 1019. Revival of Byzantine influence.

[1] Luc. de Regn. ii. ch. viii. See below, chap. xxviii, on history of Arbe.
[2] Luc. ii–ix. quotes in confirmation of this several documents in the archives of S. Grisogono at Zara, e. g. '1036. Indictione quarta die 13 Feb. Romani imperii dignitatem Gubernante Serenissimo Michaele, Gregorio Protospatario et Stratico universae Dalmatiae.'

of this time is, however, extremely obscure. In 1067 we find amicably attending the court of Peter Cresimir king of Croatia and Dalmatia at Nona an imperial officer with the title of Protospathar and Catipan of all Dalmatia, and the name of the reigning Emperor is prefixed to the royal acts[1]. Lucio conjectures that the Empire being too weak to restrain the Croatians by land, allowed their king to call himself King of Dalmatia, while he, having no navy to match that of the Empire, allowed the imperial rule to linger on in the maritime cities subject to such a tribute as they had paid with the consent of Basil I.

A.D. 1073.

The Byzantine Empire was daily losing ground. The Normans had robbed it of the theme of Apulia, and founded in its place a new kingdom of their own, and were preparing to cross the Adriatic and follow up their victory on its Eastern side. Their fleets searched the Dalmatian coast, and molested the cities, but were driven off by the Venetians, who were jealous of the interference of a new power in the Adriatic. From the expression of Dandolo that the Venetians

The Normans in Dalmatia. A.D. 1075.

---

[1] 'A.D. 1067. Regnante D. Constantino Duce magno Imperatore, Prioratum vero Iadrae retinente D. Leone Imperiali Prothospatario et totius Dalmatiae Catipano ... ego Cresimir, qui alio nomine vocor Petrus Croatorum Rex Dalmatinorumque" &c. Document cited by Luc. de Regn. lib. ii. c. viii.

Thom. Archid. says of the Kings of Croatia at this time, 'recipiebant enim dignitatis insignia ab Imperatoribus Constantinopolitanis et dicebantur eorum Eparchi sive Patritii.' ch. xiii.

exacted fresh oaths of allegiance from the Dalmatians, together with a promise that they would not invite the Normans into Dalmatia[1], it appears that the coming of the Normans was not a mere raid, but had been solicited by some of the cities. The whole incident is extremely obscure.

In the middle of this century occurred the synod at Spalato, which prohibited the use of the Illyrian liturgy, and prescribed the use of only Greek or Latin in the church services. The synod was attended by bishops from the whole of Dalmatia and Croatia, but none even of the Slav bishops protested except Gregory the bishop of Nona. The Slav priests were struck with dismay, their churches were shut and the services interrupted. A delegacy to the Pope failed to obtain relief, and the delegate of the Croatian appellants was on his return degraded, beaten, branded, and imprisoned for twelve years, while Cedèda, a Slavonic bishop ignorant of the Latin language, whom the recusant party had intruded into the see of Veglia, was ejected and excommunicated[2]. The acts of this synod illustrate the religious differences which accentuated those of race which divided the Latin from the Slav. Throughout the middle ages the Latin cities were the strongholds of Roman orthodoxy, while the Slavonic kingdoms of the interior were more or less inclined to the

Synod of Spalato, 1059.

Religious differences between Latins and Slavs.

[1] Dandolo, lib. ix. c. viii.
[2] Thom. Archid. c. xvi; vid. infra, History of Spalato, chap. x, and that of Veglia, chap. xxvi.

doctrines of the Patarenes or to those of the Greek Church.

<small>A.D. 1087.
End of Croatian kingdom.</small>

On the death of Demetrius or Zuonimir the last regular king, whose wife was sister to Ladislaus I. of Hungary, the succession to the crown of Croatia was disputed, and Ladislaus was invited to contest it with Stephen II, who had been elected by one part of the nobility. Ladislaus

<small>Hungarian conquest of Croatia.
A.D. 1091.</small>

descended into Croatia with an army, but was recalled by an invasion of Tartars before he could establish himself firmly in his conquest; and he recrossed the mountains, leaving his nephew Almus[1] as duke of Croatia to govern in his name. The Hungarians do not seem at this first incursion to have reached Dalmatia, but only to have annexed Croatia[2], a country then divided by faction and easily conquered in detail.

<small>Venetians revive their claims to Dalmatia.</small>

It is not without significance that this was the moment when the Venetians revived their dormant claim to Dalmatia. The Byzantine Empire was at this time in the throes of its struggle with

---

[1] It seems doubtful which brother of Ladislaus, Geiza or Lampertus, was father to Almus. Otto Frising., Vita Herbordi, lib. i, and de Gest. Frid. lib. vii, calls Almus brother to Coloman who was son to Geiza, but he is corrected by his annotator (ed. Pertz), who says Almus was son to Lampertus. Vid. Table of Kings of Hungary, infra.

[2] Thom. Archid. c. xvii: 'Ergo Vladislaus . . . transivit Alpes et coepit impugnare munitiones et castra, multaque proelia committere cum gentibus Croatiae, sed cum alter alteri non ferret auxilium essentque divisi ab invicem facilem victoriam Rex potuit obtinere; nec tamen usque ad maritimas regiones pervenit,' &c.

the Norman Robert Guiscard, and in the disastrous campaign of Durazzo the Venetian fleet had rendered good service to the Emperor Alexius. The Emperor was alarmed by the disposition the Dalmatians had shown to appeal to the Normans, alarmed also at the progress of Hungary towards the sea-coast, and irritated because Zuonimir the last king had sought investiture from the Pope and not from Constantinople [1]. To prevent Dalmatia falling into the hands of either Hungarian or Norman, Alexius seems to have resorted to the expedient of conferring afresh on the Doge of Venice the title of Duke of Dalmatia, which had fallen into abeyance since the time of Pietro Orseolo II. Accordingly we find Vitale Faliero [2] assuming the title 'Dalmatiae Dux,' at the very time when the Hungarians began to meditate the conquest of that country; and thus began the struggle for the possession of Dalmatia which with varying fortune raged between these two powers for the next three hundred years, till Hungary, broken by Turkish conquest, was compelled to retire from the contest and leave Venice mistress of the field.

[1] Luc. ii. x. p. 85.
[2] Luc. de Regno, lib. iii. c. ii. Vitale Faliero was Doge from 1085 till 1096.

THIRD PERIOD.

Contest of Venice and Hungary for the possession of Dalmatia,
A.D. 1102–1420.

<small>Condition of Dalmatia at this time.</small>

<small>1. The Croatians.</small>

The condition of the country and the various races that inhabited it at the opening of this new chapter in its history may be gathered obscurely from various sources. The Croatians had gradually become consolidated from a loose aggregate of semi-independent *zupanies* into a nation and a kingdom. Contact with and subjection to the courts of the two Empires had taught them to imitate the imperial offices and establishments of Constantinople and Aquisgranum. The *zupans* were latinized into *counts*, we find chamberlains palatines chaplains and judges in attendance on the king in the various places where he held his court, and Latin was the official language in state documents, at least as far back as 838[1]. There was no settled capital; royal acts and privileges are dated from Bihać Knin Novigrad Belgrad (Zara Vecchia), sometimes 'a nostro cenaculo' at Nona, frequently from Sebenico, and often from some river or fountain or church in the open country. Nona seems to have been the principal seat of the court, and the bishop of that place had all Croatia for his diocese. The bishop of Knin was scarcely less favoured; his see was

---

[1] Lucio, lib. ii. c. ii. p. 61, cites a privilege in Latin of Tirpimirus Dux Croatorum in that year.

founded at the instance of the kings of Croatia, who wished 'specialem habere pontificem,' and the bishop was the royal bishop and followed the royal court, of which he was one of the magnates[1]. All the Croatian bishops were subject to the Metropolitan of Spalato, whose province extended as far as the borders of Istria and the shores of the Danube.

The Croatians

The Croatians remained, as to some extent they still remain, lovers of the open country and haters of towns, like our own Saxon forefathers. Their towns were few and small, and the scattered population was distributed in hamlets of a few houses clustered round a humble church on the shore of some stream or beside some spring. A glimpse of the condition of the people is given by William of Tyre in his account of the march of Raymond of Thoulouse on his way to the first crusade through Lombardy Aquileja Istria and Dalmatia. He distinguishes the civilized Latin inhabitants of the maritime cities from the Croatians, who, he says, are a most ferocious people, accustomed to robbery and murder, clad like barbarians, living by their flocks and herds, and little given to agriculture[2]. 'The weather was

A.D. 1095–1096.

---

[1] Thom. Archid. c. xv. For extent of kingdom of Croatia vid. his c. xiii.

[2] William of Tyre, lib. ii. c. 17: 'Exceptis paucis qui in oris maritimis habitant, qui ab aliis et moribus et lingua dissimiles Latinorum habent idioma, reliquis Sclavonico sermone utentibus et habitu Barbarorum.' He names Zara Spalato Antivari and Ragusa as the four 'Metropoles.'

a perpetual fog, the land was mountainous and desolate, the natives were either fugitive or hostile: loose in their religion and government, they refused to furnish provisions and guides, murdered the stragglers, and exercised day and night the vigilance of the Count, who derived more security from the punishment of some captive robbers than from his interview with the prince of Scodra[1].'

2. State of the Latins of Dalmatia.

On the coast and some of the islands were the old Roman or, as they began to be called, *Dalmatian* as distinct from *Croatian* towns[2], subject in name to the Empire of Eastern Rome, tributary in fact to the kings of Croatia, but in other respects independent, governing themselves by their own laws, talking their old Latin tongue, which was already in some phase of transition towards its modern Italian form, and maintaining something of the old Latin civilization in the midst of a semi-barbarous people; 'moribus et lingua dissimiles.' No charter of privileges from a Croatian king to a Dalmatian city is known, though there are many granted to churches and convents within the city walls[3], and it is probable that

---

[1] Gibbon, Decline and Fall, chap. lviii.

[2] 'Croatos in Dalmatia maritima a Cetina flumine usque ad Istriam omnia occupasse praeter oppida maritima Iadra, Tragurium et Spalato quae cum Insulis Dalmatarum vel Romanorum nomen retinuerunt, ut Porph. tradit, et quamvis eosdem aliquas etiam Insulas occupasse constet, tamen Croatos maris usum Dalmatis et Venetis invitis habere non potuisse ex supradictis apparet.' Luc. de regn. lib. ii. c. xiii. p. 89.

[3] Luc. ii. c. xv. p. 96.

the king was satisfied with his tribute and exacted no further submission from the citizens. They began to thrive commercially; their contingent to the fleet of Pietro Orseolo had contributed in great measure to the downfall of the Narentines, and some of the island towns were quite able to protect themselves against the attacks of their semi-barbarous neighbours. Arts began to rise from the prostrate condition in which the barbarian conquests had left them, and if the buildings that have come down to us from the ages preceding the advent of the Hungarians are rude and for the most part humble, still they show the germs of future life; and one among them, the church of S. Donato at Zara, is conceived on a scale and in a style that is not easily to be matched among the contemporary works of other countries. *The Latins or Dalmatians.*

The three Dalmatian towns on the mainland within the kingdom of Croatia, Zara Traù and Spalato, had each a narrow territory attached to it, that of Zara bounded by the territories of the Croatian cities of Nona and Belgrad, that of Traù consisting only of the small plain to the north of the city with the hillsides enclosing it, and that of Spalato ceasing short of Salona and the peninsula or Vranjica or 'Piccola Venezia[1].' The Romans of Ossero Arbe and Veglia, though the rural districts of their islands were peopled by Croats, were more completely masters of the *A.D. 1195-1196.*

[1] Luc. de regn. lib. ii. c. xiii. p. 89.

soil, for the Croatian king had no maritime resources and less power of interference with them than with their brethren on the mainland.

3. State of Southern Dalmatia. The southern limit of the Croatian kingdom was the river Cettina which runs into the sea at Almissa. Beyond this lay the Serbs, the southern branch of the Slavonic family, among whom the ancient Latin culture was kept alive in the cities of Ragusa and Cattaro. Ragusa enjoyed a dubious independence, being under the nominal rule of the Eastern Empire which seldom interfered, and since the expedition of Orseolo under the more or less actively exercised influence of Venice. Cattaro was more directly exposed to Servian aggression, and when the Empire was no longer in a condition to protect her in her ancient allegiance, she placed herself voluntarily under
A.D. 1043. the protectorate of the Servian king, stipulating however that she should be allowed still to govern herself according to her ancient laws and customs.

The remaining islands of the Dalmatian archipelago, Brazza Curzola Lesina Lagosta Méleda and the rest, were either deserted, or had become thoroughly Slavonized.

4. The Hungarians described. Such was the condition of Dalmatia at the time when the Hungarians first made their appearance on the scene. Of these new-comers and their degree of civilization we may form some notion from the account given of them by a contemporary writer about half a century later[1]. Their

[1] Otto Frisingensis was a son of (Saint) Leopold, Marquis of

low stature, dusky complexion, and sunken eyes <small>The Hungarians.</small>
spoke of their Tartar descent, their manners were
fierce, and their speech to German ears barbarous. In summer-time they lived chiefly in
tents, in winter in huts of reeds, among which
were a few houses of wood, and a very few
buildings of stone. They rivalled the Greeks in
the length of their deliberations and the caution
with which they approached any new enterprize
of importance. Their obedience to their king was
absolute; and the nobles who came to attend the
court, each bringing with him his own seat, were
careful never to offend the royal ears by expressing or even whispering anything in contradiction
to the royal will. So completely was the king's
authority recognised throughout the seventy
counties of the realm that at the word of the
meanest messenger from the royal court the
highest noble would be seized in the midst of
his own satellites, loaded with chains, and subjected to the severest tortures. The whole population was liable to military service, a few
husbandmen only being left to till the ground.
The king took the field encircled by the 'hospites'

Austria, and born about 1111 or 1114. He was made bishop of
Frisinga in 1137-8, and published his Gesta Friderici, &c. about
1156-8. The monasteries near Freising had been ravaged by
Hungarians, so that Otto had some personal experience of them,
and he evidently did not love them; 'ut jure fortuna culpanda,
vel potius divina patientia admiranda sit, quae, ne dicam
hominibus, sed talibus hominum monstris tam delectabilem
exposuit terram.' Vid. Pertz, Mon. Germ. Hist. Script. vol. xx.

or princes of his court who formed his bodyguard, and who imitated as well as they could the arms and accoutrements of the neighbouring Germans, while the rest of the soldiers were squalid in person and sordid in their equipment[1].

Before this formidable and compacted nation of warriors the disorganized Croats could make little stand. Though Ladislaus was unable to return to complete his conquest, Coloman, his nephew and successor, was so far master of Croatia that in 1097 we find him at the Croatian city of Belgrad (Zara Vecchia), where he received his bride Busita, the daughter of Roger the Norman Count of Sicily. The simplicity of the times is illustrated by the celebration of the nuptial festivities in tents and huts of green boughs, there being but scanty accommodation within the city[2].

Coloman conquers Dalmatia, 1102-5

The Croats rose once more in arms to recover their independence, but were finally crushed by a fresh invasion of the Hungarians, and in 1102 Coloman was formally crowned at Belgrad king of Dalmatia and Croatia. His ambition extended to the conquest of the maritime towns which were then subject to Venice, but the moment was inopportune for a rupture with that power. The Venetian alliance was necessary to him in the

---

[1] Otto Frisingensis, De Gestis Friderici I, lib. i. in vol. xx. of Pertz's collection. Thom. Archid. ch. xxiv. tells a story curiously illustrative of the extraordinary veneration of the Hungarians for the royal person in the time of Emeric, 1196-1204.

[2] Gaufridus Malaterra, lib. 4. c. 25, in Luc., p. 111.

attack he meditated on the Normans of Apulia; the Doge was assured of his friendship, and the neutrality of the Venetians during his struggle with the rebellious Croatians was secured by his promise to respect the rights of the Republic over the maritime towns. A joint armament of Venetians and Hungarians sailed to invade Apulia; Brindisi and Monopoli were occupied, and the Normans were compelled to engage no longer to continue their incursions in the Adriatic[1].

In the year 1105 however, when the Venetians under their Doge Ordelafo Faliero were engaged in the Holy Land, and the Dalmatian cities were reduced in strength by the contingents they had furnished to the expedition, Coloman seized the opportunity to complete his scheme of conquest. Advancing into Dalmatia he laid siege to Zara, the principal city of the province, and assaulted it vigorously with a battering train. The Zaratini were aided in their resistance by Giovanni Ursini bishop of Traü, whose skill as an engineer gained him the credit of having miraculously destroyed the Hungarian engines, and to whose diplomacy the Zaratini were indebted for the favourable terms they succeeded in obtaining when further resistance became hopeless. From Zara Coloman advanced to receive the submission of the other Dalmatian cities[2]. The Spalatini, according to

Coloman acquires the Dalmatian cities.

A.D. 1104.

---

[1] Dandolo, lib. ix. c. x. pars 11.
[2] Thomas, c. xvii, says Coloman attacked Spalato first, then Traü, and lastly Zara. Lucio points out that he is mis-

Thomas Archdiaconus, astonished at the appearance of an enemy of unknown race, were disposed to resist, but finding '*that the men were Christians and that the king was disposed to deal liberally with them,*' they surrendered on condition that their ancient privileges should be confirmed; and Traü afterwards submitted on the same terms. The tower of Sta. Maria at Zara, which was built by the orders of Coloman after his triumphal entry, remains as a monument of his piety and of his desire to ingratiate himself with his new subjects. Their ancient privileges were confirmed, fresh charters were granted, and their municipal liberties were, nominally at all events, secured to them. The *Dalmatian* cities were to pay no tribute, they were to choose their own count and bishop whom the king would confirm, and to preserve their own Roman law and appoint their own judge; dues on foreign imports were apportioned between the king, the bishop, the count, and the municipality; no Hungarian or foreigner was to live within their walls against their will, and any one disliking Hungarian rule was free to depart with wife children servants and chattels[1].

Privileges of the 'Dalmatian' cities.

Not always respected.

That these charters should not always have been respected is natural, and Archidiaconus tells us how the Hungarian archbishop Manasses

taken; De regn. iii. iv. Dandolo also takes Coloman first to Spalato.

[1] Vid. Statute of Traü; Luc. de regn. lib. iii. c. iv. p. 117; also vi. c. ii.

and the Hungarian garrison which Coloman had established at Spalato—itself an infringement of the privilege—tried to make themselves masters of the city, and were defeated by the promptness of the citizens and their count. But notwithstanding occasional infringement here and elsewhere the charters remained as the foundation of civil liberty, to which appeal could always be made, and which could always be put forward when the political situation made the alliance of the cities valuable to the sovereign and concessions were more readily obtained. *Value of the privileges.*

The success of the Hungarians had been unopposed by the Venetians, who were at that time, as has been already said, engaged in the first Crusade, where the Doge Ordelafo Faliero was present in person. The Venetians however accused Coloman of bad faith, and after his death in 1114 the Doge Ordelafo Faliero invaded Dalmatia, and not only recovered the principal cities but took the Croatian towns of Belgrad Sebenico Nona and Novigrad which had never been Venetian before[1]. Arbe welcomed his arrival and volunteered her submission, Zara was taken except the castle, and Belgrad was occupied and garrisoned. In the following year, with the aid *Causes of Hungarian success.* *Recovery of Dalmatia by Ordelafo Faliero. A.D. 1115.* A.D. 1116.

---

[1] Luc. iii. c. v. p. 122. It is a significant fact that before engaging in this expedition the Venetians appealed to the Emperor Alexius, thus recognizing his nominal supremacy in Dalmatia, which the Hungarians ignored; their conquest being in fact the final severance of the tie that bound that province to Constantinople. Vid. Dandolo.

of Alexius and the Emperor Henry V, the Doge renewed the contest, defeated the Hungarian Ban, took the castle at Zara, captured and destroyed the '*impregnable*' stronghold of Sebenico, received the submission of Spalato and Traü, and returned in triumph to Venice. In the following year however he was slain in battle against a fresh invasion of Hungarians, and a truce was agreed to for some years.

<small>A.D. 1117. Death of Ordelafo Faliero.</small>

While the Doge Domenico Michieli was engaged in the Holy Land and in hostilities with the Byzantine Empire, no longer friendly to Venice after the death of Alexius, Stephen II. recovered Spalato and Traü[1]; but on his return the Doge expelled the Hungarians from both cities, took Belgrad, and entered Zara in triumph. Belgrad, where Coloman had been crowned, which had been a favourite seat of the Croatians, and which the Hungarians had endeavoured to make a rival to Zara, had awakened the jealousy of the Venetians, who took this opportunity of wreaking their vengeance on it. Belgrad was utterly destroyed, the seat of the bishopric was removed to Scardona, and many of the inhabitants settled at Sebenico, which, increased in population and wealth, and favoured by its natural advantages, began to grow in importance, and by the charter of Stephen III. in 1167 was placed on an equality with the

<small>A.D. 1127. Destruction of Belgrad by Domenico Michieli.</small>

<small>Sebenico becomes a city.</small>

---

[1] Traü had been sacked and nearly destroyed in 1123 by a Saracen fleet, and was in no condition to resist any assailant.

Dalmatian municipalities, and was thenceforth reckoned among the '*Dalmatian*' cities[1].

During the succeeding reign of Bela II, 'the blind[2],' the Hungarians made no attempt on Dalmatia, but under that of his son Geiza II, who conquered Bosnia and made it tributary to Hungary, Spalato and Traü voluntarily gave themselves to the Hungarians and received from Geiza a confirmation of their privileges, while Sebenico, as has been above mentioned, was raised by his son Stephen III. to the rank of a privileged and chartered town. *Hungarians recover Spalato, A.D. 1141; and Traü, A.D. 1151. A.D. 1167. Sebenico.*

It was at this time that the see of Zara was raised to metropolitan rank. Hitherto it had been suffragan to the ancient see of Salona or Spalato, but Spalato was now Hungarian, and it became of consequence to teach the Zaratini to look to Venice as the seat of spiritual no less than secular jurisdiction. In 1145 Lampridio, who had been elected bishop of Zara by the influence of the Venetian count Petrana, obtained the pallium from Pope Anastasius, and the new archiepiscopal see was subjected to the Venetian primate, the Patriarch of Grado. The suffragan bishops of the new metropolitan were those of Ossero Veglia and Arbe, and an attempt was made to include the new see which was at this time founded *A.D. 1145. Archbishopric of Zara founded.*

---

[1] Luc. iii. ch. viii. p. 127.
[2] Otto Frising. Vita Herbordi, lib. i: 'Bela qui a patruo suo Colomanno rege cum patre suo Almo duce diebus adolescentiae luminibus privatus,' &c. Almus however was not blinded by a *brother's* hand; vid. note above, page 34.

at Lesina[1]. But the archbishop of Spalato succeeded in maintaining his jurisdiction over that island.

<small>A.D. 1171. Invasion of the Emperor Manuel.</small> The vast designs of the Emperor Manuel, who dreamed of chasing the German Emperor beyond the Alps, and uniting the Roman world once more under a single sceptre, brought the Byzantines again, and for the last time, into Dalmatia. Milan was encouraged in her splendid resistance to Frederick by Greek gold, which enabled her to restore her demolished walls; and Ancona was laden with benefits in order to secure so convenient an entrance into Italy. These favours to the Anconitans, whom they regarded as rivals, and of whose prosperity they were extremely jealous, offended the Venetians[2], who sent a fleet and captured five galleys of Ancona. Reviving the obsolete claims of the Empire over Dalmatia Manuel sent a powerful fleet into the Adriatic, which overawed the resistance of the Venetians and received the submission of Spalato Traü and <small>His conquests in Dalmatia.</small> Ragusa. Traü, still half in ruins from the Saracen assault and capture, was in no condition to resist a siege and was speedily recovered by the Venetian fleet. Spalato remained subject to the Empire till the death of Manuel in 1180. Ragusa,

---

[1] Thom. Archid. c. xx.

[2] 'Quod Anconitani Graecum imperium nimio diligerent . . . Veneti speciali odio Anconam oderint.' Vid. Gibbon, ch. lvi. 'Hoc tempore Anconitani Emanuelis obedientes imperio Venetos ut sibi aemulos coeperunt habere.' Dandolo, ix. xv. 17.

according to the Venetian historians, was recovered by the Venetian fleet, and the imperial standards of Manuel were thrown down to make way for the banner of the republic. The wonted oaths of fidelity were exacted anew, a Venetian count was appointed, and the archbishop was compelled to accept the metropolitan of Grado as his spiritual superior[1]. But the Ragusan historians, jealous of their free traditions, dispute the accuracy of this account, as they do that of the submission to Pietro Orseolo. 'The war was terminated by an agreement inglorious to the Empire, insufficient for the republic; and a complete vengeance of these and of fresh injuries was reserved for the succeeding generation[2].' *Peace between Venice and Manuel.*

The security afforded them by the maritime supremacy of Venice in the Adriatic on the one hand, and the overthrow of the Croatian kingdom by the Hungarians on the other, had been of service to the Dalmatian cities and enabled them to develop their resources without impediment. Zara in particular had been a gainer by these revolutions; she stood foremost in wealth and population, she had emancipated herself from the ecclesiastical control of Spalato, and her territory had been increased since the destruction of Belgrad by a grant from the Venetians of the islands formerly dependent on that city[3]. *Prosperity of the Dalmatian cities.*

[1] Dandolo, l. ix. c. xv. pars 24.
[2] Gibbon, vii. ch. lvi.
[3] Thomas Archidiaconus describes the Zaratini as 'divitiis

A.D. 1171.
Sedition at Zara quelled.

In 1171, in the time of Doge Vitale Michieli II, a sedition occurred at Zara, about which there are several conflicting accounts. Lucio conjectures that it was connected with the election of the count, the privilege most jealously prized and guarded by a Dalmatian city. The Venetian count, Domenico Morosini, son of the preceding Doge, was expelled, and the countship conferred on Lampridio the archbishop, a native Zaratine. The disturbance was easily quelled and Morosini restored, but on the death of Lampridio fresh dissensions arose about the subjection of the arch-

A.D. 1178.
Refusal to submit archbishopric to patriarchate of Grado.

bishopric to the patriarchate of Grado. The new archbishop was forbidden by the citizens to acknowledge the patriarchal authority, and an appeal was made to Rome; but Alexander was under obligations to Venice, and the appeal of the Zaratini was rejected. 'It is ours to teach the people, not to obey them,' said the Pontiff in language that has the true ecclesiastical ring; and the rebellious archbishop was enjoined to submit, and punished by deprivation of the pallium and of the right to consecrate his suffragans. The

A.D. 1180–1181.
First revolt of Zara to the Hungarians.

Zaratini however forbad their prelate to obey this sentence, threw off their allegiance to Venice, and offered it to Bela III. of Hungary, who placed a garrison within the walls and strengthened the

affluentes ... superbia tumidi, potentia elati, de injuriis gloriantes, de malitiis exultantes, deridebant inferiores, contemnebant superiores, nullos sibi fore pares credebant.' This speaks for the prosperity of the Zaratini, and as to the rest it should be remembered that Thomas was a Spalatine.

fortifications in anticipation of a Venetian attack. Revolt of the other Spalato had already submitted to Hungary; Traü cities. and the islands of Brazza and Lesina successively followed its example; and the Venetians, crippled by their recent war with Manuel, were at first unable to take any serious steps to reassert their authority. Traü was for a short time occupied by A.D. 1183. the Doge Orio Mastropiero, but on his departure the city returned again to the Hungarians. The eastern half of the island of Pago, which had in some manner passed from the possession of Nona to that of Zara, was occupied and made the seat of a Venetian count; but an attempt on the city of Zara failed; the city was strong in its own resources and supported by the Hungarian alliance, and the Venetians were obliged to content themselves with holding the islands and impeding the commerce on which the prosperity of Zara depended.

But Zara was regarded by the Venetians as the key to their maritime supremacy in the Adriatic, and they never lost sight of the necessity of recovering it. An opportunity at last occurred in the time of the Doge Enrico Dandolo. After the death of Bela III. in 1196 the kingdom of Hungary was torn by the struggle between his sons Emeric and Andrew[1], and Emeric after having successfully overcome the opposition to his government was indisposed by illness for an active policy. At A.D. 1201. this juncture the fourth Crusade was proclaimed The fourth Crusade. by Innocent III, and a deputation from the levies

---

[1] Thom. Archid. c. xxiv.

in France and Flanders, in which countries alone the enterprise had been warmly undertaken, arrived in Venice to arrange for the transport of the crusaders to the Holy Land by sea. The Venetians listened to the exhortations of their blind and aged Doge, who with the ardour of a hero urged the conclusion of an agreement with the crusaders and the participation of the republic in the holy war. Venice was fixed as the rendezvous of the allies in the following year, the republic undertook to transport the entire force of 4500 knights and 20,000 foot, to provision them for nine months, and to join the expedition with 50 galleys of their own; while in return the pilgrims were to pay before their departure 85,000 marks of silver, and to engage that all conquests should be equally divided between the confederates.

A.D. 1202. Rendezvous of Crusaders at Venice. At the appointed time everything was ready except the 85,000 marks of the foreigners, of which 34,000 were still wanting; and while the French deplored the apparent fruitlessness of the toil and expense they had already incurred, the Venetians had to fear the loss of their extensive preparations and the spoiling of the provisions they *Reduction of Zara proposed.* had stored up. In this conjuncture the policy of the Doge proposed, and the necessities of the French accepted, as a way out of the difficulty, that the united forces should recover for the Venetians their revolted city of Zara, and that the services of the French in this enterprise should be taken as an equivalent to the deficient 34,000 marks.

On Oct. 2, 1202, the allies set sail from Venice. A detachment touched at Trieste and alarmed that city into an agreement to pay tribute to the republic, and the whole force then proceeded to Zara, which they reached on Nov. 10. The French troops were landed, the Venetian galleys burst the chain that closed the entrance of the harbour, and the Zaratini, finding no help was forthcoming from the Hungarians or Croatians, sent ambassadors to the Doge and offered to surrender on condition their lives were spared.

<small>A.D. 1202. Siege of Zara by the Crusaders.</small>

The Doge did not think it proper to act without consulting his allies, but when, after obtaining their consent, he returned to his tent he found the ambassadors gone. During his absence some of the French who were unfavourable to the enterprise had advised the envoys to withdraw their offer, and assured them that the pilgrims would not assault a Christian city. The envoys had accordingly returned to their countrymen and persuaded them to continue their resistance; and when the Doge called on his allies to aid him in taking Zara by force, the abbot of Vaux rose and forbad the soldiers of the cross to attack a Christian city, and several of the barons refused to fulfil their engagement.

The more politic counsels of those French leaders however prevailed who saw the necessity of carrying out their agreement with the Venetians, and a general assault on the city followed, the French attacking it by land and the Venetians by

A.D. 1202.
Capture of Zara by the Crusaders.

sea. After a resistance of five days, one of the towers being undermined by the Venetians, the garrison found themselves unable to make any further resistance, and surrendered on condition that their lives should be spared. The Venetians destroyed the town walls and towers, and according to Thomas Archidiaconus levelled all the houses, leaving nothing standing but the churches[1]. This however is not confirmed by other writers, and is inconsistent with the fact that both Venetians and French wintered at Zara, and did not sail thence to the conquest of Constantinople till

A.D. 1203.
the 7th of April in the following year. The destruction of the buildings may have been only partial, but the town was desolated, and the inhabitants mistrusting the clemency of the Doge fled in numbers to the Hungarian territory. Disputes broke out between the allies, in which the Venetians being numerically the weaker party suffered most, and peace was restored with difficulty by the leaders. Universal disapproval fell on the crusaders who had sacked a Christian city. Among the French themselves as we have seen some acted against their inclination, and one of the most illustrious among them, Simon de Montfort, departed from the camp before the assault was given. Innocent III. showered his reproofs and excommunications on the offenders, but though the French submitted and were

[1] Thom. Archid. c. xxv; Villehardouin, ch. xlix. Vid. below, Chapter iii. on Zara.

absolved, the Venetians refused to acknowledge the right of a churchman to interfere in their temporal concerns.

It was at Zara that the final treaty was made with Alexius the fugitive prince from Constantinople, and the enterprise of restoring him and his father to the imperial throne was due principally to the arguments of the Venetians, anxious to complete the imperfect satisfaction that had been made them for the injuries received from Manuel, and eager to embrace the opportunity of the presence of such powerful auxiliaries[1]. On April 7, 1203, the united armament set sail, leaving Zara overwhelmed with a ruin scarcely less complete than that which had for her sake been inflicted on Belgrad some seventy-five years before.

Treaty of the Crusaders with Alexius.

A.D. 1203. *Departure of the fleet for Constantinople.*

The exiled Zaratini lost no opportunity of revenging themselves on Venetian traders after the fleet and army had sailed, and to check their depredations the Venetians built a castle on an island opposite Zara, which was taken and destroyed by the Zaratini with the aid of ten galleys of Gaieta which were induced by the archbishop of Spalato to take the part of the exiles. The fugitive population began to return to their desolate city, to restore and inhabit the ruined houses, and to repair their shattered walls, but

Return of the fugitives to Zara and submission to Venice.

---

[1] 'Exinde Veneti sperantes refectionem damnorum ab Emanuele olim promissam sed nondum solutam Francorum auxilio se confecturos simulque inopiae militum suppletum iri,' &c. Luc. l. iv. c. i. p. 155.

hearing that a fleet was being equipped at Venice, and would be upon them before their defences were complete, they finally resolved to make their submission. The Venetians had enough on their hands elsewhere, and were willing to come to terms. Domaldus the Hungarian count was dismissed and a Venetian put in his place, the Zaratini were bound to serve against the enemies of the republic, their possessions in the islands were restored to them in return for an annual tribute of 3000 rabbit skins, and it was agreed that their archbishop should acknowledge the patriarch of Grado for his spiritual superior.

A.D. 1217.
Andrew II.
Andrew II, brother and successor of Emeric, took the cross and gathered a powerful armament for the transport of which he was obliged to have recourse to the navies of Venice, Ancona, Zara, and other towns on the shores of the Adriatic, and in recompense for the friendly offices of the Venetians he ceded to them all claims the crown of Hungary might have on Zara[1]. The rendezvous was at Spalato, whither so vast a multitude assembled that they could not be collected within the city, but encamped in the surrounding country. The king was lodged 'sumptuously' in a house called 'Mata,' outside the north gate, the Porta aurea of Diocletian's palace; ten thousand knights formed his immediate following and constituted the flower of the army, and the multitude of

[1] 'Ut jura quae Rex in Jadra sc asserit habere in Venetos transferrentur.' Dandolo, lib. x. c. iv. pars. 26.

infantry and followers appeared to the eyes of Thomas the Archdeacon innumerable. Ships could not be found sufficient to transport them all, and some had to return home and others to wait till the following year[1].

Before departing from Spalato the grateful king offered the citizens the fortress of Clissa and the countship of the neighbouring islands; and finding the Spalatines deficient in that public spirit which should have inspired them to accept at all events the fortress which stood in such dangerous proximity and commanded the passes to the interior[2], he did the best he could for the interests of the city by entrusting Clissa not to one of his nobles but to the grand master of the Templars in Hungary, with a charge to change periodically the members of the brotherhood who garrisoned it.

At this time while the Hungarians were occupied by troubles at home, and the Venetians engaged at Constantinople, the Almissans come first into notice as inheritors of the piratical traditions of the South Dalmatian Serbs. Their ranks were swelled by outlaws and political refugees from the cities, and by ruffians who wanted employment for their arms. Their attacks on Venetian com-

Almissan piracies.

A.D. 1221.

---

[1] Thom. Archid. c. xxvi. Andrew was summoned home by disturbances in his kingdom of Hungary, which he reached after a series of romantic adventures. He had been offered the throne of Constantinople by the Latins, but declined it in favour of Peter of Courtenay. Vid. Gibbon, ch. lxi.

[2] 'Spalatenses suo more ad publica nimis tardi ad privata commoda singuli intendebant.' Thom. Arch. xxvi.

merce were at first commanded or encouraged by the kings of Hungary, incapacitated at the time from taking any other revenge for the loss of Zara, but after the Hungarians and Venetians had come to terms by the treaty of Andrew II. in 1217, the pirates continued their operations on their own account.

Almissa at the mouth of the river Cetina, was protected towards the sea by the intricacy of the navigation, and towards the land by an impassable barrier of mountains; and issuing from this secret lair the Almissans preyed indiscriminately on the commerce of the Adriatic, and even stopped and pillaged pilgrims on their way to Palestine. So insecure did the navigation of those seas become that Pope Honorius III. wrote to the Spalatini urging them to unite with the other Dalmatians in a crusade against the Almissans, and he sent a legate, the Subdeacon Aconcio, to ensure attention to his mandates[1]. Spalato Traü Clissa and Sebenico united in a league against the corsairs; a naval and equestrian force was collected, and the Almissans, finding themselves attacked both by land and sea and unable to sustain the contest, made their submission, burned their boats, and swore to keep the peace for the future.

Mission of Aconcio the legate.

Almissan piracy repressed.

The Bogomiles.

But the mission of Aconcio was not only directed against the secular enormities of the Almissans: the taint of heresy which had long

---

[1] See Luc. de regn. lib. iv. c. iv. p. 162 for the letter of Honorius.

infected the Serbs Croatians and Bulgarians of the interior had extended to the cities of the coast and caused serious alarm to the Papal court.

The history of the Bogomiles[1] or Paterenes among the Southern Slavs is extremely obscure and has yet to be explored and written. The accounts of Roman Catholic historians are naturally coloured by prejudice, and even at the present day, though in Bosnia and Herzegovina there are thousands of Bogomiles who adhere with fidelity to the creed their forefathers have professed from time immemorial, and to which they have clung through trials of exile fire and blood not inferior to those of their noble brethren in the valleys of Piedmont, it is difficult to get any trustworthy account of their habits and opinions from their neighbours[2]. Like the Vaudois they are poor and illiterate, and unlike them they have not been so fortunate as to obtain defenders and excite interest in Protestant countries. They have had no Milton to implore vengeance for their slaughtered saints, and no Cromwell to stay the hand of the oppressor in their extremity, and now that they are no longer persecuted their

---

[1] The word 'Bog' in the Illyrian language means 'God.'

[2] In Dalmatia I found current even among men of cultivation stories about the Bogomiles of the same scandalous character as those that were spread about the Albigenses or Paulicians, and no doubt equally untrue. In the native 'Protestantism' of these countries a wide and interesting subject awaits the industry of some one who has mastered the Servian language, and can be trusted to write without prejudice.

very existence is almost forgotten. And yet at one time it seemed probable that their doctrines would have prevailed over those of Rome throughout the Balkan peninsula wherever the Slavs held rule, and at one time the Paterene bishop was on at least an equal footing with the Latin and Greek prelates at the courts of Servia and Bosnia.

<small>Early history of Bosnia.</small>
The history of these two countries before the advent of the Hungarians is very obscure[1]. Their inhabitants belonged to the Serb branch of the Slavonic settlers whom Heraclius brought in to dispossess the Avars, and being more removed from the superior civilization of the coast and less brought into contact with the countries of western Europe than the Croatians, they were more backward in their national development. Bosnia at all events seems to have remained in a kind of dependence on the dukes and kings of Croatia till that kingdom was itself absorbed by Hungary in 1102, after which it enjoyed a brief independence till conquered by Geiza II. in 1141, when the Ban became a vassal of the Hungarian crown.

<small>Early history of Servia.</small>
Servia was better able to preserve her independence under her own princes of the Nemagna dynasty of whom the first was Dessan, duke of Chelmo or Chulm, who obtained the throne about 1150 after a series of bloody revolu-

---

[1] A sketch of Bosnian history will be found in Mr. Evans's 'Through Bosnia and Herzegovina.'

tions[1]. Stephen Nemagna, Lord of Servia or Rascia, about 1217 exchanged his title of 'Mega Juppanus' for that of King, with the consent of Pope Honorius III. who sent his legate to crown him the first king of Servia[2].

At the courts both of Bosnia and Servia the Bogomile doctrines were regarded favourably. Not only did Culin the great Ban of Bosnia openly espouse them and protect those who professed them as his father Boric had done before him, but Daniel the Bosnian bishop declared himself an adherent, and Bosnia became the refuge of those whom persecution had driven out of other countries. The thunders of the Vatican rolled harmlessly over their heads, and the commands of the King of Hungary were unheeded; for Culin felt himself strong enough to resist any forcible interference, and the arguments of

Spread of Bogomilism in the thirteenth century.

---

[1] The duchy of Chulmia or Chelmo included the maritime district known as the Craina, between the Narenta and the Cetina, together with some of the neighbouring islands. Luc. lib. iv. c. iv. p. 160 explains 'Slavo vocabulo Crainam id est finitimam regionem dictam.' He identifies Chelmo with the Zachlumia of Porphyrogenitus.

[2] He is generally distinguished by the historians as 'Il primo coronato.' Vid. Thom. Archid. c. xxvi. The Servian crown was however nominally dependent on that of Hungary. Bela IV. in 1243 styles himself 'Bela D. G. Hungariae, Dalmatiae, Croatiae, Ramae, Serviae, Galiciae, Lodomeriaeque Rex.' Luc. p. 165. Lewis the Great in 1345 uses the same titles. Vid. Obsid. Iadr. lib. ii. c. iii. Rama included Bosnia. The King of Servia called himself King of Rascia, one part of Servia, to avoid the title used by the King of Hungary. Vid. Luc. de regn. v. iii. p. 256.

Aconcio during his mission into Bosnia produced little effect. The doctrines spread down to the coast; they were generally embraced in the territory of Cattaro; two successive counts of Spalato are described by the orthodox archdeacon as tainted with heresy[1], and the crowning sin for which he conceives Zara to have been visited with destruction in 1202 is her defection from the Catholic faith and her inclination to heretical opinions[2]. For there was according to him scarcely any man of importance at Zara who did not 'receive heretics and cherish them.' After Culin's death a Catholic Ban Zibisclave was appointed, but his influence was insufficient, and at last fire and sword were called to the aid of orthodoxy in Bosnia as they had been in Provence. For centuries Bosnian history is filled with annals of persecution and bloodshed, but Bogomilism has never been extirpated, and the number of its adherents at the present day is probably far greater than is generally supposed;

Persecution of the Bogomiles.

[1] 'Buisenus ... licet esset vir nobilis dives et potens, fautor tamen haereticorum erat.'

'Erat autem idem Petrus vir potens et bellicosus, sed non sine infamia haereticae foeditatis.' Thom. Archid. c. xxix.

[2] 'Hoc enim ad nequitiae suae cumulum addiderunt, ut Catholicae fidei normam spernerent, et haeretica se permitterent tabe respergi. Nam pene omnes qui nobiliores et majores Iadrae censebantur libenter recipiebant haereticos et fovebant.' Thom. Archid. c. xxv. Yet if this were so one may be surprised at the abstention of Simon de Montfort, and the indignation of Innocent III; the head that planned and the hand that executed the massacre of the unhappy Albigenses need not have been so scrupulous in this case.

for it is said that during the insurrection of 1876 there were among the refugees at Ragusa more than 2000 Bogomiles from the single district of Popovo in Herzegovina[1].

That the persecuted 'Protestants' should occasionally have retaliated by deeds of violence is not to be wondered at, and we are told of three brothers who were killed for their adherence to the Catholic faith near Cattaro[2]. But the tolerance of the '*heretical*' Servian kings contrasts favourably with the bigotry of the other party: we read of a Patarene bishop attending by order of Ourosh II. to witness the restoration of a relic by a Patarene who had stolen it, and at the court of Ourosh III. we find amicably seated at the same council table the bishops of the three rites, Greek, Patarene, and Latin[3].

The piracies of the Almissans had only ceased for a time and they soon broke out again, encouraged by the loose government of the Hungarians, and the factious strife of the citizens of the Dalmatian towns. Spalato, at last, tired of civil discord and disgusted with her Croatian counts, resolved, on the advice of Thomas the Archdeacon,

Renewed piracy of Almissans.

[1] Vid. Introduction to Mr. Evans's 'Through Bosnia and Herzegovina,' p. xliv.
[2] Vid. History of Cattaro, infra, c. xxii.
[3] Memorie storiche sulle bocche di Cattaro. G. Gelcich.

our historian of these times, to choose a 'Latin' podestà and to govern the city on the Latin or Italian model. Thomas himself and Micha Madii, were deputed to visit Ancona and ask that city to send one of her citizens to govern them for a year. The choice fell on Gargano degli Arsacidi, and his term of office, which was extended to a second and third year, was marked by firm and judicious administration. In his second year of office he undertook to punish and repress the Almissans. Twelve hundred armed men represented the military force of Spalato, to whom the Traürini added reluctantly a small contingent, and with this force Gargano began the campaign by seizing the island of Brazza which with that of Lesina was held by Osor and Pribislav sons of Malduco, count of Almissa. Osor the count of Brazza was nearly surprised and captured, but 'like a slimy eel' he managed to slip through the fingers of his pursuers, and raising a large force of Almissans so harassed the Spalatines that Gargano could with difficulty induce them to continue the war. Osor ravaged the island of Solta, violating churches, breaking the altars like a Pagan, scattering the relics, and throwing to the ground with daring hand the very Eucharist. But in a second foray on the island of Brazza the Almissans were surprised and worsted, Osor himself captured, and his whole force either slain or taken. The captives lay in prison at Spalato for ten months before the

Almissans could be brought to surrender their fleet and swear to abstain from piracy[1].

The Dalmatians were no sooner rid of the Almissan piracies than a fresh and more frightful visitation befel them. The earlier part of the thirteenth century was marked by the great outburst of the Moguls or Tartars. Between 1210 and 1258 China, Persia, and the Caliphate fell before the arms of Zinghis and his sons. Between 1235 and 1245 Batou, nephew of Octai and grandson of Zinghis, overran Russia, burning Kieff and Moscow, and in 1241 after penetrating into Poland as far as Lignitz, he invaded Hungary. Bela IV, son and successor of Andrew II, who had married Maria daughter of the Emperor Theodore Lascaris, was unpopular, and neither he nor his ministers seem to have made any serious preparations to resist the invasion which had for so many years been imminent. The Hungarians it is said had declined from their ancient martial character and become luxurious[2], and it was with some difficulty that an army was assembled to meet the invaders on the frontier. A disastrous

A.D. 1241. Tartar invasion of Hungary.

Defeat of Bela IV.

---

[1] Thom. Archid. c. xxxvi. His account of the affair is written with spirit. His heroes make orations to their troops in true classic style.

[2] 'Terra Ung. omnibus bonis locuples et faecunda causam praestabat suis filiis ex rerum copia immoderatis delitiis delectari. Quod enim aliud erat juvenilis aetatis studium nisi polire caesariem, cutem mundare, virilem habitum in muliebrem cultum mutare. Tota dies exquisitis conviviis aut mollibus expendebatur locis, nocturnos sopores vix hora diei tertia terminabat,' &c. Thom. Archid. c. xxxvii.

defeat in the first battle laid Hungary prostrate, and the victorious Tartars overran the whole country slaying and burning, their women and children vying with the men in cruelty and bloodshed.

The country north of the Danube was lost in a single day. The cities were laid in ruins, the churches defiled and thrown down,. the Danube itself ran with blood, and the corpses were collected in ghastly heaps along its banks to terrify the fugitive and native Hungarians on the other side whose fate it was to be devoured next. The Hungarians of a later age now expiated the atrocities of their forefathers, and as in 924 the cry had gone up from the churches of Italy 'Oh save and deliver us from the arrows of the Hungarians,' so now arose the doleful litany 'From the fury of the Tartars, good Lord, deliver us[1].'

Advance of Tartars into Dalmatia.

Bela had sent his wife his children and his treasures to the inaccessible rock of Clissa near Spalato. He himself escaped from the battle into Austria, and thence to Zagabria (Agram) where he assembled around him the remains of his shattered forces. The hard frosts of January enabled the enemy to cross the Danube. Buda was burned, and Strigonium (Gran) shared the same fate, but Alba Regalis (Stuhlweissenburg) was saved by her impassable marshes, and by the haste of the Tartar leader Caydan to overtake the king. The arrival of the invading hordes at

A.D. 1242. Flight of Bela IV.

[1] Vid. Gibbon, chapters lv. and lxiv.

the Drave was the signal for the further flight of the Hungarians. Abandoning Zagabria to its fate Bela retreated with the flower of his army and numerous magnates and bishops of the realm, and took refuge within the walls of Spalato, where he was hospitably received by the podestà Gargano and the archbishop and people. But even the stout walls of Diocletian behind which he had sheltered himself failed to give the trembling king any feeling of security: he urged the Spalatines to prepare him a galley for escape by sea, upbraided them for their slowness in completing it[1], and hastily embarking with his wife and his treasures fled to Traü; nor did he venture to rest even there, but hid himself in a neighbouring islet, still known as Kraglievaò, *the king's abode*, off the end of the island of Bua.

Meanwhile the Tartars were in hot pursuit. After a general massacre of their prisoners they descended into Croatia and appeared before the walls of Spalato. The inhabitants taking the first body of them to be Slavs, such as they were in the habit of encountering, prepared to go out and attack them, but when undeceived by the Hungarian refugees who had had experience of Tartars, a panic fell on the city.

Tartar invasion of Dalmatia. A.D. 1242.

---

[1] 'Fecerunt autem Spalat. omnia ad Regis placitum, hoc excepto quod ei quandam galeam minime potuere tam celeriter preparare quantum Rex declinans Tartarorum rabiem expetebat. Quod factum non satis acquanimiter tulit Regius animus.' Thom. Archid. c. xxxix.

Tartar invasion.
A.D. 1242.

Only a few, however, of the Tartars turned aside to Spalato; the king was the object of their pursuit, and after an ineffectual attack on Clissa, finding he was not there, they followed him to Traü. It was March, the weather was severe, and there was no grass for the horses; and Caydan was only able to bring a part of his army with him. Unable to ford the deep muddy channel which isolates Traü from the mainland, and unprovided with boats for passing it, he challenged the citizens by a messenger in the Slavonic tongue to surrender the king, and not to involve themselves in the fate of one who was only a foreigner amongst them. The Traürini, however, stood firm, and the Tartars were obliged to give up the pursuit[1]. During March they appeared five or six times before the cities, and then passed on through Bosnia and Servia to Upper Dalmatia. On Ragusa they could make no impression, but they burned Cattaro and sacked Suacia and Drivosto, putting the entire

---

[1] The channel is now a mere ditch, but was in ancient times much wider. Still it could not have been that which finally checked the Tartars, for we are told by Thomas himself (ch. xxxviii.) of their practice of making boats of osiers and skins when they came to rivers too deep to ford. The explanation of their retreat is probably to be found in their want of apparatus for a regular siege, and still more in the difficulty alluded to by Thom. Archid. of finding fodder for their horses; their force consisted of cavalry, and there is but little pasturage in Dalmatia. The narrative of the Tartar invasion by Thomas who was an eye-witness is extremely interesting. Vid. his chapters xxxvii. to xl.

population to the sword. Returning through Servia and Bulgaria they massacred their remaining captives, and finally crossing the Danube returned to the Volga and relieved Europe of their frightful presence. Famine followed their steps, for the husbandmen had been unable to sow their crops, and it is estimated that the Tartars destroyed as many by the want and pestilence which they left behind them as they had actually slain in battle or in cold blood. It is no wonder that the world of those days read in this awful visitation one of the signs premonitory of the advent of Antichrist. *Retreat of the Tartars. A.D. 1242.*

Bela, assured of his safety, emerged from his hiding-place, and leaving his queen and his youthful son Stephen at Clissa prepared to return to his capital. His two daughters Catharine and Margaret had died during the horrors of the invasion and were buried in a stone coffin over the door of the duomo of Spalato, and William, son of the Emperor Baldwin, who was betrothed to Margaret, died at the same time at Traü where he lies buried in the Cathedral. *Return of Bela IV. to Hungary.*

Bela arrived at the island of Veglia, then governed by the Frangipani as feudatories of the Venetian republic. Policy and compassion both induced Bartolommeo the reigning count to help the Hungarian cause, and it is said the force which he raised at his own expense encountered and defeated a Tartar army on the plain of Grobnico near Fiume[1]. However this may have been, it appears that the count raised 25,000 marks in coin and collected an amount of plate and other precious things which he bestowed on his royal guest, who in return granted to the counts Federigo and Bartolommeo Frangipani in 1255 the feud of Segna in Croatia. Their acceptance of this gift brought upon them the suspicion of the Venetians, who deprived them of their feud of Veglia in consequence, and did not readmit them till 1260.

A.D. 1242. Second revolt of Zara from Venetians. Either just before or at the time of the Tartar invasion Zara again revolted from the Venetians, instigated by the Emperor Frederick II, against whom the Venetians had allied themselves with the Pope. The Count Giov. Michieli was expelled, the aid of the Hungarians implored, the Venetian residents imprisoned and their property seized, though both were afterwards released and restored. The Venetians assaulted the city with a powerful fleet from both sides having burst the chain that guarded the port, but the Zaratini held out till the Ban Dionysius whom Bela had sent to command them was wounded and left

---

[1] Vid. Cubich, Notizie naturali e storiche sull' Isola di Veglia, part ii. p. 75, but he does not give his authority, and no mention of this battle or of the incredible slaughter of 65,000 Tartars occurs in Thom. Archid. or in Lucio. Bela's deed of gift in 1255 mentions the 25,000 marks and other presents but says nothing of the victory. Vid. inf. History of Veglia, ch. xxvi. There is another Grobnica or Grobnico near Zara which, according to some, was the scene of this battle.

the city, when the whole population was seized with panic, and the Hungarians first, and then the citizens, made for the gates in order to escape. The Venetians, landing their troops, allowed the fugitives to pass with impunity, and the city was recovered with scarcely any loss of life[1]. To ensure the fidelity of Zara in the future the Venetians planted a colony of their own citizens in the half-deserted city, and for their protection against the expatriated Zaratini, who had taken refuge in Nona and other towns subject to the Hungarians, a defensive league was formed between the new citizens and the islands of Arbe Cherso and Veglia, which were then feudatory counties held under the republic by the families of Morosini and Frangipani. The expatriated Zaratini, after for some time endeavouring to revenge themselves by reprisals on Venetian merchantmen, at last submitted themselves to the good pleasure of the Doge and were readmitted on liberal terms. The Venetians had enough to occupy themselves in the daily increasing perils and sinking fortunes of the Latin Empire of Constantinople, and the Pope, anxious to unite Europe for a fresh crusade, used his best endeavours to reconcile Venice and the King of Hungary. Peace was agreed to on the terms that the Hungarians should leave Venice in undisturbed possession of Zara and the

Zara recovered, A.D. 1243, June 2.

A.D. 1244. Amnesty granted to the Zaratini.

---

[1] Thom. Archid. says 'Tota civitas capta est ferme absque ulla strage alterutrius partis,' ch. xliii. Dandolo says 'absque notabili caede.'

Division of Dalmatia between Venice and Hungary.

neighbouring islands, and that the maritime towns beyond the Kerka—Sebenico Traü and Spalato—should remain subject to the Hungarian crown. An amnesty was granted to the fugitive Zaratini and they were allowed to return, but from being allies of the Republic they were reduced to the condition of subjects. The liberty of electing their own count, enjoyed by all the other privileged towns of Dalmatia, was not restored to the rebellious citizens, but they were required to accept a count appointed by the Venetians, whose term of office was to be fixed by the pleasure of the Doge, and who was to be accompanied by two councillors, also appointed by the sovereign city[1]. A garrison was placed in the castle under a Venetian castellan, and the Zaratini were forbidden to rebuild their walls without the express permission of the Doge. They were to give hostages for five years, and to contribute a contingent of one man for each house to the Venetian armament in case of a levy of more than thirty galleys for service beyond Ragusa, and to pay a life pension of two hundred Venetian lire to the count Zuanne Michieli whom they had expelled.

Relative positions of Venice and Hungary. A.D. 1244.

By the terms of this settlement and by the effect of previous circumstances Venice had now obtained all, or nearly all, that she cared to have. The possession of Zara and the islands was the

---

[1] The conditions are cited at length by Luc. lib. iv. c. vi. p. 168.

main object of her policy in Dalmatia, as the means to that dominion of the Adriatic which was necessary to her commercial and national greatness. For the security of her commerce she required the islands, for in those days of slow navigation by short stages her shipping required stations and arsenals at short distances, and it was indispensable that these should be in her own and not in foreign and possibly hostile hands. Her maritime supremacy to be sure placed the islands at all times within her grasp, but if Zara were in the possession of an enemy she was liable to lose them at any moment, whereas if Zara were hers it was of less importance who occupied the other maritime towns, and of little or no consequence to whom the country behind belonged [1]. Zara with its narrow territory on the mainland was now hers by the treaty of 1244; the island of Ossero had always been Venetian since the days of Pietro Orseolo, and was now under the hereditary government of the Morosini as feudatories of the Republic; the island of Veglia was held for her in the same way by the Frangipani; Arbe had persisted in her loyalty since the reconquest of the island by Ordelafo

A.D. 1244.

Venetian possessions.

[1] 'Iadra enim ex situs opportunitate occidentalis Dalmatiae praecipua existebat, quam dum in potestate habuerunt Veneti, omnes quoque ejusdem partis Insulas ex consequenti facile retinuerunt, et sicuti Insulas terrestribus Ungarorum viribus destitutas facile acquirere poterant, ita earundem acquisitio absque Iadra neque tuta neque diuturna esse poterat.' Luc. iii. v. p. 122.

A.D. 1244. Faliero in 1117 and was governed by elective counts, chiefly of the families of Morosini and Michieli; Lesina was to be sure still subject to the counts of Almissa, but she voluntarily sought the protection of the Republic a few years later[1], and Curzola was held as a Venetian fief by the family of Zorzi, who recovered it from the Hungarians in 1129, and whose authority had recently been confirmed. On the mainland the Venetian territory ended at the Kerka, which falls into the sea at Sebenico, and that city, with Traü Spalato and the coast southwards, remained subject to Hungary; but at Ragusa Venetian influence was supreme, and whatever Ragusan patriotism may have to say for the previous independence of the republic of S. Biagio, there can be no doubt that from 1221 till the time of Lewis the Great Ragusa was under the government of Venetian counts regularly appointed by the republic of S. Mark. Beyond the territory of Ragusa neither Hungary nor Venice had at present any matter for dispute, for Cattaro and the Bocche acknowledged the supremacy and lived under the protection of the kings of Servia.

Hungarian possessions.

Ragusa dependent on Venice.

Cattaro dependent on Servia.

Review of state of Dalmatia. c. 1250. If we turn to consider the internal condition of Dalmatia at this period and compare it with that at the time of the first coming of the Hungarians, we find that during the century

[1] In 1278.

and a half that divides the two eras the relative positions of the Latins and Croatians had been reversed. With the extinction of the kingdom of Croatia the Croats sank into the position of mere provincials of the Hungarian crown, and the maritime towns, from being their tributaries, became their fellow-subjects, on equal or rather superior terms, for they retained their autonomy under Hungarian protection. Left in possession of their municipal liberties, and relieved from the piracies which hindered their commercial development before the Venetians made the seas safe, the maritime cities rapidly grew in wealth and consequence. They had no longer anything to fear from the Slavs of the neighbourhood, whom they were able to meet on equal terms, not only on sea, but on land, for they had now an organized militia well armed and disciplined, and we have seen that the Spalatines under their podestà Gargano were able to vanquish the Almissans and put an end to their piracies without any aid from either Venetian or Hungarian. Among the other cities Zara was pre-eminent in wealth and power, and the historian of Spalato envies while he affects to deride the military ambition of the rival city and the forts and townships which she planted in her territory[1].

Military strength of the towns.

---

[1] 'Cum enim inter caeteros comprovinciales suos terra marique forent potentia et divitiis sublimati fastidio habere coeperunt nauticis lucris incumbere voluerunt militiae pompas inaniter

State of the arts in Dalmatia. c. 1250.

Concurrently with their civil development the arts had flourished within the walls of the Dalmatian cities, while among the Slavs without little or no progress was made in this respect. The architecture of the thirteenth century at Zara Traù and Spalato will bear comparison in point both of design and execution with the contemporary work in Italy by which it was principally inspired, though, as we shall see hereafter when considering it more at length, it possesses also a distinctively national character. At Zara the new Duomo was approaching completion, the beautiful basilican church of S. Grisogono had been erected and adorned with precious mosaics, and the convent of Santa Maria had been constructed, of which the fine tower and chapter-house still remain to us; at Traù the main fabric of the Duomo was well advanced and the two doorways were completed of which the western one is unsurpassed by any Romanesque portal in Europe; at Spalato the cathedral in the temple or tomb-house of Diocletian was enriched by the magnificent carved and gilded doors of Magister Guvina with their twenty-eight reliefs of subjects from the life and passion of our Lord, by the curious semi-oriental stall-work, probably from the same hand, that still adorns the choir, and above all by the exquisite pulpit of carved and inlaid marble. Ragusa during the

experiri. Constructis nempe villis et oppidis gaudebant militari equitatu volare.' Thom. Archid. c. xliii.

same period had built her cathedral, with the gifts, perhaps, of our English King Richard, a building which, to judge from the description of those who saw it[1], must have been among the most interesting on the shores of the Adriatic, but of which the disastrous earthquake of 1667 has left us only the memory. The minor arts were studied with equal care, and Lorenzo, a Dalmatian born, who ruled the church of Spalato from 1059 to 1099, was at the pains to send a servant of his to Antioch in order to perfect himself in the goldsmiths' and silversmiths' art, who on his return was employed to make several candelabra, ewers, and chalices, a pastoral staff and cross, and other things in the style of the art of Antioch, which was probably the same as that of Byzantium. Nor was literature disregarded : in the time of the same Lorenzo a scholar of Paris, on his way to study Greek at Athens, was employed by the archbishop to translate the uncouth legends of S. Domnus into polished verse, and to compose several hymns in honour of the saint ; Giovanni Ursini, Bishop of Traü, was famous for his literary and scientific acquirements, and Thomas the Archdeacon of Spalato has left us the earliest history of his country, written in a style of considerable liveliness and, in spite of the author's frequent prejudices, with some historical power.

State of the arts in Dalmatia. c. 1250.

State of literature. c. 1250.

[1] Vid. Philippi de Diversis de Quartigianis Situs aedificiorum, &c. Ragusii. Ed. Brunelli. Zara, 1882.

Temporary independence of Traü, Spalato, and Sebenico, A.D. 1242.

The Tartar invasion and the temporary disorganization of the kingdom of Hungary threw the maritime towns of Dalmatia on their own resources, and Traü Sebenico and Spalato for some time enjoyed complete independence as free republics. Unfortunately one of the first results of their liberty was a petty war between the neighbouring cities of Traü and Spalato about a disputed territory that lay between them[1].

War between Traü and Spalato.

Composed at first by the influence of the Franciscan Gherardo, the quarrel broke out again after his departure, and a naval combat took place off Traü in which the advantage remained with the Traürini, who followed it up by allying themselves with the neighbouring Slavs and ravaging the territory of Spalato. The Spalatini invoked the aid of Ninosclav, Ban of Bosnia, and with his

A.D. 1244.

aid ravaged in return the lands of Traü; but the Traürini appealed to the king Bela IV, who sent Dionysius, Ban of all Slavonia and Dalmatia[2], to put an end to the quarrel and punish the Spalatini and Ninosclav. With the entry of these champions on either side there was of course an end of the short-lived independence of the two republics.

Appearing before Spalato the Ban demanded hostages and a large sum of money, and when the citizens pleaded that this was an invasion of their

---

[1] Thom. Archid. xliv–xlvii.

[2] After the peace of 1244 the king united all his Slavonian territory under a single Ban or viceroy.

privileges he attacked the town in concert with the Traürini, captured and burned the suburb, and compelled the Spalatini to release their prisoners, pay an indemnity, give hostages, and accept a Hungarian archbishop, Hugrinus or Ugolino Cesmen, a gay and martial prelate, whom the king intended to be both pontiff and count of Spalato[1].

At this time the counts of Bribir of the family of Subich became prominent in Dalmatia. Stephen Count of Lika and Bribir was created Ban of all Slavonia and Dalmatia, and his successors under various titles held the same office till 1348. Stephen used his influence to pacify the province, and peace reigned among its various discordant elements as long as he lived. But the succeeding counts endeavoured to oppress the maritime cities, and fostered dissensions among them, and from hostility to Venice encouraged the piracies of the Almissans, which were always ready to break out when the peace of the country was disturbed.

A.D. 1247. Rise of the counts of Bribir.

[1] At this period of the history we lose the help of Thomas the archdeacon of Spalato, who died in 1268, as appears by his tombstone still existing in the cloister of the Franciscan church at Spalato. His 'Historia Salonitanorum Pontificum atque Spalatensium' breaks off abruptly at the year 1266.

The 'Historia de gestis Romanorum Imperatorum et summ. Pontificum Pars secundae partis de anno Domini MCCXC.' by Micha Madii de Barbazanis of Spalato carries the narrative of events down to the year 1330.

Both authors were edited by Giov. Lucio, and their works are appended to the 2nd edition of his 'De regno Dalmatiae et Croatiae,' Amsterdam, 1668.

A.D. 1268. In 1259 Spalato and Traü leagued themselves
Renewal of Almissan against the Polizzani, neighbours and confederates
piracies. of the Almissans ; in 1268, the Doge wrote to the
commune of Spalato to procure the liberation of
a Venetian citizen whom the Almissans had captured ; in 1274 Charles of Anjou, King of Naples,
allied himself with Spalato and Sebenico to
repress the pirates of Almissa ; and in 1277 the
Venetians besieged Almissa, and after some
trouble captured and burned the borgo or suburb,
liberated one of their captains and other Venetians whom the pirates had captured, and
received the submission of the islands of Lesina
A.D. 1278. and Brazza, which had hitherto belonged to the
counts of Almissa[1]. Notwithstanding this the
piracies continued, for Almissa was difficult of
approach, the roads outside the estuary of the
Cetina were insecure for ships in winter time,
Piracy protected by Counts of Bribir. and the Counts of Bribir who received a share of
the spoil had no inclination to discourage the
lawless enterprises by which they profited, and
their natural enemies the Venetians were the
principal sufferers[2]. In 1287 an Italian podestà
from Fermo, whom the Traürini had elected to
govern their city, was captured on his way by the
Almissans in spite of the safe-conduct of their own
count and him of Bribir, and the resentment of the
Dalmatian towns at these and similar outrages

[1] Luc. lib. iv. c. ix. pp. 179–183.
[2] 'Ex participatione praedae Comites Breberienses fautores habuisse arguunt ea quae ex scripturis eliciuntur.' Luc. Ibid.

made them listen to the overtures of the Venetians. The Republic contracted an offensive and defensive alliance with Traü and Spalato, saving the honour of the Doge on one side and the King of Hungary on the other, and in 1292 George, count of Bribir, was compelled to sign an agreement with the Doge, pledging himself and his subjects and the commune of Almissa to abstain from any hostilities and to make good any damage or injury of which the Venetians might have reason to complain. *Dalmatian league with Venetians against the pirates, A.D. 1290. A.D. 1292.*

Ladislaus III, grandson of Bela IV, was murdered in 1290, and succeeded by Andrew III, 'the Venetian,' son of Tomasina Morosini, during whose reign nothing was done to disturb the agreement between Hungary and Venice. After his death in 1301 the succession was disputed between Wenceslaus king of Bohemia, Otho duke of Bavaria, and Charles Robert or Caroberto, grandson of Charles II, king of Naples, and Maria of Hungary, sister of the murdered Ladislaus, and it was not till 1308 that Charles Robert succeeded in establishing himself on the throne to the exclusion of his rivals. The counts of Bribir had contributed to his success, and with his ultimate triumph their own position in Dalmatia was strengthened and their influence in the maritime towns increased. *Charles Robert, king of Hungary, A.D. 1308.*

Paul, Count of Bribir and Ban of Croatia, had succeeded in getting himself elected count of the maritime towns of Traü Spalato and Sebenico; *Discontent of the Zaratini.*

VOL. I. G

Zara alone remained independent of him, and he used his influence to excite the discontent of the citizens and induce them to throw off their allegiance to Venice. The Zaratini had chafed under the hard terms imposed on them by the Republic in 1244 after their last rebellion, and they listened readily to the Ban's proposals. The moment was propitious, for the Venetians were involved in various domestic and foreign troubles; their maritime power had received a severe shock by their defeat at the hands of the Genoese off Curzola in 1298[1]; the 'Serrata del gran Consiglio' in 1299 had roused the discontent of the people and provoked the conspiracies of Marino Bocconio and Bajamonte Tiepolo; the state was at war with the Pope about Ferrara; and the Pope, resorting to spiritual arms, had placed the Republic under an interdict, and in 1309 proclaimed a crusade against her which resulted in the defeat of her fleet and the interruption and ruin of her commerce[2].

Third revolt of Zara from Venice, March 1311.

The Papal bull releasing all the subjects of the Venetians from their allegiance gave the Zaratini and the Hungarians the desired opportunity, and

---

[1] It was in this battle that Marco Polo was made prisoner by the Genoese, and carried off to that captivity to which the world perhaps owes the account of his travels. The number of captives taken by the Genoese was 5000, among whom was the Venetian admiral Andrea Dandolo, who from shame and remorse dashed out his brains against the sides of the galley.

[2] '... ob interdictum Papale per proximas civitates Dalmaticas inquisitio fieret *an post prohibitionem Domini Papae aliquid Venetis venderetur vel ab eisdem emeretur.*' Luc. iv–xii. p. 201.

in March 1311 the city revolted, overpowered the garrison, and threw itself on the protection of Paul count of Bribir and ban of Croatia, whose son Mladin the citizens elected to govern them as their count[1]. The Venetian count Michele Morosini managed to make his escape in the disguise of a monk, but the two councillors Zuane Giustiniani and Marco Dandolo were caught by the people and put in prison[2]. The King of Hungary accepted the proffered allegiance of the Zaratini, reinstated them in the enjoyment of their ancient privileges, and wrote to warn the Republic not to molest them.

But Venice had now come to terms with the Pope and been relieved of the interdict, and was free to turn her attention to the recovery of her revolted subjects. A fleet dispatched under Beletto Giustiniani met with a somewhat ludicrous reverse, for under the cover of night and stormy weather the Zaratini managed to surprise the galley of the commander, who was ill and asleep below deck, and to carry him with his crew to Zara, where he died in prison before the end of the war. The fleet was afterwards reinforced, and Dalmasio, a captain of Catalonian mercenaries, was sent with a thousand horse a thousand foot and a thousand archers to invest the city by land, while the fleet under Vitale Canal blockaded the port. Dalmasio had scarcely entrenched his

[A.D. 1312. Siege of Zara by Venetians.]

[June, A.D. 1313. Siege of Zara by Venetian stipendiary Dalmasio.]

---

[1] For a table of the counts of Bribir vid. Isthuanfy, de reb. Hung.
[2] Anonymous Venetian Chronicler cited Lucio, p. 200.

Dalmasio in turn besieged by the ban Mladin.

army round the city before his camp was threatened by Mladin, who had succeeded his father Paul and was now Ban of Dalmatia and Slavonia[1], and who with an army of Slavs and German mercenaries took up a position whence he could assault the camp of Dalmasio in case the latter drew out his troops to attack the city. The summer was passed in a masterly inactivity by both sides, and the expense of maintaining an army in the field without any result began to press heavily on the Venetians. The three months for which Dalmasio had been engaged and paid had elapsed, and the Venetians knowing that he could not retire without their transports, and was therefore in a manner in their power, offered him lower terms than he asked for a renewal of his services. The effect of this was that he began to traffic with the Ban who had learned the state of affairs, and who was himself anxious to bring the war to an end being threatened in the rear by the advance of Ourosh II, king of Servia, then at war with Hungary.

Intrigues of Mladin and Dalmasio.

Mladin had already made proposals to the Venetians that they should receive the submission of the Zaratini on condition of the restitution of their ancient privileges as a free city, but the pride of the Republic refused to listen to con-

---

[1] 'Tali titulo utebatur *Mladinus Croatorum Banus, Comes Iadrae, Princeps Dalmatiae, et Secundus Bosnensis Banus.*' Luc. lib. iv. c. xiii. p. 203. His complete title was 'comes perpetuus Iadrae.' Storia della Dalmazia, Zara 1878.

ditions from her revolted subjects[1]. Foiled in this attempt, Mladin now turned to Dalmasio and offered him 1000 gold florins, and the post of governor with an annual salary of the same amount if he would himself occupy the city, promising moreover that if he wished to leave the country he and his troops should be conveyed to Apulia at the expense of the Ban. To this Dalmasio agreed, a feigned attack was made on the city, the gates were opened by arrangement, Dalmasio with his forces entered without opposition, and the Venetians in alarm went on board their ships, and, anticipating an immediate attack, put out to sea.

But Dalmasio meditated a second act of treachery, and having gained the city by betraying the Venetians he now resolved to betray the Ban and make terms with the Venetians for the surrender of the city to them. His envoys represented that he had been actuated by care for their interest in acquiring the city by stratagem after force had proved unavailing, and he induced the Zaratini to renew their offer of submission if their ancient privileges and immunities were restored. This time the Venetians listened, envoys were sent, and terms arranged, but Dalmasio did not reap any fruits from his treachery, for finding himself suspected by both

September, A.D. 1313. Venetians recover Zara.

---

[1] 'At Venetorum in Zadrenses Majestas solita cum subditis indignata pacisci nil oblatorum admisit, offensa magis libertate petita.' Albertinus Mussatus de gest. Italic. lib. ii. ap. Luc. p. 198.

sides, he claimed the promised safe-conduct and convoy of himself and his followers, and escaped to Apulia[1].

By the terms of the agreement the Zaratini regained the privilege of electing their own count subject to the confirmation of the Doge, the Venetians withdrew their garrison and dismantled the castle, the citizens were allowed to govern themselves by their own laws and customs, and were placed on the footing of allies and not as on the last occasion that of subjects[2]. Their islands also were restored to them, a matter to which the Zaratini attached the greatest importance, their territory on the mainland being closely circumscribed by the Croatians and constantly exposed to their invasion.

Tyranny of counts of Bribir. Mladin was now all-powerful in Dalmatia Croatia and Bosnia; the countship of Traù Spalato and Sebenico was held by his younger brother George, and the Venetians had been obliged to receive the Zaratini on terms which had been originally dictated by himself. His power was exercised tyrannically; he harassed the Ragusans, interfered even with the neighbouring Croatian counts of Corbavia, and oppressed the maritime cities, fomenting civil discord among them, confiscating their extramural terri-

---

[1] The whole transaction is obscurely told by Albertinus Mussatus. 'Dalmasius omnium vitandarum insidiarum astutia noctu lembum ingressus in Apuliam devectus est.'

[2] 'Veluti cum sociis aequo jure convenerunt.' Luc. iv–xii. p. 201.

tory, and ill-treating the citizens[1]. His brother A.D. 1315. George moreover openly encouraged the Almissan corsairs, granting them many immunities and regulating the division of the expenses and spoils of their piracies by a special charter[2]. The result of the oppressive government of the Croatian Ban and his brother was a revulsion of feeling in favour of Venetian rule. For a hundred and sixty years and more the Latin or Dalmatian cities of the coast to the south of the Kerka had been content to acknowledge the supremacy of the King of Hungary while their municipal autonomy and territorial rights had been respected, but no sooner were these imperilled than they at once looked round for another protector, and in January 1322 Traü and Sebenico invoked the protection of the Venetians. Mladin ravaged the lands of both cities but was summoned away to resist a rebellion against his authority in Bosnia. Allying

Chartered piracy of Almissans.

Traü and Sebenico revolt to Venice.

A.D. 1322.

A.D. 1322.

Defeat and captivity of Mladin.

[1] Micha Madii, ch. xviii. The historian's indignation is inflamed by his suspicions of Mladin's orthodoxy; 'Deum coli contemnebas et Eccles. Catholicam, quoniam ordinabas Episcopos, Abbates, et Abbatissas ... solebas frequentare legendo Bibliam, sed non observabas verba Bibliae.' Here as usual the Patarene tendencies of the Slavs are contrasted with the Roman orthodoxy of the cities.

[2] 'Item quod quando irent in cursum cum ligno 40 remorum et ultra, lignum sextam partem habeat expensarum et quintam partem lucri, et lignum a 24 remis usque ad 40 sextam partem lucri et sextam partem habeat expensarum, sed lignum x. remis usque ad 24 pro duobus hominibus partem recipiat, a decem autem remis infra de parte unius hominis contentetur.' Charter cited by Lucio, p. 204.

himself with the Vlachs and Polizzani he gave battle to the rebels, but was defeated and driven to hide himself in the fastnesses of Poglizza, whence he escaped to the king Charles Robert who was then at Knin. He was however ill-received, his loyalty was suspected, and the king carried him away with him a prisoner into Hungary[1]. Profiting by these disturbances among the Croatians, the men of Traü made an expedition against Almissa, and those of Sebenico against Scardona; both were successful, the offending towns were spoiled and burned, and their piratical boats were carried off by the victors.

Victory of Traü and Sebenico.

April, 1323. Defeat of Spalato. Though Spalato had not offered allegiance to the Venetians, her forces were united with those of Traü in the capture of Almissa, and she seems to have garrisoned and retained the place. Count George in consequence invaded and ravaged the Spalatine territory, and defeated a force of 1200 Spalatini which encountered him near Clissa with a loss of 150 men. In the following year he assembled another army meditating the conquest of Spalato, and the recovery of Almissa, which place was necessary to him as the head-quarters of the piracy by which he profited[2], but he was encountered near Knin, and routed and taken

June, 1324. Defeat and captivity of George of Bribir.

---

[1] Micha Madii, ch. xvii., xviii., xix.

[2] 'Putabas destruere Civ. Spal. et auferre Almissum, et habere ad velle vestrum, ubi esset cursus et locus piratarum.' Micha Madius, c. xxiii.

prisoner by Neliptio count of Cetina and Knin, and the voyvode George Mihovilich. In the following year the Zaratini arbitrated between the contending parties, and peace was agreed to between the Spalatini and the countess of the imprisoned George, the captive Spalatini at Clissa being released on one hand and Almissa restored on the other[1].   March, 1325.

The Spalatini in 1327 resolved to follow the example of Traü and placed themselves under the protection of Venice. The event of their late struggle with the Bribir family probably convinced them of their powerlessness to stand alone in the midst of so many warring elements, and they made their submission to the Doge on condition that their municipal autonomy should be respected, and 'saving the honour of the King of Hungary[2].' In the following year Nona, though a purely Croatian town, which had never before been subject to the Venetians, found herself obliged by the difficulties of the times, the disturbed state of affairs and the weakness of the Hungarian government, to throw herself, like the other Dalmatian towns, on the protection of the Republic[3].   A.D. 1327. Spalato submits to Venice.   Also Nona, A.D. 1328, January.

---

[1] Luc. iv. c. xiv. p. 210.

[2] Micha Madii, c. xxviii. This appears to mean that his nominal sovereignty should be respected. The name of the king was to be retained on all legal writings, and to stand before that of the Doge. Lucio observes that even under the Venetian rule the King of Hungary confirmed or refused to confirm privileges in the cities. Lib. iv. c. xv. p. 220.

[3] 'Anchor in questo tempo la Citade de Spalato e de Nona li

Dalmatia once more Venetian. The tyranny of the family of Bribir had thus forced into the arms of the Venetians those cities of the sea coast which were not hers already; and all maritime Dalmatia, including the islands, was now re-united under the banner of S. Mark for the first time since the days of Ordelafo Faliero. The policy of a commercial power like Venice was always directed towards peace, and her first endeavour was to reconcile the cities with one another and with the neighbouring Croatian counts. Though under her suzerainty—to use a word which modern politics has brought into fashion—the several cities were not her subjects, but retained their independence and had to be treated with separately. *Endeavours of Venice to pacify the country.* A treaty of alliance was therefore arranged by the Venetians between the communes of Spalato Traù and Sebenico, with conditions for mutual defence and assistance in time of war, and for the peaceful adjustment of disputes by arbitration in place of the old system of reprisals. The boundaries of the territories of Traù and Sebenico were settled in this way, and the question between count George of Bribir and the city of Spalato was decided

qual iera in estrema e chattiva condition per lo muodo che de soura e ditto de Sebenico e de Traci vegendo le ditte Cittade sottomesse al Comun de Veniesia de chativa condition esser vegnude in bona condition, e in brieve tempo, desse le do Cittade con le condition e patti delle altre do prenominade, e questo fo in 1327, che si de Spalatini in lo mese di Settembrio e foli mandado per so Conte f. Marco Fuscarini.' Ven. Chron. cited Luc. p. 210.

by the arbitration of the Zaratini as has just been related. The Venetians succeeded also in composing the civil dissensions by which Traù had been torn on the question of surrendering the city to Venice, and which had resulted in the expulsion of the losing party[1]. The *fuorusciti*, as the Florentines would have called them, were recalled and reinstated in their possessions, and the odious partisan distinction of '*ins*' and '*outs*' was terminated.

The discordant state of the Croatians of the interior enabled the Venetians to unite some of the feudal counts with the maritime cities on terms of amity or alliance. During the troubled reign of Charles Robert the authority of Hungary was but little able to make itself felt in Dalmatia, and the whole country was in disorder. The ambitious designs and oppressive arrogance of the counts of Bribir had offended the neighbouring Croatian nobles as well as the Dalmatians; and Mladin had been overthrown by a combination of Croatian counts under the Bosnian Ban Babonig. But Babonig himself next provoked the royal interference, and was defeated by the Great Ban Nicolas, whom the king had sent to pacify the country[2]. The counts near the sea coast, in order

Disturbed condition of Dalmatian Slavs under Charles Robert.

---

[1] 'Civibus in partes divisis praesertim Sebenici et Trag. mutuae caedes, familiarum expulsiones, bonorum publicationes, domorum destructiones perpetratae sunt, et extrinsecorum et intrinsecorum odiosa nomina emersere.' Luc. lib. iv. xiv. p. 205.

[2] Micha Madii, ch. xxii. The barren and inflated chronicle

Alliance between the cities and Croatian counts.

to save themselves from a similar fate, formed an alliance with the maritime towns at the instance of the Venetians, and thus supported were able to command the respect of the next Ban Mihac, who abstained from meddling with them. Among these allied counts Neliptio, count of Knin, was the most important, and in alliance with Spalato Traü and Sebenico, which places furnished a con-

A.D. 1337.

tingent of 400 foot-soldiers[1], he besieged Mladin III, son of George of Bribir, and now count of Scardona and Clissa, in his stronghold at the latter place. But Neliptio himself was guilty of aggressions on the territory of Sebenico, and the Venetians, profiting by the jealousy excited by his superior power, united Mladin and the counts of Ostrovizza and Corbavia in a league with the maritime towns, and caused Neliptio to pull

A.D. 1343.

down the fort he had erected and to sign conditions of peace.

A.D. 1342.
Accession of Lewis the Great.

But a change came over the state of affairs in Hungary which was speedily felt in Dalmatia. In 1342 Charles Robert died and was succeeded by his son Lewis, then a youth only of sixteen years,

of this author now fails us. Its value consists in the fact that Micha was an eyewitness of the events he narrates.

[1] By the conditions of the alliance in 1332 Neliptio was to defend the cities if attacked, and they were to supply when called upon a contingent of 400 men, 100 from Spalato, 140 from Traü, and 160 from Sebenico. Neliptio was to lead in person, the object was to be approved by the towns, and no hostilities were to be committed against the King of Hungary on one side, or the subjects of Venice on the other.

who soon gave promise of his future greatness. During his long reign of forty years he raised Hungary to a higher place among European powers than it had ever before occupied; to his hereditary kingdom he added, in 1370, that of Poland which was settled on him by his maternal uncle Casimir III; the princes of Moldavia, Wallachia, Bulgaria, and Bosnia were forced to submit to his arms; the Venetians were driven out of Dalmatia; and for a short time the kingdom of Naples, which he invaded to punish the murder of his brother Andrew, was at his feet, and governed by his officers.

Charles Robert, disappointed by his uncle Robert I. in obtaining the kingdom of Naples for himself, had married his second son Andrew[1] to Giovanna, the grand-daughter of Robert, and heiress to his throne. Robert died in 1342, a few months after Charles Robert of Hungary, and the youthful Giovanna succeeded at the age of sixteen, her husband being of the same age as herself. The first object of Lewis, who looked to his connexion with the kingdom of Naples for support in the vast schemes that were already working in his mind, was to obtain from the Pope, Naples being a fief of the church, the coronation and investiture of his brother Andrew not as consort of Giovanna but as heir of Carlo Martello

Alliance of Hungary with Naples.

---

[1] In 1333, July. Vid. Giannone, lib. xxii. c. iii. The prince and princess were both seven years old.

his grandfather[1], and after long negotiations at the Papal court at Avignon his ambassadors succeeded in their object, though, according to Boccaccio, not without great difficulty.

[2] This object had at first occupied the attention of Lewis to the exclusion of the affairs of Dalmatia and Croatia, but his next care was to restore order and reestablish his authority in those provinces. Neliptio was dead, but his fortress of Knin was held by his widow Vladislava for her infant son John, whom many of the Croatian counts encouraged to resist and defy the royal summons to surrender. Lewis however brought a force into Dalmatia which overawed all opposition except on the part of those who were allied with the maritime cities and the Venetians, and with the exception of Paul count of Ostrovizza, and Mladin III count of Scardona and Clissa, all the other counts of Croatia and Dalmatia laid the keys of their castles at the king's feet[3]. Having no fleet, Lewis was at present unable to attack

A.D. 1345. Lewis advances into Dalmatia.

---

[1] Giannone, Historia di Napoli, lib. xxiii. Vid. Table of Kings of Hungary, infra.

[2] The local historians of the succeeding events are the authors of the '*Summa Historiarum Tabula a Cutheis de gestis civium Spalatinorum,*' &c., and of the '*Obsidionis Iadrensis libri duo.*' Both are edited by Lucio and appended to his edition of 1668. Of the latter work he says it is a 'manuscripta historia a religioso quopiam viro qui interfuit conscripta, ut ex genere quo utitur orationis facile intelligi potest.' Its style is execrable and its matter often obscure.

[3] Obsid. Iadr., lib. 1. ch. vii.

the cities of the coast or meddle with the Croatian counts whom they supported.

The situation was one which caused the Venetians grave anxiety. The alliance of Hungary and Naples under the rule of two brothers, both young and ambitious[1], was the last political combination the Venetians would have desired. Hungary was powerful, wealthy, and warlike, her land forces were superior to any the Venetians could oppose to them, her strength was shortly to be increased by the union of Poland under the same crown, the patriarch of Aquileja was her ally, and so were the Anconitans, the hated rivals of the Republic. Naples possessed a fleet in the Tyrrhene sea; should the two powers combine to attack Dalmatia by land and sea the Venetians could not defend it; and with both shores of the Adriatic in the possession of her enemies the maritime dominion of Venice would pass into other hands. Everything now depended on the fidelity of the maritime towns, and in particular of Zara, especially since by the terms of her ancient privileges, confirmed by the late compact, no Venetian garrison could be placed within the walls. About Spalato Traü and Sebenico the Venetians felt less anxiety, for they were surrounded by the territory of the counts of Bribir, who were still resisting the king and imploring

Alarm of Venice at alliance between Hungary and Naples.

A.D. 1345.

---

[1] So says Lucio, but in fact, if Giannone may be believed, Andrew had none of the spirit of his elder brother, but was 'dato all' ozio.'

A.D. 1345. the aid of the Venetians. But Nona and Zara were enclosed by the territory of the counts of Corbavia and Knin, who had made their submission to Lewis, and they had to be carefully watched. Nona made no objection to receive a garrison, and was strongly fortified and well manned, but experience of the jealous temper of the Zaratini warned the Venetians that any proposal to place troops there would be resented as an invasion of the ancient privileges and probably provoke the very mischief that it was intended to avoid.

Prosperous condition of Zara under Venetian rule. It might be thought that interest would have attached the maritime cities to the rule of a commercial and highly civilized people speaking the same tongue and living by the same pursuits rather than that of a feudal monarch and an alien people in a lower grade of civilization than themselves, especially since they had flourished under Venetian protection as they had never done since the days of the Roman empire. The Zaratini elected their own count, had the custody of their city without the presence of any foreign garrison, governed themselves by their own laws and customs, and contracted alliances with the neighbouring Croatian counts, like the other maritime cities, with the approval of Venice; they extended their commerce into the Tyrrhene sea as far as Sardinia and Catalonia, two galleys lay in their arsenal, their harbour was thronged with craft of all sizes, and the numbers and wealth of their population were largely on the increase [1].

But the Zaratini had not forgotten or forgiven the loss of the islands of Srimaz Zuri and Jarte which they had snatched from the Sebenzani in 1323, when that people were at war with Traü, and which in 1324, after Sebenico like themselves had accepted the Venetian dominion, the Venetians had compelled them to restore [2]. When the Venetians declared war against Neliptio the Zaratini did the same, but refused to send troops across their frontier; when requested by Lewis to send galleys and boats to Segna to convey his mother the elder queen Elizabeth to Apulia, they did so without any previous communication with Venice; and when he advanced with his army into the country they sent three envoys to meet him, who came back however without effecting their purpose, for one of the envoys was a 'tyrant-hater,' and delayed his companions, and while they were on the road the king departed for Hungary [3].

Reasons for discontent of Zaratini with Venice.

The news of this abortive mission however *September, A.D. 1345.*

[1] Luc. lib. iv. c. xv. p. 217–218.

[2] Luc. iv. xv. p. 219. He gives the formal pleadings of the Zaratini when summoned to meet the plaintiffs in the chancery at Venice. They amount to a denial of the jurisdiction of the Venetians, 'quod Commune Iadrae debet habere unum Comitem qui sit de majori consilio Civitatis Ven. qui cum tribus Iudicibus roget et judicet praedictos Iadratinos ut in pactis plenius continetur, cujus rei causa ex pactorum forma non possumus nec debemus coram vobis ad judicium citari.'

[3] Obsid. Iadr. lib. i. c. vii.

VOL. I. H

Fourth revolt of Zara from Venice. A.D. 1345. decided the Venetians to anticipate the open rebellion of the Zaratini; the port was blockaded by a fleet under Pietro di Canal, and the temporizing overtures of the citizens were met by a stern demand for unqualified submission. Petitions sent secretly from the citizens to implore the aid of Lewis and that of his brother Andrew king of Naples were favourably entertained by both monarchs. Andrew received the envoys on the 17th September[1], and promised his support, and on the 8th of the same month letters arrived from Lewis announcing his approach with an army to their relief.

The Hungarians at Naples. But it was not destined that any help should reach them from Naples, for the day after his interview with their envoys Andrew was assassinated, and there was an end of the hopes and fears founded on the alliance of the two kingdoms of Hungary and Naples.

When Charles Robert of Hungary had brought his son Andrew, then a child of seven years of age, to Naples to be married to Giovanna, he had left with him as his tutor and governor one Fra Roberto, a Hungarian monk, under whose charge the prince grew up, and whose influence over the easy temper of his pupil became absolute. At the time of their accession the queen and her consort were but sixteen years old, and Fra Roberto contrived to get all the power of the government into the hands of the Hungarian party which surrounded

[1] Obsid. Iadr. lib. i. c. xix., xxiv.

the person of the king. One by one the experienced councillors of Robert I were dismissed and their posts filled by Hungarians, and the Neapolitans saw with growing discontent and repugnance that their queen was queen merely in name, and in reality the prisoner of these ' barbarians,' in whose hands her husband was as much a puppet as herself[1]. The insolence of the Hungarians and the careless indifference of Andrew provoked some of the more ardent spirits among the discontented Neapolitans to form a conspiracy, and they were encouraged by Carlo duke of Durazzo, who had married the queen's sister and was next in order of succession to the throne. The news that Lewis had procured a bull for the coronation of Andrew not as consort but as legitimate king of Naples precipitated their plans, and on the night of September 18, while the Hungarians were stupid with drink and buried in sleep, Andrew was waylaid as he left the queen's apartments in the castle of Aversa, a noose was

Discontent of Neapolitans with Hungarians.

Murder of Andrew, Sept. 18, 1345.

[1] With Costanzi and the Neapolitan historians the Hungarians are always *barbarians*, and we hear enough of their insolence, drunkenness, and 'barbari costumi.' There is a letter of Petrarch extant describing his interview with Fra Roberto. He says, 'Oh infamia del mondo, che mostro! ... un animale orrendo coi piedi scalzi, col capo scoverto, corto di persona, marcio di tempo, grosso di fianchi, coi panni logori e stracciati per mostrar a studio parte delle carne, non solo disprezzare le suppliche de' tuoi cittadini, ma con grandissima insolenza, come dalle torre della sua finta santità, non fare nullo conto della imbasciata d' un Papa.' All the rest of the Hungarian ministry, he goes on to say, are like their chief, whom he calls a 'crudele ed atroce bestia.'

A.D. 1345. thrown round his neck, and he was strangled and his body thrown out of the window. A few obscure victims were selected for punishment, but though a papal bull was launched against the principal offenders their rank and power prevented any measures being taken against them. Their impunity excited suspicion; it was whispered that Giovanna herself had been privy to the crime, and Lewis wrote to her accusing her of her husband's death, and threatening speedy vengeance[1].

A.D. 1345. Siege of Zara by the Venetians. Meanwhile the siege of Zara was pressed by the Venetians. Within the city opinion was divided: the populace, who were sailors and seafaring folk to whom Venetian rule was not unwelcome, were willing to come to terms, while the upper classes were inclined to the Hungarian alliance and determined to hold out; but the stern demand of the Venetian commander that the city should be surrendered to his discretion and the walls thrown down united all classes in a policy of resistance; they raised the royal standard of Lewis their 'natural lord and master' and exerted themselves to the utmost to put the city into a good state of defence. By sea the Venetian admiral Jacopo Ciurani blockaded them with a powerful fleet, in which were included galleys

[1] Giannone, lib. xxiii. A contemporary account of the murder of Andrew is given by Domenico di Gravina, who writes as a partisan of the Hungarians and an enemy of the queen. Muratori, vol. xii. p. 560.

from Ragusa Spalato Arbe and Traü, and smaller vessels from the other states according to their ability; the land forces, amounting to more than 16,000 men[1], were commanded by Marco Giustiniani, who entrenched himself within a stockade or bastide 200 paces long and 100 wide strengthened with thirty-four towers, leaning on the sea to the east of the city so as to communicate with the fleet, and commanding the isthmus which joins the city to the mainland. The object of this entrenchment was to resist the threatened attack of the king of Hungary, whose army was on its way to raise the siege. The winter was consumed in small engagements with varying success, and conducted with much bitterness on both sides, no quarter being given. In January the Venetians took the fort of St. Damiano on the island opposite Zara, and bursting the chain[2] forced their way into the harbour. In May they made an unsuccessful assault on the city, and in June Lewis with an army of 100,000 men of various nationalities[3] encamped at Semelnich seven miles from the city. A deputation of the citizens laid the keys at his feet, to whom he swore that he would either deliver them from the

January, 1346.

June, 1346. Advance of Lewis to relieve Zara.

---

[1] Obsid. Iadr. lib. ii. c. xii.

[2] The construction of the chain is described, Obsid. Iadr. lib. i. c. xix, 'quamdam cathenam mirae grassitiei, ex tredecim tignis ad invicem ferro connexis ac confibulatis.'

[3] 'Ungari, Croati, Bognaschi, Phylistei, Cumani, Boemi, et Teutonici seu Alemanici, et aliae plures gentes.' Obsid. Iadr. lib. ii. c. xi.

Venetians or leave his bones at Zara[1]. While there remained an enemy on their territory he declined to enter the city, but with an escort of 2000 men he approached within sight of the walls amid the ringing of bells and shouts of the populace.

July 1, 1346.
Defeat of Hungarians.

Saturday, July 1[2], was fixed for an assault on the Venetian bastide, and as the King had no military engines he borrowed some from the city. But his army was better qualified to meet an enemy in the field than to attack a fortress, and there was not space for more than a small proportion of them to come into action. Some of his miscellaneous host, moreover, were suspected of friendly relations with the Venetians, and the Ban of Bosnia, with his forces, remained an inactive spectator of the fray[3]. The Venetians were entirely successful, the assault was repelled, the engines of the assailants were destroyed and burned, and the Zaratini, on whom the brunt of the conflict had fallen, were driven back to their walls exclaiming against the treachery of their allies.

[1] 'Non semel immo saepe et crebrius cum juramento affirmasse visus est potius suum velle corpus Iadrae condere sacrofago quam constantissimos Indertinos velle desolatos relinquere.' Obsid. Iadr. ii c. ix.

[2] Obsid. Iadr. lib. ii. c. xii, 'die qui Saturno est dedicatus.' Elsewhere the reverend author enlivens his narrative by such expressions as 'existente sole immediate subsequentis diei in medio polo,' or better still 'dum Titan tertiarum hora prosignabat.'

[3] Obsid. Iadr. lib. ii. c. xii.

CH. I.]   *History of Dalmatia.*   103

On the following day Lewis burned his remain-ing engines, and the day after, July 3, broke up his camp and beat a retreat, which the Venetian historians magnify into a flight, to Vrana and thence back into Hungary [1].

July 3, 1346. Retreat of Lewis.

The Zaratini, thus abandoned to their fate, implored the king at all events to make their peace with the Venetians before forsaking them, but his proposals were naturally received by the Signory with contempt. Tumults arose in the city, the populace being as before for surrender, the nobles for resistance. Meanwhile the siege was vigorously pressed, and the castle of S. Michele on the island of Ugliano was taken or betrayed. A worse enemy soon began to make its impression on the resolution of the citizens; twenty-eight thousand souls, natives and refugees from the surrounding territory, were cooped up within the walls, of whom only six thousand were capable of bearing arms, and the ravages of famine began to drive the populace to desperation. At last in

A.D. 1346. Distress of the besieged.

---

[1] Caresinus (Murat. xii.) says, 'multisque ex Hungaris vilissime interfectis.' I have found no authority for the defeat of Lewis with a loss of 6000 killed and many more wounded, of which Sir Gardner Wilkinson speaks, vol. ii. p. 272. The author of the Obsid. Iadr. says the Zaratini were left unsupported while the Hungarian army stood and looked on, 'lucide conspicit Rex, et tota ejus turba, nemini imperat ex suis illis fidelibus Iadertinis guttam suffragii praestare, speculatur universus exercitus armis fulgidis decoratus,' lib. ii. c. xii. Lucio says that 'Rex nullo Venetis illato damno, nullo subsidio Civitati praestito, multitudine sua gravatus, fugato similis intra biduum recesserit; ita ut exinde Veneti Regem fugisse scribant.' De Regn. lib. iv. c. xv. p. 225.

December it was decided to send an embassy to Venice, and kneeling before the Doge and Signory the envoys made their unconditional submission. The gates were opened, the Venetian captains with their forces entered the city, and the standard of S. Mark was raised in the place of that of the Hungarian king.

<small>Surrender of Zara, Dec. 21, 1346.</small>

The conditions imposed on the city were more favourable than might have been expected. With the death of Andrew and the rupture between Naples and Hungary one source of danger to the Republic had been removed, and as the Venetians might now hope to retain their hold on Dalmatia they no longer desired to dismantle the fortified towns. Zara therefore retained her walls, but the citizens were disarmed, and fifty of the nobles' were sent as hostages to Venice. A garrison of 400 foot and 200 horse was placed in the castle, Marco Giustiniani was appointed count, with Marino Superanzio and Jacopo Delfin for his councillors, and the island of Pago was taken from the territory of Zara, and made the seat of a Venetian count. In other respects the Zaratini were left in enjoyment of their ancient privileges. The siege had lasted sixteen months, and cost Venice from 700,000 to 1,000,000 ducats[1].

<small>Favourable conditions granted by Venice.</small>

A variety of circumstances had combined to

---

[1] Chron. Venet. cited by Lucio, iv. c. xv. p. 224. 'Vojo che se sapia che lla dita Zara chostava al Chomun de V^a. duc. 40 fina 60 millia al mexe,' &c. Cortusii says one million. Sir G. Wilkinson says three millions, but gives no authority.

reduce this formidable expedition of Lewis to a mere military parade. The Venetian stockade could only be taken by regular siege operations, and even then with difficulty, as the Venetians had command of the sea. But Lewis had neither navy nor siege train, and the Hungarians were not expert in siege operations, while the Venetians were famous for their skill both in attacking and defending fortresses. Lewis had also to reckon with the disaffection of many of the Croatian counts; he could not expect those whom he had subdued in 1345[1] to be very zealous adherents, and Paul count of Ostrovizza and Mladin count of Scardona and Clissa still held to their alliance with the Venetians, and had not joined his army at all. The abstention of the greater part of the royal army from taking part in the battle of July 1st is ascribed by the author, who was an eye-witness of the siege, to the influence of the Croatian leaders, and especially that of the Voyvode Laccohovich[2], but it is possible that Lewis himself may have had his own reasons for not pressing it too vigorously. He was then meditating an expedition to Naples to avenge the murder of his brother and claim the kingdom for himself as the heir of Carlo Martello his grand-

Reasons for failure of Hungarians.

Designs of Lewis on Naples.

---

[1] Vid. sup. p. 94.
[2] 'Et nisi hoc fraudulentum perdimentum tunc per illos Regis Barones et praecipue per Voyvodam Laccohovich exactum fuisset sexta quidem hora ipsius diei non consummasset quod ipsa bastida ac combusta esset et in manus hostium tradita.' Obsid. Iadr. lib. ii. c. xii.

father, and it rested with the Venetians as masters of the sea to prevent or permit the passage of his army across the Adriatic. It was hinted to him that if the Venetians were not interfered with at Zara no opposition would be offered by them to the passage of his army into Apulia, and this possibly outweighed the obligations under which he lay towards the Zaratini [1].

December, A.D. 1347.

Lewis, however, was unable to persuade either the Genoese or the Sicilians to transport his army, and he finally invaded '*the Kingdom*' by land.

Jan. 17, A.D. 1348. Entry of Lewis into Naples.

On Jan. 17, 1348, he reached Aversa where he was met by the majority of the Neapolitan nobles. The queen, with her second husband, had fled to Avignon, and no resistance was offered by the people. Passing with his army before the castle where his brother had been murdered, he halted, and calling the duke of Durazzo before him asked from which window his brother had been thrown. The duke denied all knowledge of the circumstances, but his complicity was proved by the production of a fatal letter in his own handwriting, and he was immediately beheaded and his body thrown from the same window whence the unhappy Andrew had been precipitated [2]. Summary justice thus performed, and an inconvenient rival

---

[1] So Caroldus, cited by Luc. iv. c. xv. p. 223.

[2] Carlo, Duke of Durazzo, had added to his other offences that of marrying Maria, the sister of Giovanna, who had been destined for Stephen, a younger brother of Lewis. This marriage, in case Giovanna left no children, diverted the succession from the Hungarian line.

removed, Lewis advanced to Naples, which he entered wearing his helmet, preceded by a black standard painted with the figure of a strangled king, and receiving in grim silence the addresses of the trembling citizens. Many of the barons were thrown into prison, the young prince Caroberto, son of Andrew and Giovanna, was sent into Hungary to be educated by his grandmother, and Hungarian officers were appointed to the principal posts in the government.

Lewis himself, after four months, embarked on a 'bireme' at Barletta, and staying a few days at Vrana on his way northwards returned to Hungary. His departure was the signal for the revival of the party of Giovanna. The arguments of the queen, seconded by the donation or sale on easy terms to the church of the city of Avignon, had convinced the Pope that she was innocent of the murder of her first husband, and the barons of her kingdom, disgusted with the rule of the Hungarians whom they regarded as barbarians, readily accepted the Papal verdict as sufficient authority for taking arms on her behalf. Giovanna and her husband landed at Naples where they were received enthusiastically, and hostilities were at once begun. *May, 1348. Departure of Lewis from Naples.* *Return of Giovanna.*

Meanwhile the Venetians had offered Lewis terms of peace on condition that he resigned his pretensions in Dalmatia. He had at first refused to listen, but the news that reached him from Naples, the necessity of reinforcing his army there, *Aug. 5, 1348. Eight years' peace between Venice and Hungary.*

and the preparations of the Venetians to intercept his transports made him change his mind, and he consented to make peace for a term of eight years. In 1349 the young prince Caroberto died in Hungary. Lewis now hoped for his own investiture by the Pope, and as this was refused he continued the war and recovered all the kingdom except Naples and Aversa. But when at last the latter place was surrendered his forces were exhausted and he was glad to treat for peace, and professing himself ready to accept the Pope's decision that Giovanna was innocent of his brother's death, he vacated the kingdom in 1351.

<small>A.D. 1351. Lewis retires from Naples.</small>

<small>A.D. 1348. The Great Plague.</small> The year in which peace was signed between Venice and Hungary is that of the great plague which swept across Europe desolating whole countries and leaving famine and ruin in its track. Its approach was heralded by a dreadful earthquake, and, if the historian of Spalato[1] may be credited, by an eclipse, a comet, and divers portents such as the appearance of demons and even of the three furies Alecto Tisiphone and Megaera from the Stygian pool, at whose aspect men lost their tongues and ofttimes their wits, stories which serve to show the terror excited by the visitation. At Ragusa 11,000 died of it; at Florence, where it found a historian in Boccaccio, the deaths amounted to 600 a day; at Venice half the population was swept away; and in England, whither the 'black

---

[1] Hist. a Cutheis, c. i. The plague at Spalato burst out on Dec. 25, 1348.

death' in time found its way, it destroyed in its repeated visitations more than half the population of the kingdom.

During this awful calamity arms were by com- mon consent laid aside, but no sooner did it abate than the smothered quarrel of the Genoese and Venetians burst out into flame. Nicolò Pisani, defeated in the Bosphorus, retrieved his laurels near Sardinia; but the Genoese managed to equip a new fleet to replace that which Pisani had nearly destroyed, and, dexterously eluding the Venetian cruisers, their admiral Paganino Doria ravaged the coast of Dalmatia and Istria. The town of Lesina was sacked, Pola was nearly reduced to ruins, Parenzo was attacked and plundered, and these reverses so afflicted Andrea Dandolo the Doge and chronicler of Venice as to cause his death. It was of importance to the Genoese to secure the alliance of the Hungarians that they might victual their fleet from the Croatian shore, and they tried to induce Lewis to ally himself with them and attack the Venetians by land while they did so by sea. Lewis however confined himself to a demand for the restitution of the Dalmatian cities which the Venetians of course refused, but which formed a serious addition to their difficulties. They strengthened their fortifications in Dalmatia, negotiated with the king of Servia for the purchase of Scardona and Clissa, which Lelca the widow of Mladin had given him to prevent their falling into the hands of the

A.D. 1351. War between Venice and Genoa.

A.D. 1353.

A.D. 1354. Dalmatia and Istria ravaged by the Genoese.

Hungarians, and induced the Emperor to dissuade the king of Hungary from breaking the peace he had agreed to. The successor of Dandolo was Marino Faliero, and his accession was followed by the annihilation of the Venetian fleet under Nicolò Pisani by the Genoese under Paganino Doria. Disaster followed disaster; the Republic was convulsed by the conspiracy and punishment of Marino Faliero, and the first object of the succeeding Doge, Giovanni Gradenigo, was to put an end to the war. Fortunately he succeeded in concluding a peace with the Genoese and the duke of Milan their ally in 1355 before he had a fresh and still more formidable enemy on his hands.

A.D. 1355.

June 1, 1355. Peace between Venice and Genoa.

Renewal of war with Hungary. The term of the eight years' peace with the Hungarians was now at hand, and Lewis refused to listen to any proposals for its continuance. Allying himself with the patriarch of Aquileia and Francesco Carrara of Padua, both natural foes of the Republic, he invaded the marches of Treviso, while the Ban of Bosnia by his orders ravaged Dalmatia. The territories of Nona Zara and the other towns of Dalmatia and Istria were wasted, the people were driven within the walls, all cultivation of the soil was prevented, the sea was infested by pirates, and the inhabitants were reduced to the greatest straits. A fresh embassy from the Venetians offered to restore Zara to her former liberty, to restore certain places in Slavonia to the Hungarians, to pay an annual

Aug. 26, 1356.

tribute for the rest, and an indemnity for the expenses of the war. Lewis however would listen neither to the Venetians nor to his own councillors who urged him to consent to these proposals. A third offer by the Venetians to surrender all the rest if Zara alone were left to them had the effect of causing Traü and Spalato to open their gates to the Hungarians in order to gain the credit of a voluntary surrender. On July 8, 1357, the Venetian garrison and count of Spalato were surprised in their sleep and disarmed, and the soldiers shut up in various churches and crypts; at Traü the citizens shut their gates on their podestà who had gone out to a neighbouring church, whereupon he made his way to Spalato only to find himself a prisoner with his colleague. Both counts were treated honourably, and conveyed to Venice at the expense of the Spalatini, and the Ban was invited to take possession of the cities in the name of his master[1].

A.D. 1357. The Dalmatian cities submit to Hungary.

The Venetians tried to rouse the remaining Dalmatians to join them in recovering the revolted cities, but the hardships they had suffered from the ravages of the enemy and the insolence of the Venetian soldiery[2] outweighed any other

[1] Tabula a Cutheis, ch. iii.
[2] 'Spalat. vero non valentes ulterius tanta mala et damna sustinere et pati a gente Ungara ... deliberaverunt inter se insimul cum Trag. ut declinarent a dominio Ven. et reverterentur ad dominium naturale et pristinum Ung. ... Postea per aliquot dies omnes Civ. Dalm. simili modo rebellaverunt a Ven. putantes quod non esset bonum statum ipsorum sub

considerations. Sebenico sent envoys to make her submission to the Ban who was engaged in besieging Nona. The islanders of Brazza declared for Hungary; Lesina which held out for Venice was invaded and sacked by the men of Almissa Traü and Spalato in the fervour of their conversion to the Hungarian cause; and the abbot of S. Michele treacherously opened the gates of Zara and admitted the German mercenaries of Lewis who after some severe fighting made themselves masters of all but the castle. Nona and Scardona still held out, but Nona was starved into surrender after the besieged had eaten their last horse. Lewis himself came to Zara to press the siege of the citadel, but before it was taken the Venetians found it impossible to continue the contest, and a peace was agreed to by which Lewis gained everything he had contended for. The Venetians resigned all claim to Dalmatia from half-way up the Quarnero to Durazzo[1], and '*in particular the cities of Nona Zara Scardona Sebenico Traü Spalato and Ragusa on the mainland, also these cities with their adjacent territories, viz. Cherso Veglia Arbe Pago Brazza Lesina Curzola, with their islands,*' and they agreed that the Doge should drop the title of Duke of Dalmatia, while

Sept. 17, 1357.

Peace of Zara, Feb. 18, 1358. Loss of Dalmatia by Venetians.

dominio Venet. jam in fastidium effecti erant Dalmatinis Veneti propter ipsorum stipendiarios et Soldatos.' Tab. a Cutheis, c. iii.

[1] In the words of the treaty, 'renunciamus ... toti Dalmatiae a medietate scilicet guarnarii usque ad confines Duracii.'

on the other hand the king was to restore to the Republic his conquests in the Trevisan and Istria. An amnesty was to be proclaimed for the adherents of either side, the respective territories were to be transferred within twenty-two days, and a special provision was made for the repression of piracy by both parties[1]. Instructions were sent to the Venetian counts throughout Dalmatia to surrender their charge, and thus the Republic ceased to have a footing on the eastern side of the Adriatic[2].

Before pursuing the history of the fifty or sixty years that elapsed before Dalmatia passed once more and finally out of the power of the Hungarians into that of the Venetians, it will be *Reasons for the uncertain allegiance of the Dalmatians.*

[1] The text of the treaty is given by Lucio, lib. iv. ch. xvii. p. 235. It will be observed by those who argue for the perpetual independence of Ragusa, that no distinction is made between that city and the others which were subject to Venice. But vid. History of Ragusa, infra, chapter xix.

[2] '... el castello de Zara in lo qual iera stado f Andrea Zane Cap. e mo jera Cap. Piero Badoer, e Scardona della qual se haveva dominio fo messa in le man del Re de Ongaria, apresso fo scritto a f Iacomo Corner Conte de Arbe, e f Iacomo Ziuran Conte de Pago, e f Nicolo Corner Conte de Cherso e Ossero, e f Nicolo Corner Conte de Liesina, e a f ... Zuzi Conte de Cursola, e a f Marco Sanudo Conte di Ragusi che de li detti luoghi se dovesse remover con tutta la famegia e vegnir à Venexia e de quelli plui non se impazar.' Chron. Ven. in Lucio, p. 235.

Cattaro threw herself on the protection of Lewis in 1370, the Servian kingdom having sunk to so low an ebb as to be unable to protect her from the lords of Zenta.

VOL. I. I

Policy of the Dalmatian cities. useful to pause and consider how these repeated changes of master were regarded by the Dalmatian cities, and what occasioned the apparent fickleness with which they so readily transferred their allegiance from one side to the other. The causes which led to the successive rebellions of the Zaratini, will throw light on the revolutions that occurred in the other cities as well. Their first revolt in 1180 was provoked by the subjection of their archbishop to the Venetian primate; the causes of the second in 1242 are obscure, but may no doubt be found in the close subjection in which they were held since the conquest of 1202; their third revolt in 1311 was made at the instigation of the counts of Bribir, with the prospect of regaining under Hungarian rule those ancient privileges of which since their previous outbreaks the Venetians had deprived them; and their fourth in 1345 was occasioned by irritation at the loss of the islands which the Venetians compelled them to restore to the Sebenzani. In all these cases the offence was given by interference either with their municipal autonomy and independence, or with the territorial rights of the commune.

Autonomy their real desire. The real object of the policy of Zara and every town of the Dalmatian pale, was to be allowed to live under its own laws, to choose its own magistrates, to govern itself on its ancient democratic basis, and to regulate its own internal affairs without interference from any superior authority. These privileges were secured to the citizens by the ancient charters, which were confirmed from time to time by the successive rulers under whose dominion they passed. They are all to the same effect; the citizens were exempted from tribute; they had leave to elect their own count and bishop[1] whom the suzerain, Hungarian or Venetian, was to confirm; they were to use their ancient Roman laws, and to appoint their own judges; no alien, even if he were of the ruling nation, was to reside within their walls except at their pleasure, a stipulation by which they were protected against the intrusion of a foreign garrison; no castle or fort was to be built on their territory without their leave; they were not to be called upon to give hostages; and no citizen could be cited to appear before any foreign tribunal or before any judges but those of his own city. So long as these privileges were respected and they were allowed to govern themselves in their own way the municipalities of Dalmatia considered that they were free[2], and it is in the prospect of better preserving their freedom and autonomy under the protection of one ruler or the other that we must seek the explanation of the readiness with which they

Nature of their ancient privileges.

---

[1] M. Guizot remarks that it was the general characteristic of Roman municipalities,—of cities properly so called,—that the clergy in concert with the people elected the bishop. Hist. of Civilization in France, Lect. xvii.

[2] 'Suis enim legibus vivere idem erat quod integra libertate frui, nam leges civibus modum vivendi statuentes a cujuslibet alterius jurisdictione cives eximebant.' Luc. de Regn. lib. iv. c. ii. p. 273.

turned from Venetian to Hungarian, and from Hungarian to Venetian, rather than in any preference for one over the other.

Their need of protection by a great power.

What the cities really desired was to be left alone and to have as little as possible to do with either or any of their powerful and dangerous neighbours; but unhappily their weakness and isolation made them necessarily dependent on that neighbour who was for the time being the most dangerous and powerful. For the cities of Dalmatia had no cohesion among themselves; had they been able to league themselves together like the free cities of Lombardy they might perhaps have defied Croatian, Venetian, and Hungarian; but except now and then under the leadership of Venice the relations of city to city were seldom amicable and often hostile. Too small to stand alone they naturally sought the protection of the most powerful friend they could find, and so long as their internal autonomy was respected and their territorial rights were not infringed they were willing to serve as allies and to send a contingent of ships and men to the forces of the power whose flag they hoisted.

Difficulty of their position.

The difficulty of the position of these maritime cities between the rival powers of Venice and Hungary was extreme. Their position on the sea coast, their commercial pursuits by which they lived, and their possessions on the islands that lay off their shores placed them at the mercy of Venice in time of war, and it was to

Venice that they had to look in time of peace for security against the piratical Slavs who infested those seas. On the other hand their territory on the mainland, surrounded by the feudal estates of Slavonic counts, or the lands of Croatian cities like Nona and Belgrad, was at any time exposed to be invaded by the Ban to whom they were seldom able to oppose any adequate resistance. Their allegiance to one side or the other was obviously a matter to be decided more by interest than by affection, and in time of war when neither party could protect them against the other except on his own element their case was pitiable.

The instincts of race, and the ties of a common language and culture naturally inclined the Latin population of the cities towards Italy rather than towards Hungary. Between the Latins and the Croatians, in spite of the intermixture that naturally took place during the lapse of centuries, there was little sympathy. As the towns grew in wealth and importance, and developed the arts of civilisation in their midst, the Croatians seemed to them more and more left behind in comparative barbarism. The municipal governments were moulded on the model of the towns of Italy; the chief magistrate or podestà was generally an Italian; at Spalato immediately after Coloman's conquest we find the rector was a Trevisan; in 1200 the citizens made an Italian from Perugia their archbishop: they refused the rectorship of

Their natural inclinations towards Italy.

the city to Reles, duke of Croatia, because they spurned the idea of being governed by a Slavonian[1], and in 1239 they invited a podestà from Ancona. It was the same in the other cities, and even under the tyranny of the Slavonic counts of Bribir the office of podestà was filled by Italians generally chosen from the march of Ancona[2].

<small>Autocratical government of Hungary.</small>

Between the Latins and the Hungarians there was even less affinity than between them and the Croatians. From both Latins and Croatians the Hungarians were aliens in race, language, and customs. The free democracies of the cities, whose acts were issued in the name of '*the count with the judge and the whole body of the people*[3]', were unintelligible to them. Monarchical themselves they treated the Dalmatians autocratically, and the privileges which the Hungarian kings confirmed were in effect often infringed. The Bans, subservient to the king themselves, loved to lord it in their turn over the provincials, and the privileges of the towns were a constant source of vexation to the Bans who could not oppress the citizens as they did the Croatians.

---

[1] 'Detestantes prorsus regimen viri Sclavigenae experiri.' Thom. Archid., c. xxi.

[2] 'Potestates autem, qui ex Marchia Anconitana ut plurimum voluntate tamen Comitis eligebantur,' &c. Lucio de Regn. lib. iv. c. xiv. p. 205.

[3] A.D. 1174. 'Ego Joannes Spalatensis comes pariter cum Petro judice, et cum toto ejusdem Civitatis Populo pari voluntate et communi consilio decrevimus,' &c. Luc. lib. iii. c. x. p. 132, and so passim. Vid. also quotations from statutes of Ragusa, infra, chapter xix.

The Venetians therefore might have been expected to attract the sympathy and command the allegiance of the Dalmatians more readily than the Hungarians. Under the rule of the Republic the provincials paid no tribute or taxes beyond the 'strena or strinna' which perhaps represented the nominal acknowledgment retained to the Empire in the time of Basil I[1], their ancient constitutions were respected, and they were treated as allies rather than as subjects[2]. The Venetians might have made sure of Dalmatia had their protection been as powerful by land as it was by sea. Lucio observes that there always had been, and were even in his own day, 'two classes of men in the cities of Dalmatia, especially those of the continent, one living by terrestrial pursuits and industries, the other by navigation and fisheries; from which difference two parties grew up in each state, the landed party attaching itself to the Croats and Hungarians, the maritime party to the Venetians, and the maritime party prevailed until as time went on the territory on the mainland increased in extent, when the landed party either equalled or overmatched the maritime[3].' The landed party, whose farms and estates were at the mercy of the Bans, naturally wished to keep on good terms with them and the Hungarians, and the frequent

Character of Venetian government.

Two parties in every city.

Reason of Hungarian influence.

---

[1] Vid. supra, p. 23, and Const. Porphyr. de adm. Imp. c. xxx.
[2] Lucio, lib. vi. c. ii. p. 275-6.
[3] Ibid. p. 227.

and prolonged absences of many of the maritime party on trading expeditions threw more power into the hands of those who were always at home. It required the tyranny of the counts of Bribir to unite both parties in opposition to the Croats and Hungarians and to force them into the arms of Venice.

<small>A.D. 1358. Dalmatia under Lewis the Great.</small>

The rule of Lewis did not give universal satisfaction in Dalmatia, nor did it remove the grievances which had been felt under the government of Venice. Spalato Traü and Sebenico which had voluntarily surrendered to him received a confirmation of their privileges[1] and liberties, but some jealousy was felt at the same favour being extended to the other places which had been taken by force or given up by the Venetians. The Zaratini alone were excluded <small>Character of the rule of Lewis in Dalmatia.</small> from the king's liberality; the island of Pago was not restored to them, nor those of Srimaz and Zuri which were given to the Sebenzani, nor were they reinstated in their ancient privileges of which the Venetians had deprived them, nor was the castle pulled down as they had hoped it would have been, but on the contrary it was garrisoned with Hungarian troops. A new rule provided an appeal to the king from the decisions of the judges which was rightly felt to cut at the

---

[1] Vid. text of confirmation of those of Sebenico. Lucio, iv. xvii. p. 234.

root of their autonomy[1], and the Queen-mother, Elizabeth 'the Elder,' whom Lewis sent into Dalmatia as regent with plenipotentiary powers, set herself to work with the barons who were associated with her to clip and shape all the customs and privileges of the country to an uniform pattern, the object of the king being to obliterate the ancient distinctions of Dalmatian, Croat, and Serb, and to govern them all by the same code[2]. On one point he was forced to give way; the possibility of having the decision of their municipal courts upset by appeal to the king made the other privileges worthless, and Lewis was at last obliged to listen to the remonstrances of the citizens and substitute for an appeal to himself one to four colleges in Italian states friendly to himself.

It was not only in these respects that the liberties of the cities suffered under a king accustomed to absolute rule. He interfered with the election of the counts, refusing to confirm those chosen by the citizens, and appointing others of his own choice; he exempted certain citizens from the municipal jurisdiction, and imposed heavy dues, especially creating the state monopoly of salt, an abominable institution that has survived under various governments down to our own day[3]. From this monopoly he derived great profit, and he tried to export salt to Ferrara and Padua,

Abridgment of privileges by Lewis.

[1] Luc. vi. c. ii. p. 276.   [2] Luc. v. c. i. p. 238.
[3] Luc. vi. c. vi. p. 276.

but was prevented by the Venetians who had by treaty with those places a monopoly of their own in that article.

A.D. 1378. War of Chioggia. In the deadly struggle between the republics of Venice and Genoa, which from its principal incident is known as the War of Chioggia, the Hungarians with the Carrara lords of Padua and the patriarch of Aquileia were allied with the Genoese. In the abasement of Venice and the destruction of her supremacy in the Adriatic Lewis saw his way to form a navy of his own, and to secure a safe and easy communication between his Dalmatian conquests and that kingdom of Naples which still eluded his grasp. This is not the place to follow the history of that six years' struggle in which Dalmatia played no part *Dalmatia ravaged by Venetians.* but that of a sufferer at the hands of the Venetian admiral Vittore Pisani, who made havoc of the unhappy maritime cities which were now subjects of the Hungarian enemy. On Aug. 17, 1378, he sacked Cattaro but spared the citizens and restored the city to them, leaving a garrison in the castle; on Oct. 17 he sacked and burned Sebenico, where he also left a garrison; from Zara, which he watched with his main force, he sent on Nov. 7 a detachment to Arbe, whose citizens, now as always inclined to be loyal to the Venetians, delivered their keys to the Captain Ludovico Loredano[1]; and on Nov. 17 Pisani with

---

[1] 'Confestim Arbenses clavibus exhibitis ad suum verum Ducale Dominium redierunt.' Caresinus in Muratori, vol. xii.

the whole fleet moved from Zara to Traü, where he found seventeen galleys of the Genoese but was unable either to cut them out or assault the town.

After the surrender of the Genoese fleet, which from blockading Venice had itself become blockaded in the lagunes, Arbe was retaken by Maruffo, who commanded another squadron of the Genoese, and the Venetians sacked and burned Segna, recovered Veglia[1], and burned Buccari. *A.D. 1380.*

When peace was at last restored by the mediation of the Duke of Savoy Dalmatia was once more ceded to the King of Hungary, and the reconquests which the Venetians had made were given back. The Hungarians were prohibited by the terms of the treaty from trading with ports north of a line drawn from the point of Istria to Rimini, and the Venetian triremes were forbidden to enter any royal port which was closed by a chain. Such chains were placed at the entrance of the harbour of Sebenico and many others, as for instance in the bocche di Cattaro, where the channel which it closed is still known as 'le Catene.' *Aug. 8, 1381. Peace of Turin.*

Lewis, in failing health and no longer young, was obliged to leave to a more youthful and *Succession to crowns of Naples*

---

[1] 'Galeis inde recedentibus Veglienses laesi fuerunt sed modice quia statim ad obedientiam devenerunt.' Caresinus.

The islanders generally preferred Venetian rule, having less to fear from the Hungarian ban than the citizens of the continental towns.

and Hungary. vigorous arm that conquest of the kingdom of Naples which had been the dream of his life, and to which the acquisition of Dalmatia had been a stepping stone. For a long while he had been childless, and had brought up at his court and destined as his heir the orphan nephew of that Carlo duke of Durazzo on whom he had wrought such summary vengeance at Aversa. Giovanna was also childless; in case of her death her realm devolved on Lewis as direct heir of Carlo Martello, and the young Carlo della Pace as he was called was destined by him to inherit and unite the two kingdoms of Hungary and Naples. The birth of his daughter Maria caused Lewis to change his plans. The crown of Hungary was reserved for his daughter, and that of Naples for Carlo della Pace, who was forthwith married to his cousin Margarita, posthumous daughter of the duke of Durazzo, so as to unite her claims to the crown of Naples with his own.

Charles III of Naples. In 1376, at the invitation of Urban VI, Lewis sent Carlo into Italy to dispossess Giovanna, who had offended the Pope by siding with the antipope. The resistance of Otto her fourth husband was speedily overcome, and Giovanna surrendered to her rival, by whom she was imprisoned *A.D. 1382. Murder of Giovanna.* and shortly afterwards put to death. It is said that Carlo wrote to Lewis to ask what he should do with her, and was answered that her end ought to be the same as that of her husband Andrew. She was smothered in the castle of Muro in the Basilicata, in the year 1382[1]. Her murderer succeeded as Charles III of Naples.

In the same year, on Sept. 12, Lewis died at Ternova and was succeeded by his daughter Maria, then scarcely twelve years old, who was crowned '*king*' on the 17th of the same month at Alba Regalis or Stuhlweissenburg[2]. Elizabeth, widow of Lewis, known in history as 'the younger,' to distinguish her from his mother Elizabeth 'the elder,' had acted for her husband during his last illness, and she continued to administer the kingdom during the minority of her daughter. At first the reign of the two queens was undisturbed, but signs of discontent soon showed themselves. The warlike nobles of Hungary and Croatia despised the government of a woman, resented the influence of the Palatine Nicolò Ban of Gara, and disliked the idea of subjection to Sigismund of Luxembourg, king of Bohemia and marquis of Brandenburg, the son of the Emperor Charles IV, to whom Maria was promised in marriage. A party was formed to revive the pretensions of Charles III of Naples, of which the leaders were Paul bishop of Zagabria or Agram, Stephen vaywode of Transylvania and

Sept. 12, 1382. Death of Lewis.

Regency of Elizabeth the younger.

Conspiracy against Maria. A.D. 1383.

[1] Giannone, lib. xxiii. c. 5.

[2] '1382, 17 mens. praesentis D. Maria filia senior antedicti Regis in Civ. praedicta coronata fuit in Regem.' Mem. Pauli de Paulo, Patricii Jadrensis. The reader will remember the 'Moriamur pro rege nostro Maria Theresa' of the Hungarians in 1741.

his brother, Giovanni Palisna prior of the Knights Hospitallers at Vrana, and Horvat ban of Dalmatia. The suspicions of the queens were aroused; they went in person to Zara, Palisna and Horvat were removed from their offices, and Vrana which had openly revolted was recovered. On Nov. 4 the queens visited Vrana and afterwards returned to Buda. In the following year the conspiracy continued to gain ground. Four persons whose treason had been discovered were beheaded in the piazza of Zara in July, fresh oaths of allegiance to the queens were exacted from the citizens, and Horvat was sent out of the way into Italy on pretence of supporting Charles in his struggle with Lewis of Anjou. This seems to have been injudicious, for Horvat abused his opportunity to persuade Charles to undertake the easy task of dispossessing the youthful queen and making himself king of Hungary. The bishop of Zagabria followed with the same request; Charles listened eagerly to the proposal, and on Sep. 12, 1385 he sailed from Barletta in Apulia with only a small body of adherents, anticipating a welcome reception and little opposition. Zara was held by a Hungarian garrison, and the Dalmatians generally remained faithful to Maria; passing them by therefore, Charles made for Segna, whence he reached Zagabria six days after leaving Barletta. Here he stayed some days to issue his proclamations, which were highly garnished with promises of immunities and privileges; all Hun-

A.D. 1384.

A.D. 1385.
Arrival of Charles III in Hungary.

gary and Croatia rallied to his standard, the queens were deserted by nearly everyone but the Palatine Nicolò, and on the arrival of Charles at Buda they were kept in an honourable captivity and obliged to affect submission and compliance.

In one point they had been too quick for their rival; he had intended to marry Maria to his son Ladislaus, but on the news of his landing Sigismund had been summoned and his marriage with Maria celebrated before the Neapolitan party could prevent it, and as Charles approached Buda Sigismund retired before him into Bohemia. *Marriage of Maria to Sigismund.*

In the following year, however, by the contrivance of the Ban Nicolò, Charles was waylaid and murdered in the apartments and presence of the two captive queens[1], his Italian suite was dispersed, and the populace shouted for 'King Maria,' as loudly as they had a few days before shouted for her rival. *A.D. 1386. Jan. 1. Murder of Charles III.*

The rebellion was however continued in Croatia by Horvat and Palisna, who collected a party to meet the queens as they were on their way southwards to reestablish their authority. The encounter took place 'prope Diacum'; the queens were accompanied apparently only by their ordinary suite[2] and were unprepared; their followers

---

[1] For further particulars of this affair vid. infra, Novigrad, chapt. v. The story is given at length by Giannone, lib. xxiv. c. 2.

[2] Caresinus, 'Cum Nicolao magno Comite Palatino et aliqua Comitiva.' Lucio says, 'solitis Aulicis comitantibus,' lib. v. c. ii. p. 253.

fought bravely, Nicolò of Gara and Blasio Forgac, by whose hand Charles had fallen, were killed, and the queens were taken prisoners and conveyed to the castle of Novigrad near Zara. Here Elizabeth ended her days, though whether she was drowned in the Bozota, or dispatched by the sword, or whether, as some say, she died of grief remains shrouded in mystery. The heads of Nicolò and Forgac were sent to feed the vengeance of Margarita, the widowed Queen of Naples, and Maria was reserved to be sent after them, a living victim on whom a still sweeter revenge might be taken.

<small>Jan. 1387. Death of Elizabeth. Captivity of Maria.</small>

Sigismund, who advanced from Bohemia to the rescue of his bride, was driven back by the Croatians, and the case of Maria would have been desperate but for the assistance of the Venetians, who though they owed little to her family, saw probably that in her survival and marriage with Sigismund lay the strongest barrier against the union of Naples and Hungary.

<small>Coronation of Sigismund.</small>

The ambassadors of the Republic persuaded the Hungarian barons to accept Sigismund for their king, and he was crowned at Alba Regalis on March 31, 1387. Meanwhile the Venetian admiral Giov. Barberigo, Captain of the Gulf, watched Novigrad to prevent the threatened abduction of Maria, and their land forces so pressed Palisna, the prior of Vrana, that he was obliged to release his captive. On June 4 Maria was brought to Nona, where she received dele-

<small>June 4, 1387. Release of Maria.</small>

gates from Zara, among whom was Paolo de Paoli, as he records in his journal[1]; on the 15th she reached Segna, a feudal possession of the Frangipani counts of Veglia, who were among her supporters, where she stayed till July 1, and on the 4th of that month she rejoined her husband Sigismund at Zagabria.

During these disputes the Dalmatian cities remained quiet, preserving their allegiance to the queen, so far at all events as to take no part with the Croatian insurrectionists. For the usual 'Regnante Regina Maria' at the head of their public acts, the Spalatini, in 1385, substituted 'impedita Reg. Maria[2],' nor did they prefix the name of Sigismund after his coronation until he was formally associated with Maria on the throne. *Attitude of the Dalmatian cities.*

The rebellion however was not yet at an end; Sigismund sent a force to punish Horvat and the prior Palisna, who invited the assistance of Tvartko King of Bosnia, and thus brought a new disputant into the field. Bosnia from being a banat of the Hungarian crown had, under the reign and by the permission of Lewis, been ad- *The rebellion continued.*

---

[1] '1387. Die. 4 men. Junii de mane Sereniss. Princeps et D. nostra naturalis D. Maria R. Ung. liberata fuit a captivitate, et exivit de Castro Novigrad in quo detinebatur et die Veneris sequentis ivi ad eam Nonam, et die crastina die Sabbathi locutus fui Majestati suae, et die lunae immediate recessi a Nona licentiatus ab ea,' &c. Memoriale Pauli de Paulo, Patritii Jadrensis.

[2] Lucio, p. 253.

vanced to the rank of a tributary kingdom[1]. The Ban Stephen Tvartko was cousin to Queen Elizabeth the younger, and enjoyed the royal favour; and after he had been employed about the year 1357 to humble the neighbouring kingdom of Servia or Rascia, he was allowed to assume the title of King of Rascia and Bosnia[2]. His ambition aspired to the dominion of the sea coast as well, and in the appeal made to him by the insurrectionary Croatians he saw an opportunity to attain his object and to shake off what remained of the Hungarian yoke at the same time. Advancing into Dalmatia he made himself master of Cattaro Clissa and Almissa, and attacked Ragusa and Spalato. Palisna had been driven back by the Zaratini with the aid of the count of Segna and Modrussa, and was beleaguered in the stronghold of Vrana. Tvartko raised the siege, captured Nona and Ostrovizza, and again attacked Spalato Sebenico and Trau. Disappointed in their appeals for aid to Sigismund and Maria, the citizens consented to treat with the Bosnian king, stipulating only that time should be allowed for the return of their messengers from Hungary that they might save their reputation for fidelity. The time elapsed,

Bosnian kingdom of Tvartko I.

A.D. 1389. *Conquest of Dalmatia by Tvartko.*

A.D. 1390.

---

[1] Lucio de Regn. lib. v. p. 256. The assumption of royalty by Stephen Tvartko was about 1376.

[2] He was the first Bosnian prince since Culin (d. 1216) who coined money, and his reign marks the high tide of Bosnian history. That country had never been so great before, and its decline set in immediately afterwards.

no help was forthcoming from their liege lords, and the three cities made their submission to Tvartko, stipulating, as usual, for a confirmation of their privileges. The islands of Lesina Brazza and Curzola admitted his lieutenants, the sea coast of the ancient duchy of Chelmo was his by conquest, and Tvartko could now style himself *D. G. Rasciae, Bosniae, Maritimaeque Rex.* His forces under Palisna repulsed an army of Sigismund which attacked the fortress of Knin, and Zara and Ragusa alone defied his arms.

A.D. 1391.

In the succeeding year, however, Palisna died (Feb. 16, 1391); Tvartko himself died a month later, and his Dalmatian kingdom fell to pieces as rapidly as it had been formed. His successor, Stephen Dabiscia[1], had to contest his throne with

A.D. 1391. Death of Tvartko and decline of Bosnia.

[1] The succession of the Bosnian kings is very obscure. The list given by Nic. Isthuanfy (*de reb. Ungar*) is incorrect. The following table is I hope accurate; it has been collected from various sources.

Stephen, Ban of Bosnia, d. 1310.

Stephen Cotroman, Ban. d. 1357.	Wladislav.	Ninoslav.
Elizabeth, wife of Lewis the Great of Hungary.	STEPH. TVARTKO I, King of Rascia and Bosnia, 1376. d. 1391.	STEPH. DABISCIA, 1391. d. 1396.
	STEPH. TVARTKO II, illegitimate, disputes throne with Ostoya, 1396–1435. Reigns alone 1435. d. 1443.	STEPH. OSTOYA KRISTIĆ, disputes throne with Tvartko II. d. 1435.
	Catharine, dr. of Steph. Cosaccia.	= STEPH. THOMAS KRISTIĆ, 1443. Murdered, 1461, by

STEPHEN TOMASOVIĆ, his illegitimate son, who was flayed alive by Mahomet II, 1463.

a rival, and when this difficulty was overcome he had enough to do to keep his kingdom against the Turks, and he resigned the reversion of his rights in Croatia and Dalmatia to Sigismund without a struggle, reserving for himself only a life possession.

<small>A.D. 1395. Death of Maria. Disputes about the succession.</small>

In the same year died Maria queen of Hungary. The question now arose whether the succession was vested in her consort Sigismund, or whether it did not pass to Hedwig or Edviga, queen of Poland, the surviving daughter and sole descendant of Lewis; and for a time the acts of Spalato Sebenico and Traü contain no royal name at their head, but are issued in the name solely of the Rectors and Judges[1]. But Edviga and Sigismund were not the only claimants of the throne; a third pretender was put forward by the

<small>Croatian disaffection.</small>

insurgent Croatians, whose resistance to the authority of Sigismund had never been overcome. Their revolt had obviously less to do with the question of succession than with that of the dependence or liberty of Croatia. In the rivalry of Maria and Carlo III the Croat leaders had seen an opportunity of freeing themselves from the Hungarians, and by their alliance with Tvartko and his conquest of Dalmatia they had partially succeeded. When the Bosnian power declined

---

[1] '1394, Aug. 14. Spalatenses autem decreverant *quod a morte Tuertichi Regis citra non fiat mentio de aliquo Rege nec de aliquo alio nisi solummodo de Rectoribus et Judicibus*,' &c. Luc. v. iii. p. 258.

the Croatian leaders looked around for another ally, and fixed their eyes on the young Ladislaus of Naples, son and successor of Charles III, whom they invited to revive his father's claims. But while Ladislaus hesitated[1], Sigismund acted with promptitude; his Ban Nicolò Gara defeated and slew Horvat, the leader of the rebellious party since the death of Palisna, and recovered the maritime cities, and for the next few years Ladislaus was too much occupied by domestic disturbances to think of the Hungarian succession. *Pretensions of Ladislaus of Naples put forward by the Croats.*

It is time to turn our eyes to a new power that was steadily making its way towards the Dalmatian seaboard, and a new danger that threatened not only Hungary but Christendom itself. A century had nearly elapsed since Othman conquered Prusa, and the Ottoman Turks first made their appearance in history. Orchan the son of Othman achieved the conquest of the Asiatic provinces of the Empire and the ruin or subjection of the seven Apostolic churches. The Turks owed their first introduction into Europe to the same discord among the Christians by which their empire was in after times cemented, and the Emperor John Cantacuzene inflicted on the Empire 'its deep and deadly wound' by inviting the aid of the Ottomans against his ward and rival John *THE TURKS. A.D. 1299. A.D. 1312.*

---

[1] 'Sed juvenis, paternae necis memor, accedere verebatur.' Luc. v. iv. p. 259.

Palaeologus. Once established in Europe they speedily overran Thrace, and Amurath I. (Murad) fixed his capital at Adrianople. Postponing the fate of Constantinople he attacked the kingdoms of Bulgaria, Servia, Bosnia, and Albania, and from the hardy youths of those countries whom he captured and reared in the Moslem faith he formed the invincible corps of Janizaries. The crisis, which decided the fate of Christendom in the Balkan peninsula, was reached in 1389, when Lazarus Grebelianovich, king of Servia, combined his forces with those of the kings of Bosnia and Bulgaria, and encountered Amurath at Kossovo. Treachery and discord as usual ruined the Christian cause; the allied forces were disastrously routed; and though Amurath himself fell by the hand of a desperate Servian after the battle was over, the knell of Servian and Bulgarian liberty was sounded on the fatal field of Kossovo. Zenta or Montenegro preserved a doubtful and obscure independence among her mountains, and from this day her separate history begins. The Bosnian forces alone escaped the rout; they retired in good order from the field, and Tvartko was able again to meet the Turks and to wipe out his defeat by a victory which for the time saved his kingdom[1]. From this time

---

[1] He reports this triumph to his subjects at Traü on Aug. 1, 1389, 'iuito cum eis bello die 20 Mensis Junii proxime praeteriti, Dei dextera adjutrice et nobis propitia assistente, obtento penitus cum triumpho campo confliximus, devicimus, et humi

Servia and Bulgaria sank gradually into the condition of Turkish provinces; but it was not the policy of the Turks to reduce their conquests instantly to slavery; Servia was for a time governed by despots appointed by the Sultan, and it was not till 1459 that it was reduced to a mere province of the Turkish Empire.

After the death of Tvartko a fresh advance of the Turks on Bosnia alarmed and united the Hungarians Germans and French by a sense of their common danger. A crusade was preached, and an army of 100,000 soldiers of the cross assembled under the leadership of Sigismund to meet Bajazet Ilderim at Nicopol on the Danube. The day was lost by the rashness of the French chivalry, the crusaders were disastrously defeated, and Sigismund with difficulty escaped by a small boat down the Danube to the Black Sea, whence he reached Constantinople, and was conveyed by the Venetians to Ragusa. He passed the winter at Knin to which place he granted a 'privilege,' and reached Hungary in the following spring. *A.D. 1396. Crusade against the Turks. Sept. 18, 1396. Battle of Nicopol. A.D. 1397.*

The invasion of Timour, the defeat of Bajazet at Angora in 1402, and his captivity and death, interrupted the victorious career of the Ottomans and gave Europe a short breathing space. The sons of Bajazet were occupied by civil wars, and the Ottoman Empire was not reunited till the reign of Amurath II. (1421–1451).

prostravimus interemptos, paucis demum ex ipsis superstitibus remanentibus.' Luc. v. iii. p. 257.

Pretensions of Ladislaus of Naples.

Meanwhile the Croats continued their resistance to Sigismund, and their invitations to Ladislaus of Naples. Ostoya the new king of Bosnia and the Voyvode Hervoye were drawn into the same cause, and the cities were divided by factions, some favouring Sigismund and some the Neapolitan pretender. Sigismund had become an alien in Hungary since his wife's death, and his reputation had been ruined by the defeat of Nicopol. Many of the Hungarian nobles were favourably disposed towards his rival, and for a short time he was a prisoner in the hands of an insurrectionary party. In Dalmatia his excessive taxation had disgusted the cities, especially Spalato, and Zara had not forgiven him for depriving her of her territory on the island of Pago, to which he had conceded the same liberties which were enjoyed by the other cities of Dalmatia.

A.D. 1400. *Ladislaus invades Dalmatia.*

Ladislaus had now finally triumphed over Lewis of Anjou, his rival for the throne of Naples, and was free to listen to the overtures of the Croats. Hervoye was constituted his lieutenant and in his name confirmed the privileges of the Dalmatian cities.

A.D. 1401.

His admiral Aloysio Aldemarisco arrived with a fleet at Zara, the citizens were won over by the promise of the restitution of Pago, on Aug. 27 his standard was hoisted in the piazza, and the example of the Zaratini was speedily followed by the other towns and islands. The Ban of Croatia, who was approaching to support the cause of Sigismund, was defeated near Bihać; Vrana was taken by Hervoye, and with the exception of Ragusa and Cattaro the whole of Dalmatia and its islands accepted the dominion of Ladislaus. His pretensions were supported by the Pope, and a legate was sent to meet him at Zara where he was solemnly crowned King of Hungary, Dalmatia, and Croatia. He confirmed the privileges of the various towns, and yielded to the objections made by the Traürini and Sebenzani to the construction of a castle within their cities as a violation of their liberties. Hervoye was constituted his viceroy and voyvode, and was made count of Spalato, and of the islands of Curzola, Lesina, Lissa, and Brazza; and, leaving his new kingdom in his lieutenant's charge, the king returned to Naples in November. A.D. 1403. Ladislaus crowned at Zara.

His departure revived the sinking cause of Sigismund. Veglia Segna and Modrussa received back their Count Nicolò Frangipani who supported Sigismund, and under his guidance Arbe was recovered, but soon after lost again to the Neapolitan admiral Giovanni di Lusignan. But Ladislaus was occupied with another war in Italy and could send no troops to Dalmatia, Bosnia was torn by a struggle for the succession to the throne, and was powerless, and the party of Sigismund gained adherents every day. Finally Hervoye himself made his peace with Sigismund and transferred his support to that side, and soon there remained to Ladislaus of all his acquisitions in Reaction in favour of Sigismund. A.D. 1408. Defection of Hervoye from Ladislaus.

Dalmatia only the city of Zara, the castles of Vrana and Novigrad, and the island of Pago. To save himself from absolute discomfiture he resolved not to wait till these places fell into the hands of the Hungarians, but to sell them to the Venetians, and thus, though driven off the field by his rival, he could feel that he left his sting behind[1]. A hundred thousand ducats was the price which the Venetians were glad to give to recover once more a footing in Dalmatia; a fleet was sent to take possession of Zara, the indignation of the Neapolitan soldiery was appeased after some disturbance, a garrison was introduced, and the defences of the city were strengthened by cutting through the isthmus which joined it to the mainland. Pago was placed as before under the separate government of a Venetian count.

June 9, 1409. Venetians buy Zara, &c.

A.D. 1409. Zara recovered by Venice.

Sigismund did not remain passive; his armies invaded Friuli and Dalmatia, but without any success. The Venetians opposed his journey to Rome to receive the Imperial crown, and allied themselves against him with the Duke of Milan, and finally compelled him to conclude a truce for five years. At Sebenico the city was rent by factions: the nobles favoured the Venetians and were expelled by the populace, who were for Hungary; but

A.D. 1411.

---

[1] Luc. v. v. p. 262 has preserved the deed of sale. 'Ladislaus, &c. ... et ex aliis causis justis moventibus mentem suam Regiam vendere et alienare Civitatem Iadrae ... cum et sub specificatione Novigradus Insulae Pagi et aliorum districtuum ipsius nec non terram Lauranae cum fortalicio et castro ... pro ducatis centum millibus.'

finally, in 1412, weary of internal dissension, the exiles were recalled and the city handed over to the Venetians. At Spalato Hervoye, who was convicted of intriguing with the Turks, was disgraced and expelled[1], and retired to Cattaro, where he died in 1415. In 1420 the islands of Lesina Brazza and Curzola gave themselves to the Venetians, Traü was bombarded and captured by their admiral Pietro Loredano, Spalato surrendered to avoid a like fate, and Cattaro, which had for long implored the protection of the Republic against the Balsa of Zenta, was for the first time in its history admitted to the dominion of Venice.

A.D. 1412. Sebenico recovered by Venice.

A.D. 1420. Traü and Spalato, and the islands recovered by Venice.

The whole of maritime Dalmatia was now in the possession of Venice except Ragusa, Almissa, and Veglia. Almissa gave herself to the Republic in 1444; Veglia continued independent under her counts of the Frangipani line, subject to the protection of Venice, till 1480, when the tyranny of the last count Giovanni or Ivan caused his deposition, after which the island was governed, like the other Dalmatian states, by a Venetian count. Although the Emperor did not formally cede his rights till the peace of 1437, he never succeeded in recovering any of the maritime cities; and by the terms of that peace, while the towns of the interior, Knin Verlicca Sign Scardona Clissa and others were left to the Hungarians, Novigrad

Peace of Prague, July 29, 1437.

Final recovery of Dalmatia by Venice.

---

[1] 'Vafritiem Demetrii Pharii imitatus Ducatum Spalati consecutus.' Lucio, p. 267.

Nona Zara Sebenico Traù Spalato with their respective territories, and all the islands except those which belonged to Ragusa, were recognized as Venetian.

<small>Ragusa becomes independent.</small>

Ragusa alone had no share in these changes. Of all the cities of Dalmatia she alone was possessed of resources sufficient to qualify her for independence. Till 1358 she had acknowledged the dominion of Venice and received a Venetian count; since that time she had lived under the protection of Hungary, and accepted a count from the king. But now that Hungary was in no condition to interfere, the Ragusans, while carefully maintaining the useful shadow of Hungarian protection, gradually advanced to complete practical independence, and formed their state into a miniature republic on the model of Venice. As such it survived almost to our own time, protected first by the kings of Hungary and afterwards by the Empire, and its interesting independence might have continued even to the present day but for the whim of Napoleon who, in 1808, thought fit to declare that the Republic of Ragusa had ceased to exist.

<small>Venetian rule a barrier to Turkish conquest.</small>

'Thus,' says Lucio at the end of his great history, 'whatever is included by the name of the Dalmatian kingdom[1], except Ragusa, by the good

---

[1] Lucio here as elsewhere limits the 'Dalmatian kingdom' to the old Roman cities, and the more recently chartered towns like Sebenico, which being put on the same footing he considers as placed within the Dalmatian pale.

fortune of Dalmatia, passed into the hands of the Venetians. For the Turks spreading their Empire wider every day, having taken Constantinople, seized the kingdom of Bosnia and its dependencies after the murder of Stephen, the illegitimate son of King Thomas Ostoya, and occupied the greater part of Hungary and Croatia, and day by day wasting the territories of the maritime cities themselves, acted over again the period of the occupation of Dalmatia by the Slavs, except that this time things were better in one respect, namely that through the precautions of the Venetians the Turks occupied none of the islands, nor were they allowed to practise piracy; so that the Dalmatians lead a more tolerable existence, and form a barrier against the passage of the Turks to the neighbouring shores of Italy, the country which they declare it is their principal aim and desire to conquer[1].'

FOURTH PERIOD.

From the final acquisition of Dalmatia by the Venetians in 1420 to the downfall of the Republic in 1798.

By the establishment of Venetian rule throughout Dalmatia an end was put to the civil dissensions which had agitated the maritime cities since

[1] Luc. de Regn. lib. v. c. v. p. 270. This was written about the middle of the seventeenth century, while the Venetians were still occupied in driving the Turks back from Dalmatia into Bosnia.

Unsettled state of Dalmatia previous to the Venetian acquisition.

the death of Lewis in 1382¹. For nearly thirty years they had been tossed to and fro from one master to another, and whatever the shortcomings of Venetian rule may have been—and they were not few nor unimportant—it was at all events something gained for the provincials to know who was their master. The pretensions of Charles III of Naples to the throne of Hungary, the captivity of Queen Maria, and the outbreak of the national movement of the Croats towards independence had shaken the reliance of the Dalmatians on the protection of Hungary, and left them uncertain to which side it would be most politic to attach themselves. In 1390 they submitted to the Bosnian king Tvartko; five years later they returned to Sigismund, but only to doubt whether the death of Maria did not determine their allegiance to her husband; five years later again the whole country embraced with something like enthusiasm the cause of Ladislaus of Naples, only to find it had grasped at a shadow.

Civil factions in the cities.

The result of these struggles and changes was to divide the citizens into hostile factions which favoured different sides and plotted and intrigued against one another with all the animosity that civil discord alone can inspire. Most of the towns had their *extrinseci* and *intrinseci*, the weaker

---

¹ Farlati remarks of the end of the fourteenth century, 'Incredibile dictu est quanta in conversione rerum et perturbatione in temporibus illis tum Dalmatae omnes tum vero Arbenses versarentur, sic prorsus ut inter paucos annos ex aliis ad alios Dominos et transierint et redierint.' Tom. v. p. 248.

of the two parties being driven into exile, and ever watching from beyond the border for an opportunity of return and vengeance on the triumphant faction. Theirs is the old story of the banished citizens of the Greek commonwealths, the fuorusciti of the Italian republics, the émigrés of revolutionary France, who were more formidable in exile than they would have been at home, always intriguing with the neighbouring powers and ready to sacrifice their country to their own political objects. All this was now at an end, and in spite of the terror of Turkish invasion which from this time forward hung like a cloud over the country till the Turkish power itself began to decline, Dalmatia under the settled government of a great commercial power advanced rapidly in wealth and prosperity. The arts flourished, noble buildings sprang up, the treasuries were enriched with beautiful work of the goldsmith or silversmith, and while artists from the other shore of the Adriatic were invited into the country, the native Dalmatians proved themselves by no means deficient in power both of design and execution, and some among them attained celebrity and eminence among the artists of Italy herself.

Pacification and prosperity of the province under Venice.

From this time till the eighteenth century the history of Dalmatia is simply a narrative of resistance to the westward progress of Turkish conquest. To the policy no less than the resolution of the Republic of S. Mark, and the stubborn valour of her Dalmatian subjects, Europe is indebted for the safety of Italy, the country for which the Turk ever hungered, but on which, except for a moment at Otranto, he never set foot.

The Ottoman power soon recovered the shock of Angora; '*the massy trunk was bent to the ground, but no sooner did the hurricane pass away than it rose again with fresh vigour and more lively vegetation*[1].' The empire of Bajazet, torn by the civil wars of his sons, was reunited by Amurath II in 1421; in the next year he assailed Constantinople; in 1444 he defeated Ladislaus IV and his general John Corvinus Huniades on the fatal and perjured field of Varna; and in 1453 Mahomet II, son of Amurath, took Constantinople and extinguished the last feeble spark of the Roman Empire.

A.D. 1453. Constantinople taken by the Turks.

A.D. 1428. Servia meanwhile had regained a brief independence. But the country was agitated by disputes about the succession to the throne, and when Lazzaro II, Brancovich, the fourth Despot of Servia, died in 1458, his widow Helena obtained from the Pope the investiture of the kingdom as a fief of the Church. Enraged at this concession to the Romish Church, which they detested, the Servians appealed to the Sultan Mahomet II; the Turkish armies crossed the frontier, and in 1459 Servia and Rascia lost their last traces of independence and sank into the condition of a

A.D. 1459. End of Servian kingdom.

[1] Gibbon, chap. lxv.

province of the Ottoman Empire. Helena escaped into Hungary, and thence retired to Ancona, Ragusa, and Venice, where she died in exile.

Bosnia also was torn by dissensions about the succession to the throne between Ostoya and Tvartko II. Tvartko invited the Turks to his aid and Ostoya the Hungarians, and though the former succeeded in triumphing over Ostoya, it was at the expense of allowing the Turks to obtain a footing in the kingdom. In 1443, after the death of both rivals, Stephen Thomas Kristić, son of Ostoya, was elected king, but he was obliged to purchase the acquiescence of the Turks by an annual tribute to Amurath of 25,000 ducats. His illegitimate son Stephen Thomasović, who murdered him and succeeded to the throne in 1461, having refused to pay the tribute, was flayed alive by Mahomet II, and the kingdom of Bosnia became, like Servia, a Turkish province. *End of the kingdom of Bosnia, A.D. 1463.*

One Slavonic principality still remained to be swallowed up. In 1440 the Emperor Frederick III had made Stephen Kosac, known to the Italians as Cosaccia, Herzog or Duke of S. Saba, the modern Herzegovina[1], which at that time included within its boundaries the highland republic of Poglizza, and the Craina or sea-coast from the Cetina to the Narenta. Almissa was induced to *End of Duchy of Herzegovina, A.D. 1465.* *A.D. 1465.*

---

[1] 'Herzegovina received its name from the title of Herzog, Duke, or Voivoda. .... It was also called the duchy of Santo Saba, from the tomb of that saint.' Sir G. Wilkinson, ii. p. 96; vid. also Lucio, lib. v. c. v.

submit to the Venetians in 1444, and the republic of Poglizza, while retaining its autonomy, accepted the protection of the Republic, agreeing to pay a small annual tribute by way of acknowledgment, and to supply recruits for the Venetian garrisons of Spalato Traü and the other maritime cities. The rest of the duchy was overrun by the Turks in 1465–6, and Cosaccia finding himself unable to defend the Craina, made it over to the safer keeping of the Venetians[1]. In 1475 his son Ladislaus gave them the fortress of Vissech on the Cetina about three miles above Almissa, to prevent its falling into the hands of the Turks[2], and with these exceptions the duchy of Herzegovina shared the fate of Servia and Bosnia.

<small>Reasons for ease of conquest by Turks.</small>

The ease with which the Slavonic principalities were conquered by the Mahometans is to be explained by two causes. Principally, no doubt, it was due to their internal dissensions, in all of which the Turks took care to mix themselves up, and out of which they never failed to reap advantage. Another reason that has been given is a religious one. The majority of the people were Bogomiles or Patarenes, who had been persecuted with fire and sword by the king the nobles and the clergy, and who were driven in despair to look to the Turks as deliverers[3]. We have seen

<small>1. Dissensions among the Christians.</small>

---

[1] Sir Gard. Wilkinson, vol. ii. p. 196. Storia della Dalmazia (Zara, 1878), p. 200, 209.
[2] Luc. de Regn. lib. v. c. v. p. 270.
[3] Vid. Introd. to Mr. A. Evans's 'Through Bosnia,' &c.

how in Servia, where the people were attached to the Greek Church, they voluntarily called in Mahomet II to defend them against the pretensions of the Church of Rome; and in Bosnia it is laid to the charge of the Romish propaganda and its system of persecution that the people to so great an extent became, and still remain, Mahometan. In 1459, while his kingdom was tottering to its fall, Stephen Thomas Kristić, who had himself renegaded from Bogomilism, and whom the grateful Catholics have rewarded with the title of 'the Pious,' expelled 40,000 innocent Bogomiles, who took refuge with the Herzog of S. Saba their co-religionist. Already in 1450 the Bogomiles had turned to the Turks for protection and invited them to enter the country, and it was then that the tribute of 25,000 ducats had been imposed as a condition of peace; and now on the final invasion of Mahomet II the people offered no resistance. Radić, the Patarene governor at Jajcze, persuaded the parricide king to surrender himself, the '*Manichean*' governor of Bohovac gave up the keys, seventy strong places and cities opened their gates without a struggle, and in a week the whole of Bosnia passed into the hands of Mahomet II.

2. Persecution of Bogomiles by Catholic kings.

Bogomiles driven to seek protection from the Turks.

A.D. 1462–1463.

Of the Christian population, both Latin, Greek, and Patarene, a large portion preserved their faith and have kept it to the present day; but many of the Bosnians, especially of the aristocracy, renegaded to Islam, in order to preserve

Bosnian nobility not Turkish but Slav.

their ascendancy, retain their feuds, and triumph over their ancient Catholic foes. It must not be forgotten in considering the history of Dalmatia from this time that the Moslem population of Bosnia and Herzegovina are for the most part not Turkish intruders but descendants of these renegade Slavs, speaking the same language and belonging to the same race as their Christian neighbours; and it is said the begs, or feudal nobles, of Bosnia have all along kept with reverent care their old title-deeds and pedigrees in readiness for the return of Christian supremacy [1].

Advance of Turks into Dalmatia. By the fall of these ultramontane kingdoms, the outworks of Christian Europe, Dalmatia was left exposed to the immediate attack of the Turks, who advanced wreaking every kind of cruelty on the unhappy people. In 1467 they penetrated so far as to threaten Segna and ravage the territory of Sebenico and Zara, and the Traürini to protect their coast built the succession of castles along the shore of the Sea of Salona, which gave it the name of the Rivièra dei Castelli. Numbers of refugees from Bosnia and Croatia flocked into the

The Morlacchi.

---

[1] It used to be said (vid. Mr. Evans's 'Through Bosnia,' &c.) that the Begs would become Christian again if Bosnia passed to a Christian power. This condition has now come to pass, but hitherto at all events no such conversion has followed. On the contrary, something like an exodus is taking place. When I was in Dalmatia in 1884 and 1885 the steamers were crowded with Mahometan Bosnians with their wives children and substance on their way to Trieste, whence they go to Asia Minor where the Sultan gives them a settlement and grant of land.

Venetian territory, the ancestors of the Morlacchi who constitute the peasantry of Northern Dalmatia, an agricultural and pastoral race, hardy and warlike, deadly foes of the Turks, and invaluable recruits for the armies of the Republic[1]. Watch-towers and beacons were planted on every point of observation, on mountain-top or highland pass, and on the approach of the marauding infidels the alarm was given by smoke in the daytime or fire by night, so that the people might take refuge in the fortresses or cities or arm themselves for defence.

Matthias Corvinus, son of Huniades, who had been elected King of Hungary in 1458, recovered

A.D. 1465.
Temporary recovery of

---

[1] The origin of the name Morlacco is obscure. Luc. lib. vi. c. v. believes the Morlacchi who at this time descended into the plains retiring as the Turks advanced, to be Vlahi, Vlachs, or Wallachs, descendants of the population which preceded the Slavonic conquest in the seventh century. Vlah, he says, will be found among all the Slavs to mean Roman, Latin, Italian, names which became terms of contempt and reproach with the victorious Slavs. He quotes the Presbyter Diocleas who, writing before 1200, says the Bulgarians conquered 'post haec totam Provinciam Latinorum qui illo tempore Romani vocabantur modo vero Moroulachi hoc est nigri Latini.' He adds that Moldavia was in later times called by the Greeks Maurolahia. The Morlacchi however, if they ever were Romans, have not preserved their Latin language like the Roumanians, but speak Illyrian, and it remains to be explained why they should have been called *black*. Others derive the name from *Mor*, 'sea,' and *Vlah*, inhabitant, 'dwellers along the sea'; not however the Adriatic, but the Black sea, whence they originally came. Vid. Sir G. Wilkinson, ii. 295. This seems far-fetched in every sense of the word. There are various other derivations of the name besides these. Fortis devotes a chapter to the subject.

Bosnia by Hungary. a large part of Bosnia in 1465, almost as rapidly as it had been lost, and the Banat of Bosnia maintained itself in dependence on Hungary till 1527.

The condition of Dalmatia was deplorable; the raids of the Turks across the frontier were continued even during the time of peace; Ladislaus of Hungary, who received an annual subsidy of 30,000 ducats from the Venetians to enable him to protect the frontier, was unable to fulfil his engagements; his bans and viceroys vied with the Turks in ravaging the Venetian territory in Dalmatia and Istria; and finally the league of Cambrai, which reduced the Republic to the last extremity, caused the recall of all the Venetian forces in Dalmatia for service at home, thus leaving the defence of the province to its own unassisted resources.

A.D. 1508–1509. League of Cambrai.

By the time that the Republic emerged from these perils which had well-nigh swamped her, and found herself once more in smooth water though with shattered forces and half-ruined commerce, it was no wonder that the Dalmatians had begun to look for help elsewhere, and that a Hungarian party had been formed in several of the cities. Envoys from Zara and Traü had been sent to Buda, and commotions had taken place in those cities, and also at Sebenico and Lesina; but severe measures were taken against the leaders of disaffection, and the authority of the Republic was re-established.

History of Dalmatia.

Meanwhile the incursions of the Turks continued. Clissa and the Polizzani were compelled in 1515 to pay tribute; the invaders burned the suburbs of Knin, besieged Jajcze, and captured Karin, and, though often driven back with severe loss, returned with undiminished ardour to the attack. Even the Montenegrins in their inaccessible fastnesses could scarcely maintain their doubtful independence, and the last of the Tzernoievich dynasty, despairing of further resistance, abandoned his country and retired to Venice with his wife, who was of the family of Mocenigo, and sank into obscurity as a Venetian patrician. The defence of his principality was boldly taken up by the bishop, or Vladika, of Cetinje, the first of the line of episcopal and princely heroes who have so gallantly maintained their independence to our own day. At this time however they were obliged to pay an annual tribute to the Porte, and a century elapsed before they were strong enough to refuse it.

A.D. 1515. Progress of Turkish conquest.

A.D. 1516. Montenegro forced to pay tribute.

The Vladika.

The condition of the Croatians and Bosnians was desperate. They could obtain no aid from the Hungarians, their own forces were exhausted, and their Ban Berisclavić had been slain. The Croats turned their eyes towards Venice and proposed to place themselves under the protection of the Republic, but Venice was occupied by the war of Cyprus, and was obliged to decline even to take over the fortresses of Scardona and Clissa which were offered her. Knin, the prin-

Croats offer themselves to Venice.

A.D. 1522. Knin and Scardona occupied by the Turks.

cipal Croatian fortress in Dalmatia, surrendered to the pacha of Bosnia in 1522, and the inhabitants of Scardona fled to Sebenico abandoning their city to the enemy, but the Croatian garrison still held out in Clissa, though hardly pressed by the besiegers.

A.D. 1526.
Battle of Mohacz.

Hungary was at this time torn by the struggle for the throne between Lewis II and John Zapolya the Voivode of Transylvania, and the Sultan Solyman thought the moment had arrived for finally conquering the country which had so long barred his way. Invading Hungary with an enormous army he was met by Lewis with a very inferior force at Mohacz on the Danube. The Hungarians were routed, Lewis himself was among the slain, Buda was obliged to open her gates, and the whole country along the Danube was ravaged before the conqueror returned to Belgrad. Ferdinand of Austria, brother of Charles V, who was elected to succeed Lewis II, had enough to do to secure his throne against the party of Zapolya, and he was in no condition to send any assistance to Dalmatia or Bosnia. Zapolya who had been crowned by his own party at Alba Regalis allied himself with Soly-

A.D. 1529 and 1530.

man, to whom he offered to make his kingdom tributary, and the Turkish armies advanced as far as Vienna before they were compelled to retire.

A.D. 1527.
Bosnia recovered

Meanwhile Jajcze had been surrendered to the Turks in 1527, and with it the whole of Bosnia passed once more, and irretrievably, into the power of the Sultan. Sign Verlicca and Nučak in Dalmatia were betrayed by their commandants, who had been won by Turkish gold, and in 1536, after their heroic commandant Peter Krusić had fallen, the garrison of Clissa were compelled to surrender that place to the pacha of Bosnia. The castles of Vrana and Nadin were surrendered in 1538, and though the Venetians captured and destroyed Scardona, and with the aid of the fleet of Charles V took Castelnuovo in the Bocche di Cattaro, the latter place was recovered directly by Haireddin Barbarossa, who put the Spanish garrison to the sword. When peace was concluded between the Republic and the Sultan in 1540, no part of continental Dalmatia was left to the Venetians except the cities; while the rest of Dalmatia was made a Turkish province under a Sangiac who fixed his residence at Clissa. *by the Turks. A.D. 1536. Turkish conquests in Dalmatia. Peace of 1540. All Dalmatia except the cities ceded to the Turks.*

An illustrious modern writer on Dalmatian history[1] attributes to the crowding of the cities at this time with refugees who left the open country from fear of the Turks the introduction of the Illyrian language within the walls, where it has since remained the tongue of the populace, Italian being the language only of the upper classes, except at Zara and Spalato which have retained a thoroughly Italian character down to our own times.

[1] Storia della Dalmazia. Zara, 1878, p. 243.

The Uscocs at Segna. The garrison expelled from Clissa was composed in great part of 'Uscocs,' or *refugees* from the countries in the interior, who on the surrender of the fortress retired to Segna on the Croatian shore of the gulf of Quarnero, where Ferdinand readily gave them a settlement on the understanding that they were to defend the frontier against the Turks. Active mountaineers, and well acquainted with the country, they formed very effective guerilla troops, and their forays across the border kept the Turks in a constant state of alarm. But they were a wild race, accustomed to eke out the poor livelihood derived from a barren and miserable country by deeds of robbery and violence, and being unused to control or discipline they were almost as formidable to their *The Uscocs become pirates.* friends and allies as to their enemies[1]. Once settled at Segna they became no less expert by sea than they had been on the mountains, and their constant attacks on the shipping and maritime possessions of the Turks exposed the Venetians, who were responsible for the safety of the seas, to complaints and recriminations which threatened to disturb the peace. Venice complained in her turn to Ferdinand, Segna being in Croatia and therefore within his dominions,

---

[1] Vid. Palladius Fuscus Patavinus, A. D. 1540. 'Incolae uno omnes vocabulo Morlachi vocantur qui ferinum potius quam humanum aspectum prae se ferentes lacte caseoque victitant, et prope vias abditi viatores alienigenas adoriuntur atque dispoliant, denique summam laudem esse putant ex rapto vivere.'

but her remonstrances met with little attention, and the Uscocs, finding their movements watched and impeded by the Venetians, extended their depredations to the property and territory of the Republic, and rapidly degenerated into mere bloodthirsty corsairs whose name has become infamous in Dalmatian history. The piracies of the Uscocs gave occasion to Selim II, who had succeeded his father Solyman the Magnificent in 1567, to break the peace with Venice, and reopen the war in Cyprus and Dalmatia. Zemonico near Zara was taken by his troops and Novigrad assaulted, and the renegade Uliz-Ali king of Algiers entered the Adriatic with a powerful fleet. After ravaging the islands of Zante and Cefalonia, he invaded Albania, took Dulcigno Budua and Antivari, unsuccessfully assaulted Curzola where he was daunted by the courage of a slender garrison aided by the heroism of the women, and landing at Lesina gave a great part of the city to the flames. *A.D. 1570. War reopened between Venetians and Turks.*

Meanwhile Cyprus was invaded by an overwhelming force of Turks; Famagosta and Nicosia fell after a heroic defence, and the whole island passed into the possession of the enemy on the 4th of August, 1571. *A.D. 1570. Cyprus conquered by the Turks.*

On the 7th of October however the sinking fortunes of Christendom were retrieved by the victory of Lepanto, when the united squadrons of Spain Venice and the Pope, under the command of Don John of Austria, utterly defeated *A.D. 1571. Battle of Lepanto.*

156   History of Dalmatia.   [CH. I.

the Turkish fleet and sank eighty of their galleys. Uliz-Ali with about thirty galleys forced his way through the enemy's lines and made his escape, but otherwise the success of the Christians was complete and decisive. The Dalmatian contingents had their share in the honours of the day, and in the churches of Veglia and Arbe may still be read the epitaphs of the captains who commanded the triremes of those islands[1].

Diary of Venetian agents, 1571–4.
Sir Gardner Wilkinson gives extracts at considerable length from the diary and reports of Venetian agents at Spalato and elsewhere in Dalmatia during the years 1571–4, which are extremely interesting and throw much light on the nature of the harassing and desultory warfare of that time. They show that although the Turks were guilty of great cruelties to the peasantry, yet the hostilities between the regular combatants were marked with something of chivalry and courtesy. There are challenges to single combat; joustings between Captain Giorgio and the Red Turk. Captain Giorgio complains that his foe has killed his horse contrary to knightly usage, and the Red Turk promises to give him another, after which they embrace and part. In the middle of all this comes the news of the victory of Andrea Doria and Don John at Lepanto, and great rejoicings are made at Spalato, Zara, and Traü, much to the perplexity of the Turks

[1] Vid. infra, Veglia, chapt. xxvi, and Arbe, chapt. xxviii.

outside, who send a cavalier into Zara to enquire what has happened. Six cavaliers of the Turks challenge six Christians to tilt. They kiss each other first on the forehead. There are love affairs between the two sides; a Turk requests leave to enter the churches and hear mass, but is refused because he is suspected of being enamoured of the Marquis's daughter. *[Diary of Venetian agents, 1571–4.]*

From these and similar stories we gather that the Turks, though rude and overbearing, were not without generosity. As the Venetian agent says, 'no nation are all evil alike, seeing how some of them are without conscience, laws, or honour, while others are true and loyal cavaliers.' The Turks respected a foe who showed a bold front, and always gave him fair play. 'Whenever any of our Dalmatians before turning his back to fly like his neighbours wheels round upon his adversary and gives him a sound drubbing, using his fists and heels lustily, they always stand round and allow him a fair fight. Moreover they always remember the names of such individuals and relate their prowess among themselves, and these men can always go with impunity among the Turks even unarmed, because the respect which they have inspired renders them inviolate[1].' *[Character of the Turks.]*

Peace was signed between Venice and the Porte in 1573, each party regaining what it had lost during the war, except that the Turks retained *[A.D. 1573. Peace with Selim II.]*

---

[1] Sir G. Wilkinson, vol. ii. p. 344. Sir G. W. says that this description applies to the Turks of the present day also.

Uscoc piracies countenanced by Austria.

Zemonico. For the next seventy-two years no direct hostilities occurred between the two powers, but the irregular warfare carried on by the Uscocs was continually on the verge of embroiling them, for though the Venetians used every means to restrain the Uscocs by force, and induce the emperor to remove them from the sea coast, they were unable to succeed in either case, and the Turks accused them of complicity with their tormentors. The position of the Venetians was a very difficult one; their great object was to maintain peace with the Turk, but the Uscocs could not be crushed without invading Croatia, which would have involved hostilities with the emperor.

A.D. 1596. Uscoc attack on Clissa.

In 1596 a party of Uscocs and Poglizzans surprised Clissa, but the Turks speedily recovered it, and routed the Croatians with the loss of many of their number, among whom was Antonio de Dominis, bishop of Segna. This gave occasion to the Porte for fresh complaints against the Venetians who punished those who had taken part in the affair, and renewed their remonstrances with

The Uscocs embroil Venice and Austria.

the emperor and his archduke of Styria, in whose province Croatia was included. Matters grew worse, and at last the murder of a Venetian officer by the Uscocs with circumstances of the most brutal atrocity brought matters to a crisis. The Venetians attacked and destroyed Novi on the Croatian coast, and war broke out between them and the Austrians which raged for three years in Friuli till terminated through the mediation of

France in 1617 by the peace of Madrid. The Uscocs were removed in the following year to Carlstadt in the interior of Croatia, their fleet was destroyed, and Segna was garrisoned by German troops[1].

A.D. 1617. Peace of Madrid.

War again broke out between the Venetians and Turks, and the pasha of Bosnia invaded Dalmatia with a large army. Novigrad was surrendered by the Governor Conte Soardo after a brief bombardment, and Sebenico was besieged by the pasha, but without success. Leonardo Foscolo, who was sent into Dalmatia as Provveditore, recovered Novigrad, took and destroyed Scardona, and captured Zemonico after a desperate resistance by the Sangiac Ali-beg of Vrana. Fresh forces under Tekely, the new pasha of Bosnia, advanced to besiege Sebenico, the command of which place was entrusted by Foscolo to Degenfelt, who repelled the Turks with a loss of 4000 killed. Disease had incapacitated 5000 more, and the pasha was obliged to retreat to Dernis, and thence into Bosnia. In the following year, at the head of 6000 Morlacchi and 700 horse, Foscolo assaulted and took Dernis, advanced to Knin which he found abandoned by the enemy, and captured Verlicca. His proposal to rebuild and fortify Knin was unwisely rejected by the Senate, and they had reason before long to regret their decision. Clissa still held out,

A.D. 1645. War with Turks renewed.

A.D. 1647. Successes of Leonardo Foscolo.

A.D. 1648.

---

[1] A more detailed account of the Uscocs will be given with the description of Segna. Vid. below, chapter xxvii.

and an attempt to relieve it was made by Tekely Pasha, but he was defeated, and the garrison surrendered on condition that they should be allowed to depart without arms. In the following year Foscolo attacked the Turks in the Bocche di Cattaro and took and destroyed Risano.

A.D. 1649.

The war continued several years with varying success; Knin, which had been reoccupied by the Turks, was unsuccessfully assaulted, but the Morlacchi under Smiglianich gained several brilliant victories over the enemies of their race, till their leader fell in 1654. Had the defence of the province been confided more to the natives and less to the Italian mercenaries, it is probable that the Turks would have done far less mischief. The Venetian agent at Spalato in 1574 wrote to the Signory that '*the principal defence of their own country ought to be committed to those brave people who verily have no care for their lives against the Turks, but set on them like mad bulls; and truth compels me to say (albeit with grief) that we have been vanquished in more than one important skirmish through the cowardice of the Italian infantry*[1].' The Provveditore Andrea Corner in 1660 had the same opinion of the native militia, and declared to the Senate that the peasants were the principal defenders of the province[2]; but the Venetians seem to have inherited from the Byzantine empire the jealous

Gallantry of the native Dalmatians.

A.D. 1660.

---

[1] Cited Sir G. Wilkinson, vol. ii. p. 344.
[2] Storia della Dalmazia, Zara, 1878, p. 265.

mistrust which refused to the provincials the defence of their own frontier.

The history of Ragusa since 1420 is so distinct from the general history of Dalmatia that it is reserved for a special chapter. It is impossible, however, not to notice in its chronological place the fearful earthquake by which 5000 Ragusan citizens, including the Rector Ghetaldi, were buried in the ruins of their houses, and many of the principal buildings of the city were thrown down. The earthquake was felt as far as Cattaro, where great damage was done to the cathedral and other buildings. *A.D. 1667. Great earthquake at Ragusa.*

Peace was at last arranged between the Porte and Venice; Candia, which after a defence of twenty-nine years had been forced to capitulate, was yielded to the Sultan, but the Venetians were secured in the possession of Clissa and the forts they had occupied in Dalmatia. Disputes arose as to the possession of the forts which the Venetians had destroyed but not occupied, and the Turks claimed and retained under this head the castles of Zemonico Vrana Ostrovizza Dernis Knin and Douare. Hostilities again broke out with Kara Mustapha, the Grand Vizir, but his defeat by Sobieski before Vienna, and his subsequent disgrace and execution, relieved Dalmatia of a dangerous enemy. The Venetians took advantage of the Turkish reverses, and in the following year they had recovered Ostrovizza Plavno Perusić Bencovaz Scardona Obbravazzo *A.D. 1669. Peace between Venetians and Turks.* *A.D. 1683. Siege of Vienna raised by Sobieski.* *A.D. 1684–8.*

<small>Venetian conquests in Dalmatia.</small> and Dernis, and the only places still held by the Turks were Sign and Knin. Their fate was however only deferred, for Sign was taken in 1686 and the garrison put to the sword, and Knin and Verlicca were obliged to surrender in 1688.

The tide of Turkish conquest had turned. Buda was taken by the Christian forces in 1686, after having been 145 years in the possession of the Moslem, and the soil of Hungary was once more cleared of the invader. In 1690 the Venetians completed the conquest of the Morea, and having driven the Turk back from the seaboard of Dalmatia, they pursued their successes <small>A.D. 1699. Peace of Carlovitz. All Dalmatia secured to Venice.</small> in Herzegovina and Bosnia. The war was closed by the peace of Carlovitz between the Emperor the Republic and the Sultan, by the terms of which the Venetians gave up their conquests beyond the frontiers of Dalmatia, but were confirmed in the possession of all Dalmatia except the territory and city of Ragusa, which remained independent under the nominal protection of the Empire, and the more real defence of the Turks, to whom the Ragusans paid a tribute.

<small>A.D. 1714. War renewed.</small> The Turks were not disposed to rest long under terms so disadvantageous to them, and they declared war again against Venice in 1714 on the ground that the Republic had allowed piracy and favoured the Vladika of Montenegro their enemy. <small>A.D. 1717. Siege of Belgrade.</small> The Emperor offered his alliance to the Republic, and Prince Eugene advanced into the Banat and

besieged and took Belgrade, a success which partly compensated Christendom for the loss of the Morea, which was regained by the Turks in 1715. The peace of Passarovitz confirmed the Republic in the possession of the whole of Dalmatia, excepting as before the territory of Ragusa which extended from Klek on the Canale della Narenta to Sutorina in the Bocche di Cattaro. At these two points Ragusan jealousy of the Venetians, whom the little Republic feared more than the Turks, had stipulated that a narrow slip of territory should be conceded to the Turks to divide her by an impassable barrier from the dangerous proximity of the Venetians. Beyond Sutorina the Venetian territory began again with Castelnuovo, and the province of Venetian Albania, as it was called, extended from this point southwards, beyond Cattaro and Budua.

A.D. 1718. Peace of Passarovitz. Venetian possession of Dalmatia confirmed.

Dalmatia from the mountains to the sea was thus finally united under the government of the Republic, and the Turks never again invaded it. From this time till the fall of the Venetian Republic there is little or nothing to record. The policy of the State was to preserve its neutrality and avoid occasion of quarrel with its more powerful neighbours, and to prevent any excitement or outbreak in its provinces, and the Dalmatians were involved in the political and moral stupor that gradually paralysed the Venetian commonwealth.

Turkish invasions finally cease.

Venetian rule in Dalmatia.

Fall of the Republic of Venice. A.D. 1797. Dalmatia ceded to Austria.

On the fall of the Republic of Venice the Dalmatian troops were sent home, disbanded, and distributed among their families without any disturbance. Dalmatia was ceded to Austria by the treaty of Campo Formio, together with the rest of the Venetian territory. Some disturbances followed at Spalato and Traü, where the Garagnin palace was sacked by the mob, and also at Sebenico Lesina and Macarsca, but the arrival of the Austrian officials and troops put an end to all idea of resistance, and order was re-established without difficulty.

Peace of Presburg, Dec. 26, 1805. Dalmatia ceded to France.

The remainder of the history of Dalmatia may be briefly dismissed. After Austerlitz, Dalmatia was by the terms of the peace of Presburg ceded to France, but before the French could arrive to occupy it the Russians had seized the Bocche di Cattaro, garrisoned Castelnuovo, and induced the Montenegrins to rise in arms to support them. The French under Molitor reached Knin on Feb.

A.D. 1806. Conflict of French and Russians.

12, 1806, occupied Zara and Sign, and advanced towards the Bocche by way of Traü, Spalato, Macarsca, and the Narenta. The small independent state of Ragusa unhappily lay in their path, and as the two combatants could only get at one another by traversing Ragusan territory the government of that state was unable to remain neutral. To allow the French to pass would bring on the Ragusans the vengeance of Russia, to refuse would cause an instant rupture with France. It was a dilemma in which either alternative meant ruin; the despair of the citizens was extreme, and Count Caboga proposed that the Republic should beg from the Sultan, their protector, some island in the Aegean whither they might migrate and where they might continue to live under their own laws as heretofore. These councils of despair were not heeded; the French were allowed to enter, and in consequence the Ragusans found their commerce laid under an embargo in the ports of every European country which was at war with France. The Russians and Montenegrins ravaged their territory, and their delicious suburbs with the gardens and villas of their aristocracy were reduced to a wilderness. A report that the French were advancing in force caused the Russians and Montenegrins to retire, but the ruin of Ragusa was effectually accomplished. *Danger and despair of Ragusa.*

In the following year the Russians took Curzola, but were repulsed by the French in an attempt on Lesina. The little peasant republic of Poglizza in the fastnesses of Mount Mossor rose in arms, but the French made short work of its rustic militia; those who could not escape to the Russian ships had to witness the destruction of their homes and the massacre of their kindred in cold blood by the brutal French soldiery, who marched through their country for three days destroying the villages and putting the inhabitants to the *A.D. 1807. Destruction of Republic of Poglizza.*

sword. A price was set on the head of the Great Count and the other officials, and the Republic of Poglizza 'ceased to exist.'

Peace of Tilsit, July, 1807. The French administration of Dalmatia after the peace of Tilsit, when they were left in possession of the country, was tyrannical and severe, and the prisons were crowded with political offenders who were afterwards transported to France where they languished in captivity till the downfall of the Empire.

A.D. 1808. End of Republic of Ragusa. In 1808 it was decreed by Napoleon that the Republic of Ragusa, which had been ruined in his service, had 'ceased to exist.'

At this time our own countrymen contribute a chapter to Dalmatian history. England had sent a detachment of her fleet under Captain Hoste into the Adriatic, which made its principal station at Lissa, the outermost island of the Dalmatian *The English at Lissa.* archipelago. Under the protection of the British flag Lissa rapidly became an emporium for British commerce, and the goods of Manchester, Leeds, and Birmingham, prohibited in every port under French control, were smuggled across the Dalmatian frontier and so through Bosnia into Germany. The population of the island rose between 1808 and 1811 from 4000 to 12,000, and the profits made both by Lissans and Dalmatians were immense. In the temporary absence of the English squadron a French fleet under Dubordieu sailed from Ancona, and entering Lissa under English colours landed a body of troops unopposed and burned sixty-four merchantmen with their cargoes. A rumour of the return of the English fleet caused the French to make a hasty retreat, and they sailed again the same night for Ancona. In the spring the French fleet was strengthened and a resolute attempt was made to expel the English from Lissa. Dubordieu's force consisted of four frigates of forty-four guns, two corvettes of thirty-two guns, a sixteen-gun brig, a schooner, two gun-boats, and a xebec, carrying in all 284 guns, and a body of infantry destined to occupy the island. The English fleet, under Captain Hoste, consisted of four ships, the Amphion Active Cerberus and Volage, mounting altogether 156 guns. The numbers were 880 men on the English side against 2500 French and Italians, but notwithstanding the odds against them the English obtained a complete victory. Three frigates and one corvette of the enemy struck their colours, and the French admiral Dubordieu was among the slain. *Battle of Lissa, March 13, 1811.*

In the following year Lissa, and in 1813 Curzola, were regularly occupied by the English, who appointed a governor and established a system of administration under native officials in each island, which continued till July 15, 1815, at the end of the war, when both islands, together with Lagosta, which had also been occupied by the English, were handed over to the Austrians. *A.D. 1812-15. English occupation of the islands.*

In 1809, the French troops having been withdrawn from Dalmatia, the Austrians re-entered; but by the treaty of Vienna, Oct. 14, 1809, the

Severity of French government in Dalmatia. province was restored to France and united to the Illyrian kingdom. A military commission sat at Sebenico which tried, shot, and imprisoned those who had been implicated in bringing back the Austrians, and the fort S. Nicolò at the entrance of the harbour was crowded with political prisoners. The clemency of Marmont, who commanded in the province, is in agreeable contrast to the severity of the French government which he served, and it was owing to his humanity that the town of Scardona was spared the destruction to which it had been condemned for a demonstration in favour of Austria.

A.D. 1814. After the Russian campaign, and the other disasters that befel the French arms, the combined efforts of Austria and England drove the French from Dalmatia, which has since remained under the rule of the Austrian Emperor, and so, as it were by accident, has once more returned to the dominion of a Hungarian king.

Condition of Dalmatia under the Venetians, A.D. 1409–1797. From a review of the character of Venetian dominion in Dalmatia since the final occupation of the country by the Republic, and of its effect on the condition of the people, it may be gathered that however little the Venetians desired to promote the interests of their subjects, and however badly they may have governed them in some respects, the province, and more especially the cities, made on the whole a rapid advance in material prosperity under the settled government of the Republic, and that arts and letters flourished in spite of the absence of any encouragement from the State. The worst feature of Venetian government was its jealous hatred of any political vitality in its subjects, and the terrorism of the secret police by which it guarded itself against popular combinations. So great was the moral terror inspired by the secret machinery of the State that it is said one or two sbirri were enough to carry out any sentence of the law, and that a man condemned to the pillory would sit out the term of his punishment without any guard being necessary to prevent his escape. *Dalmatia under the Venetians, A.D. 1409–1797.* *Terror of political police.*

The government agents kept the Senate informed of everything that took place, and of everything that was said; those who had gone far enough to be dangerous disappeared, and their fate was wrapped in mystery which added terror to its warning for others; young men of family who had travelled and imbibed liberal notions at Padua, Oxford, Brussels, or Rotterdam, and had been overheard indiscreetly drawing unfavourable comparisons between their own government and that of other countries, were sent for to Venice and appointed to some post or employment '*which would keep them away from the fire,*' and the local authorities of the various towns were warned not to hesitate '*to cut away certain poisoned members to preserve the sound part from infection*[1].'

[1] Documenti Storici, published by Solitro from the Records

Dalmatia under the Venetians, A.D. 1409–1797.

The youths of Dalmatia and Istria were withdrawn from their own country where they might have been dangerous, and drafted into the forces of the Republic serving in Italy, while Dalmatia was defended by Italian troops, who, as we have seen, made a much weaker barrier against the Turks than would have been opposed by those whose hearths and homes were threatened[1]. The Church itself was made to feel the restraining hand of the State; it was allowed no secular power, the patronage of benefices and even bishoprics was virtually possessed by the government, the representative of the Republic was enthroned in the cathedral in a position of equal dignity with the archbishop or bishop[2]; and when at last the Senate was induced to allow the establishment of the 'Holy Inquisition' within its dominion, the permission was accompanied by the condition that lay assessors appointed by the State should sit with the inquisitors, and that the sentences should be revised and confirmed by the Council of Ten[3].

State control over the Church.

in the Library of S. Mark, class. 7, cod. ccx. quoted by Sir G. Wilkinson, vol. ii. p. 344.

[1] The Dalmatian levies amounted to 12,000 men out of a population of 250,000. Stor. della Dalm. p. 280.

[2] Cubich, Veglia, part ii. p. 116. See also below, description of duomo of Zara, chapt. iv.

[3] Romanin, Stor. di Ven. v. c. 6. The result was that very few cases of capital punishment for heresy occur in the annals of Venice. 'La saggia Venezia voleva frenare il soverchio zelo ed eventuale fanatismo degl' inquisitori e raccommandava mitezza nelle pene; sicchè rarissimi furono i casi di condanne a morte che altrove abbondavano.' Franceschi, L' Istria, p. 291.

At the final re-entry of Venice into Dalmatia the ancient privileges of the cities seem to have been confirmed in most respects, but the liberty of electing the count was not restored to them, the appointment being thenceforth vested in the State. The Gran Consiglio also, originally a democratical assembly in each little commonwealth, as it had been in Venice before 1299, was now as in the ruling state a close aristocratical body, to which the people had no access, and which served the central government as an obedient instrument for carrying out its ends. In other respects the municipal liberties seem to have been maintained, and justice on the whole fairly administered between rich and poor; but the distance from the central government threw too much power into the hands of the Provveditori, who during their thirty-two months of office were almost absolute rulers, especially on the islands, and who sometimes exercised their authority in an arbitrary and despotic manner. The taxes were onerous, and as the object of the government was to keep the country poor and dependent the burden was so arranged as to press heavily on the few native industries it possessed. The monopoly of salt placed, as it still does under the Austrian government, insuperable difficulties in the way of the fisheries, which if properly developed would be a mine of wealth for the maritime Dalmatians, especially the islanders. Nowhere is there a more abundant supply of fish than at Lissa, and yet for

Dalmatia under the Venetians, A.D. 1409–1797.

Excessive power of the governors.

The salt monopoly.

Dalmatia under the Venetians, A.D. 1409–1797.

political reasons no magazine of salt was allowed on that island, so that when the fishermen had a great take of fish they were obliged to row thirty or forty miles to Lesina to get salt; and if contrary winds or bad weather prevented their going thither, fifty or a hundred thousand fish would sometimes have to be thrown into the sea and wasted[1].

Industry repressed.

In some instances the government attempted to destroy the resources of the country by more direct means. The silkworm had been cultivated in Dalmatia from early times[2], and silk and olive oil had been among the chief products of the country. An iniquitous decree of the Senate ordered that all the mulberry trees and olives should be cut down, and a great number of the former had been destroyed when it was found that the people were determined to resist a measure which meant nothing less than ruin to them, and the olive trees which are scarcely less important to the Dalmatian farmer than his vines were saved.

Education discouraged.

Education, if not prohibited, was discouraged, and no public schools existed in the province except one seminary at Spalato which was founded in 1700 by archbishop Stefano Cosmi Comasco, and endowed with the funds of two religious establishments at Traü[3]. The youths of the higher

---

[1] Fortis, Viaggio in Dalm.
[2] E.g. at Arbe; vid. sup. p. 31, and infra, chapt. xxviii.
[3] Storia della Dalmazia, p. 408.

classes had to go to Italy to study in the universities of Padua, Pavia, or Bologna, or else to content themselves with the teaching of the clergy at home, while the peasantry were left in the lowest depths of ignorance and barbarism. It will scarcely be believed that the printing press was not introduced at Zara till 1796, when the Republic was on its deathbed.

Dalmatia under the Venetians, A.D. 1409–1797.

The country swarmed with ecclesiastics, and the number of conventual establishments almost exceeds belief. The island of Arbe, with a population of some 3000 souls, had at the time of Abbate Fortis's visit no fewer than three convents of friars, and as many of nuns, besides sixty priests who were poorly endowed, and whose sustenance fell on the already impoverished islanders. Out of 3000 inhabitants of Cherso at the same period there were 120 ecclesiastics, including a convent of friars, and a monastery of nuns, '*an excessive number to say the truth in a place where arms are so precious.*' At Pago Fortis found no fewer than two convents for men and one for women within the walls, and at a short distance another for Franciscan friars, '*a race of men who under various names and disguises infest every place where credulous ignorance can be persuaded to maintain the idle and superstitious*[1].'

Excessive number of ecclesiastics.

Of the condition of the Morlacchi at the time of his visit he gives a very interesting account. He found them honest, generous, simple, and con-

Social state and superstition of the Morlacchi.

[1] Abbate Fortis, Description of island of Pago.

Dalmatia under the Venetians, A.D. 1409–1797.

fiding, and easily imposed on by the Italians. There were no beggars among them poor as they were, and they were never wanting in hospitality to strangers. Their superstition was abject, and the mendicant clergy were either as ignorant and superstitious as their flock or else traded on the ignorance of the people for their own profit. The Morlacchi both of the Greek and the Latin church believed in witches, fairies, enchantments, nocturnal apparitions, and vampires[1] or spirits of dead persons who suck the blood of infants. When any dead person was suspected of becoming a vampire the body was ham-strung and pierced with pins which prevented its wandering, and many persons on their deathbed, afraid of becoming vampires, implored their relatives to serve them in this way after death. Morlacca girls

Treatment of women among Morlacchi.

were carried off by their suitors with their own consent, in order to escape the attentions of those they intended to reject. Before marriage Fortis says the girls were neat, but when married they neglected their persons and became filthy and repulsive. Women were treated as inferiors; if the husband possessed a bedstead the wife lay on the floor; and a man never spoke of his wife without an apologetic 'by your leave,' or 'begging

Their cottages.

your pardon.' Their cottages were seldom roofed with anything but thatch or shingles; beds were rare, the people generally lay on the ground wrapped in goat's hair blankets, or in summer out

[1] Called *Vukodlak*; or in the island of Cherso *Bilsi*.

of doors the better to escape the attacks of vermin. The walls of the huts were built without mortar, the door was the only opening, and the smoke had to find its way out without a chimney. The interior was varnished black and loathsome with smoke, the savour of which pervaded everything, hanging about the persons and clothes of the inhabitants and flavouring the milk and everything they ate or drank. The only point about which they were nice was that of sanitary cleanliness, as to which they seem to have been scrupulously exact, but they were content to share their houses with the beasts, and a slight wattled partition plastered with clay or dung was all that separated the human inmates from their pigs and oxen and horses. They had an extreme abhorrence of snakes, founded on Pagan traditions. In the beginning they say there were three suns, the heat of which being excessive the serpent resolved on getting rid of them. He succeeded in absorbing two and a half, but the remaining half sun, whose light we now enjoy, proving too much for him, the serpent, unable to bear the light, hid himself among the rocks. The sun incensed at the attack that had been made on him applauded every one who killed one of the serpent race, and threatened to punish him who failed to do so when he had the chance. When Fortis was ascending Monte Biocovo above Almissa a viper crossed the path of his guides. '*They both ran furiously to kill it with stones; our interces-*

sion to let it alone had no effect; they said it was a malefick demon disguised in that form, and even turned in horrour from the way they thought it might have touched.' His companion Signor Bajamonte having taken it up in his hand and approached them to show them it was dead, they presented their muskets at him and bade him stand off at the peril of his life.

Dalmatia under the Venetians, A.D. 1409-1797.

Still more curious were the superstitions about tempests and the mode of averting them. At Pago one of the Dominican friars was in Fortis's time elected by the people to the office of exorcising storms, and keeping the island clear of the summer rains which damaged the salt works, and of hail which destroyed the vines. At Novaglia also the clergy were expected to exorcise the evil spirits and the Vukodlaci or witches who raised the storms, and they had to stand in their sacerdotal dress with the holy water in their hand exposed to wind and rain. 'The impostors,' he says, 'appeared to act this scene very seriously, making a thousand motions and grimaces and leaping from one side to the other as if pursuing some Vukodlak. I knew one of them who ran after the devil into the sea up to the middle, and in that strange position continued his crosses, aspersions, and conjurations. The islanders, while the priest mutters his prayers, discharge their pieces towards the place pointed at by him as if to kill the witches or put them to flight. What sillier customs can there be among the

Superstition fostered by the clergy.

Lapponians!' At Verbenico on the island of Veglia the priests '*are obliged to sleep under a lodge open on all sides and contiguous to the steeple from St. George's Day to Michaelmas, that they may be ready at any time to drive away the storms of hail by ringing the bells, and if the storm continues it is their duty to go out into the open air bareheaded to conjure it.*' The Abbate goes on to enlarge on the shameful ignorance and superstition of the priesthood in the rural districts. At Castelmuschio he was shown two pieces of willow and told they were parts of Moses' rod, and two links of a chain which were said to have bound S. Peter. The saints were represented by frightful images scarcely resembling anything human, to which the people were so devoted that it would have been dangerous to attempt to deprive them of them[1].

Dalmatia under the Venetians, A.D. 1409–1797.

The degree of cultivation among the upper classes, less dependent on local conditions than that of the peasantry, was not inferior to that of Italy or the rest of Europe, and a very creditable list may be made out of Dalmatians who distinguished themselves in arts and letters during the fifteenth, sixteenth and seventeenth centuries. Sebenico, the youngest of '*Dalmatian*' towns, produced more illustrious sons than any except perhaps Ragusa, and Fortis declares that in the sixteenth century the arts and sciences flourished

Cultivation of the upper classes.

[1] I saw a frightful but highly venerated image of S. Gaudenzio at Ossero in 1884.

Dalmatia under the Venetians, A.D. 1409-1797. Illustrious Dalmatians.

there more than in any other town of Dalmatia. From this city sprang the four Veranzii, of whom the eldest Antonio (b. 1504 † 1573), rose to the dignity of Archbishop of Gran, Primate of Hungary, and Viceroy of the kingdom, and left behind him valuable materials for the history of his country; the Illyrian poet Difnico and the historian Tomco Marnavich were also Sebenzani, and so were Schiavone the painter, whom Titian condescended to imitate, and Martino Rota the engraver. Giorgio Orsini also, the architect of the wondrous vaults of the cathedral, was an inhabitant of Sebenico, though probably a native of Zara, and he may be claimed as a naturalized Dalmatian though descended from a Roman stock. The island of Cherso produced Francesco Patrizzi or Patrizio, the first to unfold the military system of Rome, from whom Lipsius is accused by Scaliger of plagiarizing[1]; Arbe gave birth to Nimira an accomplished though self-taught mathematician, and the famous Marc Antonio de Dominis the first to explain the solar spectrum, whose theological wanderings have almost made the world forget his achievements in the field of natural science; Zara alone has no illustrious progeny to boast of unless, as seems probable, the architect Giorgio Orsini was born there. Spalato during this period can only point to the name of Marco

---

[1] Vid. Hallam, History of Literature, vol. i. p. 526, vol. ii. pp. 6, 371, and Fortis, Saggio d' osservazioni sopra l' isola de Cherso ed Osero. Patrizio was born in 1529, and died in 1597.

Marulo the historian, but Traü may glory in having given birth to Giovanni Lucio, the father of Dalmatian history, whose great work is as remarkable for critical sagacity as for the industry and research which have gone to produce it.

Dalmatia under the Venetians, A.D. 1409–1797.

Ragusa, whose independence dates from the period when the rest of Dalmatia passed finally under the dominion of Venice, has a still more brilliant roll of worthies to display. Elio Lampridio Cervo, the poet laureate, and Ludovico (Tubero) Cerva of the same family, the historian of his own times, flourished in the fifteenth and earlier part of the sixteenth century: Gian. Francesco Gondola (b. 1588 † 1638) achieved the great literary triumph of the Illyric language by his epic poem of the Osmanide, in which the subject is taken from contemporary history, and the hero is a sultan of those Turks whose friendship strangely enough was the bulwark of Ragusan independence at the time that they were generally regarded as the natural foes of Christendom. At the same time Marino Ghetaldi was pursuing those experiments in natural science which gained him an European reputation, while the Ragusan peasantry thought him an enchanter and dreaded to approach the cave which served him for a laboratory; and in the eighteenth century the achievements of Ruggiero Giuseppe Boscovich as a mathematician and natural philosopher shed lustre on his native city[1].

Ragusan worthies.

[1] Both Ghetaldi and Boscovich travelled to England, and the

Dalmatia under the Venetians. A.D. 1409-1797.

Material prosperity shown by architectural activity after 1420.

That in point of material prosperity the maritime towns and islands of Dalmatia flourished under the dominion of Venice is proved beyond a doubt by the public and private buildings which began to spring up on all sides as soon as the political transition was effected. Zara completed her cathedral and the basilica of S. Grisogono; Sebenico began her new cathedral and raised it nearly to the cupola; Curzola completed her duomo and raised the campanile, and built the Badia with its graceful cloister which is one of the gems of Dalmatian art; a new cathedral was begun at Ossero; and the cathedral at Traü was enlarged and adorned by its western tower and by the sumptuous sacristy baptistery and chapels that render it the most magnificent church in Dalmatia. Throughout the province the churches and convents were fitted with handsome stalls, and the treasuries furnished with beautiful plate and embroideries, reflecting the taste of the ruling city and probably generally the handiwork of Venetian artists. Palaces and public buildings that remind one by their architecture of the Grand Canal sprang up in the streets of every seaport town of the mainland or islands; the streets and squares were paved, and the walls

latter was made a fellow of our Royal Society. Boswell mentions him more than once; he met Dr. Johnson at dinner at the houses of Sir Joshua Reynolds and Dr. Douglas, afterwards Bishop of Salisbury, where 'that celebrated foreigner expressed his astonishment at Johnson's Latin conversation,' ch. li.

and gates rebuilt or strengthened; the harbours were improved, arsenals were established, and the dockyards were crowded with shipping in course of repair or construction. In the principal piazza of each city was erected the loggia or tribunal, where sat the judges, and where the principal public business of the place was transacted; in front of it a pillar supported the flag-post from which floated the banner of the Republic, while the Lion of St. Mark, in marble or stone, looked down from every gateway, bastion, and public building, significant of the watchful argus-eyed government seated on the distant lagunes whose vigilance nothing could escape.

As the commercial greatness of Venice declined towards the end of her career, the prosperity of her dependencies naturally passed away at the same time. Decay and torpor set in, ship-building declined, the ports were deserted and the trade came nearly to a standstill. The arts were neglected, and the series of architectural works was closed, except at Ragusa, which still preserved its liberties and some remains of its former prosperity. The palaces of the rich Venetian and native merchants were deserted or neglected, and many of them fell into the ruin which now meets the eye at every turn. *Decline of Venice felt in Dalmatia.*

Such was the state of Dalmatia when the province came into the hands of the Austrians, and such to a great extent it remains to the present day. Something has undoubtedly been done by *Dalmatia under Austria.*

<small>Dalmatia under Austria.</small>

the present government, and it is no light benefit to the province that a perfect system of police has been established, that the Haiduks or bandits have been suppressed, and that notwithstanding the vicinity of the Turkish provinces the traveller may move about in the remotest corners of Dalmatia as freely as he would in England, and with a security that is unknown in the south of Italy or Spain. Blood feuds among the Morlacchi have also been repressed, and the practice of carrying arms put under control, and above all a regular system of education in all its grades, both elementary and advanced, except that of the University, has been introduced into every part of the country. For all this Dalmatia may well feel grateful to her present masters; but there is still much that she may fairly ask to be done for her. Her trade and productions are hampered by vexatious customs and monopolies, and the peasants still plough the land with instruments compared to which the Virgilian plough was a masterpiece of ingenuity. 'Ah, Signore,' said a Dalmatian tradesman to me, 'it is a wretched country you have come to visit; the Venetians made a *Morlaccheria* of it, and though the present government has done a little for us of late years, things are not much changed for the better.'

<small>Present condition of the population.</small>

In the interior of the country the Morlacchi still inhabit the huts described by Fortis a hundred years ago, without window or chimney, black with smoke, and serving as in Ireland for cottage and pig-stye in one, men women and beasts occupying the same tenement, with scarcely any partition to divide them. The belief in witchcraft and fairies is as strong as ever, brides are still carried off by the favoured suitor and brought home again after an interval to be formally espoused, and firearms are still supposed to be efficacious against the demon of the storm. The abuse against which Fortis declaims of an extravagant number of ecclesiastics and convents still exists, and the number of the latter is scarcely diminished since his time. Of the adult population of the country not less than 33 per cent. are non-productive, consisting of priests, monks, nuns, idlers, mendicants, and rogues [1], and consequently it is no wonder that more than half the cultivable land of the province should be lost to agriculture, serving merely to afford scanty pasturage to sheep and goats, and that Dalmatia should be the most backward and the poorest province of the Austro-Hungarian dominions.

Modern Dalmatia.

During the past two years a fresh movement has taken place in Dalmatia which is driving the most intelligent and cultivated of its inhabitants to something like despair. In the preceding pages the dual element in the population of the country

Distinction of Latins and Slavs in modern times.

[1] Schatzmeyer, La Dalmazia. Trieste, 1877. He divides the adult population of Dalmatia thus:—Agriculturists, 50%; industrials, 3·75%; commercialists and mariners, 2·50%; proprietors and government employés, 2·50%; servants, 7·50%; and '*i restanti, vale a dire più di 33% di tutti gli abitanti rappresentano una populazione improduttiva, che consiste di preti monaci e monache oziosi mendicanti malviventi,*' &c.

which has existed since the seventh century, and has survived all changes of government down to our own days has been put forward as the key to the proper understanding of Dalmatian history. Side by side through all the alternations of Venetian and Hungarian rule the Latin and the Slav have remained as two distinct elements, mixing at the edges as it were, but never fusing into one another. In the old Roman cities the old Roman traditions, and no doubt the old Roman stock survived the shock of Slavonic conquest, and though the Croat was lord outside the city walls and beyond the narrow territory claimed by the citizens, within the gates the *Dalmatian* people retained their old Roman customs, governed themselves by the old Roman law, and spoke the old Latin tongue, which they still speak at the present day in its modern form.

Erroneous idea as to origin of this distinction. Those who have not acquainted themselves with Dalmatian history are apt to think that the Latin fringe which borders the Slavonic province has derived its language and customs from Venice, to which it was so long subject. Nothing can be farther from the truth; Zara Spalato Traü and Ragusa were Latin cities when as yet Venice was not existent, and they remained Latin cities throughout the middle ages, with very little help from her influence until the fifteenth century. The Italian spoken in Dalmatia before that time was not the Venetian dialect; in some parts it had a distinct form of its own, in others it resembled the form into which Latin had passed in the south of Italy or Umbria, and it was only after 1420 that it began to assimilate itself to the Italian of Lombardy and Venetia[1]. At Ragusa it never became Venetian at all, and to this day resembles rather the Tuscan dialect than any other, while the patois of the common people is a curious medley of Italian and Illyric, with traces of rustic Latin, Vlach or Rouman.

It is to the Latins of Dalmatia that we must look for evidences of culture and intellectual progress, and not to the Slavs. Those Croatian towns that, like Sebenico, emerged from semi-barbarism did so by being gathered within the Dalmatian pale, and by copying the institutions and customs and adopting the language of the older cities of Latin descent. Ragusa, the Dalmatian Athens, has sometimes been held up as an example of Slavonic culture, but this is only partially the case, for the history of Ragusa is uniformly that of a Latin rather than a Slavonic city. The public acts were recorded either in Latin or Italian, never in Illyric, except in case of correspondence with a Slavonic power; Italian appears as the language of the records and laws as early as the fourteenth century[2]; the pleadings in the law-courts in the fifteenth century were not in Illyric but in a *Dalmatian culture in the Middle Ages confined to the Latins. Adherence of the Dalmatian cities to Latin traditions.*

[1] Vid. Luc. lib. vi. c. ii.
[2] Vid. Statutes of the Dogana of Ragusa in Eitelberger's Dalmatien, p. 374, ed. 1884.

Rouman or debased Latin dialect[1]; the rules of the lay confraternities of goldsmiths carpenters and other trades are drawn up in Italian at least as far back as the year 1306, an incontestable proof that Italian was then the vernacular language of the working classes[2]; and when, in 1435, the little republic set an example which many greater states might worthily have imitated, and instituted public schools, it was from Italy that she invited her professors. Cattaro, the remotest of Dalmatian cities, which lived till the fifteenth century under the shadow and protection of the kings of Servia, preserved her Latin traditions as jealously as the rest; it was from Italy that she invited her public teachers ever since the thirteenth century, and it was to the colleges of Rome Padua or Bologna, and not to the court of Rascia, that an appeal was provided from her municipal tribunal.

Venetian rule favourable to the Latins.

This *Latin*—it would be incorrect to call it *Italian*—element which the Venetians at their advent found already existing in Dalmatia naturally became preponderant over the Slavonic element when both parties passed under the rule of an Italian power. Under the Venetian government Italian was the official language throughout the entire province, from the sea-shore to the

---

[1] De Diversis, ed. Brunelli, p. 70. Zara, 1882; vid. also infra, History of Ragusa, chapter xix.

[2] Le confraternite laiche in Dalmazia. G. Gelcich, Ragusa, 1885, p. 30, &c.

crests of the Vellebich mountains; Italian officials were appointed to every office in both urban and rural districts, and the Illyric language was left to boors and husbandmen. And when the Austrians came in and established a system of public instruction throughout the country it was given in Italian, even in places where the population was entirely Slavonic and the Italian language understood by only a minority. This was clearly unjust, and could not be expected to outlast the period of Slavonic depression and servitude. All this is now changed: the achievement of independence by Servia and Bulgaria, the successful revolt of Bosnia and Herzegovina from the Turks, and the virtual incorporation of those provinces into the Austro-Hungarian Empire, have given an impetus to the Slavs of Croatia and Dalmatia, and they too have begun to dream of forming an independent state, federally attached to the Austrian Empire, but enjoying the same kind of autonomy as Hungary. The Croats are agitating for the separation of that tie which has bound them to the Hungarian monarchy since the days of King Coloman, and among the Dalmatians a party has sprung up which clamours for union with Croatia and a share in her anticipated 'Home Rule.' *Preponderance of Slavs in modern times.*

Unfortunately the fervour of their new-born national life has brought the Croats of Dalmatia into violent collision with the Latins. The Croat party insists on the thorough Slavonizing of the whole province, whether rural or urban; they *Present antagonism of Latins and Croatian Slavs.*

Demands of the Croat party. demand that Illyric shall be the official language, and the vehicle for all education, in the cities as well as in the country, even in the higher grade schools, and in the case of those whose mother-tongue is Italian.

These demands of the Croat party probably partake of the nature of a rebound from former depression. It is hard to say what Dalmatia is to gain by the extinction of her ancient Latin culture, and the suppression of a native language which is understood by most educated men in western Europe, and which makes her merchants and sailors at home in every port of the Mediterranean. It is not as if the Illyric language were not understood in the cities, and had to be introduced there; every educated person in Dalmatia is bilingual, and though he may generally talk Italian in his own family, he has also talked Illyric from his cradle. The double language places no barrier between the citizen and the countryman, for both can talk Illyric, though both may not be able to talk Italian. So far as a common language goes there is nothing to prevent the Latin and Slav from combining to form a Dalmatian nation, and to a foreigner it appears absurd that politics should have been dragged into a social and educational question. For there is no question in Dalmatia of 'Italia irredenta,' as there is in Istria; the Latin element numbers only ten per cent. of the population, and the merest visionary could hardly dream of an-

History of Dalmatia.

nexation to Italy. All that the Latin population desire is that Italian should be retained as the language of school instruction for those who desire it and in those towns where Italian is spoken by everybody, while in the rural schools the instruction might be given if preferred in Illyric; and in this demand it is difficult for an outsider to see anything unreasonable [1]. *Demand of the Latin party.*

The educational question touches the Latins alone, but the political question touches one branch of the Slavs also. For the Dalmatian Slavs themselves are not of one family, nor at present of one mind. Northern Dalmatia is peopled by Croats, and Southern Dalmatia by Serbs, the division between them being the river Cettina as it was in the times of Heraclius and Porphyrogenitus; these two branches of the Slavonic race speak a slightly different dialect of their common Illyric language, and have different political aspirations, for while the majority of the Croats are Roman Catholics and are agitating for the annexation of Dalmatia to Croatia, in order to form a single powerful Slavonic province with an independent constitution like that of Hungary, the majority of the Serbs belong to the Greek Church, and are bitterly opposed to the idea of sinking their nationality in that of the Croats, and incline rather towards union with Servia and Montenegro. The *Views of the Serb party.*

---

[1] It should be observed that by the Austrian law private schools are rendered practically impossible, and children have no alternative but home education or the state school.

The autonomous party.

common danger has for the present united the Serbs and Latins in opposition to the Croats, and they form what is known as the *autonomous* party whose primary object is to defeat the union of Dalmatia and Croatia and maintain their separate national existence.

Recent educational laws in favour of the Slavs.

The Government however is fighting the battle of the Croats, by suppressing hostile municipal boards and appointing others, and by manipulating the elections as a paternal government well knows how. It is the policy of Austria, which seems preparing for itself a retreat from Germany into the Slavonic lands of the Balkan peninsula, to ingratiate itself with the Croats, and the Croats have had their way in this and every question between them and the Latins. Except in Zara, a place which is so thoroughly Italian that the change has been found impracticable, and one or two places like Traü, where the Latin element was strong enough to insist on the change being optional with the parents of the children, the whole education of the country is now conducted through the Illyric language. Even in the Ginnasi or schools immediately below the grade of the University it is the same, and those who wish to study Italian literature must do so through the medium of Illyric, even though Italian be their mother-tongue. Slavonic literature there is next to none; it is a matter of the future; it consists at present of little more than one epic and a mass of lyric poems and national songs, and is in-

ferior in interest to the ancient literature of Wales.
The most ardent Croat can hardly wish to substitute this for the 'Divina Commedia,' and it is
scarcely possible to take him seriously when he
replies to the objection by telling you that the
Italian poets will still be read through the medium
of excellent translations into Illyric. It remains
to be seen what will be the outcome of this mode
of education at second hand; meanwhile it is
difficult for a foreigner to view without regret
a needless attempt to extinguish an ancient culture and to silence an ancient language which can
boast an uninterrupted descent from the days of
the Roman Empire [1].

The political future of Dalmatia is necessarily
and inevitably Slavonic; Dalmatia is the natural
sea-board of the great Slavonic populations behind
her; but there is no reason why the regeneration
of the Slav should mean the extinction of the

[1] The violent measures by which the Government was obliged to introduce this and similar changes favouring the Croat party, make one suppose that they were unwelcome not only to the Latins, but to the majority of the Dalmatians. I never talked with a seafaring man who did not speak with bitterness of the change, and dilate on the hardship of his children not being taught Italian, a language in which a sailor can make himself understood throughout the Levant, and in almost every port of the Mediterranean. Indeed, when talking with gentlemen who were extreme partizans on the side of the Croats, I never found one who did not admit that the extinction of the Italian language would be a loss to the country, although in their public and collective capacity they are doing all they can to bring about that of which in private they deplore the contingency.

Latin. The best hope for the formation of a Dalmatian nation lies in a policy of conciliation, and not in the vain attempt to turn the Latins into Croats. The race distinctions of Latin and Croat will probably never be effaced, but there is no reason why if they mutually respect one another they should not live as contentedly under one government as the various races of England Scotland and Wales.

TABLE OF

THE KINGS OF HUNGARY

DOWN TO THE TIME OF

THE AUSTRIAN DYNASTY

TABLE OF THE KINGS OF HUNGARY,
DOWN TO THE TIME OF THE AUSTRIAN DYNASTY.

Arpad, settled on Danube, c. 887.

Solton, 907-961 (?).

Toxun, 956-971.

GEISA, 971-997, baptized 989.   Michael.

1. STEPHEN I, 997-1038,   Sarolta = Samuel Aba,   Gisela.   Ladislaus the Bald, d. a. 1031, acc. Lucio, son of Geisa.
crowned first King of Hungary   who disputed the throne
1000, canonized 1083.   with Peter.   2. PETER, 1038,   3. ANDREW I, 1047-61.   4. BELA I, 1061-3 (?)
 Emeric, d. 1031,   deposed 1041,
 canonized 1083.   restored 1043,   Sophia = 5. SALOMON, 1063 (?),
 deposed and   daughter of   deposed 1074,
 blinded 1047.   Emp. Henry III.   died 1087.

6. GEISA I, 'the Great,' 1074-77.   7. LADISLAUS I, 1077-95,   Lampert (?)
 canonized 1192.
8. COLOMAN, 1095-1114.
 9 STEPHEN II, 1114-31.   Almus, acc. Lucio, and others, son to Geisa I.
   10. BELA II, 'the Blind,' 1131-41.

11. GEISA II, 1141-61.   Stephen, disputed the throne with Stephen III, 1161-63;   Ladislaus, disputed the throne with Stephen, 1161-64;
 by some reckoned as Stephen IV.   by some reckoned Ladislaus II; d. 1172.

12 STEPHEN III, 1161,   13. BELA III (Alexius), 1173-96.
dethroned 1162,
restored 1163,   14. EMERIC, 1196-1204.   Gertrudis = 15. ANDREW II, 1204-35 = Beatrice d'Este.
died 1173.   'of Jerusalem.'

 16. LADISLAUS II, 1204,   Maria, daughter of = 17. BELA IV, 1224-70.   Coloman.   Stephen, = Tomasina
 'the Infant.'   Emp. Theod. Lascaris.   posthumous.   Morosini.

18 STEPHEN IV, 1270-2 (by some reckoned as Stephen V).   Anne = Rotislav.   Elizabeth = Henry of
    Bavaria.
Elizabeth, = 19. LADISLAUS III,   Maria, m. Charles the Lame,   Coumenned = Ottone II, King of   22. OTHO, Duke   20. ANDREW III,
sister of   1272, murdered 1290.   d. 1292,   afterwards Charles   Wenceslaus IV,   of Bavaria,   1290-1301.
Charles II.   II, King of   King of Bohemia.   abdicated 1308,   Last male descendant
   Naples   died 1312.   of Arpad.
   (of Anjou).

   Casimir, Duke of Cujavia.   21. WENCESLAUS V, of Bohemia,
   elected King of Hungary 1301, abdicated, 1304, assassinated 1306.

   Sigismyal.   Charles Martel, b. 1271,   Robert, King   John, Duke of
    opposed to Andrew III,   of Naples,   Durazzo.
   Ladislaus IV, of Poland, 1320-33,   died at Naples 1301.   1309-1343.
 Stephen, Ban of   Lokietek or the Dwarf.
 Bosnia.   Casimir.   Casimir III, 'the Great,'   Elisabeth 'the   23. CHARLES   Charles, Duke
  of Poland, d. 1370.   Elder,' d. 1380.   ROBERT,   of Calabria,
 Ladislaus, Stephen Ostroman, = Elisabeth.   1308-1342.   d. 1328.
 Ban of Bosnia,
 d. 1357.
 Stephen   Elisabeth 'the Younger,' = 24 LEWIS I, 'the Great,'   Andrew = Joanna I, Queen   Maria = Charles, Duke   Louis, Count   Robert,
 Tvartko I.   murdered or died in   King of Hungary 1342,   mar. Sept.   of Naples, de-   of Durazzo,   of Gravina,   killed
 King of   prison at Novigrad   King of Poland 1370,   1333,   posed and mur-   put to death   died at   in France
 Bosnia,   1387.   died 1382.   murdered   dered by Charles   1348 by   Naples in   1356.
 Rascia and the   Sept. 1345.   III, 1382.   Lewis I.   1362.
 Primorie 1376,
 died 1391.   27. SIGISMUND,   Caroberto,   Margarita, = 26. CHARLES III, King of
 Son of Emperor   = 25. MARIA, 1382, Hedwig = Jagellon, Grand Duke   posthumous,   d. 1412.   Naples, crowned King of
 Charles IV, associ-   married 1385,   of Lithuania, elected   died a boy in   Hungary 1386, murdered by
 ated 1388, alone   died Sept. 1395, s. p.   King of Poland 1386   Hungary.   Elisabeth 1386.
 1395, Emperor 1411,   = 2nd wife, Barbe de Cilley.   as Ladislaus V.
 died 1437.
   28. ELISABETH, = ALBERT OF AUSTRIA,   29. LADISLAUS VI. of Poland,   LADISLAUS, King   Joanna II,
   1437, died 1442.   associated 1437, died 1439.   1434; IV of Hungary 1440;   of Naples, disputed the   of Naples,
   fell at battle of Varna 1444.   throne of Hungary with   1414-35,
   Sigismund. Crowned at   born at
 John Muniades, died 1456.   Elisabeth = Casimir IV of Poland.   30. LADISLAUS V. 1445-57.   Zara 1403, retired 1409,   Zara 1373.
   died 1414.
31. MATTHIAS CORVINUS,   32. LADISLAUS VI,
 elected King 1458, died 1490.   King of Bohemia 1471,
   died 1516.
34. FERDINAND I of Austria, = Anne, married 1521,   33. LEWIS II, King of Hungary and Bohemia 1516,
 brother of Charles V, elected   died 1547.   fell at battle of Mohacz 1526.
 King of Hungary and Bohemia 1526,
 King of the Romans 1531, Emperor 1558.
 Since whom the succession has continued in
 the House of Austria.

CHAPTER II.

Dalmatia.

The Country, the People, and the Architecture, with a chronological list of the principal buildings.

DALMATIA though nominally a kingdom has never had any independent national existence. It has never since its first appearance on the stage of history been the home of a single united nation, and it is not so much a distinct country as a convenient geographical expression. Even its geographical boundaries have been differently fixed by different writers and at different times; for while Pliny[1] gives to Liburnia the coast from the River Arsia in Istria round the head of the Quarnero as far as the Titius or Kerka at Sebenico, and to Dalmatia the coast southwards to Lissus on the Macedonian frontier, Constantine Porphyrogenitus[2] in the tenth century

---

[1] 'Nunc finis Italiae fluvius Arsia,' lib. iii. c. xix. 'Liburniae finis et initium Dalmatiae Scardona in amne eo.' v. c. xxii.

[2] De adm°. Imp°. c. xxx. He divides the theme as follows:—

(1) *Diolcea*, from Dyrrhachium and Antivari to Decatera (Cattaro), and inland to Servia.

(2) *Terbunia*, from Cattaro to Ragusa and inland to Servia, corresponding to the district of Canali.

(3) *Zachlumia* (*Za*=behind, *Chlum* the name of a certain mountain), from Ragusa to the Narenta; afterward the Serb duchy of

confined the theme of Dalmatia to the coast south of the Cettina, which enters the sea at Almissa. In the middle ages after the irruption of the Croats and Serbs the name *Dalmatian* was for a long time confined to the Latin inhabitants of a few maritime towns and islands, the whole of the country beyond their narrow territory being considered Croatian[1]. In modern times Dalmatia is the strip of lowland or sub-mountainous country between the Alps and the sea, as well as the whole archipelago of islands that lie off its shores, reaching from Albania on the south to the opening of the gulf of Quarnero on the north, and including the islands of Pago and Arbe within that gulf. For this length of nearly 300 miles it has an average width of some twenty or twenty-five miles, varying from barely a mile at Cattaro to not quite forty miles at Knin. It is divided from Croatia Bosnia Herzegovina and Montenegro by the high range of the Dinaric Alps

Chulm or Chelmo, known also as the Primorje (or sea-coast) of Stagno.

(4) *Pagania*, from the Narenta to the Cettina at Almissa, known afterwards as the Craina, or the Primorie *par excellence*, the country of the Pagan Narentines, to which belonged the islands of Melita, Curzola, Brazza and Lesina, nearly deserted then, but used as pastures.

(5) *Croatia*, northwards from the Cettina round the Quarnero, as far as Albona in Istria.

Pliny's Dalmatia included the first four of these divisions and part of the fifth, as far as Sebenico. The rest of Porphyrogenitus' Croatia is Pliny's Liburnia.

[1] 'Iadra, Tragurium, et Spalato quae, cum insulis, Dalmatarum vel Romanorum nomen retinuerunt.' Luc. de Regn. lib. ii. c. xiii. p. 89, et passim.

which go by various names in various parts of their extent, between which and the Adriatic the land lies in a succession of ridges running parallel to the mountains and the sea with intervening valleys and plains. As the general level falls westwards the sea enters between the last parallel ridges, and the result is that strange shoal of long narrow islands, the crests of half sunken mountains, which fringes the coast of Dalmatia, and which we knew so well in our school atlas.

The natural scenery of Dalmatia is as singular as its geographical formation, and is in the strongest contrast to that of the opposite shores of Italy. The luxuriantly wooded mountains of Umbria, and the lagunes and marshes of Romagna and Venetia, are confronted in Dalmatia by stony deserts and mountains of an arid whiteness which at the first view seem covered with new fallen snow; while the muddy sea that beats on the flat shores and harbourless coast of Italy is exchanged on the opposite side for sapphire depths of crystal clearness which interlace an intricate network of natural breakwaters and penetrate into countless havens of matchless security. To the traveller from central and western Europe the sterility and barrenness of Dalmatia suggest the deserts of Arabia rather than any part of his own continent. It is true that there is some appearance of fertility in some of the islands, on the Riviera of Traü, and at the entrance of the Bocche, but still the general impression which the country leaves on the mind is one of bare white mountains, and fields covered with loose splintered rocks which the land 'grows' faster than they can be picked off it, although the great heaps that divide field from field cover more ground than they leave exposed for cultivation. In those parts of the interior where the mountains recede from the coast there are extensive peaty moors and unwholesome swamps, seed-beds of agues and fevers which are extremely prevalent throughout the province. These moors and swamps are due to the curious conformation of the surface, which is honeycombed with pits punch-bowls or basins of all sizes, some so small that you may jump over them, and others many miles in diameter, which are known by the various names of foibe, doline, or polje. Into these basins the rain washes down all the vegetable earth, and forms an alluvial stratum which is the cultivable soil of Dalmatia. At the bottom of each little crater is a potato bed or a patch of corn land, and the large plains which form the floor of the greater punch-bowls are the best pasture lands. From these hollows there is often no natural outlet, or none that is sufficient to carry off the drainage, and violent or long continued rain often reduces them to the condition of a lake. With the return of dry weather they become dry land again, and the damp effluvium from the mud and decaying vegetation is extremely pestilential[1]. But the malaria is not

---

[1] These singular hollows in the soil of Dalmatia and Istria have

confined to the interior: many of the maritime towns enjoy an equally bad reputation. Sebenico is said not to be free from malaria, nor Traü either, though the air there is more wholesome than it used to be; but Scardona Nona and Ossero are regular hot-beds of ague and tertian fevers, and till a few years ago Pola and Parenzo in Istria were no better. It is curious that all these places are old Roman towns, which once supported large and flourishing communities, and which it may be presumed were in ancient times wholesome to live in. Pola has become so once more since the establishment of the arsenal there and the enormous increase of its population with corresponding attention to sanitation; and at the other places I have named the cause of malaria is patent enough and so is the remedy; for behind or around their walls lie festering in the sun filthy deposits of mud and sewage, half sea and half marsh, that exhale deadly mists at sunrise and sunset to which no stranger can expose himself with impunity, and of which the effect may be seen in the ghastly complexions and lack-lustre eyes of the natives.

The absence of running water lends another element of strangeness to the landscape. There are some few rivers of considerable size, and after rain there are mischievous torrents that wash away the scanty soil and run dry in a few hours, but there are no brooks or springs, and most of the

never been satisfactorily accounted for. Vid. Reclus, Nouvelle Géographie Univ. vol. iii. p. 216, &c.

people have no water to drink but such as falls from the skies and is collected in cisterns. The limestone rock of which the country is composed, honeycombed with chasms and fissures, swallows up the rainfall, and streams plunge into καταβοθρα as they do in Greece, continuing underground for many miles and bursting forth again into daylight at a great distance off with the volume of a full-grown river.

From so unpromising a soil it might seem hopeless to expect much return, and yet Dalmatia is literally a land of oil and wine. The oil may be compared favourably with that of Lucca, and however poorly the traveller may fare otherwise he will never have reason to complain of the wine. An immense quantity is exported annually from Spalato and elsewhere into France, and Englishmen would be surprised to learn how much Dalmatian wine they have drunk under the name of claret since the partial failure of the Bordeaux vintage. When the results achieved by Dalmatian farmers with their present appliances are considered, there seems no reason to doubt the capabilities of the soil under better conditions, for their plough is a simpler instrument than that described by Virgil, and probably the same as that employed by the ancient Illyrians in the time of king Agron before the Romans first crossed the Adriatic [1].

In the maritime cities of the mainland, and on most of the islands the traveller may well imagine himself in Italy; for the language, architecture,

[1] Vid. illustration, Fig. 17, in ch. vi.

manners and dress of the citizens are the same as on the other side of the Adriatic. It is not among the Latins that he will find anything of that brilliant and picturesque costume for which Dalmatia is famous. It is the Slav who arrays himself in broidered garments and blazes with silver and gilded ornaments, and preserves in his attire the magnificence and bizarrerie of the middle ages. In some parts of South Dalmatia, especially on the bocche di Cattaro, the national costume is worn by all classes just as it is in Montenegro where the Prince and Princess and their family wear it habitually; and in some parts of Northern Dalmatia, on the island of Pago for instance, the fashion has set in for the upper classes to give up the dress of the 'borghese' and wear the national garb, which in point of appearance certainly carries the day over the humdrum coat waistcoat and trousers of Western Europe. Interesting costume, however, is confined to the mainland and to the country districts, except on market days when the country folk come into the towns to sell their poultry, eggs, and other farm produce, and make their purchases of necessaries or finery in the gay little shops that line the narrow streets. On the islands there is little or no costume to be seen, for though, with the exception of Veglia Ossero and Arbe, they were repeopled by Slavs, and have no Latin descent to boast of, their long subjection to Venice and the sea-faring life led by most of their male population, which brings them into constant contact with Italy, has pretty thoroughly Italianized them in manner, costume, and language[1]. Of all the towns in Dalmatia none will make the visitor fancy himself in Italy more completely than Lesina, a place which was entirely repeopled by Slavs who occupied the deserted site of an ancient Greek colony, but which, nevertheless, seems less Slavonic than many towns of Latin origin. Of all the Dalmatians the islanders have the reputation of being the most intelligent, industrious, and prosperous, and the standard of civilization is certainly higher among them than among the peasantry of the mainland. One never sees on the islands the rags and dirt that are common among the Morlacchi of the interior; on the contrary, there is a general air of comfort and respectability, and though no doubt poverty exists there as it does everywhere, it does not seem to exist in an extreme form. Though the soil is probably worse on the islands than on the continent it is better cultivated, and the people have the sea to help them to a livelihood as well as the land. Many of the islands have a considerable trade in ship-building; Curzola is unrivalled in the make of small craft, while at Lussin-piccolo large vessels of 1200 or 1300 tons are constructed, and indeed in the number and tonnage of the ships launched annually from her yards Lussino is inferior to Trieste and Fiume alone among the ports of Austro-Hungary.

[1] In the remoter villages and districts of the islands, however, we found Italian was only understood by the men, and not by all of them.

As one turns one's back on the sea-coast and advances into the interior towards the old Turkish frontier, both country and people become ruder and less cultivated. In the few miserable towns of inland Dalmatia there are no doubt a certain number of residents of a better class, 'impiegati' and others, among whom the traveller will find accomplished and highly educated gentlemen, but they seem lost amid the semi-barbarism that surrounds them. The huts in which the Morlacchi live are the same as those described by Fortis; the women are strange half-savage looking creatures, with elf locks hanging over their weather-beaten faces, dressed in thick embroidered leggings that give them the appearance of Indian squaws, and among the men are to be seen rags and tatters, and sometimes half-naked figures with nothing but a blanket to shield them from the weather as they tend their flocks on the bleak highland moors. Yet, poor as they are, most of them appear on festival days with silver coins beads and buttons hung so thickly over their wretched rags that as they journey on their little asses or ponies over the mountains to the fair, they blaze in the sunshine like a troop of cuirassiers. The contrast between this idle wealth and the misery of the tatters below serves but to give a deeper tinge to their barbarism.

The architecture of Dalmatia has so much in it that is peculiar and distinctive that it is entitled to rank as a style by itself among the various national styles of mediaeval Europe. It is entirely urban, and confined to the maritime cities, for the sea has in all ages been the parent of Dalmatian civilization; the history of the country is in fact the history of the maritime towns, and it was in them alone that art and letters found a congenial soil and took root. The Slavonic conquerors came in as barbarians with everything to learn and nothing to teach; they gradually received the religion and in a rude way imitated the art of the Byzantine Empire to which they paid a nominal subjection, but they never developed an art of their own, and the silversmith's work which has been produced in purely Slavonic districts in modern times is but little removed from the Byzantine art of the eighth and ninth century[1]. The Dalmatians of the maritime cities on the contrary were brought into contact with the nations of western Europe, and above all with Italy, and though their architecture bears traces of Byzantine influence as late as the twelfth century, they developed after that period a native art of their own, and have left us a series of architectural monuments not inferior in interest to those of any country of Europe. Their style is principally based on that of Italy—it is only natural that it should be so—but nevertheless it has about it something distinctive that is not altogether Italian, shewing that the Dalmatians were not mere copyists. Something there is about it that reminds one of Northern

[1] E.g. the silver plate in the convent of Savina; vid. infra, ch. xxiii.

Gothic, which may be due to the influence of Hungarian rule, for though the Hungarians were not an artistic people themselves they employed artists from France and Germany, and some masters of those nations may have followed the track of Hungarian conquest in Dalmatia. It is said that among the various 'maestri' whom the Dalmatian cities or the various confraternities of artizans from time to time invited from other countries, the painters carvers masons and master architects were commonly brought from Hungary and Austria[1]. Other elements there are that may be traced to the influence of Slav or Albanian; for though the Slav developed no art of his own, he no sooner came down to the coast and mixed with the Latins either as a settler within their walls, or by imitating, as at Sebenico, their municipal constitutions, and gaining for his Croatian city admission to the Dalmatian pale, than he shewed a capacity for art which proved his backwardness to be due only to the want of good example. Many of the Dalmatian artists whose names have come down to us seem by their names to have been Slavs, and others were Albanians, of that still more ancient stock in which it is supposed the old Illy-

[1] 'I salariati (*maestri*) sono per lo più chiamati d' Italia; i notari però, i trombettieri ed i musici assai più spesso d'Ungheria, e qualche volta anche dalle provincie dell' Austria centrale. I doratori, i fabbro-ferrai, i pittori e gli intagliatori dall' Ungheria, e dall' Austria, donde s' ebbero anche degli scalpellini e dei maestri architetti.' Le Confraternite laiche in Dalmazia, p. 25. G. Gelcich. Ragusa, 1885.

rian race survives. Of these the work of the Albanian is the most singular; that of the Slav is fresh and vigorous but not especially characteristic, his talent being for adopting and imitating rather than for originating; that of the Northerner, be he Hungarian, Teuton or Gaul, is tempered by southern influences till only a faint flavour of peculiarity remains; and the work of one and all is practically based on that of Italy, the country to which the Dalmatian cities looked ever for support and instruction, and from which they often invited artists to come among them as they did their podestà or their schoolmaster even during the period of Hungarian dominion.

The history of Dalmatian architecture is an epitome of that of southern Europe. In the palace of Diocletian at Spalato we have one of the earliest, perhaps the earliest, step towards that new departure in architecture which resulted in the development of the styles of modern Europe. Here we see the first relaxation of the strict rules of ancient classic art; the proportions of the different members of the order are varied and arbitrary; some members are omitted entirely; new forms of ornament, such as the zigzag, which was to play so large a part in Norman architecture, make their first appearance; and the arches are made to spring immediately from the capitals without an intervening entablature. Other irregularities occur in this building which shew the decline of the age towards barbarism, and for perhaps the first time in classic architecture columns and fragments of older buildings are adapted and used up second-hand in the new one[1]. It is impossible to overrate the interest of this building to the student either of ancient or modern art. To the one it will be the last effort of the dying art of antiquity, still majestic in its proportions, still dwarfing into insignificance by its huge masonry the puny works of later ages, which are already crumbling into ruin while it seems destined to stand for eternity, but at the same time fallen from the perfection of the classic age, and stamped with the seal of returning barbarism. To the other it will seem the new birth of that rational and unconventional mode of building in which the restless and eager spirit of the regenerated and repeopled Roman world has found free scope for its fancy and invention; which places fitness before abstract beauty, delights to find harmony in variety, and recognizes grace in more than one code of proportions. Both will be right; the palace of Spalato marks the era when the old art died in giving birth to the new.

The date of Diocletian's building is from 284 to 305. Of the architecture of the next five centuries Dalmatia has not a single perfect example remaining. In Istria and Friuli, however, the continuity of examples is better preserved, the irruptions of the barbarians having been less disastrously destructive there than on the eastern side of

[1] This seems to me obviously the case; I do not know whether it has been observed before. Vid. infra, ch. xi.

the Adriatic. At Parenzo still stands the magnificent basilica of Euphrasius, built between 535 and 543. At Grado the duomo of Elias was completed between 571 and 586, and we may still admire the wondrous pavements and grieve over the shattered capitals of the original building. The magnificent basilica of S. Maria di Canneto at Pola has unhappily disappeared, and its rich columns of marble and oriental alabaster must be looked for at Venice, but at Trieste there are still some remains of early Byzantine architecture in the apse of the church of S. Giusto.

It is a wide bound from the architecture of Spalato to that of these examples, so wide indeed that in the interval a new art had time to arise and perfect itself. The church of Euphrasius is a specimen of the Byzantine style at its best. Classic tradition survives in the basilican plan, the long drawn ranks of serried marble columns, and in the horizontal direction of the leading lines. But the capitals with their crisply raffled foliage, emphasized by dark holes pierced with a drill which recall the fragility and brilliancy of the shell of the sea echinus, belong to a new school of sculpture, and the massive basket capitals which are found among them, as well as the second capital or impost block which surmounts them all, were novelties in architecture at the time of their erection. These buildings belong to the best school of Byzantine art, and were erected at the same period as those at Ravenna and Constantinople, which they resemble in every detail; and in the church of Parenzo especially one might imagine oneself in the ancient capital of the exarchs.

Dalmatia, as I have said, has nothing to shew that belongs to this period. There must have been buildings in this style of equal importance with those just mentioned, and the half-excavated basilica of Salona seems to have been worthy to rank with those of Istria and the lagunes. But in the seventh century the province was swept by barbarian hordes, the cities were depopulated and laid in ruin, and when the trembling Latins ventured once more to return and inhabit their desolated homes they found their ancient monuments prostrate, and had to reconstruct them little by little as well as their poverty and weakness enabled them.

The series of Dalmatian examples begins at the opening of the ninth century with a remarkable class of buildings of which the church of S. Donato at Zara is the most important. From Parenzo and Grado to S. Donato is a wider bound than the last, and the change is proportionately greater. We find ourselves now landed in a much ruder age; the traditions not only of good architectural design but even of good building construction are forgotten; the buildings are generally small and the masonry of the roughest. It was beyond the humble powers of the builder to make capitals or columns for himself, and his only resource was to pilfer them from the surrounding ruins of which there was then no lack. The columns were used just as they came to hand; some were longer and some thicker than the others, and they were crowned with capitals that never belonged to them, and were often much too small to fit them. If the supply of capitals ran short a fragment of a cornice or a moulded base upside down was made to serve instead, and in at least one instance the architect has not hesitated to place the square capital of an ancient pilaster upon a cylindrical column, with the sublimest indifference to the grotesqueness of the effect.

In the plan of their churches and such simple bits of original detail as the builders of the period trusted themselves to execute we find the influence of Byzantine art still governing them. The Eastern Empire was still nominally supreme in Dalmatia, and remained so till the twelfth century; from time to time its power was still felt in the Adriatic, and Venice herself at this period professed submission to the 'King of the Romans,' and borrowed her art from Constantinople. In a rude way and generally on a miniature scale the two classes of Byzantine churches, the domed church and the basilica, are represented in the buildings of Dalmatia erected during the remainder of the Byzantine period from the ninth to the twelfth century. Of the basilican type are the churches of S. Pietro vecchio S. Lorenzo and S. Domenica at Zara, S. Barbara at Traù, S. Stefano and S. Giacomo in Peline at Ragusa, to which may be added that of Muggia vecchia near Trieste. The churches at Ragusa consist of simple naves; S. Pietro vecchio at Zara has the peculiarity of a double nave divided by a central arcade; and the others have a nave with two side aisles. They are generally covered with waggon vaults strengthened by flat ribs of stone at each column, and the vaults are finished with a semidome at the east end. The ground plan, nevertheless, is not apsidal but square, and the corners are filled up at the springing level of the semidome with little squinches which bring the square plan to a semicircle from which the semidome rises. This is a peculiarity I have observed in no other country, and the Dalmatians were so fond of it that the aisles of S. Lorenzo at Zara are vaulted with a succession of semidomes constructed in this way facing sideways to the central nave. The largest basilican church (ναὸς δρομικός) of this period of which any traces remain in Dalmatia is the duomo of Zara, S. Anastasia, which is described by Porphyrogenitus as decorated with painting and paved with mosaic, and constructed with columns of white marble and cipollino, which were no doubt the spoils of ancient buildings. If, as seems likely, the apse and the eastern part of the crypt of the present duomo are parts of this basilica, and have survived the rebuilding of the greater part in the thirteenth century, the older church probably dated from the ninth or tenth century, for the work is too rude to be attributed to the palmy days of Byzantine art in the sixth or seventh. Other examples of basilicas of this period are to be seen in Istria, at

S. Lorenzo in Pasenatico, and in the duomo of Trieste.

Of domed churches there are several varieties. At Nona the churches of S. Nicolò and S. Croce are small cruciform buildings, barrel vaulted, apsidal, and with a central cupola rudely carried on pendentives, the invention of which feature is the crowning triumph of Byzantine art, and the middle of the church is carried up so as to form a kind of central tower which conceals the exterior of the cupola. The size of these buildings is generally insignificant; S. Croce was the cathedral of Nona, but its dome is only about eight feet in diameter, and each arm of the cross is only about eight feet long. At Cattaro the two churches of S. Maria and S. Luca, which though rebuilt in later times probably retain their original plan, have cupolas rising from the centre of an elongated nave which finishes with an eastern apse.

The ancient baptistery of Zara and the churches of S. Trinità at Spalato, and S. Orsola at Zara of which only the foundation exists, are still more curious in plan; they consist of a circular central space or nave covered with a cupola, which is surrounded by six apses applied to the external drum, and opening to the central space by round arches. At S. Orsola one of these apses is interrupted to form a short nave ending with a campanile. I cannot but think that the singular plan of these churches is derived from that of the duomo of Spalato, and affords one instance among many of the influence exercised on Dalmatian art from first to last by the buildings of Diocletian's palace. The baptistery at Zara is polygonal externally like the temple, from which it differs only by being hexagonal instead of octagonal, and having all the niches round instead of round and square alternately (comp. Figs. 1 and 29).

Of the date of these buildings all that can be said with certainty is that they were built at some time between the year 800 and the year 1100. During this long period architecture stood still here as it did pretty well throughout all Europe. Some of the buildings are ruder than the rest and contain no original details, and these may be attributed to the earlier part of this dark period; to this class S. Pietro vecchio may certainly be joined. Others contain not only fragments from old Roman buildings, but also capitals and cornices carved originally for their place, the first timid efforts of native Dalmatian art, and these may safely be placed towards the end of the period; of this class S. Domenica at Zara is the best example. But it would be dangerous to attempt to fix the date of each building more precisely.

Fortunately the finest church of this period that has descended to us is also the one about whose date there is least doubt. The grand round church of S. Donato at Zara was undoubtedly built about the year 810 by Donato bishop of Zara, and in its rugged simplicity and elephantine proportions it supplies an admirable illustration both of the rudeness and the promise of that age. It will be fully described in the next chapter.

With the opening of the twelfth century new political factors began to operate in Dalmatia; the last tie which bound that country to Byzantium was severed, Venice and Hungary were left to contend for possession of it, and its architecture was for the future based on the styles of Italy or Germany instead of that of Constantinople. Venetian art, it is true, still continued to cling to Byzantine example, but it was Byzantine with a difference, while the art of France and Germany which had been adopted by the Hungarians, and that of Lombardy also, belonged to the other branch of round-arched architecture, the Romanesque. The influence of Venice was predominant at Ragusa and in the islands, where her possession was seldom disturbed during the twelfth, thirteenth, and first half of the fourteenth centuries, and it is in precisely those parts of the province that the impress of Byzantine feeling remained longest, though even there Romanesque details began from an early date to make their way. The transition from pure Byzantine work towards the round-arched styles of Lombardy or Germany, in other words from the eastern to the western form of Romanesque architecture, may be observed in the interesting church of S. Giovanni Battista at Arbe. There we have the old basilican nave and aisles with closely set columns and with the impost block or second capital above the first, but the apse with its semi-circular ambulatory, and the narrow arches

Examples of Early Dalmatian Work

Plate I

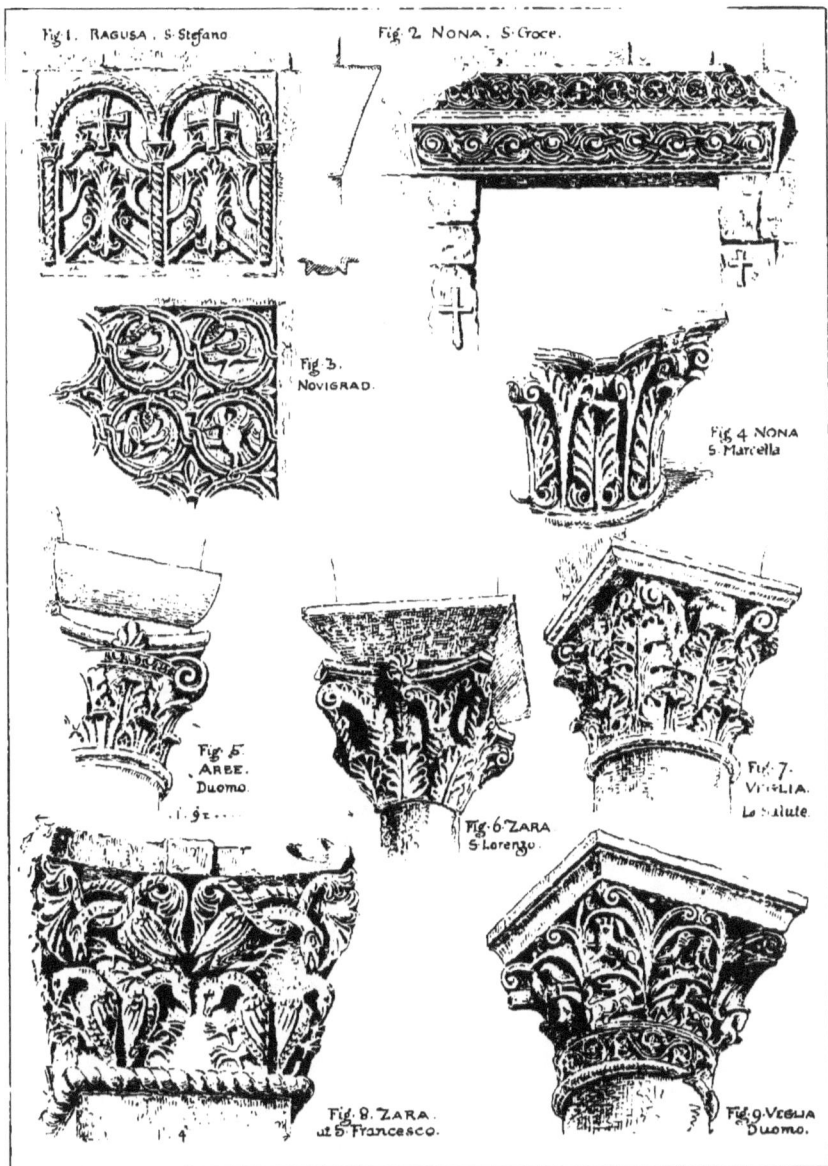

opening into it, with their coarsely carved capitals, have nothing about them that can be referred to the art of Constantinople, and remind one rather of the Romanesque art of France or England.

In Plate I. I have collected a number of examples to illustrate the progress of Dalmatian art from the end of the seventh century to the end of the twelfth. The panel from Ragusa, Fig. 1, has a thoroughly Byzantine character, which disappears gradually in the succeeding examples, though there are traces of it in Fig. 7, which is probably coeval with Fig. 9, and if so dates from 1180–1190.

Of the part played by Hungary in the modification of Dalmatian art it is difficult to speak very precisely. At the time of their first coming into the country the Hungarians were a much ruder people than the Dalmatians of the cities, among whom the arts and letters had already begun to recover themselves: they were perhaps even ruder than the Croatians, living as they did in huts in winter and tents in summer, and possessing scarcely any buildings of more durable materials[1]. To the Latin races the Hungarians seemed barbarians down to a much later day: their unpolished manners and overbearing conduct, their drunkenness and *'barbari costumi'* made them odious to the Neapolitans of the fourteenth century[2]. On the capital of the

---

[1] Vid. supra, p. 40, the account of Otto Frisingensis who describes the Hungarians of his own day, c. 1156–8, half a century after their arrival in Dalmatia.

[2] Vid. supra, p. 99 note, extract from letter by Petrarch.

ducal palace at Venice, of which the poles are occupied by the Greek and Latin, the Hungarian figures with his tall cap and untrimmed locks among Turks Tartars Goths Egyptians and Persians; and to the Ragusan Ludovico Tubero, writing about the year 1500, the Hungarians are still a Scythian race, to whose overbearing pretensions it is safer to oppose a bold front than to make concessions[1]. Such a people as the Hungarians were at the time of their conquest of Dalmatia in 1102 were not likely to bring with them new artistic ideas to influence the art of a people who were superior to themselves in the arts of civilized life: and though their luxury and extravagant living of which we hear in the middle of the thirteenth century[2] may imply some advance towards refinement of manners, we find them after their country had been desolated by the Tartars dependent on artists from France and Germany for the reconstruction of their principal buildings. Villars de Honnecourt, architect of the cathedral of Cambrai, was in Hungary directly after the retreat of the Tartars, and is supposed to have built the cathedrals of Gran and Kaschau and the church of S. Elizabeth at Marburg[3]. French in-

[1] 'Quandoquidem Hungaris tutius est vel pervicaciter obluctari quam eorum cedere contumaciae. Quoniam naturae ut plerique Scytharum magis ferocis quam fortis animi sunt.' Lud. Cervarius. Tubero, vol. i. p. 180.

[2] Thomas Archid. vid. supra, p. 65.

[3] He tells us on one leaf of his sketch-book, 'when I was drawing this, I was sent for into Hungary, and therefore I like it all the better;' and on another page containing a sketch of

fluence may be detected in several other churches of Hungary, and the west portal, as well as sundry details of the curious church of Ják, has a look of French design about it. Elsewhere throughout Hungary the influence of German Romanesque is plainly seen in the earlier architecture, and that of German Gothic in the later, and it is difficult to trace any of the artistic ideas of Hungarian architecture to a distinctly Hungarian source[1].

But, if the Hungarians were not an artistic people themselves, they gave abundant employment to artists from other countries, and it is probably to the influence of these foreigners, from whatever country they came, that the peculiarities of Dalmatian architecture should be attributed when they cannot be traced to Italian sources. One peculiarity, however, must be accounted for by the conditions and sentiment of the Dalmatians themselves, and that is their persistence in the Romanesque style long after it had passed into Gothic in most parts of Europe. In France and England round-arched gave way to pointed architecture at the end of the twelfth century; in Germany the new ideas took root more slowly, but Gothic architecture

a pavement, he says, 'I was once in Hungary, and remained there many a day. There I saw a church pavement made in such a manner as this.' Sketch Book of Villars de Honnecourt, plates 19, 29, &c.

[1] Elaborate drawings of several Hungarian churches may be seen in the Mittelalteliche Kunstdenkmale des Österreichischen Kaiserstaates, by Heider, Eitelberger, and Hieser. Stuttgardt, 1858. As to Hungarian architecture vid. chapter xiv, infra.

began to supersede Romanesque about 1230 or 1240; in Italy churches arose between 1220 and 1300 at Assisi, Venice, Verona, Siena, Orvieto, and Florence, in which Italian Gothic reached its fullest development; but in Dalmatia we find the people contentedly working on at Romanesque architecture through the whole of the thirteenth and well into the fourteenth century before any signs of transition to the pointed style begin to manifest themselves. This singular unchangeableness may be due to several causes, among which it is natural to place first the backwardness of a remote and poor country, hemmed in on one side by semi-barbarous kingdoms, and subject to distant powers, which, whether Venetian or Hungarian, never showed any disposition to encourage and promote the well-being of the provincials for their own sake. Something also may be put down to the influence of Italy, a country in which the round arch was never entirely abandoned, especially in the brick buildings of Lombardy. Nearly half a century after the Gothic west front of Siena was completed the campanile of St. Gottardo at Milan was erected in a round-arched style, differing but little from the earlier Romanesque. But the principal reason was no doubt the actual preference of the Dalmatians for the earlier style, and the influence which never failed to impress them of Diocletian's mighty building at Spalato. Down to the last they built their doorways with the straight lintel below a semicircular arch and tympanum, of which the Porta Aurea and the Porta

Ferrea furnished the prototypes, and they never tired of imitating with various alterations and modifications the round waggon roof of the temple of Æsculapius.

From this it may be gathered how difficult it is to guess with anything like certainty the date of any Romanesque building in Dalmatia, and how largely the evidence of the building itself, which in other countries is a better guide even than documentary evidence, requires in this to be fortified and confirmed by records. Fortunately Dalmatian architects have been tolerably liberal in the matter of inscriptions and shields with armorial bearings; and as the heraldry of the country has been well studied and illustrated, a clue is often obtained in that way to a date which is surprisingly different from what the building itself would have suggested: but even this is sometimes wanting, and nothing but vague traditions exist to help the puzzled antiquary out of his difficulties.

The Romanesque architecture of Dalmatia bursts suddenly into life with the splendid campanile and chapter-house of the convent of S. Maria at Zara, the work of King Coloman and his repudiated wife the abbess Vekenega between 1102 and 1111. They correspond in style with the contemporary Romanesque of Lombardy and Germany. The church of S. Grisogono at Zara, which, though its date is disputed, seems to belong to the latter part of this century and to have been consecrated in 1175, is a very refined and highly finished piece of Lombard architecture resembling the churches at Lucca. At the end of the twelfth century we have the magnificent campanile of Arbe, with the three other steeples its satellites in the same style, a triumph of Romanesque architecture. Contemporary with this are the duomo and other buildings at Veglia, in which Byzantine feeling is still perceptible. The duomo of Zara, which belongs to the thirteenth century, has an archaic look that would mislead the unwary to attribute it to the eleventh or twelfth ; and the cathedral of Traü, with its superb portals and sombre nave, which was building at the same time as that of Zara, is round-arched and Romanesque, though in beauty of design and technical merit it does not lag behind the Gothic work of its age. I shall have occasion to point out the correspondence of this building with examples of architecture in Hungary (vid. chapter xiv).

The great work of the fourteenth century is the campanile of Spalato, which was begun probably soon after 1300, and was not finished when the century expired, the work having been interrupted for a long time after the death of Maria of Hungary, the widow of Charles II of Naples. This wonderful tower, begun some thirty years later than the angel choir at Lincoln, and barely finished before Brunelleschi started upon his dome at Florence, is throughout of good honest Romanesque work that might have been put together in the twelfth century, with columns carried on the backs of lions, Corinthianizing capitals, billet moulds, and acanthus foliage, as if the architect had never heard of any other style. It is remarkable also how many of the ornamental details are copied from those of Diocletian's work, in the midst of which the tower stands.

Contemporaneously with this round-arched work the pointed arch begins to appear occasionally[1], and with the beginning of the fifteenth century came the final Venetian occupation of Dalmatia, and Romanesque architecture finally melted away and made room for the contemporary art of the mistress city. The upper central parts of the fronts of the duomo and S. Grisogono at Zara are probably the latest instances of the expiring round-arched style, which actually prolonged its existence into the fifteenth century, when on the other side of the Adriatic the Italian Renaissance had fairly set in, and round-arched architecture had once more come into fashion. Venice, however, did not accept the Renaissance so soon as central Italy, and the architecture which she brought with her into Dalmatia was that form of Gothic which she had invented and refined, and which as a domestic style has never been surpassed. The streets of every Dalmatian town on the sea-board or islands are filled with the same graceful semi-oriental ogee windows and the same lovely balconies that meet the eye at every turn in the mistress city, the churches are fitted with rich tabernacle work that

---

[1] It should be observed that the earliest buildings in Dalmatia in which the Gothic style was thoroughly developed are the convents of the mendicant orders.

recalls the choir of the great church of the Frari, and it does not need the ever-present symbol of the Evangelist to remind us that we are treading the soil of an ancient Venetian province. It is, however, chiefly in private buildings that Gothic architecture prevailed in Dalmatia; besides the earlier part of the duomo of Sebenico (1430) there are but few churches in that style, and the most important public building is the palace of the Rectors of the Republic of Ragusa, which was begun in 1435 by a Neapolitan and not a Venetian architect. The sculpture in this palace is of a very high order, and will be fully described and illustrated in its proper place.

Gothic architecture, however, had but a short reign in Dalmatia; it was adopted very late, and abandoned very early for the Renaissance, a style for which the Dalmatians showed a natural and almost precocious liking. Its introduction is due to Giorgio Orsini, or Giorgio Dalmatico as his admiring countrymen like to style him, the scion of a Zaratine family which claimed descent from the princely Roman house, and an architect of original genius who may fairly be styled the Brunelleschi of Dalmatia.

In 1441 he was entrusted with the completion of the duomo of Sebenico, which had been begun by another architect in a style of very good Italian Gothic. Giorgio at once threw over the plans of his predecessor, and built the eastern part of the church in a picturesque variety of the early style of the Renaissance, which he treated with great originality. Thorns and brambles, as he might have said, of the old Gothic art clung to him, and among his classic columns and in his windows and vaults is to be found tracery-work that belongs rather to the style he had abandoned than that he adopted. But in spite of these incongruities Giorgio has produced a masterly design, and no one who has seen his church will easily forget it. His greatest triumph was achieved by the roofs, which consist of waggon vaults of stone, visible outside as well as inside; an idea perhaps suggested by the semicircular vault of the little temple at Spalato which was in the same way visible externally, but which when carried out as it is at Sebenico, on so vast a scale, at so great a height, and with such comparatively slender materials, may fairly be considered original, and cannot fail to excite surprise and admiration[1].

The handiwork of Giorgio will be met with elsewhere in Dalmatia, and notably at Ragusa, where in 1464 he repaired the front of the Rector's palace, placing the round arches of the present arcade with their festoons of leaves and ribbons upon the old colonnade of Onofrio de la Cava. He was highly honoured by his fellow-citizens and entrusted by them with an embassy to Rome, and in the old quarter of Sebenico may still be seen the doorway

[1] I assume here that the idea of roofing the church in this way is to be attributed to Giorgio, although he did not live to see the vaulting completed; vid. infra, Sebenico, chapter ix.

of the house he built for himself, with the bear of Orsini on the lintel, and the mallet and chisel of his sculptor's craft on the door-posts surrounded by clusters of flowers.

Contemporary with Giorgio was another Dalmatian architect, whose fame attracted the attention of one of the leading princes of Italy. In 1468 Federigo da Montefeltro, Duke of Urbino, set about building that palace in his capital which is one of the gems of Renaissance architecture; and having searched Italy, and in particular Tuscany 'the source of architects,' for an artist worthy of the occasion, he finally selected Messer Lutiano of Laurana or Vrana, in the territory of Zara, to whom the work was entrusted and by whom the oldest remaining part of the palace was designed and erected. I am not cognizant of any work by Luciano di Laurana in his native country. He settled at Urbino and died at Pesaro about 1481[1].

When we observe that Giorgio's 'Renaissance' work at Sebenico in 1441 preceded that of Leo Battista Alberti at Rimini by nine years, and was contemporary with the Gothic Porta della Carta at Venice, we shall be struck with the willing reception of the new art in Dalmatia, and with the prominent position to which Giorgio is entitled as a leader of the new movement. The early Renaissance work of Pietro Lombardo on the Chiesa dei Miracoli at Venice is forty years later, and the Cancelleria at Rome, which marks the turning-point of the Re-

[1] Vid. infra, under description of Vrana, chapter viii.

naissance from its semi-Gothic to its purely classic phase, was not built till sixty years afterwards in 1500. In France the Renaissance did not begin to affect the current Gothic art till about 1508, nor in England till about 1520, while the castle of Heidelberg, in the Renaissance style of Germany, was not built till 1556.

Once established in Dalmatia the new style soon prevailed over the older Gothic art for all buildings of importance, though it would seem that private houses were still built in Venetian Gothic. An Albanian architect, Andrea Alecxi of Durazzo, was employed at Traù Spalato and Arbe, and the names of a few Italian architects from Venice or Florence, and occasionally of a German, have come down to us. It is singular, however, that though the Dalmatians adopted the style of the Renaissance almost as soon as it appeared, they did not advance it like the Italians to pure Palladianism. Of the cold severe formal architecture of that school Dalmatia hardly contains an example; the picturesque freedom of Gothic which continued to inspire the earlier phases of Renaissance art, and which give it its life and charm, never forsook the style in Dalmatia till the seventeenth century was well advanced, when the art suddenly sank into the slough of the 'Barocco,' in which it was fatally engulphed.

The following chronological list of the principal buildings in Dalmatia of which I have been able to ascertain the dates, or to conjecture them with anything like certainty, will I hope be of use to the student of the architecture of the country. I have added a few Istrian buildings to complete the regular sequence of examples.

ROMAN PERIOD.

A.D.		
284–305.	Spalato. Palace of Diocletian.	Irregular classic. Old columns, &c. used up secondhand.
Fourth or fifth century.	Salona. Basilica and Baptistery. Destroyed 639.	Classic passing into Byzantine.

BYZANTINE PERIOD, 535–1102.

535–543. 546.	Parenzo. Duomo. Pola. S. Maria di Canneto consecrated (now destroyed).	Pure Byzantine as at Ravenna. do. do. do.
571–586.	Grado. Duomo of patriarch Elias.	do. do. do. but some fragments of old buildings used secondhand.
809.	Cattaro. Original duomo of Andreasci.	Only fragments remain. Interlacing knots and barbarous animals.
c. do.	Cattaro. La Collegiata (since rebuilt).	Original plan probably retained. Byzantine.
c. do.	Zara. S. Donato.	Grand but rude domed church with old fragments employed.
857.	Pola. Duomo of Handegis (since rebuilt).	Fragments remain of Byzantine design.
Ninth to eleventh century.	Zara. S. Pietro vecchio.	Barbarous. Made up of fragments of older buildings.
,,	Nona. S. Nicolò.	Plain and rude. In plan Byzantine. Small cruciform church with cupola.
,,	do. S. Croce.	do. do. do.
,,	S. Lorenzo in Pasenatico, duomo.	do. Details original.[1] Basilican in plan.
,,	Trieste. Duomo (southern part perhaps older).	do. do. do.
,,	Zara. S. Lorenzo.	do. A few original details.
,,	do. Baptistery.	Byzantine. Cupola surrounded by apses.
,,	do. S. Orsola.	do. do. do.
,,	Spalato. S. Trinità.	do. do. do.

[1] By this I mean that the sculpture was designed and worked originally for the building, not used up secondhand from older buildings.

Dalmatian Architecture.

A.D.		
Ninth to eleventh century.	Zara. Apse and crypt of Duomo. (Rest rebuilt.)	Plain rude work. (Date uncertain.)
,,	Ragusa. S. Stefano.	do. Scale very small.
	do. S. Giacomo in Peline.	do. do. do.
,,	Traù. S. Barbara.	Byzantine. More original in details, showing an advance in art.
,,	Zara. S. Domenica.	do. do. do.
,,	Arbe. Baldacchino in duomo.	Byzantine. Knotwork and animal grotesques approaching Romanesque.
,,	Muggia vecchia.	Building rude. Knotwork, &c. in screens approaching Romanesque.
,,	Arbe. S. Giovanni Battista.	Basilican nave, but Romanesque apse and ambulatory, showing transition.
1026–31.	Aquileia. Poppo's rebuilding.	Byzantine passing into Romanesque. Capitals finely executed.

VENETIAN AND HUNGARIAN PERIOD, 1102–1409.

1105.	Zara. S. Maria. Campanile and Sala Capitolare.	Lombard or German Romanesque, well designed and executed.
1111.	do. do. Tomb of Vekenega.	do. do.
1123–1166.	Cattaro. Duomo rebuilt.	Clustered or articulated piers alternating with columns. Romanesque, rude.
1175.	Zara. Apse and south wall of S. Grisogono.	Lombard Romanesque, highly finished.
1186–90.	Veglia. Duomo.	Byzantine passing into Romanesque.
c. 1200.	Arbe. Great campanile.	Romanesque, excellent workmanship.
1213.	Traù. South doorway finished and probably nave of Cathedral generally.	do. do.
1214.	Spalato. West doors (wooden) of Duomo by Guvina. Stalls of same date and probably by the same hand. Also the marble pulpit.	Transitional or refined Romanesque, highly finished.
1240.	Traù. West portal finished by Radovan.	Transitional Romanesque, exquisitely finished.
c. 1250?	Zara. Nave of Duomo (consecrated 1285).	Ruder than the above. Old capitals occasionally used up. Piers and columns alternately.
1251.	Parenzo. Canonica.	Lombard Romanesque.
1277.	do. Baldacchino in duomo.	Arches bluntly pointed. Capitals Byzantine.
1287.	Arbe. Duomo mostly rebuilt.	Byzantine in character. Plain.

A.D.		
c. 1300–23.	Spalato. Two lower stages of campanile.	Romanesque.
1306.	Ragusa. Dominican church.	Italian Gothic.
c. 1312 (?)	do. Sponza, two lower storeys of court.	Plain early pointed work.
c. 1317.	do. Franciscan cloister by Mycha di Antivari.	Transitional Romanesque.
1324.	Zara west front (upper central part is still later).	Romanesque.
1330–1385.	Trieste. Central nave of duomo.	Italian Gothic.
1332.	Zara. Baldacchino in duomo.	Pointed arches, but capitals Romanesque.
c. 1348.	Ragusa. Dominican cloister and convent.	Romanesque mixed with Italian Gothic. Details later in character than general design.
1360–1416.	Spalato. Upper part of campanile by Nicolò Tverdoj.	Romanesque like the lower part.
1365.	Aquileia. Duomo remodelled by patriarch Marquard after earthquake.	Pointed arches of Italian Gothic. Venetian foliage. Poppo's capitals retained.
1380.	Zara. Silver ark of S. Simeone. By Francesco di Milano.	Italian Gothic.
1394–95.	Zara. Stalls in S. Francesco. By Giov. di Borg. S. Sepolcro.	Venetian Gothic.
c. 1407.	Zara. Central upper parts of west fronts of duomo and S. Grisogono.	Romanesque, but attenuated and meagre.

VENETIAN PERIOD, 1409–1797.

1420–50.	Zara. Choir stalls in duomo. To the same style and period belong the stalls at Cherso Lesina, Parenzo, Mezzo, S. Maria in Zara, Traü, and Arbe. The last-named is dated 1445.	Venetian Gothic, resembling that of the woodwork in the Frari at Venice.
1422.	Traü. Campanile above portico by Matteo and Stefano. (Top part later.)	Good Italian Gothic, well-moulded and elaborated.
1427.	Spalato. Altar of S. Doimo by Bonino of Milan.	Italian Gothic of excellent workmanship.
1430.	Sebenico. Earlier part of nave with the arcades, aisle vaults, and two principal doors by Antonio di Paolo.	Fine Italian Gothic. Giottesque in character.
1435.	Ragusa. Palazzo Rettorale rebuilt by Onofrio de la Cava. A great deal remains.	Fine Italian Gothic. Sculpture of a very high order.
1437.	Ragusa. Public fountains by Onofrio de la Cava.	
1438–65.	Curzola. Campanile.	Round arched below. Elaborate Gothic belvedere above.
1441.	Sebenico. Eastern part, upper vaults, and cupola begun by Giorgio Orsini.	Renaissance of an early type, but mixed with Gothic details.

A.D.		
1447.	Traü. Sacristy.	Italian Gothic.
1448.	Spalato duomo. Altar of S. Anastasio by Giorgio Orsini.	Italian Gothic, but Giorgio was directed to make the altar like that of S. Doimo, v. sup. 1427.
1452.	Sebenico. Sacristy by Giorgio Orsini.	Renaissance of an early type.
1457.	Ragusa. Chiesa delle Danče.	Italian Gothic.
1460.	Zara. Silver pastoral staff of archbishop Valeresso.	do. do.
1464.	Ragusa. New arches to front of Rector's palace by Michelozzo and Giorgio Orsini.	Renaissance of an early type.
1465–98.	Ossero. New duomo (? by Giorg. Orsini).	Renaissance of an early type.
1467.	Traü. Baptistery by Andrea Alecxi of Durazzo.	Renaissance. Early in character with *pointed* barrel vault.
1468.	Traü. Chapel of S. Giovanni Ursini by Andrea Alecxi.	Renaissance. With round vault, rich in figure sculpture.
1477.	Curzola. Cloister of Badia.	Venetian Gothic, passing into Renaissance.
1490.	Arbe. Duomo, west door.	Renaissance.
1520–36.	Ragusa. San Salvatore.	do., but mixed with Gothic features.
1543.	Zara. Porta di Terra firma by Sammichieli.	Classic renaissance fully developed.
c. 1540–50.	Lesina. Loggia by Sammichieli.	do. do. but treated with freedom.
1571–4.	Lesina. Three campanili and restoration of churches.	Renaissance, but mixed with some Gothic features.
1600.	Zara. Facade (unfinished) of S. Rocco.	Classic fully developed.
1642–59.	Savina. Church plate in Greek convent, brought from Bosnia.	Byzantine; resembling but for a few suspicious details the work of the sixth or seventh century.
1642–59	Ragusa. Chiesa del Rosario.	Barocco.
1667.	Cattaro. Western towers.	do.
1671–1713.	Ragusa. New duomo.	do.
1699–1715.	do. Chiesa dei Gesuiti.	do.
1715.	do. S. Biagio.	do.

CHAPTER III.

Zara.

Description of the city.   History.   Roman remains.

Zara is naturally the place where the traveller will first touch Dalmatian soil, and first be introduced to the people, the scenery, and the arts of South-Eastern Europe. Though it may be reached either from Ancona or Fiume the more usual route is by way of Trieste and Pola, and the exigencies of the time-table generally bring the steamer into port early in the morning, so that the traveller begins his new experiences just as the day is breaking and the sleeping city awaking to fresh life. And no lack of new experiences will be felt by those who have never before crossed the Adriatic and trodden the border lands of European civilization. It excites a thrill of interest to find oneself for the first time within reach of the Turk, at whose dread coming four centuries ago Christendom trembled, kingdoms fell, and the last fragment of the Roman Empire crumbled into ruin. Though driven out of Dalmatia he has left his mark on many a ruined castle and half-deserted town; and as the steamer ploughs her way in the morning stillness along the Canale di Zara, and the dawn brightens over the jagged crests of the Velebić mountains, the thought rises that behind that rugged barrier is the land where the Turk still bears rule in name, and where it was but yesterday that the despised Christian obtained equal rights with his Moslem conqueror.

The Turk it is true will not often be met with in Dalmatia now-a-days, but a stranger will find enough in the Christian population to surprise and perplex him. The first sounds of the Illyric tongue, the first glimpse of the gorgeous costume of those who speak it, the appearance of the Eastern form of Christianity on an equality with the Latin branch, and in southern Dalmatia almost on a superior footing, tell him of a very different land from the well-known countries of western Europe. He will wonder at the extremes of civilization he encounters, ranging from high culture to something lower than semi-barbarism; and, above all, he will be perplexed by the existence, unaccountable to those who have not studied Dalmatian history, of the two elements in the population,—Latin and Slavonic,—which for twelve centuries have lived on side by side without losing their difference, and which are now forced more sharply asunder than ever by the policy of the present rulers of the country.

It was with the pleasant sensation of having realized a day-dream of many years that I woke one morning to find myself steaming down the Canale di Zara, a channel perhaps three miles wide, with the low irregular coast of the mainland backed up in the distance by the Velebić mountains on the left hand, and the mountainous island of Ugliano on the right. Straight before us lay Zara, where we were to make our first acquaintance with a Dalmatian town, and our curiosity was I confess mixed with some anxiety as to the sort of accommodation we should find ; for there are no Dalmatian guide-books, and the reports that had vaguely reached us of Dalmatian inns were not encouraging. Zara makes little show from a distance, and, before we well knew we were there, we were entering the historic harbour where the French and Venetians landed after the galleys of St. Mark had burst the chain that closed the entrance. We saw nothing indeed of the mighty walls whose strength made the crusaders wonder at their own success, for they were long ago removed to make way for the more modern fortifications of the Venetian engineer Sammichieli, and these in their turn have on the sea front of the town been demolished to form the handsome promenade of the Riva nuova, much to the advantage of the city in point of airiness. Toward the harbour however the bastions and curtains of Sammichieli remain standing, with a wide quay, at which the steamers are able to lie close to the shore in deep water.

We entered the town by the Porta San Grisogono, above which the Lion of St. Mark still keeps guard, though the town is his to guard no longer. The streets along which we followed our porters were narrow and smoothly flagged for foot traffic like

those at Venice, and might very well have been on
the island of the Rialto ; a church we passed was in
the familiar Romanesque style of Italy; and many a
window met the eye with the well-known ogee arch
and billet moulding of Venetian architecture. At
first sight the town itself is thoroughly Italian, and
one is inclined to be disappointed to find so little
novelty in it ; but the crowds that throng the busy
little streets are strange enough to Western eyes
and soon bring home the fact that the Adriatic lies
between Zara and the shores of Italy. The native
Zaratini to be sure are Italian in language, garb, and
habits, but the country people of whom the town
was full when we first saw it, just at vintage-time,
show plainly in all three particulars that they belong
to a different race, which has not yet lost the picturesqueness of the Middle Ages in the humdrum of
the nineteenth century. The splendour of their embroidered garments, and the wealth of silver ornaments and coins displayed on their persons, may
perhaps smack slightly of semi-barbarism, but they
are not the less interesting on that account to those
who like to see civilization in the making ; and
though the native Dalmatians of the Latin stock
object to these gay costumes being considered
national, a foreigner may enjoy their picturesqueness,
in which point it must be admitted the advantage is
all on the side of the Croatians. The men wear
trousers of blue cloth gaily worked at the pockets,
tight to the leg and often fastened up the back of
the calf by a row of silver hooks and eyes ; and they

are shod with the opanka, a kind of sandal well adapted to the sharp rocks they have to encounter, made of a sole of thick leather turned up and stitched to form a toe, and laced over the instep with knotted and twisted thongs of leather. In the markets and bazaars the peasants may be seen bargaining for the sole leathers, which are cut for them then and there from the hide and sold by weight [1]. Above the opanka they wear a kind of spat of gay embroidery reaching a little above the ankle. The waistcoat is buttoned across on one side, and has a wide border of braid or needle-work, and the jacket has stripes of bright colour on the lappets, and an abundance of knots and tassels of coloured wools. The true Morlacco fashion is to have the hair plaited behind into a pigtail, and to wear the shirt outside the trousers, but this is less commonly to be seen in the towns now than formerly [2]. On gala days the jacket of the true Morlacco is still more splendid, made of scarlet or blue cloth richly worked with birds and flowers in coloured threads at the seams and shoulders, in the same place as the uniform of our hussars or horse-artillerymen, which is but a

[1] Wheler gives a drawing of a Morlacco or Dalmatian peasant from which it seems that the costume has changed a good deal since 1675. But the opanka was the same then as now; '*for shoes they have only a piece of Leather or sometimes of a dried Skin fitted to, and by thongs, or strings, going crossways over the back of the feet, are tyed fast to their soles.*' Wheler's Journey into Greece, p. 9.

[2] The 'gamins' of Zara amuse themselves by shouting 'izvadi košulya,' 'out with your shirt,' after those gentlemen who are known to be partisans of the Croat movement.

distant and vulgarized copy of the national garb of the Slav. A jaunty and becoming little scarlet cap with a bluntly pointed crown and a tuft of black fringe over one ear completes the costume. Both jacket and waistcoat are thickly hung with silver ornaments; zwantzigers of Maria Theresa and her husband dangling at the end of a link, buttons of filagree work or plain metal ranging from the size of a nut to that of a small hen's egg, and smaller studs sewn thickly together and several rows deep. The women wear a smock of homespun linen fastened at the throat with a filagree button, and embroidered in front and at the shoulders and wrists; a waistcoat of blue cloth open in front; a short petticoat of the same; and an apron worked in coloured wools so solidly as to be as stiff as a piece of carpet; and they have opankas and embroidered spats like the men, the latter often continued as leggings half way to the knee, and having the effect of trousers. The unmarried girls wear a scarlet cap like that of the men, but covered with embroidery and spangles, and on festivals hung round with a fringe of pendent coins. Married women change this for a large white handkerchief of homespun linen beautifully worked at the corners and edges, which covers the head, is tied under the chin, and hangs over the back and shoulders. The women are not behind the men in the profusion of their silver ornaments, and round their waists they often wear several coils of a leather band thickly studded with bright metal knobs, and sometimes with coarse stones set in brass. They wear large golden or silver gilt earrings, and on their fingers large rings of filagree, and on grand occasions their heads are thickly set with pretty filagree-headed pins. They would rather go without bread than part with their jewelry, and consequently it is not often that any of it comes into the market. Those among them who are too poor to afford silver ornaments have imitations of them in tin and brass, and some are reduced to deck themselves with cowrie-shells instead of studs and buttons, which they sew thickly over their ragged garments for want of something finer. Among the crowd were many figures so ragged, unkempt, and filthy, as to seem more than half-way to savagery.

Zara occupies a level peninsula, slightly raised above the sea, lying parallel to the mainland, and embracing a natural harbour of deep water with its entrance towards the north-west. Sites of this kind, convenient for maritime pursuits and easily secured against attacks from the landward side, abound on the coasts of Istria and Dalmatia, and were eagerly seized upon by the early colonists. Of all the Dalmatian ports however none were found to combine so many advantages as that of Zara, and none were so jealously guarded by the Venetians or thought so necessary to the security of their marine. Cattaro, in the innermost recesses of her winding 'bocche,' was a secure haven for her friends, and difficult of attack by her enemies, but she was inconvenient of access; the harbour of Ragusa was small, and lay within the city walls; that of Spalato was not safe during the storms of winter; that of Traü, though both safe and spacious, would be untenable if an enemy occupied the island that enclosed it; the magnificent haven of Sebenico was inadequately defended by fortifications; but that of Zara, lying between the mainland and the long peninsula of the city, was capacious, though the mouth was not too large to be closed by a chain, and was nearer to Venice than the rest, more roomy than most of them, and more easily defended[1]. A possession so valuable has always been strongly fortified. The Crusaders of 1202 speak with astonishment of the prodigious walls and towers that they were asked to attack[2]; and Lucio, who saw fragments of these defences, describes them as resembling the Roman walls of Spalato, and supposes that Zara was at the time of the siege still enclosed by the curtains and bastions of Roman Jadera, which were destroyed by the Crusaders after their capture of the city[3]. Of the mediæval fortifications which succeeded to these one noble tower remains, the torre 'Bovo d'Antona' near the public gardens, a picturesque pentagon with a salient angle towards what was once the open country but is now enclosed within the later lines.

[1] Their relative advantages are thus summarised by Lucio, de Regn. v. i. p. 240.
[2] 'Si virent la citè fermée de haus murs et de grans tours, et pour noient demandissiés plus bele cité né plus fort: et quant li pélerin la virent si s'en esmaièrent moult et distrent li uns à l'autre "Comment porroit estre tele cité prise, sé nostre Sires meisme ne le faisoit?"' Villehardouin, ch. xliv.
[3] De Regno, iv. p. 155.

The existing fortifications were designed by Sammichieli, and were constructed between 1543 and 1570 when Zara was considered to be in danger from the Turks. They consist of earthworks faced with masonry, and were protected by a ditch cut across the peninsula in 1409 when the Venetians for the last time recovered the city[1]. One gate alone communicated with the terra-firma, and this gave Sammichieli an opportunity of showing himself an architect as well as an engineer. It is a grand piece of simple architecture, with a spacious central arch and two lateral doorways of rusticated Doric; but its effect has been seriously injured by the filling up of the ditch which formerly washed the walls. The lower part, which is now hidden, was of fine masonry bevelled and raised in diamonds, forming a solid basement to the upper part, which now seems deficient in this respect. I am told by those who remember the gate in its original state that at least one third of its height is concealed. It used to be reached by a long bridge of wooden beams on stone piers which approached it obliquely, and not like the present road directly; and it is said the architectural effect has suffered by this change of approach. Over the arch is the Lion of St. Mark, and an inscription records the erection of the gateway in 1543[2].

[1] 'Isthmum, quamvis e saxo, perfodere, marique immisso Civitatem in Insulam redigere decreverunt.' Lucio, l. v. c. v. p. 263.

[2] Michele San Michele was born at Verona in 1484, and was much employed by the Venetians and their General the duke of

By these fortifications Zara remained enclosed till a few years ago, when their inutility under the altered conditions of modern warfare became evident; those towards the sea have now been entirely removed, and those toward the port laid out as a public garden, which affords one of the most agreeable lounges in Dalmatia. The town which was formerly very close and airless, a network of narrow streets hemmed in on all sides by earthworks that overtopped most of the private buildings, has benefited very greatly by the change.

Two main thoroughfares intersect the town, the Calle larga, leading from the Porta di Terra firma to the Piazza dell' Erbe, and the Corso parallel to it, leading from the Piazza dei Signori to the duomo. As in all ancient municipalities the piazza is the heart of the city and the centre of its life. Here are the public clock tower, the Communal palace, not now architecturally remarkable, and the loggia where the judges used to sit, and where the public acts were ratified. The latter is a dignified building of classical architecture, once open on two sides with a series of lofty arches,

Urbino as a military engineer. After repairing and renewing their forts on the Italian side, he was sent to do the same with those in Dalmatia Cyprus and Candia, and being unable to do all himself he left the execution of his plans to his nephew Giov. Girolamo, who, according to Vasari, carried out the work at Zara. The nephew died in Cyprus in 1558 or 1559, perhaps by poison, and was buried at Famagosta, and the uncle died in 1559 of grief at the extinction of his family, according to Vasari. *Vita di San Micheli.*

but now enclosed with glazed sashes and turned into a town library, endowed by the munificence of a citizen of Zara, and named after him the Bibblioteca Paravia[1]. In the interior may still be seen the stone bench and table of the Venetian judges with the Lion of St. Mark on the wall above. In this piazza is the principal caffè, with two rows of tables in front under an awning, between which flows the full tide of the life of Zara. Morlacco peasants with hand trucks and wine skins and sometimes even carts, Austrian officers in full uniform, contadini gay with embroidery and silver ornaments, civilians of Zara, ladies and gentlemen, in ordinary European garb, rural police in scarlet jackets like the peasants, but laden to an incredible extent with buttons and even balls of massive silver, priests of the Latin Church in black, Franciscan friars in brown, Greek priests with wide blue sashes round their cassocks, shovel hats, and flowing beards, all pass in a never-ending procession through the two lines of guests who sit breakfasting or drinking coffee in front of the Caffè agli Specchi, and form a never-failing source of interest and amusement to the traveller who takes his place among them.

The military bands play at night in the piazza, which is then crowded with the townsfolk, while

---

[1] I must express my sense of the obligations I am under to the authorities of the Bibblioteca Paravia for the liberal use allowed me of their collection, which contains many books rarely to be found beyond the limits of Dalmatia.

perhaps the moon lights up one-half of the square and falls brilliantly on the Torre dell' Orologio, and one may sit and listen and be reminded of Florian and the arcades of the Procuratie of St. Mark.

A short way eastward from the Piazza is the Campo di San Simeone with a single Roman column standing in the open space, and beyond that are the public gardens, and the cinque pozzi which supply the city with water. They were constructed by Sammichieli, and are supplied with water from sources outside the city which passes through an elaborate system of filtering beds before reaching the wells from which it is drawn[1]. Branches are led from this supply to other parts of the town, but for the most part I believe the inhabitants depend on the water that runs from their own roofs. The sky is the only source from which fresh water is obtained in the smaller towns of Dalmatia, and especially on the islands, where there are neither springs nor streams; and as even in this dry country the supply rarely fails, one may believe what has been said of the sufficiency of the water from our own roofs in England for all our domestic wants. In the courtyards of the houses and in the cloisters of the convents the whole area is excavated to form an immense cistern; a wall is built round it, and the bottom and sides are puddled with clay; a cylinder of dry masonry or

[1] Sammichieli's plans have been engraved, and the contrivance they show of filtering beds and subterranean channels is curious. A copy is in the possession of an architect living at Zara.

brickwork is raised in the middle as high as the ground level; and the area of the cistern round the cylinder and within the puddled walls is filled with sand which is wetted repeatedly till it has sunk to the utmost. The yard is then paved over, and holes are left in the paving to allow the water from the surrounding roofs to soak into the sand, through which it finds its way, filtered from all impurities, into the central cylinder, which is in fact the well from which it is drawn. On the top of this well is set the well-known Venetian 'pozzo' of marble or Istrian stone, which adorns the centre of every campo and the cortile of every house in Dalmatia as it does in Venice, where the same mode of constructing cisterns and filtering the rain water has prevailed for centuries[1]. It is only necessary to change the sand periodically in order to ensure a supply of water which is probably safer and purer than any derived from springs or rivers, although the latter are not exposed to contamination as they are with us, for in Dalmatia so far as I have observed there are no house drains.

Following the Corso westward we arrived at the Duomo, a building which in point of design and execution need not fear comparison with the Lombard churches of Italy which it resembles, and which as the first great church we saw in Dalmatia raised our expectations of the architecture

[1] Wheler describes the construction of cisterns on this plan at Venice in his time. Journey into Greece, p. 13.

of the province. Near it is the other great square, the Piazza dell' Erbe or vegetable market, the best place in Zara to see the Croatians and Morlacchi in their picturesque costume. Here there is another isolated Roman column with a tablet and cross of Byzantine workmanship attached to the front of it, beside which dangle some chains with hinged rings to clip the neck hands or feet of culprits condemned to the 'berlina' or pillory, who sat here in the fetters of the Law with the Gospel cross over their heads. These grim instruments have swung in the wind so long that the arcs they describe at the end of their chains are graven deeply in the marble of the column.

From the Piazza dell' Erbe the outer or seaward shore of the peninsula is now reached directly, all the fortifications having been removed on this side. In their place vast many storied-buildings are rapidly rising, such as are to be seen in the new quarters of any Italian town. A really magnificent promenade with rows of acacias is being formed along this shore, which when finished will be a very agreeable addition to the resources of the place. The channel of the sea which it borders is here perhaps three or four miles wide, and the opposite shore is formed by the long narrow island of Ugliano, which rises into a chain of miniature mountains, one of which is crowned by the ruins of the castle of S. Michele, which played an important part in the history of Zara.

The history of Zara is in fact the history of

Dalmatia, for Zara was throughout the middle ages the most important city of the province, and the principal object of dispute between the Venetians and the Hungarians. It is, therefore, unnecessary to do more than recapitulate briefly the principal events and revolutions of which Zara was the scene, referring for details to the general history of the country already given.

Jadera, already in alliance with Rome, received a Roman colony in the year 78 B.C. Its prosperity under the Empire may be conjectured from the remains of splendid buildings that are still to be seen there, but it was probably eclipsed by the older capital Salona. It may be safely conjectured that Jadera did not escape the Avars, but perished like the other cities of the coast; and the conjecture is supported by the story of Archidiaconus that some refugees from Salona found their way to the harbour of an ancient but ruined town which they inhabited and named Iadria after their own river Iader, whose delicious waters bathed the walls of their deserted Salona[1].

Zara, however, recovered from her ruin, and received again the Latin population that had fled to the islands, and in 752, when the Lombards took Ravenna, the Byzantine fleet was removed

---

[1] Thomas Archid. c. ix. I must not omit an equally original derivation of the name of Zara by Constantine Porphyrogenitus. ὅτι τὸ κάστρον τῶν Διαδώρων καλεῖται τῇ 'Ρωμαίων διαλέκτῳ ἰὰμ ἔρατ, ὅπερ ἑρμηνεύεται ἀπάρτι ἦτον· δηλονότι ὅτε ἡ 'Ρώμη ἐκτίσθη, προεκτισμένον ἦν τὸ τοιοῦτον κάστρον· ἔστι δὲ τὸ κάστρον μέγα. ἡ δὲ κοινὴ συνήθεια καλεῖ αὐτὸ Διάδωρα. De adm. Imp. c. 29.

to Zara, which became the capital of the province and seat of the Byzantine duke. Her submission to Pietro Orseolo II in 998 did not interfere with the nominal sovereignty of the Empire, which was only broken down by the Hungarian conquest of 1105.

The Venetians recovered Zara in 1116, and from that time forward the retention of that city was the mainspring of their policy in Dalmatia[1]. Four times the Zaratini rebelled; the first revolt was in 1178, when they threw themselves on the protection of the Hungarians, and were not reconquered till 1202; they rebelled a second time in 1242, but were recovered with little bloodshed after a few months; in 1311 they rebelled a third time, but were forced to submit in 1313; and their fourth revolt, in 1345, was crushed in 1346, in spite of the assistance of Lewis of Hungary. In 1357, however, the Hungarians were treacherously admitted within the walls by the abbot of S. Michele, and in the following year the peace was signed at Zara by which Venice ceded to Hungary all her rights in Dalmatia. In 1403 Ladislaus of Naples was crowned at Zara king of Hungary with all its dependencies, and on the failure of his attempt in 1409 he sold Zara with Pago Novigrad and Vrana to the Venetians, in whose possession it remained till the downfall of the Republic in 1797. Thus during the eight centuries that followed the expedition of Pietro Orseolo Zara was only

[1] Vid. sup. History, chapt. i. pp. 51–72.

eighty years in all out of the possession of the Venetians.

Of Roman architecture there are abundant traces at Zara, though for the most part they consist of fragments. There are the two antique columns in the piazze, of which the most important is that in the Piazza dell' Erbe, which according to one theory is actually standing where the Romans placed it, though Professor Hauser believes it to be an antique column set up by the Venetians where we now see it, to carry the Lion of St. Mark, whose image adorns the top[1]. It is a fine Corinthian column, more than four feet in diameter and thirty-four in height, not fluted, still retaining its defaced capital, and it evidently belonged to the peristyle of a temple of considerable grandeur and magnificence. Wheler, who visited Zara in 1675, speaks of a second column standing with this one[2], which confirms the theory of its being in its original place.

The column in the Piazza di S. Simeone, or 'della colonna,' at the opposite end of the town, is a fluted Corinthian column less perfect than the other; it has been sawn into lengths, and the lower part is missing, so that the flutings run out on the modern base without being properly stopped.

---

[1] Vid. Hauser e Bulić, Il tempio di S. Donato in Zara, pp. 6, 16. Sp. Artale. Zara, 1884.

[2] 'Near the Greek church dedicated to Saint Helie are two Corinthian Pillars, whose first Chapters and Bases are of very good work.' Wheler, p. 11.

This also no doubt once carried the Venetian lion.

Close by this column I was fortunate enough, in 1884, to see exposed the base of a Roman building which seemed to have been a triumphal arch of considerable grandeur. The pedestal, or rather basement, of one side of the arch remained, and on it were lying in disorder various fragments of the architraves and other members of the upper part. The excavations had not been carried down to the base, but the original level of the ground on which the arch stood could not have been less than eight or nine feet below the present level of the piazza. This interesting fragment of Roman magnificence was only exposed for a short time, and on my return a few weeks afterwards I found it had been covered up again.

Another piece of Roman antiquity is the gateway, or rather fragment of a gateway, now forming the inner face of the Porta S. Grisogono, though evidently brought there from elsewhere. It consists of an archway flanked by Corinthian columns, whose lower half is imperfect, which carry a horizontal entablature. The frieze bears this inscription :—

MELIA ANNIANA IN MEMOR. Q. LAEPICI. Q. F. SERG. BASSI MARITI SVI EMPORIVM STERNI ET ARCVM FIERI ET STATVAS SVPERPONI TEST. IVSS EX IIS $\overline{\mathrm{DCDXX}}$. P. R.[1]

[1] Prof. Bulić interprets the last words *ex sestertiis $\overline{DC}$ deducta vigesima Populi Romani*. That is to say, there was a handsome market-place adorned with statues formed at the cost of about

There is a tradition that this gateway was brought to Zara from the old Roman town of Aenona nine or ten miles off. It would be curious if it should prove instead to have belonged to the triumphal arch near S. Simeone.

In the public gardens are to be seen several old Roman inscriptions and fragments of classic work, and there are many others in the museum that has been formed in the disused church of S. Donato. But perhaps the richest and certainly the most curious collection of Roman remains is that which recent discoveries have brought to light under the very walls of that church, and which we shall presently describe. They have been traced by the industry of Prof. Hauser to at least four distinct buildings, all of a magnificent character, and two of them on a magnificent scale. There are also pedestals among them of elaborate workmanship, which must have carried seated statues either for worship within the temples or for adornment of the public squares. All this together with the remains above ground, which have been already described, shew that Jadera must have been a city of wealth and consideration, adorned with handsome buildings, and not unworthy of comparison with some of the great provincial cities of Italy.

600,000 sesterces. Wheler by the simple confusion of sestertii and sestertia makes the cost '*six hundred and thirty Sestertia, which is a piece of money that weigheth about Two pence halfpeny, and amounts to near Twelve pounds sterling; which was a great deal of money in those days.*'

CHAPTER IV.

Zara.

The churches of S. Donato, S. Pietro vecchio, S. Lorenzo, S. Domenica, S. Orsola, the cathedral of S. Anastasia, the church of S. Grisogono, the convents of S. Maria and S. Francesco, the church and silver ark of S. Simeone, etc., etc.

Zara possesses a tolerably complete series of architectural examples of every period from the eighth century downwards. It is particularly rich in buildings of the earlier styles, although with one notable exception they have to be hunted for and discovered under various disguises as magazines hay-lofts and cellars; but that one exception, the Church of the Holy Trinity, now known as S. Donato, is not likely to be overlooked by the most casual visitor. From the interior of the town this church is not much seen it is true, being enclosed by the cathedral on one side and the houses of the Piazza dell' Erbe on the other; but from a distance the lofty central drum with its pyramidal roof is the most conspicuous building that appears above the walls.

During the past hundred years it has been put to a variety of uses. In 1798 it ceased to be used for religious purposes, the pictures were dispersed, the altars sold, and the Austrian government turned it into a military store, inserting a floor to divide it into two stories. In 1870 it was restored to the authorities of the cathedral who let it to the 'Società enologica di Zara.' In 1877, chiefly in consequence of the attention directed to it by the publications of Professor Eitelberger, it was rescued from the neglect into which it had fallen; the modern floor was removed, and the building is now devoted to the purposes of a museum for the numerous objects of antiquity discovered at Zara, which had previously no home.

S. DONATO (vid. Plan, Fig. 1)[1] is a round church of the same type as that of S. Vitale at Ravenna and the cathedral of Aix-la-Chapelle, though it differs from both in many particulars. It has a circular space in the centre surrounded by a circular aisle, and from the aisle three apses project eastward, of which the middle one is larger than the other two. This principal apse does not open to the church as at S. Vitale by a lofty arch of the height of the central space, but all three apses are vaulted at the lower level of the circular aisle. Above this aisle and the apses is an upper story like a triforium, opening to the central space, and it is to this upper gallery or triforium, which has three apses of its own over the others, that Constantine Porphyro-

[1] For my plan, Fig. 1, I have reduced to the same scale and put together the plan of S. Donato by Prof. Hauser, and that of S. Anastasia by Prof. Eitelberger, and supplemented them by additions and corrections of my own.

genitus refers when he says there was a second church over the first[1]. The ascent to this upper

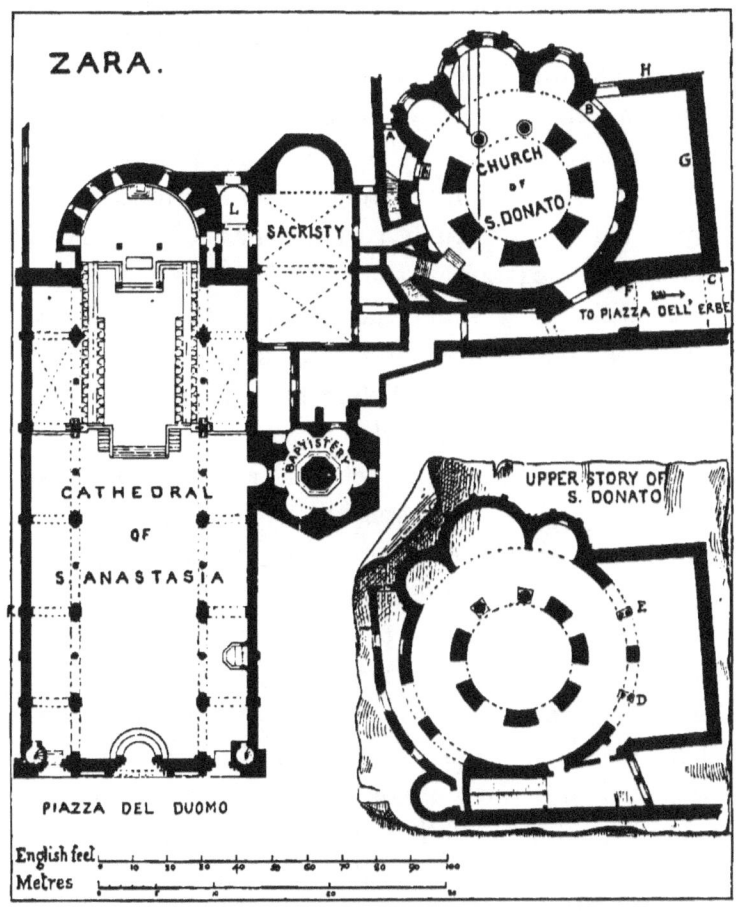

Fig. 1.

[1] Ἔστι δὲ καὶ ἕτερος ναὸς πλησίον αὐτοῦ (sc. the church of S. Anastasia) εἰληματικός, ἡ ἁγία Τριάς· καὶ ἐπάνω τοῦ ναοῦ αὐτοῦ πάλιν ἕτερος ναὸς δίκην κατηχουμένων, καὶ αὐτὸς εἰληματικός, εἰς ὃν καὶ ἀνέρχονται διὰ κοχλείας. Const. Porph. de adm. Imp. ch. 29. The church was originally dedicated to the Trinity.

church is διὰ κοχλείας, by a stair that winds round the outer wall, and now falls in with another stair that has been contrived below it, after which the two together form a grand flight for the rest of the ascent, landing in a kind of atrium or antechamber from which the upper church is entered. The second stair however is evidently a subsequent addition, for it cuts through and obliterates the lower part of a circular turret which was probably the campanile; and as the stairs have been used for a 'Santa Scala' which the devout ascended as at Rome on their knees, the second stair was no doubt added for convenience of descent while the first was being used for ascent in this manner.

This gallery or upper church probably was, as Porphyrogenitus suggests, the church of the catechumens, and it had its own distinct entrance from the outside of the church by a little doorway at A. (vid. plan) at the foot of the staircase[1]. This is now blocked up, but those who have the enthusiasm proper to archaeologists, and do not mind into what dirty places they go in search of their object, may see, as I did, the outside of it with its curiously carved hoodmould, which is remarkable as the only original architectural detail in the building (Fig. 2), every other piece of carving—and there are but few—being stolen from Roman Jadera.

[1] The present door leading from the church to the stairs is modern, dated 1733. Whether the upper church were intended for catechumens or for women it would be equally in accordance with ancient usage to provide a distinct entrance to it outside the church. Vid. also Mr. Butler's Coptic Churches, vol. i. p. 20.

Indeed nothing could well be ruder than the construction of this great church. Externally it is perhaps no plainer than S. Vitale at Ravenna, or other buildings of the age of Justinian, but *they* are as superbly and delicately finished within as they are simple without, while S. Donato is no finer inside than it is outside. The central space, as has

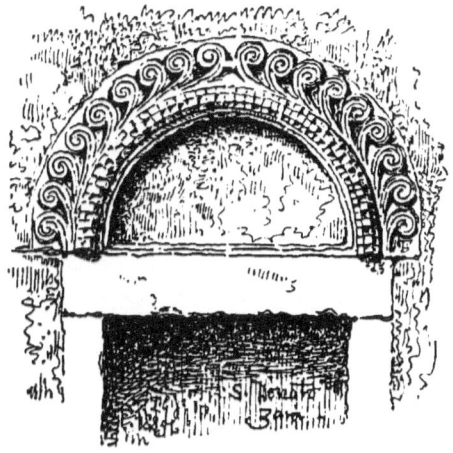

Fig. 2.

been explained already, runs up the full height of the building and was covered by a dome which has now fallen in; the circular aisle opens into the central space by eight round arches, and is ceiled with an annular barrel vault which forms the floor of the upper gallery. The original stair is ceiled in the same way. Six of the eight piers on each floor between aisle and central area are huge masses of plain masonry which are actually wider than their intercoluminations, and the remaining two, which carry the arches opening into the apses, are ancient monolithic columns with ancient capitals. The two columns on the ground floor have preserved their full proportions and bear composite Roman capitals, similar, Prof. Hauser observes, to those of the arch of Septimius Severus at Rome[1]. The upper pair of columns are truncated in order to fit the height allowed for them; one of their capitals is Corinthian, and the other was once composite, but its lower part seems to me to have been rudely cut again in Byzantine times in order to reduce it to the necessary diameter, only the upper part of the original composite capital remaining as the Roman workman left it.

The central dome is now gone, and the wooden roof with its tiling is exposed to view from within the church; the circular aisle of the upper church also has lost its vaulting, if it ever had any as the καὶ αὐτὸς εἰλημματικός implies, though there is little evidence for it in the building itself.

The circular gallery of the upper floor is not so simple in plan as that of the lower. In the first place it has on the north side a second or outer aisle communicating with it by arches, and occupying the space over the staircase; in the next there may be seen on the south side at D—E (vid. plan of upper story) some columns and arches now walled up, but evidently shewing there was once something beyond on this side also. I believe Prof. Hauser has conjectured that there was a second

[1] Il tempio di S. Donato in Zara. Hauser e Bulić. Zara, 1884.

κοχλεία on this side, but there is no evidence for this, nor does it seem as if it could have arrived at the upper level soon enough to land at these arches. Some further explanation is required; and a clue is furnished by an impost moulding at C (vid. plan) in the wall of a house adjoining the church which resembles those of the interior, and seems to imply that the wall F—C is coeval with and part of the church itself. In company with Monsignor Bianchi and Professor Smirich, the Imperial Conservator of Monuments at Zara, I penetrated a dense net-work of courts and houses to the south of the church, and by hunting in cellars and mounting to attics succeeded in tracing at H and G walls four feet thick, forming a square building of the full height of the double-storied aisle. This building had no opening to the church on the ground floor except by the doorway at B (vid. plan) which though blocked is still visible, but on the upper floor it evidently opened to the gallery or triforium by two pairs of arches springing each from a central column D—E (vid. plan of upper floor) which may be seen even more plainly on the outside of the wall than the inside. This made a large addition to the area of the upper story, and rendered it worthy to be described as *another church above the first*, an expression which seems hardly applicable to a mere gallery such as it now is. The central columns of the arches of communication would, I believe, be found if the wall were opened to be double, one behind the other, for a column is visible close to the surface both inside and outside of the wall, which is much thicker than the diameter of a single shaft. The capital of one of them can be reached from an attic window and proves to be nothing but a classic base reversed, so that though the architectonic idea of these arcades was graceful their execution was probably very coarse and inartistic.

The same criticism may be applied to the other scanty examples of architectural detail that the building contains. The walls of the aisle are decorated, if it can be called decoration, by curious elongated niches, which run up the whole height of the story, and are really not so much niches as prodigious flutings of the surface, and the impost mouldings from which the vaulting and arches spring are meagre in the extreme.

Such is the church of the Holy Trinity, a structure rude almost to the verge of barbarism, but which does not fail to derive a certain simple dignity from its ponderous construction (vid. Plate II). Many theories have been broached as to its age and builder. Some writers of daring but uncritical imagination have seen in these rough walls a veritable temple of the polished age of Augustus, converted as they suppose to Christian uses by Donatus I, who was bishop of Zara in the fifth century. This theory requires no comment. Another theory is that it was built by Bishop Donatus II, at the end of the fourth or beginning of the fifth century, which would make it older than S. Vitale, a church which is much more likely to have

ZARA   Plate II.

T.G.J   S Donato

been the model from which it was imitated, for the comparative rudeness of the work at S. Donato points to a ruder and later age than that of Justinian. The most probable theory is that the church was built by Bishop Donatus III, at the beginning of the ninth century. This prelate, who has been called the Ambrose of Zara, accompanied Beato Doge of Venice in 804 as envoy from Charlemagne to the Emperor Nicephorus at Constantinople, to compose the quarrel that had arisen between the Empires out of the Frank conquest of Dalmatia. In the year 806 he visited the court of Charlemagne at Thionville in company with 'Paulus dux Jaderae,' as an envoy from the Dalmatians, bringing their submission and laden with offerings to their new master[1]. The treaties of 810 and 812 between the two Emperors, by which the maritime cities of Dalmatia were restored to the Eastern Empire and Zara became the capital of the Byzantine province, may have given a stimulus to new building plans, and Donatus, whose extensive travels had acquainted him with the churches of Constantinople and Italy, and probably that of Aquisgranum, was better qualified than his predecessors to originate so vast a scheme as that of the church of the Holy Trinity.

But we have not yet exhausted the wonders of S. Donato; the most curious part is still to come. Built into one of the piers close to the entrance may be seen a large marble block, between six and seven

---

[1] Vid. General History in chapt. i, p. 22, note.

VOL. I. S

feet long and three feet high, with the following inscription in a panel surrounded by an arabesqued border:—

IVNONI · AVGVSTAE
APPVLEIA · M · FIL · QVINTA
SVO ET · L· TVRPILII BROCCHI
LICINIANI · FILII · NOMINE
TEST ·   PONI ·   IVSS

This inscription, which was known and published as long ago as 1435[1], misled the earlier antiquaries into taking the existing building for classical work, but recent explorations have explained the history of this stone, as well as that of the classical columns and capitals in front of the apses. In 1877 the old pavement of the Christian church was taken up and the area excavated to the depth of about four feet. At this level was found the ancient pavement of a Roman street or forum, and running diagonally across the area of the church were the two lower steps of what had evidently been a flight leading up to a portico (vid. Fig. 1). But the most surprising spectacle revealed by this excavation is that of the foundations of the Christian work. They consist of huge fragments of more than one magnificent classic building, entablatures with Corinthian enrichments, marble columns cut or broken into lengths and laid simply on their side, rich friezes with running scroll-work in the best style of Roman architecture,

[1] By Ciriaco Anconitano. Bulić, p. 8.

dedicatory inscriptions, mouldings, and string courses, all thrown flat on the pavement of the Roman town, some on their sides, some upside down, and some arranged cornerwise or awry with a rough approximation to the plan of the superstructure. The whole mass of these fragments was filled in with earth and rubbish, and covered over with the pavement of the Christian church, so that till now their existence was not even suspected. The two pairs of columns that were saved and used in front of the apses were probably spared not from any admiration or respect, but simply from the difficulty of making new ones in that rude age. The rest seems to have been trodden underfoot with an ascetic scorn for the meretricious splendour of Pagan rites and Pagan temples, and with a sublime irony to have been made to carry the simple piers and coarse masonry of the Christian church. It reminded me of the figure of St. Gereon at his church in Cologne, making a pedestal of the crouching figure of Diocletian his ancient persecutor,—pride spiritual crushing pride temporal.

By a systematic examination of the fragments Prof. Hauser is led to conclude that there are among them the spoils of at least four public buildings. Two of these were of magnificent dimensions, their columns being about thirty feet in height; both were of the Corinthian order, one with fluted and the other with plain columns, corresponding respectively with the two columns now standing in the two squares of Zara. The block with the inscription '*Junoni Augustae*,' and a companion one dedicated by the same lady '*Jovi Augusto*' which the recent discoveries have unearthed, were probably pedestals of sitting statues of the two divinities, but whether the divinities were really Jupiter and Juno, or Augustus and Livia under those titles, is a question which archaeologists will probably debate without ever arriving at an unanimous conclusion.

The fact that the fragments of classical architecture on which S. Donato rests belonged not to one but to several buildings disposes of the old story that a temple of Augustus and Livia standing on this site was purposely thrown down to make way for it. In the ninth century Zara was no doubt full of ruined buildings, of which a temple so dedicated may have been one; and they no doubt served the townspeople as a quarry, that being the general use to which buildings of '*the Pagans*' were put in the middle and dark ages. To form the foundations of the new church the largest blocks that could be found would be collected from various parts of the town and rudely arranged on the old Roman pavement, while the smaller fragments would be used in building the superstructure as ordinary walling stones with their wrought faces inwards. In all probability the upper walls are largely composed of old materials of this kind, and in fact several pieces of Roman moulding may be observed in the old walls right and left of the corridor by which the church is approached from the piazza.

It is singular that the builders of S. Donato

should have trusted so confidently to the solidity of the Roman pavement as to build their vast walls and piers upon it without any foundation. The pavement has stood this unfair test better than might have been expected, and has carried the church for a thousand years, but settlements have nevertheless taken place, and there are serious fissures in the wall in several places.

The old pavement has been traced under the adjacent buildings for a considerable distance: I found it everywhere within the area F C G H on the south of the church, and the walls G and H were built just like those of the church on fragments of Roman architecture simply thrown down on the ancient flagging.

In size the church of S. Donato is inferior to its companions at Ravenna and Aix-la-Chapelle, and in point of workmanship it is as far inferior to Aix-la-Chapelle as Aix-la-Chapelle to S. Vitale. The area of the points of support at Zara is far greater in comparison to the voids, and the proportions are far less pleasing, the central space under the cupola being so narrow in relation to its height as to resemble a lofty hollow tower rather than a domed area. For both these reasons it is very difficult to get any satisfactory view of the interior, and the difficulty is increased by the insufficient light. In its original state the church must have been darker even than it is at present, for most of the windows are modern insertions, and even now the church is badly lighted.

S. PIETRO VECCHIO, which according to some

opinions is the oldest church in Zara, is now a storehouse forming the ground floor of a private dwelling in a street near the Piazza dei Signori[1]. It consists of a double nave with a central arcade, a

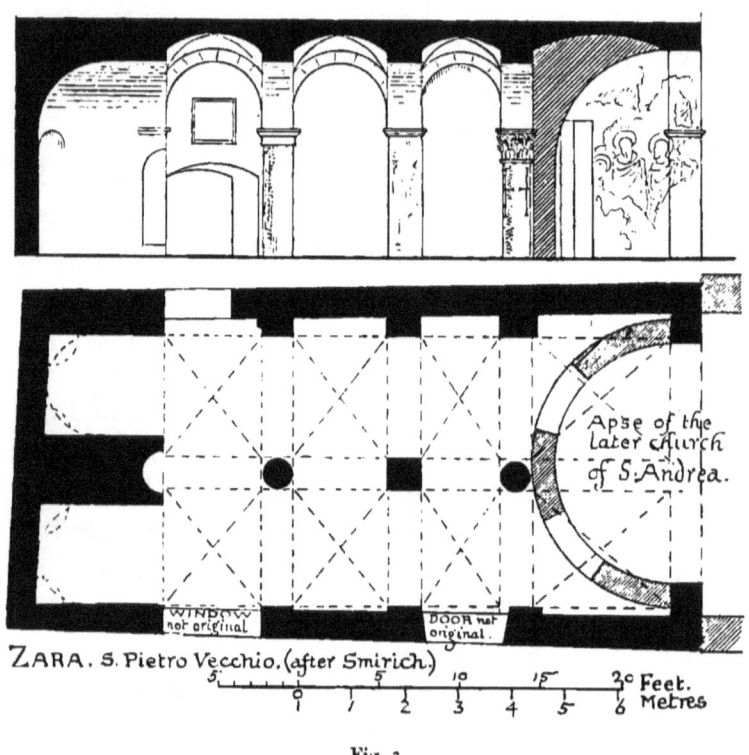

Fig. 3.

very unusual plan in this country and at this date. The east end of both the naves is square, but the angles of the square are brought into a semicircular plan at the springing of the vaults by squinches,

[1] I am indebted to Prof. Smirich of Zara for the plan and section of this building, Fig. 3.

and the vaulting thus finishes with a semidome just as if the plan had been apsidal. This device is very common in Dalmatia[1]. The western part is destroyed to make way for the apse of the later church of S. Andrea, itself now desecrated and turned into a magazine. This apse has traces of fifteenth-century painting. The arcade dividing the two naves is made up of fragments of Roman work clumsily adapted, one round column being actually fitted with a capital that belonged to a square pilaster, while the other has by way of capital what looks like a classic base upside down. The capital of the western pilaster is raffled in the Roman way. The other imposts from which the arches spring are simply moulded, and the vaults are very unskilfully formed and ill-shaped. This church might be of any age up to the eighth century. It is said to be mentioned in a will of the year 908[2].

S. LORENZO is a church partly destroyed, and partly in tolerable preservation, now serving as a lumber room to the house of the Austrian Commandant in the Piazza dei Signori. (Plate III.) It is said to be mentioned in a document of the year 919[3]. The architectural features of this church are partly made up with antique fragments, but there is some original work among them as well, and this may perhaps be taken to show that it is of somewhat later date than those churches which are entirely

---

[1] E.g. S. Croce at Nona, S. Barbara at Traü. See above, page 211.
[2] Bianchi, Zara Cristiana, vol. i. p. 380.
[3] Ibid. p. 447.

made up of stolen odds and ends. At A (vid. Plate III) is a granite column, diminished with entasis, and carrying a Byzantinesque cap which has no necking. The impost block above it seems to be the base of an antique pedestal, being moulded on three sides but plain on the fourth, as if it had stood against a wall. B has the capital of which I give a separate drawing (Plate I. Fig. 6). Though rudely cut it is not without character, and looks like work of the ninth or tenth century, and as it fits its shaft correctly it was no doubt worked for its place. The capital of C is apparently of the same date, but it is placed on an old granite column which is too large for it; one leaf is carved with the figure of a saint, perhaps S. Lorenzo, and it has the traditional caulicoli of the antique Corinthian capital, but otherwise resembles B. D has an antique capital of purely Roman character.

The apse has disappeared, and the western part of the church is shut off by a wall with a grating, behind which it is said were the Venetian prisons, the grating serving to allow condemned criminals to hear mass.

The vaulting is singular: that of the nave is a plain barrel with a transverse rib at each bay springing from an animal now too much defaced for recognition, but the little aisles are strangely vaulted with a succession of semidomes on squinches facing sideways. The original north door, which has been removed for security to the museum in S. Donato, has jambs decorated with a Romanesque

ZARA. Plate III

T.G.J. S. Lorenzo

running pattern, and a lintel formed like a pediment with a representation of Our Lord within an oval wreath supported by an angel on either hand. The form of this door-head resembles that of the old duomo at Pola which bears the date 850 (vid. inf. chap. xxx. Fig. 103). The windows were rounded headed slits, one to a bay, but all are now blocked.

S. DOMENICA, once S. Giovanni in Pusterla[1], is artistically the most interesting church of this group, though probably not so old as the preceding. It is raised on a cruciform crypt, and the upper church consists of a nave and aisles, cross vaulted and tied with iron rods, and reached by an external stair with a door in the side wall, which is ornamented with Romanesque scroll-work. The imposts of the vaults are carved with knot-work of the same style and period. The east end is square externally but formed into three apses internally, the side ones so small as to be mere niches. Built into the exterior wall is a bas-relief of the ninth or tenth century, representing the salutation, the nativity, the adoration of the shepherds, and the visit of the Magi, in groups under seven arches, and corresponding in style and dimensions with another carved slab in the museum so closely that they are supposed to have formed the front or back of the same altar.

---

[1] It was dedicated to S. Giovanni Battista, and stood near the postern gate. 'In scrittura infatti del 1446 leggesi, Chiesa di S. Giovanni Battista ovvero di S. Domenica.' Bianchi, Antichità Romane e Medievali di Zara. Zara, 1883, p. 36.

The church has a picturesque little campanile on one side. It is now desecrated and belongs to the family Stermich or Strmić: the crypt serves as a cellar and the church as a hayloft.

A smith who lives opposite invited us into his house to see an old wooden crucifix which he said once hung in this church. The figure is about four feet high, and though now black was once painted naturally. The feet are placed side by side, not crossed. The style is that of the thirteenth century, but this in Dalmatia is not conclusive as to its date.

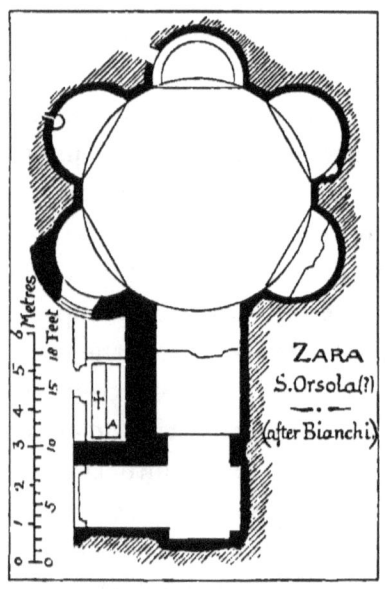

Fig. 4.

S. ORSOLA. The foundations of another very curious church, resembling in plan the ancient baptistery of the Duomo, and supposed to have been dedicated to S. Orsola, were discovered in 1883, when the sea-front of Sammichieli's fortifications was demolished to make way for the Riva nuova. At A (vid. Fig. 4) was found a sarcophagus consisting of a fragment of a large fluted column hollowed out just as savages hollow out the solid trunk of a tree to form a boat, and covered with a coped lid on which was carved a cross. Inside there was a skeleton which apparently had never been disturbed.

The foundations of the church were covered up again because they came inconveniently in the middle of a roadway, but their outline may still be traced obscurely on the surface of the ground. The sarcophagus has been removed to the yard at the east end of the duomo. From the plan of the church it seems probable that there was a campanile over the western end[1].

S. VITO, a very early and interesting church, has lately been destroyed to make way for a new shop. It is described by Monsign. Bianchi and Professor Freeman.

THE DUOMO. The cathedral of Zara, dedicated to S. Anastasia, is one of those buildings that perplex the antiquary who is new to the architecture of Dalmatia. He would, to be sure, see at once that it is not the church which Porphyrogenitus describes as floored with marvellous mosaics and decorated with paintings that were ancient even in the tenth century[2]. Some of the columns of cipoll-

---

[1] The plan was taken by Prof. Smirich and published by Monsignor Bianchi in his Antichità Romane e Medievali di Zara. Compare La Trinità near Spalato, Fig. 40, and the Baptistery at Zara, Fig. 1. See also above, p. 212.

[2] Ὁ δὲ ναὸς τῆς ἁγίας Ἀναστασίας ἐστὶ δρομικός, ὅμοιος τῷ Χαλκοπρατίων ναῷ, μετὰ κιόνων πρασίνων καὶ λευκῶν, ὅλος εἰκονισμένος ἐξ ὑλογραφίας ἀρχαίας· ὁ δὲ πάτος αὐτοῦ ἐστὶν ἀπὸ συγκοπῆς θαυμαστῆς. Const. Porph. de adm. Imp. c. xxix. The church of the Θεοτόκος in Chalcopratcia, a district of Constantinople, was originally a syna-

ino and white marble which he mentions may perhaps still be doing duty in the nave arcades, and fragments of the famous mosaics are still to be seen in the floor mixed with the pavements of a later age; but the heavy cushion capitals in the nave resembling our earliest Norman work, the alternation of clustered piers with single columns dividing the nave into double bays, and the arcading which covers the west front and runs along the north side recalling the duomo of Pisa, all belong evidently to a later period than the Byzantine, though they might still be taken for work of the twelfth century. It seems, however, tolerably certain that the present building was not begun before the thirteenth, and as that century opened with the capture and partial destruction of Zara by the crusaders it is natural that tradition should connect the rebuilding of the cathedral with the ruin of the city at that time. According to one story therefore the crusaders, prompted by remorse for their destruction of a Christian city and the reproaches of Innocent III, rebuilt the duomo, or rather, we must suppose, left funds behind them for rebuilding it, for they sailed from Zara after four months' stay. But although it is true that Innocent in his letter to the Doge Henrico Dandolo accuses him of having destroyed churches, on the other hand we have the statement

gogue granted to the Jews by Constantine, and was consecrated as a church 130 years later by Pulcheria. Theophanes, p. 158, ed. Bonn. It is curious to find in πράσινος an equivalent to the Italian 'cipollino.'

of Thomas Archidiaconus, who was an eyewitness of the rebuilding of Zara, to the effect that the crusaders 'left nothing but the churches standing,' from which it would seem that the old cathedral survived that disaster[1]. Whatever uncertainty, however, may exist as to the reason of the rebuilding and the date when it was begun, we know for certain that the new cathedral was consecrated by Archbishop Lorenzo Periandro, a native of Zara, in the year 1285[2], and taking into account the slow

[1] 'Diruerunt enim omnes muros ejus et turres per circuitum et universas domos intrinsecus, nil nisi solas Ecclesias relinquentes.' Thom. Archid. ch. xxv. Lucio says, 'Ecclesias etiam intactas relictas ipsarum antiqua structura adhuc incolumis declarat,' de Regno. iv. p. 154; but we do not know by what rule he measured their antiquity. The extent to which the city was destroyed seems to have been exaggerated. Dandolo simply says, 'maritimos muros circumquaque dirui fecit et ibidem hyemare disposuit.' Had the city been so far destroyed as to have been made uninhabitable, it would hardly have been represented as suitable for the army to winter in. 'Et lors vint li dus as contes et as barons, et leur dist: "Seigneur, nos avons ceste ville conquise, la merci Dieu et par la vostre! or est yvers entrés, et nos ne poons mais de ci movoir devant la Pasque, quar nous ne troverions mie chevance en autre leu, et cette ville si est moult riche et moult bonne, et de tous biens garnie,"' &c. Joffroi de Villehardouin, c. xlix.

[2] Lorenzo writes thus in 1285 to Gregorio, Bishop of Traü, 'Cum pridie, seu noviter, quando placuit vobis consecrationi ecclesiae nostrae personaliter interesse, praesentibus venerabilibus patre domino fratre J. archiepiscopo Spalatense, et vobis cum aliis suffraganeis ejus, atque nostris' . . . Farlati says the rebuilding was entirely the work of Lorenzo, who conceived the project as soon as he was made archbishop in 1247, 'vetus quippe . . . erat male materiata et ruinosa neque magnitudine neque structura neque elegantia dignitati sedis archiepiscopalis respondebat.' The new church was built on the same site as the old. Illyr. Sacr. Tom. v. pp. 8, 80.

rate of building during the middle ages, and more especially in a poor country like Dalmatia, we may safely assume that the work was begun at least forty or fifty years, if not more, before that date, and perhaps not very long after the opening of the century.

The plan of the cathedral (Fig. 1) is basilican still, though the age of basilicas was gone by on the opposite shores of the Adriatic; but the traditional proportions of the ancient basilicas are forgotten or neglected, for the nave is three times as wide as the aisles. Piers with semi-attached shafts alternate with cylindrical columns, forming double bays, two in the aisle to one in the nave. There are four of these double bays with a single bay beyond at each end, and they are defined by flat pilasters at each pier run up as high as the string course over the triforium. The half-columns attached to the piers have heavy cushion capitals, but the columns in the centre of the pair of arches of each double bay are of beautiful antique marble, and have capitals either of debased Roman Corinthian work or imitated from it, which probably belonged to the former basilica.

The pier at the entrance of the choir is now disguised by a stucco casing carrying a stucco arch, added absurdly in modern times to mark the division between choir and nave. This pier is richer than those in the nave, and has on three of its sides two attached columns instead of one, while on the fourth side towards the choir was a single attached column with a Corinthian capital as was ascertained during my visit by opening the stucco pier. This column and a similar one on the pier farther east ran up like vaulting shafts, though it is clear no vaulting was ever contemplated. The capitals are either of debased Roman work, or rude imitations of it in later times. They are all Corinthian in type, and have the strong Gothic abacus fully developed.

In the last double bay westward the marble columns are fluted spirally.

Above the nave arches is a string course carved with a curious leaf ornament (Fig. 5), which occurs also at Spalato and Traü, but is, so far as I know, peculiar to Dalmatia. Above this is a regular triforium of small arches springing from square piers of stone, in front of which were once coupled colonnettes supporting the moulded impost[1]. The little arches have alternate voussoirs of white stone and red breccia marble, and in their openings is a balustrade with a deceptively early look. The upper part of the walls with the roof and ceiling are modernized.

Fig. 5.

A spacious apse ends the nave eastwards. It is lined with red breccia marble to half its height; a marble seat for the clergy runs round the wall, and

---

[1] In 1885 the stucco mouldings which disguised these piers were being removed under the direction of Professor Smirich, exposing distinct traces of a pair of little columns in front of each square pier. They seem to have had square capitals and no bases.

in the centre, raised on five steps, is the bishop's seat, a marble chair of Byzantine character, ornamented with round arched panels divided by coupled shafts. The apse is lighted by six very narrow round-headed slits splayed both inside and out, so that here, as in the adjacent church of S. Donato, and several others in Istria and Dalmatia, the central space is occupied by a pier and not by a window, an arrangement somewhat strange according to our northern notions, but suggestive of the use of the wall rather than the window as a field for decoration in southern Europe. The paintings which once adorned the apse have now disappeared.

The exterior of the apse is now disguised with smooth yellow stucco, and has lost all traces of antiquity; Professor Smirich, who has seen it uncovered, tells me the masonry is not of smooth ashlar but hammer-dressed, and if this were restored to view it would not only be a great improvement artistically but might lead to some interesting discoveries. The ruder construction of this end of the church and the smallness of the windows suggest that the apse may be a relic of the older basilica.

Below the apse is an extensive crypt, to which two flights of steps descend, one on each side of the nave. The plan of the crypt is irregular, for while the apsidal end coincides with the apse walls above, the rest is much narrower than the choir, and varies in width in three places. The capitals of the stunted columns are plain, fudged out simply from the round shaft to the square of the impost, except one which

Interior of Duomo.

is carved in the style of the ninth or tenth century. Old bases of debased Roman work are used up again, and one base rests on a slab carved with interlacing knot-work laid flat on the ground, an evidence that that part at all events of the crypt is not so old as the Byzantine basilica. Another slab of the same kind, much worn, is laid in the southern flight of steps which ascends to the nave.

In the crypt is an altar formed of an imperfect slab with a relief of S. Anastasia bound to two stakes between palm trees, emblematic of her martyrdom. Her name is inscribed in Lombardic lettering of the thirteenth century, and although this may of course have been added afterwards, the style of the figure which has the feet, neck, and other parts well and naturally modelled, seems to me to point to that century rather than to an earlier one.

The choir is splendidly furnished with stalls on either hand and a magnificent marble baldacchino over the high altar, and though the rest of the interior is somewhat bare of architectural detail, this part of the church is fully worthy of the metropolitan see of Dalmatia (vid. Plate IV).

The baldacchino is on a grand scale, loftier, as the Zaratini boast, than the famous one in St. Mark's, and though it dates only from the fourteenth century it preserves all the chaste severity of an earlier style. It rests on four columns of beautiful cipollino marble which are ornamented something after the manner of our Elizabethan chimneys, the front pair being

VOL. I.   T

richly diapered with sunk work, and the back pair fluted, one of them spirally and the other in zigzags. Their capitals are imitated from classic; and one of them has little half-length figures cleverly enough contrived in the place of caulicoli. The four arches are pointed, and enclose a quadripartite vault with diagonal ribs, and the whole is crowned by a horizontal cornice of acanthus leaves[1]. The execution and detail of this splendid canopy are worthy of all praise. An inscription in Lombardic lettering on the front records its erection in the year 1332 in the archbishopric of Giovanni di Butuane (Fig. 6).

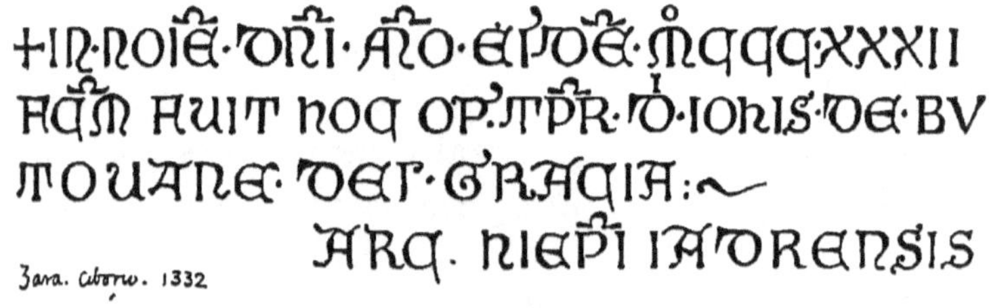

+IN·NOIE·DNI·ANO·EPOE·MCCCXXII
HCM HUIT HOC OP.TPR·O·IOHIS·DE BV
TOUANE·DEI·GRACIA:~
              ARC. NIEPI IADORENSIS

Zara. Ciborio. 1332

Fig. 6.

The choir stalls (Fig. 7) are undoubtedly the most magnificent examples of a class of woodwork that abounds in Dalmatia and the Littorale, resembling the well-known stalls of the Frari at Venice. At Parenzo Cherso Arbe Lesina Traü Spalato and Mezzo there are stalls that might almost be attributed to the same hand as these, and in Zara itself at S. Maria and S. Francesco there are two other choirs similarly furnished. The stalls of Arbe have

---

[1] The flat dome and figure of our Lord which now surmount the baldacchino are not original.

CH. IV.]   *Zara: the Duomo.*   275

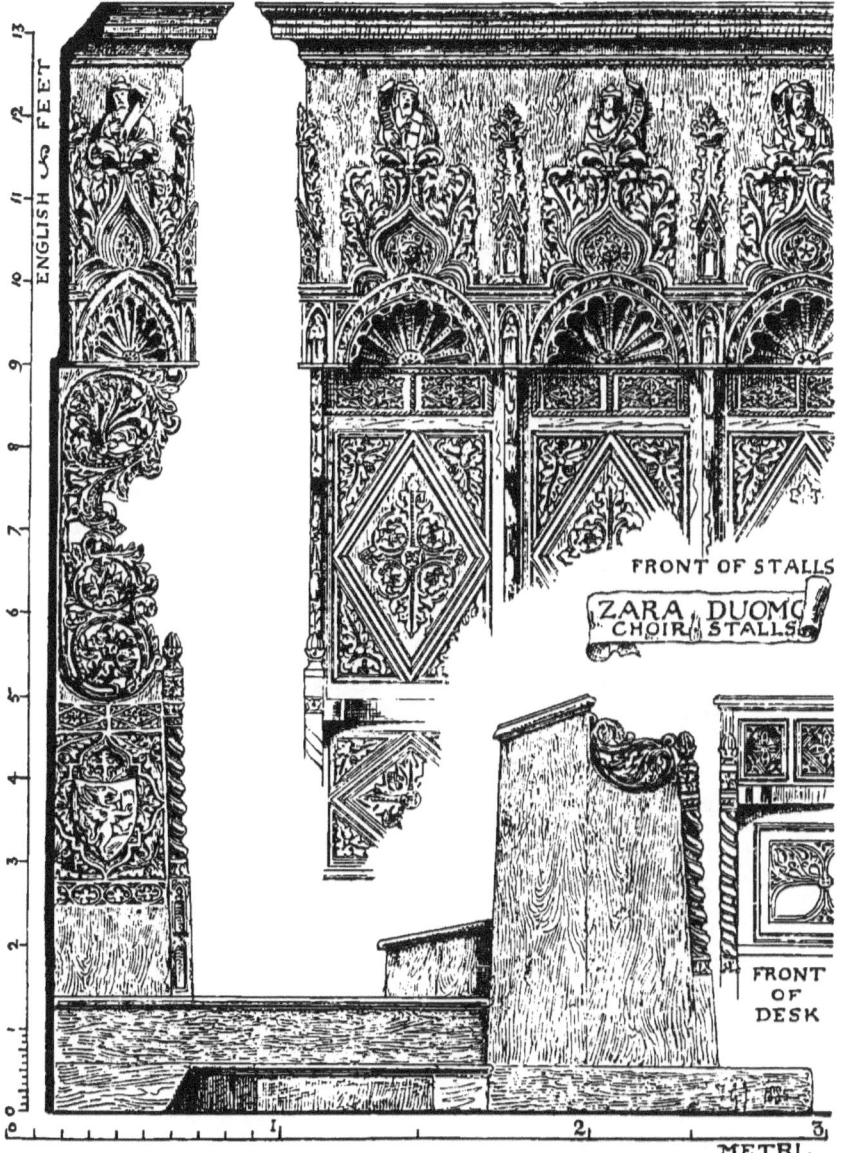

Fig. 7.

the date MCCCCXLV. upon them, and these at Zara bear the arms of four successive archbishops whose episcopates cover the period from 1400 to 1495[1]. They may be attributed to the earlier half of the fifteenth century, their date extending probably from about 1410 to 1450. In all these ten examples there is a similarity that is a little monotonous, and a coarseness of execution that is a little disappointing. They will not compare in respect of fancy and refinement with the best examples of French or German woodwork, least of all with our English work, which in point of artistic feeling for the nature of the material, and luxuriant fancy in the mode of treating it, is perhaps unrivalled. But all the same these Dalmatian carvings have a splendid freedom in their lines, and a luxurious fulness in their scrolls and flourishes that is very effective, and they shew a facility in drawing and technique that was perhaps itself a snare to the workman and a hindrance to his artistic growth. They are all no doubt the work of Venetian carvers; for we know those at S. Francesco in Zara were made by an artist born indeed in Tuscany but settled and naturalised at Venice; and though the names of the artists of the other stalls may not be known they all belong to the same Venetian school.

There are seventeen stalls on each side of the

---

[1] Luca da Fermo, 1400–1420, a griffin holding a book; Biagio Molino, 1420–1427, a mill-wheel; Lorenzo Venier, 1428–1449, six bars gules and argent; Maffeo Valaresso, 1450–1495, azure six bendlets or.

choir, including that of the archbishop on the north and that of the Venetian provveditore opposite on the south[1]. Each stall is divided not only by elbows but by shades of elaborately carved and pierced scroll-work reaching up to and supporting the canopy. The canopies are formed like fluted shells, and are surmounted by ogee gables; little half-length statuettes of prophets from Adam downwards form their finials, each holding a scroll with his name, and in the lower part of the pinnacles are still smaller figures of saints in little niches, which, like the prophets, have all been painted and gilt. The arms of the four archbishops are carved on the elbows of the standards, the lion of St. Mark appears in the canopy of the stall of the provveditore, and the shield of Maffeo Valaresso over the stall of the archbishop. The influence of the coming renaissance is observable in many of the details, and the arms of Valaresso are supported by two amorini that have quite burst free from Gothic tradition.

The exterior of the duomo is far finer than the interior. The facade (Plate V) is the finest in Dalmatia, and its round-arched portals, and tiers of arcading that fill the whole upper part of the wall and the gables, are equalled in their own style only

---

[1] The Venetians insisted on their governor being accorded a seat of equal honour with the bishop in the provincial cathedrals; the provveditore was to be 'incensed,' and treated with the same ceremony as the bishop, and he received the '*pax*' from a priest of the same degree and title and vested in the same way as the one who performed the same function for the bishop. Vid. Cubich, Veglia, Part ii. p. 118, 145.

in the churches of Pisa Lucca or Pavia. The contrast between the plainness of the lower story and the rich detail of the upper part is very good; and the same artistic subordination is preserved in the side wall next the Corso or High Street, which has a plain wall below surmounted by an open arcaded story just below the eaves. The whole is beautifully executed in a white compact limestone that may almost be considered a marble, and though it has undergone restoration it is on the whole in an admirable state of preservation.

The doorways are square openings with jamb shafts, some of them spirally fluted, which carry semicircular arches enclosing a tympanum. In the tympanum of the two lateral doors is the lamb and flag, carved in an archaic style, and in that of the central door are three niches of Italian Gothic evidently of a later date than the rest, with the Madonna and child in the centre between two saints. A wide border of Romanesque scroll-work surrounds the opening of the doorways. A few statues carved in the solid stone of the pilasters flank the doors, and the north-east angle is decorated with some incised ornaments filled in with black cement in the manner of the facade of the cathedral of Lucca.

The arcaded part above has evidently been disturbed by several alterations: the lowest tier of arcades, extending quite across the facade, has capitals of an early Romanesque character, and the arcades in the half gables of the aisles, with the great stone beasts at their lower ends, are also in that style; but

Plate V.

ZARA.

The Duomo

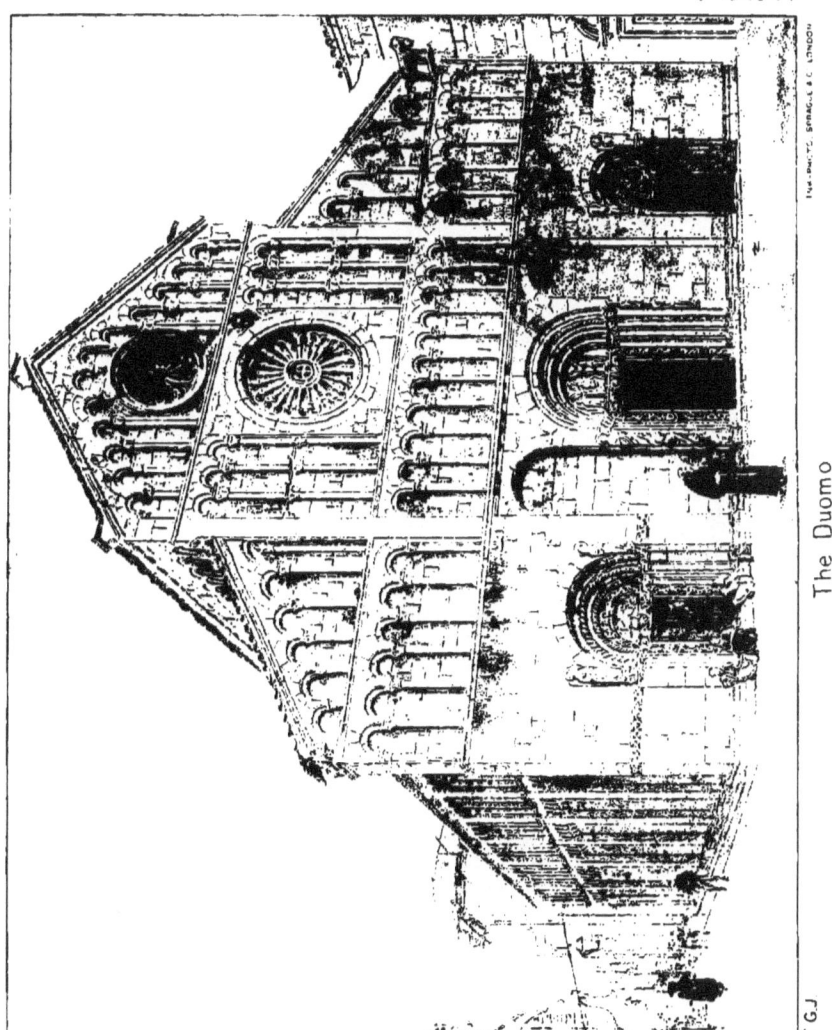

the arcading of the three upper tiers of the nave or central part is very different, the shafts are much thinner and are placed in couples, and their capitals are later in character. Other irregularities, one by one, catch the eye ; in one aisle the columns of the upper tier are over those of the lower, but in the other over the centre of the arches; the pilasters that divide the central part from the wings cut off half the arch on the north side ; and the displaced column is set up naïvely in the centre of the arch it should have carried. The two rose windows are evidently of different dates, and the coping of the central gable is clearly not of the same period as that of the half gables of the aisles.

An inscription in Lombardic letters on the lintel of the great door tells us that this Romanesque facade is not even so old as the rest of the church, but was actually built in the year 1324, a hundred and fifty years after Romanesque architecture in England and France began its transition to Gothic.

AÑO · D · MCCCXXIIII · TPR · DNI · IOHĪS · DE · BVTVANE · DI · GRA · IADRN · ARCHIEPI.

As the cathedral was only consecrated in 1285, we can hardly suppose the west front needed rebuilding forty years later in the episcopate of Giovanni di Butuane, and we can only suppose that he either completed what Lorenzo Periandro had left imperfect, by adding a west front, or that he extended the church further westward, for which there is some slight evidence in a change of the courses of masonry of the side wall[1].

[1] Farlati merely says the Basilica, 'inchoata olim a Laurentio

To his work belongs no doubt the greater part of the facade with the lower rose window, but the upper rose, and the three upper tiers of arcading of the central part with their coupled shafts and the gable above are probably work of the fifteenth century.

The north wall, with its arcaded gallery and the little cushion capitals from which the arches spring, has undoubtedly an early look, and I was tempted to assign it to the time of Lorenzo, until I detected on several of the little cushion capitals the shield and arms of Archbishop Valaresso (1450–1495). Still more perplexing is it to find on one of the shallow buttresses at K (vid. Fig. 1) the arms of Archbishop Pesaro and those of Giov. Minotto and Francesco Foscari, the Count and the Captain of Zara between 1513 and 1515, and to observe that westward of this buttress the masonry changes its character, and the lancet windows become pointed instead of round-headed. I cannot but believe that these arms, as well as those of Valaresso, refer rather to restorations more or less extensive than to the original construction, which from the character of the work can hardly, even in Dalmatia, be later than the thirteenth or early part of the fourteenth century.

The sacristy is an apsidal building, perhaps formerly a church and of greater antiquity than the present duomo, although it is now ceiled with perfectly developed rib and panel vaulting. A short

Periandro et magna ex parte perfecta demum absoluta fuit sub pontificatu Johannis.' Illyr. Sac. Tom. v. p. 93.

passage, now walled up, formerly led from this chamber to the adjoining church of S. Donato[1].

The passage at L (vid. plan) between the sacristy and the duomo, now opening to the yard, is evidently an ancient chapel, though many of its original features are obliterated. It has still a barrel roof, strengthened by flat underlying ribs, and it ends with a semi-dome over a square end, with squinches in the angles like the early churches already noticed at Zara, and several others throughout Dalmatia. The east end of this building has lately been modernized, but in the process the interesting discovery was made of two windows filled with slabs of perforated stone, of which examples exist at S. Lorenzo in Istria, and at Grado (vid. ch. xxxii. Fig. 115, and ch. xxxvi. Fig. 128).

In the Corso, a few yards distant from the east end of the duomo, stands the unfinished campanile, begun in 1480, a magnificent project of Archbishop Maffeo Valaresso, which the jealousy of his relations who did not choose that he should spend his substance in that way prevented him from completing. Defeated in this intention he diverted his extravagance to building a small castle or palace on a rock in the bay of Cassione, some six or seven miles south of Zara, of which the ruin still remains.

The most perfect 'souvenir' of this magnificent prelate which Zara possesses is the very beautiful

---

[1] The apse of this sacristy was formerly visible from the cathedral yard, but it is now hidden by an unhappy building which had sprung into existence between my last two visits to Zara.

and quaint pastoral staff which he gave to his cathedral (vid. Plate VI). It is of silver, parcel gilt, and bears this inscription :—

R + D + MAFEVS + VALARESSVS + ARCHIEPVS HVADRENSIS + FACIENDVM + CURAVIT · M · CCCCLX +

From the circumference of the crook radiate eleven little figures; in the centre is the figure of Christ standing on a rock, and on each side of him are five little half-length figures springing out of flowers, and facing alternately to each side of the staff. Each holds a scroll with his name, ELIA · P̄ — SIMON · · PA — AMOS · P̄—IEROBOAM, whom one is surprised to find in such good company, TVBIA—MOSE · P̄— IEREMIA · P̄.— DANIEL · P̄.—ARON · P̄—IACOBE[1]. In the centre of the crook are statuettes of a female figure, crowned and holding a book, and a bishop with a pallium, who holds out a book with his right hand. These have been variously supposed to be the Virgin Mary and Archbishop Valaresso the donor, or S. Donato and S. Anastasia the patron saints of Zara. It may be objected to the latter interpretation that Donato was not an archbishop, and would not have the pallium.

The neck immediately below the crook has been modernized, but all the rest of the pastoral is perfect and original. The next stage is a rich piece of tabernacle work, triangular in plan, with a pinnacle at each corner, and two stories high. In the upper stage the three faces are occupied by St. Peter, St. Jerome (?) and a bald saint holding a

---

[1] The labels with TVBIA and IACOBE are not original.

ZARA. PLATE VI.

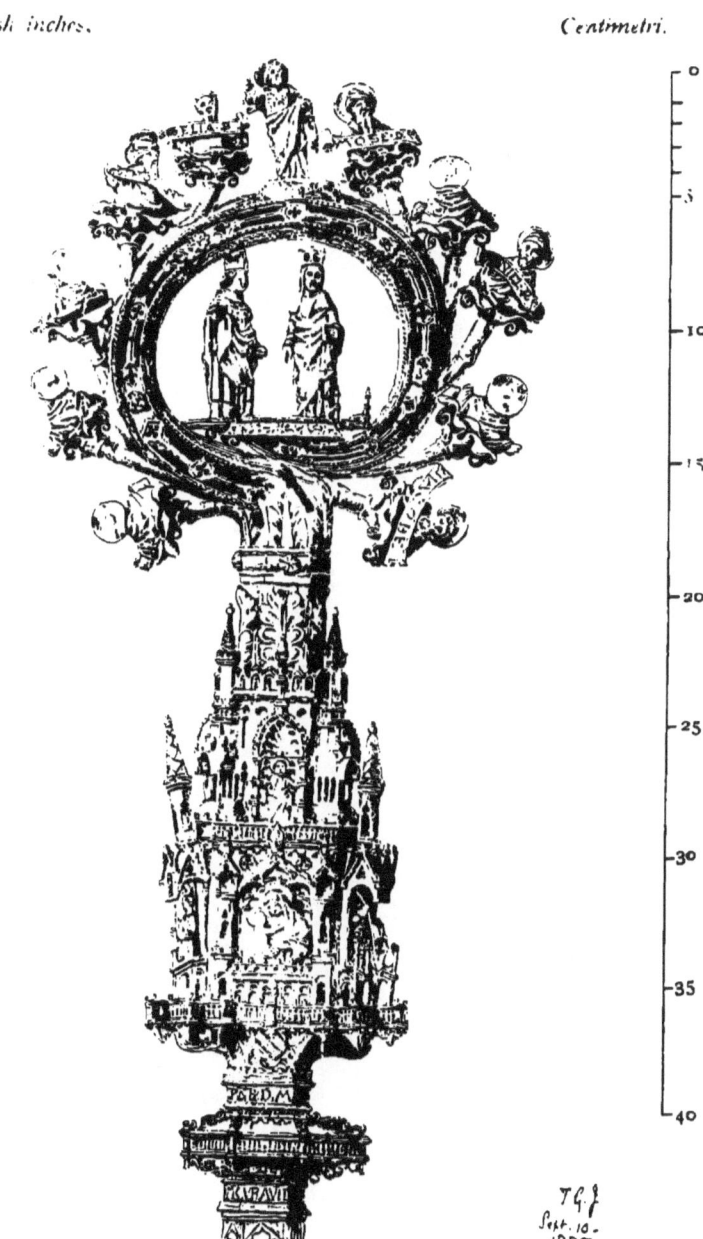

PASTORALE OF ARCHBISHOP VALARESSO.
A.D. 1400.

book; in the lower by a Madonna with the Holy Child, a figure of our Lord issuing from the tomb, and a saint also apparently stepping out of a tomb. St. George and two female saints occupy niches in the angle pinnacles. The staff is plated with silver, and the total height of the pastoral is six feet six inches. The workmanship is very fine; the little figures are cast and engraved with a tool, and the foliage of the flowers out of which the prophets emerge is beautifully finished with file and graver.

The treasury of the Duomo is very rich in church plate, of which the following are the most remarkable pieces :—

1. A reliquary supported by four dragons, which have lost their wings, and whose tails raised in air meet in the centre and form a base for the upper part. This begins with a cube of crystal surrounded by cast and pierced metal work, bearing the figure of a man in civilian dress blowing a horn, alternately with that of a knight tilting. The knight has a falcon, and a tree is introduced behind him. This part bears the inscription—HIC EST SPONGIA DÑI QVA. POTAT FVIT IN PATIBVLO CRVCIS. Above is a band of natural leaves with birds, and still higher is a crystal tube containing the relic and surmounted by a crucifix. The relic is labelled 'the holy thorn,' by some one who apparently has not taken the trouble to read the inscription on the reliquary.

2. A coffer containing the head of 'S. Giacomo Interciso,' a martyr apparently of the fifth century.

Round the ring of the domed top is this inscription:—

+ EGO BOSNA IVSSI FIERI ANCH CAPSAM AD ONOREM SCS IACOBI MARTIRIS OB REMEDIVM ANIME CHASEI VIRI MEI ET ANIME MEE.

Nine saints surround the drum, each under a round arch supported by columns, fluted, twisted, and diapered; they bear their names—S. Petrus, S. Paulus, S. Andreas, S. Jacobus, S. Tomas, S. Jacobus, S. Filippus, S. Bartolomeus, S. Mateus. On the lid in round medallions are these six figures—Christ, with the monograms I.C.—XC, Jachbus martyr, Judas, Simon, Johannes, Maria. Monsign. Bianchi[1] says there was a prior of Zara named Chaseus or Chaseo in the year 1096, who might very well be the person mentioned in the inscription, for the lettering is not unlike that of the epitaph of the princess Vekenega at St. Maria (vid. Fig. 12, infra), who died in 1111, and the style of the figures and draperies is quite consistent with that date. The whole work is in silver, the ground left plain, and the figures gilded. The classic head with flying hair in the crown of the casket cannot have belonged to it originally.

3. The reliquary of S. Grisogono or Chrysogonus is a long casket with three oval medallions of enamel on the lid. The figures are beautifully drawn and delicately chased in silver; the ground is filled in with a deep rich blue enamel, and there

---

[1] Zara Cristiana, vol. i. p. 155. There is an illustration of this reliquary in Eitelberger's Kunstdenk. Dalmatiens, p. 150. ed. 1884.

is a cypress on each side of the figure chased in silver and glazed with a transparent green enamel. On the front are two square enamels in the same style. The rest of the casket is covered with embossed work of vine leaves in scrolls in a style which is extremely common throughout Dalmatia. Round the lid is the following inscription in Lombardic letters of silver on a red enamel ground :—

+ HOC OP · FVIT · FACT · TPR · NOBILIV · VIROR · VITI · CADVL · VVLCIN · MARTINVSII · ET · PAVLI DE GALCIGN · ANN · D · MCCCXXVI.

4. The reliquary of S. Orontius, an oblong box covered in front and at both ends with silver plates, is perhaps the most interesting piece in the treasury. Ten arches, embossed on the front and sides, supported by columns either fluted or twisted, contain each a figure which is bearded, long haired, and dressed in oriental vestments, and holds a small cross before his breast. Each has a nimbus, and his name in characters which are a mixture of Greek and Latin :—

(A) CABINIANϓC — (A) ϕEΛIZ — (A) BITAΛIC — (A) CATOPϓC — (α) PEΠOCITϓC — (α) CEΠTIMI-NVC — (α) IANϓAPIϓC . — (α) APωTATIOC . — (α) ONωPATϓC . — (α) ϕωPTVNATIANVC.

On the back is now only a plate with the inscription in Roman characters + SERGIVS · F · MAI · NEPOS · ZALLAE · FECIT · HANC · CAPSAM · SC̄O · CAPITI · ARONTII · MARTIRIS. On the top is the scutcheon of Archbishop Pesaro (1505–1530), when some repairs were probably effected. The industry of

Monsign. Bianchi has traced the names of Madius and Zella in documents of 1067 and 1096[1], and that of Sergius tribunus in one of 1091, who most probably is the person mentioned as the donor on the loose plate affixed to the back. But the front and end plates with their Greek saints are probably Byzantine works of an older date than this, and have evidently once belonged to a different casket, for they do not fit the present one at all well, as may be seen in Prof. Eitelberger's illustration[2]. They most likely date from the eighth or ninth century, and were adapted to the present casket by Sergius, who gave it to the church at the end of the eleventh. From a calendar of 1516 it appears probable that this reliquary was once at Grado: 'Ebreduni in Gallia S. Orontii. Mart. qui in persecutione Diocletiani martyrio coronatus est, et ejus caput ex Gradensi Ecclesia Iadram translatum[3].' This is especially interesting because at Grado also inscriptions exist in which Latin and Greek letters are used indiscriminately[4].

5. A reliquary professing to contain a finger of St. John Baptist, made in the form of an arm, with plaques of transparent enamel in the midst of scrolls of vine leaves. It is inscribed in Lombardic letters,

---

[1] The name Zella appears among those of the witnesses to a deed of Cresimir in 1072, conveying certain crown lands to the convent of S. Maria at Zara. Luc. de Regn. ii. ch. xv.

[2] Kunstdenk. Dalm. p. 153, ed. 1884.

[3] Bianchi, Zara Cristiana.

[4] Vid. infra, chapt. xxxvi, on Grado.

DIGITVM · SANCTI · IOHANNIS · BAPTISTE, and dates probably from the fourteenth century.

6. Another reliquary in the form of an arm, with this inscription round the wrist in raised Lombardic letters :—EGO CHACIA VSOR DIMITRII · FECI · FIERI · HOC · OPVS. The arm is of plain metal, enriched with filigrana and set with stones and patterns in cloisonné enamels. The triangular base is of cast metal, raised on three feet, reminding one by its form of the great candelabrum at Milan. Each side has in the centre a winged figure with sceptre and orb in the midst of open scroll-work of twelfth-century character. Monsign. Bianchi says that Demetrius, husband of Chacia, was prior of Zara in 1162, a date which is full early for the workmanship. This is the best of the numerous *arms* in the Treasury.

The Baptistery, adjoining the cathedral to the north (vid. plan, Fig. 1), is evidently a building of great antiquity, and belongs by its plan to a class of churches of which Dalmatia contains several examples[1]. The destroyed church of S. Orsola at Zara (vid. Fig. 4), which has been described, and the half-ruined church of SS. Trinità, near Spalato (vid. Fig. 40, infra), correspond with this baptistery not only in plan but in dimension, the three having almost to an inch the same diameter of twenty feet for the central dome, which would seem to have been the standard measurement for this class of building. They consist of a circular chamber covered

[1] Vid. sup., account of Dalmatian architecture, p. 212.

with a dome, and surrounded by six apses, each covered with a semi-dome, but while at Spalato the curved walls of the apses shew outside the church, here at Zara the building is a hexagon externally, and the walls are consequently more massive. It has now three doors, but none of them are original, and that to the north is as late as the time of Archbishop Valaresso, whose arms it bears within a renaissance wreath. The original door was no doubt through the south apse, opening direct into the Duomo. The interior is lighted by six windows, one over each apse arch.

The red breccia marble font is very curious, and though standing within a hexagonal building it is octagonal. The sides are ornamented with shallow romanesque arcading, like the archbishop's throne in the tribune of the cathedral.

THE CHURCH OF S. GRISOGONO is the most interesting in Zara after the Duomo. It was the church of an abbey which dated from remote antiquity and ranked as one of the most important conventual establishments in Dalmatia. Originally dedicated to S. Antonio, and served by Egyptian monks, it was rededicated in 649 to S. Grisogono, when the relics of that saint were brought from Aquileia, and when he was formally adopted as patron of the city[1]. A testament of 908 contains a

[1] Bianchi, Zara Cristiana, vol. i. p. 296. It is said that the cavalier who appears mounted on a black horse in the arms of the city represents S. Grisogono, and that the device dates from this period.

bequest for repairing the church and convent; and in 986 they were rebuilt by Majo or Madius, rector of Zara and governor of Dalmatia, who reorganized the brotherhood under another Madius, a Benedictine monk, whom he invited from Monte Cassino. The new church is described as large and splendidly furnished with marbles and precious metals. It was again rebuilt in 1175 by Archbishop Lampridio, whose reconsecration of the church was recorded by an inscription on the 'triumphal arch' of the apse, which will be referred to presently. There was

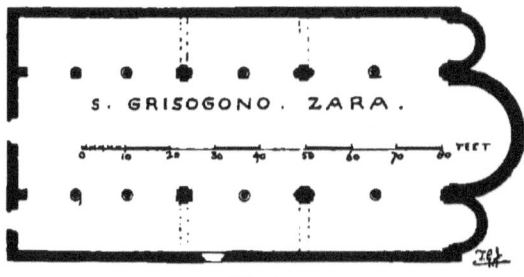

Fig. 8.

another consecration of the church in 1407, and it is important to ascertain how much of the church belongs to the latter date, and how much, if anything, to the former.

The plan is so far basilican (Fig. 8), that it has a nave with two aisles, wooden ceilings, and three apses at the east end; but here, as at the Duomo, the arcades spring from columns and piers alternately, and consequently are not strictly according to the old basilican type. The piers are square with semi-columns attached to them, and there are cross arches thrown from the piers to the outer wall. The isolated columns are of beautiful marble, possibly antique, though they scarcely seem diminished properly according to classic rule, and they carry capitals of early romanesque design. Over the arcades is a string of dentils sunk in the wall face as at Spalato and Traù and the church of Jàk in Hungary.

The exterior of the church is more interesting and better preserved than the interior. The apses are extremely beautiful (Plate VII)[1], the open gallery with its delicate colonnade being equal to anything of the kind in the Lombard churches of Italy. The south flank of the church next the street is beautifully arcaded with shallow round-headed arches resting on attached columns spirally fluted and bearing capitals of an early character. These arches consist of a single square order, a horizontal string course runs above them, and the upper part of the wall is pierced by small round-headed windows deeply splayed from the outside to the middle of the wall. The arcaded gallery of the apse has little cushion capitals and two plain square orders which are eccentric, the outer order being stilted so as to make the inner one wider at the crown than at the springing, a very common device in Italian romanesque work, and one that is employed at the Duomo also. Thus

[1] In the gable over the principal apse is inlaid a cross of coloured majolica tiles which it is not easy to discover, and which I unfortunately did not see till my drawing had been lithographed.

ZARA. Plate VII.

S Grisogono

far everything corresponds with the architecture of the end of the twelfth or beginning of the thirteenth century. The details are similar to many in the Duomo, which date probably from the middle of the thirteenth century, and it is difficult to assign the work at S. Grisogono to a later date than this. It is true Dalmatian art lagged behind that of western Europe, but even if we suppose the present building to be the church of 1175 it would still be a century later than very similar work at Pisa, and it is impossible to believe that a design so purely romanesque, and so free from suspicious traces of the later styles, which would be sure to have crept in had the building been an anachronism, can really be the work of the fifteenth century. The latter view, however, is seriously maintained by some writers, and among others by Professor Eitelberger, who takes the opportunity of reading a lesson on the unprogressiveness of the arts in Dalmatia. On the other hand, Monsign. Bianchi gives some particulars which confirm the conclusions to which the architectural style itself would naturally lead us. According to him the principal apse was once adorned with a mosaic like those at Rome Ravenna and Parenzo, which existed till 1791, when the church had the misfortune to be restored, and the mosaic with many other matters of interest was destroyed. Fortunately a drawing of it which was made in 1771 has been preserved, together with copies more or less complete of the inscriptions it contained, which suffice to fix its date. The following is Monsign. Bianchi's account[1]. ' *The mosaic represented the Saviour with the Virgin on his right, and St. John the Evangelist on his left. Below them a band, which ran round the whole semi-circle, contained an inscription which could not be deciphered, and beneath it in twelve pictures were seen the figures of the Apostles with their proper names, some of which were still legible. The epoch of the work was precisely indicated by certain inscriptions, while below the figures of the Apostles Simon and Judas could be traced the following words :—*

HOC OPVS FIERI IVSSIT STANA FILIA COMITIS PETRANA IADERαE ET *Dalmatiae Proconsulis*

... It should be observed that in a document of 1134 *mention is made of Pietro, called also Petrana, count of Zara. Besides this, round the front arch ran the following legend, which being much damaged by time, has perhaps in some parts been not very well copied, and which we will attempt to complete as well as we can in italic letters*[2] *:—*

SVMMA MAIESTAS TVA TVAQ · POTESTAS
OMNIA GVBERNAS PVGILLO CVNCTA SVSTENTAS
ANNO MILLENO XPI DECIES QVOQVE DENO ET DECIES SEXTO TER QVINTO MSEQ · MAIO *die* EIᴜsDEm MeNSIS QV*arto* Lam*pridius archiepisco*pus METROPOLITAN*us hanc ecclesiam de*dicavit s*ancto ch*RISOGONO QVO GAVDET IADRA PATRONO XPO REGNANTE Q*uinque* SECᴜLA FVIT DE ANTE * * * *

[1] Bianchi, Zara Cristiana, vol. i. p. 301.
[2] The original seems to have run in rhyming hexameters which

However imperfect this record of the vanished mosaic may be, it seems clear that it bore the date of the consecration of the church in the year 1175, and the name of the donor Stana or Anastasia daughter of Petrana or Pietro count of Zara whose name is found on a document of 1134, who is also well known as the Venetian count of Zara at whose instigation the see was raised to an archbishopric in 1145[1]; and this seems to dispose of the theory that the apses though romanesque in style were really built at the end of the fourteenth or beginning of the fifteenth century.

The apses carry with them the south wall with its arcades and deeply splayed windows, all of which, if the evidence of the drawing of 1771 may be believed, date from the latter part of the twelfth century.

The case of the west front is somewhat different: the ends of the south aisles with their half gables are in the same style and of the same date as the side wall, and have preserved their original copings, which are carved with a series of rosettes, and supported by grotesque beasts at their lower end, just like those at the Duomo. But the central part forming the west end of the nave is of much later workmanship, and though it still preserves the round arches and the tiers of arcades of roman-

the copyist and Monsign. Bianchi in his conjectural restoration have lost sight of.

[1] 'Comes vero civitatis erat eo tempore Petrana.' Thom. Archid. c. xx.

esque architecture, the details and proportions belong rather to the fifteenth century than to the twelfth, and this part may very likely date from the time of rededication in 1407. The west door has a lintel with round arches above it inclosing a tympanum, the arches consisting of four shallow square orders slightly horseshoed, and surmounted by a pediment. At some height above this is an arcade extending across the front, with round arches springing from slender coupled columns like those in the upper part of the facade of the Duomo, which as I have already remarked are evidently later than the rest. Here, however, there is no central rose window, and the back wall of the arcades is not flat but hollowed out into a series of shallow niches.

On the tympanum of the west door is an inscription in Lombardic lettering which is now almost obliterated, having unfortunately been only painted on the stone and not incised. According to Monsign. Bianchi it recorded the rebuilding of the town walls, which was begun in 1298, and it might have been read as follows :—

AD HONOREM DNI XPI SALVATORIS
SANCTIQVE CHRYSOGONI IADERAE PROTECTORIS
MVRVS VRBIS IADERAE FVIT INCHOATVS
DIE XII ADSTANTE NOVEMBRIS
INDICTIONIS BIS SENAE ORDINE LABENTIS
SVB ANNIS XPI MILLE DVCENTIS
NONAGINTA OCTO PLVS COMPVTI LEGENTIS
EXISTENTE COMITE LEONARDO CHRYSOGONO

but I cannot believe this doorway as old as the date of the event recorded upon it. The whole of this later work, doorway, arcading, gable, and coping, is of an attenuated and meagre character, poorly designed, and contrasting very unfavourably with the earlier work of the south aisle and apses.

Whatever may be the date of the church of S. Grisogono, it is, with the exception of the west front, a perfect example of romanesque architecture at its best. Though not large, it is on a scale sufficient for dignity, the nave measuring about ninety-five feet by twenty-five, and the nave and aisles together being about fifty-two feet in width ; it is admirably proportioned according to the rule which seems to have been generally accepted as proper for basilican churches, the nave being approximately four times as long as it is wide, and twice as wide as the aisle; the details are well studied and refined, and their execution is nearly perfect.

To the north side of the small churchyard in front of the west end is the campanile, once among the loftiest in Zara, but now barely overtopping the surrounding buildings, the upper part having been so damaged by a fire in the neighbouring houses in the year 1645 that it was found necessary to take it down. The date of its construction is given by an inscription on the south side in lead letters beaten into the stone.

> AD LAVDEM · DEI · ET B · CIRY
> SOGONI   BERNARDVS   IADR
> ENS.   MONACHVS · HVIVS · AE
> DIS · PRIOR · SVA · ALIORVMQ
> MONACHORVM · CVRA · ET
> IMPENSA   ·   M · D · XLVI.

The floor of the eastern part of the church is full of carved sepulchral slabs, among which is one of Giovanni Rosa, bishop of Veglia, who died in 1549, bearing his effigy in relief and his arms charged with a rosette. An interesting crucifix of painted wood hangs on the aisle wall.

The adjoining convent was suppressed in 1807; its buildings which had been repeatedly reconstructed were destroyed in 1822, and on its site were erected the buildings now occupied by the Ginnasio and the Scuola reale of Zara.

CONVENT OF S. MARIA. The church of S. Maria and the convent of Benedictine nuns attached to it can boast an antiquity scarcely inferior to that of the convent of S. Grisogono. The church of S. Maria minore which stood on its site is mentioned as far back as the year 906, and in 1066 it was granted by the Benedictine monks of S. Grisogono to Cicca, sister of Cresimir king of Croatia and Dalmatia, who purposed founding a nunnery of their own order. Cicca rebuilt the church, and retiring from the world after the death of her husband, was herself the first abbess of her new foundation. Special privileges were granted to the monastery by Cresimir her brother in 1066[1]; and in 1072 the new buildings were consecrated by Andrea, bishop of Zara, with the assistance of the bishops of Arbe Nona Veglia and Belgrad (Zara-Vecchia), and of Giovanni Ursini bishop of Traü and four Benedictine abbots, who happened to be assembled in a provincial council. Another instrument of king Cresimir dated in this year conveys to the convent certain royal lands, and speaks of the 'monasterium S. Mariae Monialium rogatu sororis meae, quod noviter factum est Iadere, Cichae, &c.'; and a third document, dated also 1072, 'in die consecrationis ejus basilicae,' contains a grant of the island of Selve to the abbess Cicca and her sisterhood by the prior clergy and people of Zara[2]. These privileges and concessions were confirmed in 1102 by Coloman of Hungary after he had assumed the style of king of Dalmatia and Croatia[3]; and his triumphal entry into Zara in 1105 was commemorated by the erection of the campanile of the convent which is still standing,

---

[1] 'Anno Incarn. D. N. I. Christi, 1066. Dubcyzi (sc. *Constantine Ducas*) Constantinopolcos Imperante. Ego Cresimir Rex Croatiae et Dalmatiae filius Stephani Regis, concessione Laurentii Spalat. Archiepiscopi, omniumque nostri Regni Episcoporum, et laudatione nostri Ducis Stephani, caeterorumque Croatiae Comitum, do Regiam libertatem monasterio S. Mariae Jadrensis, quod soror mea Cicha fabricavit,' &c. &c. Luc. de Regn. ii. c. xv. p. 98.

[2] Idem, p. 102.

[3] Idem, p. 113.

and on which till a few years ago might be read this inscription:—

ANNO INCAR DNI NRI IHV XPI MIL CV
POST VICTORIAM ET PACIS PRAEMIA
IADERÆ INTROITVS A DEO CONCESSA
PROPRIO SVMPTV HANC TVRRIM
SCÆ MARIÆ VNGARIÆ DALMACIÆ
CHROATIÆ CONSTRVI ET ERIGI
IVSSIT REX COLOMANVS[1]

Cicca died in 1096, and her daughter Vekenega, who was married to Coloman but had been repudiated by him[2], following her mother's example took the veil, and became abbess of S. Maria in her stead. She died in 1111, and her tomb with its contemporary inscriptions, which is still to be seen within the walls of the convent, is one of the most interesting historical monuments in the city.

The church is flanked by the Calle Larga, from which a door leads into a forecourt which, like that at S. Grisogono, may perhaps have been at one time an atrium preceding the basilica. The church retains nothing of its original character, for though the shell may possibly be of Cicca's building, it has been clothed in the garb of the renaissance, and its antiquity, if it has any, is not recognizable. The facade and the south side which flanks the street are gracefully designed in the style of the Lombardi, and probably put on their present form at the end

[1] Vid. Lucio, de Regn. iii. c. iv. p. 115, and Bianchi, Zara Cristiana, vol. i. p. 315.
[2] Bianchi, Zara Cristiana, vol. i. p. 322.

of the fifteenth or beginning of the sixteenth century. The interior has suffered restoration still more recently, and is now smothered in rococo ornaments of stucco. There is in fact nothing whatever to be seen at S. Maria except within the precincts of the convent, and as this is still inhabited by Benedictine nuns who are not allowed to see or be seen by the outside world it is of course inaccessible to ordinary visitors. However, by the kindness of his Excellency the Archbishop of Zara I was allowed the rare privilege of entering the convent, and was shewn everything it contained which was worth seeing; a privilege which I believe has only been extended to one or two laymen beside myself.

We were first shewn some handsome altar-cloths which were brought into a parlour outside the cloister precincts in order that my wife might see them, for curiously enough women are even more rigorously excluded from the interior of the convent than men, and I was told that even Madame Ivanovitch, the wife of the governor of the province, had never penetrated beyond this parlour. The older of the two 'antependia' is embroidered with figures in gold on a red ground. The lines of the drapery are traced in a red line on the gold, and the faces have the lights worked in shades of flesh colour, the red silk ground being left for the darker tints. This dates probably from the fourteenth century. The other altar-cloth is the finer of the two, but a little later in date.

Passing the porter's lodge after being scrutinized

through a grating, I was received by the abbess and another nun and conducted to the inner court of the convent, which is spacious and prettily filled with flowers. The greater part of the surrounding buildings are modern, but on one side a simple cloister remains, consisting of columns supporting a wooden architrave and a pent roof. This once ran along the western side also, but has within the last twenty or thirty years been replaced by a large modern building containing rooms for the nuns, which is by no means an addition to the architectural beauty of the quadrangle. Worst of all, this great intruding block of building hides the lower part of King Coloman's campanile, which rises in the corner of the courtyard and was formerly visible from the ground upward; and with inexcusable carelessness the end wall has been allowed to conceal the inscription on the tower which records Coloman's triumphal entry into Zara, and his erection of this very campanile as a memorial of the event. Surely an opening might have been left in the new wall to expose this precious piece of history in stone, or at all events some note might have been made of its position, which is now lost, and could only be recovered by demolishing the side of a staircase.

The tower (vid. Plate VIII) is a fine example of that romanesque type of campanile which runs through Italy and Germany, from Rome to Verona, and from Verona to Cologne. It has the same straight unbuttressed outline; the same groups of windows, increasing in number as the tower rises

ZARA. Plate VIII.

T.G.J.
S. Maria

stage above stage, and set in shallow panels between flat pilasters; and the same window shafts set back to the middle of the thickness of the wall, and carrying imposts that project fore and aft to take the thickness of the wall above. The last-named feature of the romanesque campanile survived in Dalmatia at least till the seventeenth century, and I am not sure that if there were a tower to be built there now the Dalmatians would not build it in the same way.

To the south of the quadrangle, interposed between it and the church, is the Sala capitolare or chapter-house, a building of the highest architectural importance, being coeval or nearly so with the foundation of the monastery; which, though sadly disfigured by modern alterations, preserves under its disguise of stucco and colour-wash the romanesque work of the days of Cicca and Vekenega. It is a hall about thirty-six feet long and eighteen wide (Fig. 9), with four windows and a central door on the north side, the party wall of the church on the south, in which there is a grated window generally closed by shutters, the campanile at the west end, and the party wall of other conventual buildings at the east. It is covered by a barrel vault strengthened by four underlying transverse ribs of plain squared stone springing from pilasters or vaulting-shafts. The back of this barrel vaulting may be seen from the stairs that lead to the upper part of the tower, and from the regularity of its masonry, and the stone channelling for rain-water which is formed between

302   Zara: S. Maria.   [Ch. IV.

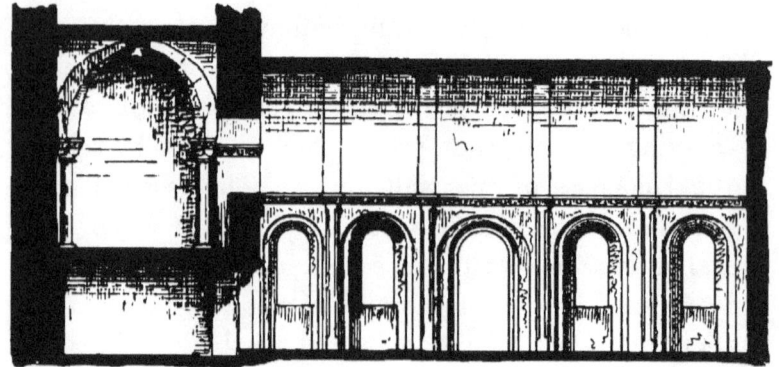

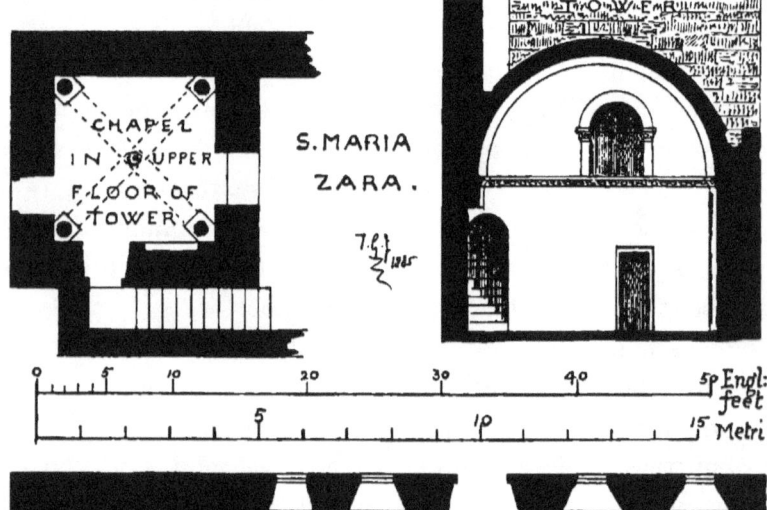

S. MARIA ZARA.

NORTH AISLE OF THE CHURCH OF S. MARIA
Fig. 9.

it and the side wall of the church, it seems that the exterior was intended to be exposed to view without any roof over it. The idea of a semi-cylindrical covering, vault and roof in one, had a great attraction for Dalmatian architects : at Sebenico we shall see it triumphantly realized on a stupendous scale, and at Spalato we shall find its origin in the little shrine of Diocletian's palace.

At the springing level of the barrel vault a cornice or stringcourse runs round the hall, which is en-

Fig 10.

riched with a simple romanesque leaf-pattern (Fig. 10), which is also to be found in a stringcourse at St. Mark's in Venice. All the windows and the door are round-arched of course, and seem to have been quite plain, but they are now so disguised by stucco mouldings that it is difficult to tell what they were like originally.

In the south-east corner of the hall is the monument of Vekenega, the daughter of Cicca, and repudiated wife of Coloman, who buried herself and her sorrows in this convent, and succeeded her mother as abbess. It consists of a recess in the wall, which probably once penetrated its whole thickness, and opened into the church as well as into the chapter-house. The front is formed of two small arches

Fig. 11.

within an including arch (Fig. 11), and has four sunk panels with inscriptions, of which that over the arch is the epitaph of Vekenega, who died in the year 1111 (Fig. 12), which with its puzzling abbreviations expanded reads as follows:—

> *LAVDE NITENS MVLTA · IACET · HIC VEKENEGA SEPVLTA*
> *QVAE FABRICAM TVRRIS SIMVL ET CAPITOLIA STRVXIT*
> *HAEC OBIT VNDENO CENTVM POST MILLE SVB AEVO*
> *QVO VENIENS CHRISTVS CARNIS GESTAVIT AMICTVS*
> *NOS HABET EST ANNVS QVINTVS QVO REX COLOMANNVS*
> *PRAESVL ET EST DECIMVS QVO GREGORIVS FVIT ANNVS.*

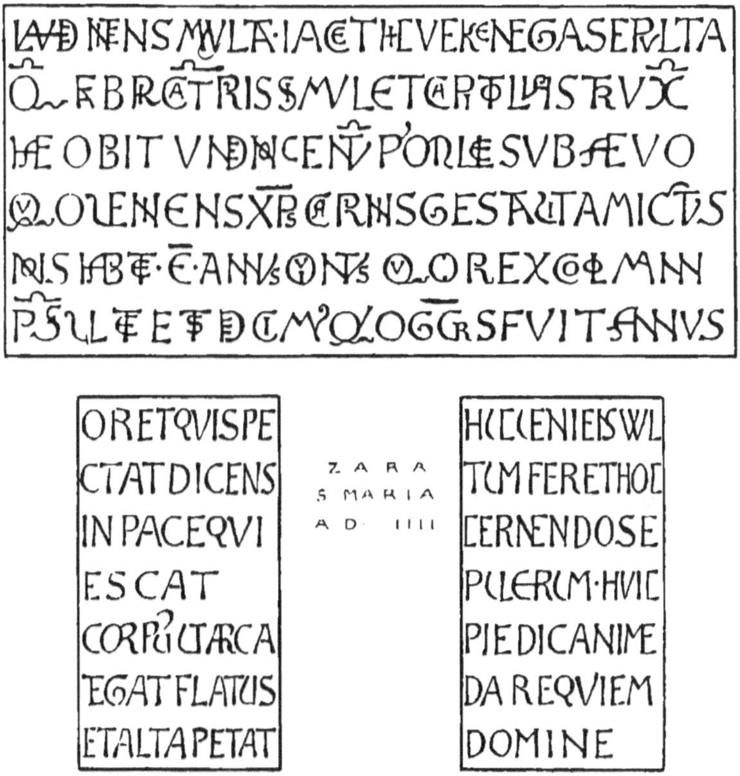

```
LAUDENS MULTA IACET HC VEKENEGA SERLTA
Q  FBRCTRISSMVLETERPLASRVX
HE OBIT VNDNCENTPORIE SVB EVO
Q OLEMENSXR ERNSGES AUTAMICUS
NLS HBE E ANNONS Q OREX CL MN
PSUL E F D CM Q OGG SFVIT ANVS
```

```
ORETQVISPE       HCCENIEISWL
CTATDICENS       TCMFERETHOC
IN PACEQVI       CERNENDOSE
ESCAT            PCLERCM·HVIC
CORPU CARCA      PIE DICANIME
EGATFLATUS       DA REQVIEM
ETALTAPETAT      DOMINE
```

ZARA
S MARIA
A D IIII

Fig. 12.

Vekenega's claim to have been the builder of the tower and the chapter-house probably means that they were built while she was abbess and under her supervision; the tower at all events was built, as we have seen, by her quondam husband Coloman, at his own expense, as he was careful to record, not only outside the tower by the inscription which is now unhappily invisible, but also on the inside, as we shall see presently.

The lower tablet contains five elegiac couplets in

honour of Vekenega, written in the same character and of the same date.

> RES FLVITANT CVNCTAE MVNDI VELVT IMPET VNDAE
> QVICQV̄D ET EXORITVR LABĪT ET MORITVR
> MENTE DEVM PVRA SEMPER VEKENEGA SECVTA
> NON PENĪT MORITVR SED MORIENS ORITVR
> NAMQ̄. PROBOS MORES CVPIENS SERVARE SORORES
> ACTIB · EXCOLVIT VOCE Q̄D HAS MONVIT
> HOSTIS AB INSIDIIS ADITVS BENE CAVIT OVILIS
> QVAQ̄ · REGENTE DOMVS CREVIT ET ISTE LOCVS
> IN FESTO SACRI COSMAE MIGRAT ET DAMIANI
> VT SIT IN ARCE DEI VITA PERENNIS EI.

A narrow doorway through nearly four feet of masonry in the west end of the capitular hall admits to the basement of the tower, a low vaulted chamber containing nothing but the tomb of the last abbess, who was by special privilege buried here in accordance with her dying request. The vaulting of this chamber forms the floor of a small chapel contained within the tower, which opens into the capitular hall by a window where, according to tradition, Vekenega used to sit to hear mass. This chapel is reached from the capitular hall by a narrow stair, for which just enough space is left between the tower and the church, and which finishes with a square landing, whence a square doorway under a round arch admits to the interior of the tower. The chapel is very curious. In each corner there is a detached column standing well away from the wall and carrying a massive cushion capital with a heavy abacus carved with a leaf ornament. Two of the columns are cylindrical and two octagonal, and on the four cushion faces that are turned towards the centre of the chamber are distributed the letters of the royal name of Coloman (Fig. 13). From these capitals spring two heavy diagonal ribs of plain squared stone, underlying a vault which is almost a dome in construction. From the intersection of the ribs depends a boss or rosette of a kind not uncommon in the romanesque buildings of Dalmatia.

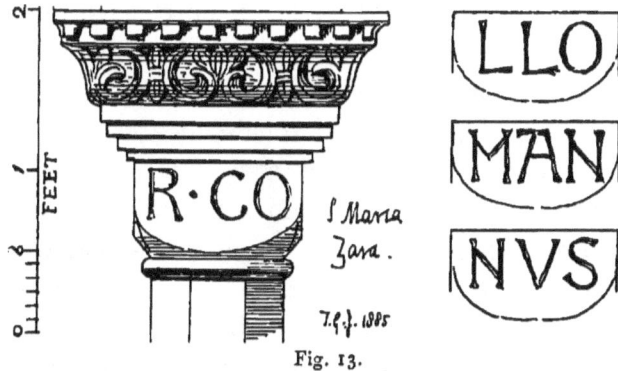

Fig. 13.

The little window in the south side of this chapel has for a lintel a fragment, set upside down, of a classic frieze carved with dolphins. The upper part of the tower is worth studying for the largeness of its window openings and the hardihood of its construction. Several pillars of the upper stage have decayed, and have been replaced by others not altogether like the original, though fortunately their defects are not observable from the ground, and very few ever see them at a less distance.

Above the aisles of the church is a spacious triforium, which is returned in the form of a wide gallery across the west end. In this gallery is the nuns' choir, which is fitted with handsome stalls of the same kind as those at the Duomo, though perhaps rather later in style. They now surround three sides of the gallery, but have evidently once formed two simple rows right and left of a choir in the usual place on the floor of the church, and they have suffered a good deal by the process of adaptation to their present position. The scroll-work dividing the stalls is not all of one style or date, that of the southern stalls being much slighter than that of the northern, and the back of the abbess' stall is different again, being of pronounced renaissance work. The standard end of her stall is also of that date, and bears the inscription ARTIFICIO IOHANNIS CORCYRAE M·C·C·C·C·L·XXXV, recording possibly the year when the old choir was dismantled, and the name of the artist employed in adapting the stalls to their present place. The renaissance panel to which his name is attached is sufficient proof that he was not the artificer of the stalls themselves, which abound in flowing Gothic traceries, and correspond in the style of their carving with the stalls at Arbe, which are dated fifty years earlier.

The window-openings from the triforium to the church are filled with good wrought-iron grills, which deserve to be noticed.

THE FRANCISCAN CONVENT AND CHURCH claim the honour of having been founded by S. Francis himself when he visited Zara in 1212. The church was dedicated in 1282, but has been extensively modernized, though it still retains a few traces of Italian Gothic architecture. In the interior the only feature of any architectural interest is the woodwork of the choir stalls, which is of unusually good design and execution. The stalls are not now in their original condition, nor in their original place. They are now behind the altar, but according to Fabianich they were originally in front of it, and were only moved to their present position in modern times. These stalls are among the finest we saw in Dalmatia, and are earlier in date and in a purer Gothic style than the others. They were made in 1394–5 by Giovanni di Borgo San Sepolcro, a Tuscan settled at Venice, and they cost 456 golden ducats, of which 200 were bequeathed by Giorgio de Matafari, a noble Zaratine, to whose executors a receipt was given for that sum by Fra Benedetto, the custos of the convent[1]. Among the scrolls of

[1] Fabianich gives the following agreement between the Friars and their artist: 'Millesimo trentesimo nonagesimo quarto, Indictione ii die vigesima mensis maij. Praesentibus Jacobo q. Petri Blundi e Iadra, et Nutio Pacini de Florentia habit. Iadre testibus et aliis.
'Magister Joannes q. Jacobi de Burgo Sancti Sepulcri, habitator et civis Venetiarum, fuit confessus et contentus penes se integraliter habuisse et recepisse a Fratre Benedicto Custode Fratrum et Conventus monasterii S. Francisci Ordinis Minorum de Jadra ducatos auri quadringentos quinquaginta sex, in auro puro, et in ratione Chori facti et nondum expediti et expediendi in dicta

pierced foliage which as usual form shades or screens between stall and stall are introduced figures of St. George on horseback, St. Francis receiving the stigmata, and St. Benedict and other saints of the Franciscan order (Fig. 14).

In a side chapel is a very large picture by Vittore Carpaccio, representing the church militant and the church triumphant.

In the sacristy of S. Francesco are preserved several fine pieces of old church plate and some good embroideries. There are in all five very good chalices of various dates and styles, two of which, with part of a third, are shown in Plate IX.

Near the west door, upside down and serving as a base to an 'acqua santa,' is a singular romanesque capital, which must have belonged to a building long anterior to the foundation of this convent. I could learn nothing of its history (Plate I. Fig. 9).

ecclesia S. Francisci; de quibus idem magister Joannes fecit dicto Fratri Benedicto finem securitatem et quietationem generalem et pactum de ulterius non petendo. Et promisit insuper dictus magister Joannes venire ad dictum laborerium expediendum hinc ad unum mensem cum dimidio proxime futurum, cum pactis modis et conditionibus habitis inter ipsas partes hactenus usque in praesentem diem sub poena quarti, &c. &c.

Actum Iadrae in Cancelleria inferiori
Ego Florchus de Artico.'

The text of the receipt to the executors of Matafari is also given in full by Fabianich, Storia dei frati minori in Dalmazia e Bossina, vol. ii. p. 51.

Also the text of a contract in 1443 between the convent and Magister Marcus ab Organis de Venetiis for a new organ. The new organ was to be five feet wide, and the builder was to receive fifty-six golden ducats and the old organ.

Fig. 14.

It may be compared with the capitals of the pulpit of Spalato (vid. Fig. 32, infra), which, though romanesque in style, probably date from 1200–1220.

S. SIMEONE. This church was originally the collegiate church of S. Stefano, the establishment of which was suppressed in 1393, and it changed its name when the ark and relic of St. Simeon were moved hither in 1625. The church is a simple building of the early renaissance, pleasing but not remarkable, and the campanile, which has a fairly good outline, was built as lately as 1707.

The glory of this church is the great silver gilt ark, in which lies the body, as the Zaratini believe, of Simeon, who held the infant Christ in his arms at the Presentation in the temple. After various vicissitudes and removals this magnificent piece of silversmith's work, the largest it is said [1] in the churches of the Austrian Empire, is now to be seen above and behind the high altar, supported by two bronze angels, and reached by a narrow flight of stairs from each side, so that the faithful who come to adore the saint may ascend on one side to see the relic and kiss the shrine, and descend on the other. This they may be seen doing all day long; but on the feast of St. Simeon, October 8th, they come in enormous numbers, and each pilgrim receives a '*bombace*,' or little tuft of cotton-wool in a paper envelope, which has been shut up in the ark and

[1] Eitelberger, p. 157.

Plate IX.

ZARA.

Chalices at S. Francesco.

T.G.J.

has thereby imbibed virtues which are miraculous in cases of toothache or earache or other minor ills to which cotton wool is applicable, and with which the nerves and the imagination have much to do. For three months beforehand the business of making these *bombaci* goes on; no less than 25,000 were ready when we were there, filling three large chests, some in pink envelopes for the Zaratini, the rest in white for pilgrims from without. We were presented with a handful as a reminiscence, and thereby some poor Croat was perhaps consigned to the pangs of hopeless toothache, if the number happened to fall short.

The story of the arrival of the relic, which Fondra its historian in the seventeenth century[1] candidly admits he was the first to put in writing, is this. Either in 1213 or 1273 a ship was driven to Zara by a tempest, having on board a nobleman who during his stay deposited in the cemetery the body as he said of his brother, which he was taking home for burial. The nobleman however died at Zara, and from his papers it was discovered that the body was none other than that of Simeon the Just, who had held Christ in his arms in the Temple. Dreams and portents were not long wanting to confirm the discovery, and the body was taken to the collegiate Church of S. Maria, where, by the expulsion of devils from demoniacs and other satisfactory

---

[1] Istoria delle insigne reliquie di San Simeone, &c. Scritta da Lorenzo Fondra. Zara, 1855. p. 36.

miracles of the same kind, it sufficiently asserted its sanctity[1].

In 1371 Lewis the Great of Hungary with the elder and younger Elizabeth, his mother and wife, visited Zara after his conquest of Dalmatia. The younger queen, so says the legend, was so desirous of possessing a piece of the relic that she broke off a finger and hid it in her bosom, but she instantly lost her senses and only recovered them on restitution of her theft. The finger miraculously attached itself to the body, and the bosom of the queen which had begun to mortify and breed worms was no less miraculously healed.

After this we at last touch historical ground. Elizabeth wrote to certain nobles of Zara to have a rich ark of silver made to contain the relic: they entrusted the work to one Francesco d' Antonio di Milano, a goldsmith of Zara, with whom they entered into a contract in 1377; and the ark was finished in 1380, as we know by the inscription on the back, in which Francesco di Milano has recorded his own name as the artificer. The ark is an oblong coffer with a coped roof and a gable at each end, and is long enough to contain a human body at full length. The front is hinged and falls down, disclosing in the interior behind a glass panel the ghastly and withered mummy of some poor son of earth, whoever he may have been. Both within and without the

[1] This is not the only legend relating to the arrival of the relic in Dalmatia. Ragnina connects it with Ragusa rather than Zara. Vid. Brunelli, notes to De Diversis, p. 102.

whole ark is covered with silver plates, embossed with figure subjects, and chased with diapers and ornamental borders. The effigy of Simeon lies on the slope of the roof towards the church, and the rest of the surface is occupied with various scenes of the arrival of the relic at Zara, and of the miracles it performed there, the only historical subject being the Presentation in the temple which occupies the central panel of the front. Of the other subjects different persons give different explanations, and some are generally admitted to be inexplicable. Fondra finds in one group on the back of the lid the story of Elizabeth and the rape of the finger; his editor believes this to be nothing of the sort, but finds the story of the stolen finger in the group at the left-hand end of the ark, which Fondra on the contrary takes to be merely a representation of the solemn entry of King Lewis and his queen into Zara. When two such faithful doctors disagree we may perhaps be allowed to question whether either of these pictures represents the story of Elizabeth, and even whether the origin of the story itself may not be found in the attempt of some ingenious person to explain pictures of which the true history had been lost.

The various compartments are divided by spirally twisted shafts supporting canopies of Italian Gothic design. The gable ends bear the royal escutcheon of Hungary impaled with the lilies of France, and the cypher L. R. (vid. Plate X). The embossed figures which occupy the several compartments are in bold relief and effective, but like all silversmiths' work seem ruder and more archaic than coeval work in wood or stone, owing to the difficulty of getting true lines and exact forms by means of embossing. A short examination is enough to shew that the ark is not in its original state. Some of the cusped arches are queerly distorted and do not complete themselves, and the interior has had the back lined with new plates in renaissance times. That it should have needed repair is not to be wondered at, for it has seen strange vicissitudes of fortune. Its original home was not the church where we now find it, but the collegiate church of S. Maria to the north of it, where the ark stood over the high altar supported by four silver angels. St. Mary herself yielded precedence to her ancient admonitor, and her church came to be known as the church of St. Simeon. This church was demolished to make way for the new fortifications of 1543 and 1570, a small chapel only being left standing, where the body remained in its ancient humble ark of cypress wood, the silver one being consigned to the safe keeping of the nuns of S. Maria[1].

In 1572 an attempt was made to raise funds for a temple worthy of so famous a relic, but money came in slowly, and in 1600, when the facade was half finished, the attempt was abandoned. In 1623 more modest counsels prevailed. Not far from the site of S. Maria stood the once collegiate church of S.

[1] The nuns gave a formal receipt for it which is cited by the annotator of Fondra's history.

Stefano, and hither it was proposed by Archbishop Garzadori that the relic should be conveyed. An outbreak of plague in 1630 awoke in the minds of the superstitious a recollection of the neglect into which the cult of St. Simeon had fallen; the church was hastily prepared by the addition of a new chancel, and in 1632 all was ready for the translation. The silver ark had been found, black and dirty, in a corner of the nunnery, and was repaired by Benedetto Libani, a goldsmith, who reduced the length by four and the width by three fingers, an alteration which explains the puzzling irregularities now visible. The translation took place amid public rejoicings on May 16, 1632, and Simeon has since then reigned as patron of the city. Other towns have made inconvenient pretensions to possess parts of St. Simeon, but it is the special glory of Zara to be able to shew his entire body, and Fondra with relentless logic extinguishes the claims of the rival churches[1].

The subject on the southern end of the ark is especially interesting as shewing the costume of the Hungarians in the fourteenth century (vid. Plate X). We see here Lewis himself with his queen and in the middle of his courtiers, and, from the variety of expression and feature in which the artist has indulged himself, we may almost believe that he has attempted actual portraiture of the principal personages. The king is bareheaded, and wears his

[1] An arm of St. Simeon was one of the relics with which Charlemagne endowed his church at Aix-la-Chapelle. Vid. Dandolo, Chron. lib. vii. c. xii. pars 21.

hair on his shoulders; his upper lip, which is long
and rather deeply indented, is shaven, and his beard
is cut to a point. He wears a long-waisted jerkin
and tight hose, and on his collar is a motto, of which
the letters 𝖛𝖆 ///// 𝖛𝖆𝖓𝖙 can be made out. The
Queen, to whom he is talking, wears an embroidered
underdress and a long cloak reaching to her heels,
and her head is enveloped in a hood or coif turned
up and bordered with fur. The Hungarian nobles
have long hair and flowing beards, and some of them
wear tall pointed caps with plumes of feathers.
Except for the feathers their head-dress corresponds
exactly with that of the Hungarian who is carved
on one of the pillars of the ducal palace at Venice,
who is also represented with long hair and beard and
a conical cap.

On the central panel of the back in raised Lombardic lettering is this inscription :—

SYMEON : HIC IVSTVS · Y
EXVM · DE · VIRGINE · NAT
VM · VLNIS · QVI · TENVIT
HAC · ARCHA · PACE : QVIE
SCIT · HUNGARIE · REGI
NA POTENS · ILLVSTRI
S : ED · ALTA : ELYZABET · I
VNIOR : QVAM · VOTO : CON
TULIT · ALMO · ANNO · MI
LLENO : TRECENO : OCTV
AGENO

✝𝔥𝔬𝔠 𝔬𝔭𝔲𝔰 𝔣𝔢𝔠𝔦𝔱 𝔉𝔯𝔞𝔫𝔠𝔦𝔰𝔠𝔲𝔰 𝔡𝔢 𝔐𝔢𝔡𝔦𝔬𝔩𝔞𝔫𝔬.

ZARA. PLATE X

ARK OF S. SIMEONE.
A.D. 1380.

This ark is not the only relic of Queen Elizabeth the younger to be seen in the church of S. Simeone. In the sacristy is a very beautiful chalice presented by her to the church, and bearing on the buttons of the knop and in a medallion on the base the arms of Hungary impaled with the lilies of France, surmounted by the crowned eagle and waving plumes that appear as the royal crest in the gable end of the ark. The arms of Hungary and France impaled appear also on the ark (Plate X). The latter coat was derived from the Angevine kings of Naples from whom Lewis was descended, and to whose kingdom he pretended as the rightful heir of Carlo Martello [1].

Of the other churches in Zara little need be said. That of S. DOMENICO has an interesting western doorway with a square lintel under a pointed tympanum, on which is a figure of the archangel Michael weighing souls in a balance and repelling with his spear the demon who attempts to claw the scale down [2]. On one side of this group is St. George, and on the other a female saint. It dates probably from the latter part of the fourteenth century. The rest of this church has been rebuilt in later times.

In another part of the town, between S. Simeone and the harbour, may be seen the imperfect façade of

[1] Vid. tables of Kings of Hungary, sup. p. 193. Also General History above, pp. 93 and 105.
[2] Professor Eitelberger gives an illustration of this door-head, Plate xiii. Fig. 1.

the great church which was to contain the ark and relic of St. Simeon.   The promoters of the scheme got

Fig. 15.

so far as to raise the doorway and half the great columns of the order, and on the lintel we read their names, which, after all, are only associated with a failure, for the church rose no higher :—

C. IVLIO CHRYSOGONO FEDERICI F · ET THOMASO CIVALELLO GREGORII · F · PATRICIIS PROCVRANTIBVS M. CCCCCC.

In remains of domestic architecture the streets of Zara are not so rich as those of many other Dalmatian towns. Still there are several good windows and doorways to be found, and not a few gracefully arcaded cortili. Fig. 15 shews a balconied window near the Piazza dei Signori, which is interesting as an example of Dalmatian eclecticism, combining the trefoiled arch and ogee canopy of Gothic architecture with the shell ornament the amorini and the swag of the Renaissance. One of the prettiest court-yards is that of an old palace or convent, no one can say which, near the church of S. Simeone, which is surrounded by two stories of cloisters, the upper one with a brick parapet in which are introduced some panels of simple tracery. In the centre is the usual Venetian well with a coat of arms. Those who say the building was a palace assign it to the families of Cernizza and Adobbati, but the coat is not that of either of these houses. In the jamb of the entrance doorway is a fragment of a Roman mortuary inscription built into the wall upside down.

CHAPTER V.

NOVIGRAD.

QUEEN ELIZABETH the younger of Hungary forms so conspicuous a figure in the history of Northern Dalmatia, and her story is so romantic and tragic, that a visit to the old castle of Novigrad, where she came by her mysterious death, follows very appropriately the study of her silver ark and enamelled chalice at Zara.

Novigrad, civitas nova, the Novgorod of the Russian, may be reached from Zara with a pair of horses in three and a half hours, by roads that steadily deteriorate from good to bad, and from bad to worse, till at last they amount to little more than a track across a stony desert. The excursion is an interesting one, and gives a fair glimpse of the interior of the country and its Slavonic population. The castle was a royal residence of Croatian and Hungarian kings, and a frontier fortress of the Venetians against the Turks, and it plays an important part in the history of the country on several occasions. But the incident which naturally rises in the memory in connection with Novigrad is the tragic death of Queen Elizabeth, which took place either within or near its walls in 1387.

Elizabeth was the daughter of Stephen Cotroman Ban of Bosnia. Her hand was sought by Stephen Dushan the great Czar of Servia for his son, who afterwards succeeded him as Ourosh V, and also by Lewis of Hungary then a childless widower. The proposals of Stephen Dushan were declined and the Hungarian alliance preferred, and the Servian czar avenged the slight by invading the province of Bosnia. Cotroman however with his daughter took refuge in the castle of Bobovaz, and Elizabeth shortly afterwards became the wife of Lewis. Two daughters were the issue of their marriage, Maria the elder who was crowned '*King*' of Hungary on the death of her father in Sept. 1382, and Hedwig who married Jagellon Duke of Lithuania, afterwards King of Poland under the title of Ladislaus V. For two years Elizabeth, as guardian of the youthful Maria then espoused to Sigismund of Luxembourg, reigned in peace, but discontent with female government, and jealousy of the power of the Palatine Nicolas Ban of Gara, provoked a conspiracy, the object of which was to transfer the crown to Charles III, King of Naples, who before the birth of Maria had been destined by Lewis as his successor[1]. Charles, who had secured his possession of the throne of Naples by the murder of Giovanna in 1382, landed at Segna and penetrated through Croatia to Buda, where he was crowned King of Hungary in 1385. The two queens were kept in an honourable captivity; few of the Hungarian nobility

[1] See above, General History, p. 124.

remained faithful to them except the Palatine Nicolas; the recent fate of Giovanna was fresh in their memory, and they were obliged to feign compliance and even to attend the coronation festivities. Under the disguise of this submission however they harboured thoughts of revenge, and when Nicolas the Ban of Gara suggested the assassination of Charles as the only remedy for their misfortunes they eagerly entered into the project[1]. On Jan. 1, 1386, the trap was laid, and Charles was invited into their rooms in the castle of Buda to listen to proposals from Sigismund, who they pretended was ready to follow their example and surrender his claims to the kingdom on condition that Maria should be released. While he was talking with them the Ban Nicolas entered with one Blasius Forgac[2], a '*persona intrepida*,' who cut the king down with a Hungarian sword. The approaches of the castle were guarded by partisans of Maria, and the populace were soon shouting for King Maria as lustily as they had a short time before shouted for King Charles.

The dying king was carried to the castle of Vissegrad, where poison is supposed to have completed what the sword had begun. But the party who had supported him determined to avenge his death, and as the two queens were on their way through

[1] 'Queste parole furono avidamente pigliate dalle due Regine e ad un tempo risposero che non desideravano cosa al mondo più di questa.' Giannone, xxiv. 2.

[2] So Lucio. Giannone calls him Brasio Torgas.

Croatia towards Dalmatia they were met by the Ban John Horvad and Giovanni Palisna the Prior of Vrana[1], who overpowered their escort after a desperate struggle, in which the Count Palatine Nicolas, and Blasius Forgac were slain, and carried them captive to the castle of Novigrad. Here Elizabeth met her death, but whether by the sword, or by drowning in the Bozota, or as some say from mere grief and despair, remains wrapped in impenetrable mystery. Maria was detained by her captors at Novigrad, whence she owed her escape to the interference of the Venetian government, as has been related in the general history[2].

The first part of the route from Zara to Novigrad lies along the great post road that traverses the whole province as far as Spalato, with branches to Knin Sign and the passes over the mountains into Bosnia. The first village is Zemonico, where are the remains of a fortified cavalry station, built by the Venetians as an outpost against the Turks. In most parts of Dalmatia there is but little scope for the movements of cavalry, but here there is a considerable plain called *Grobnica*, where according to one account the Tartars were defeated in the thirteenth century[3].

The next village is Smilcich, perhaps the place where Lewis of Hungary encamped in 1346 on his way to attempt to raise the siege of Zara, and where

---

[1] Lucio, v. ii. p. 253, ' prope Diacum.'
Vid. sup. Chapter i. p. 128.
Vid. General History in Chapter i. pp. 69–70.

he received the envoys of the citizens[1]. It has a modern church standing on an open green, and to our surprise there was a very decent-looking inn. From Smilcich the main road runs on to Karin, the Roman Corinium, where I believe there are some ruins to be seen, and thence over the hills to Obbrovazzo. We however left the high road, and struck into a very rough country track across rock and bog, which threatened to jolt our frail carriage to pieces, and tried the endurance of our little scrambling steeds to the utmost. It was a lovely day; the distant Velebić mountains wore their tenderest hues, and the air was full of the scent of aromatic plants that seem to flourish best where the ground is most rocky and sterile. There were multitudes of birds resembling a large lark or thrush, which were very bold, waiting till the carriage was close to them before taking to the wing, from which we inferred that the Sunday 'chasse' of the Gaul and Italian is not an institution among the Croats.

Before reaching Novigrad we met a substantial yeoman of that place to whom we had an introduction, which was to facilitate our plans and ensure us a good reception. He had married a girl from Oltre on the island of Ugliano, though not in the usual manner of the contadini, with whom it is still the custom for the lover to carry off the girl from her home, and bring her back after a few days

---

[1] Obs. Iadr. lib. ii. c. ix. 'in confinio Semelnici districtus Iadrae distans ab urbe fere per spacium septem milliarium castra metatus est.'

to be formally married[1]. The person we now encountered was however of a better condition than the ordinary peasants, and his wedding had been conducted in a more regular fashion. We were much impressed by his easy graceful carriage and polished manners; the Dalmatian type of humanity is a very noble one, and the national costume is well calculated to set it off.

At last, on our right, emerging from a hollow

Fig. 16.

ravine we saw the castle of Novigrad, a huge mass of yellow wall, so splintered and shapeless that it might almost have been a natural cliff (Fig. 16) It was perched on a promontory of rock surrounded by ravines which gradually disclosed themselves as we approached, and revealed in their depths the sea of Novigrad encircling the castle rock on three sides, and the little town of Novigrad lying far below us on the slopes of the hill, within its old walls, which

---

[1] Vid. sup. Chapter i. pp. 174, 183

stretch up the hill side to meet the fortress above. A long descending zigzag brought us to the water's edge, and rounding the end of the haven we soon reached the level quay of the town on the further side.

The castle covers a good deal of ground, but shews no evidences of taste or splendour, and must always have been much more castle than palace. It is not a castle of the same kind as Conway Carnarvon or Carew, built first indeed for defence, but secondarily for royal state or princely magnificence; in its ruin at all events it reminds one more of the robber castles on the Rhine and the Danube than of any more civilized home of chivalry. It can only be reached by a rough path up the rocky hill-side, through narrow gateways, and finally by two rude flights of external stairs which lead to the massive keep that occupies the summit of the hill. The entrance is at the head of the second flight, by a small doorway, close to which an iron ball from a Turkish cannon still lies imbedded in the solid masonry. The innermost enclosure of the keep is spacious, but the buildings are so dilapidated that little can be made of them. The natives point out the site of the little chapel, and there are many vaults below the level platform of the area, some of which have fallen in, but exploration was dangerous on account of the swarms of angry bees that infested the ruins. We were however rewarded for our climb by the magnificent view; to the right were the bare crags of the Velebić mountains, and in front the blue sea of Novigrad famed for its tunny fishery; while beyond was the open sea with its islands, and the channel by which, as our guide sapiently observed, you can go from Novigrad to all parts of Europe.

Returning to the town we put ourselves under the guidance of the Parroco, or Curè, the personage in whom when wandering in remote parts of the country the traveller will generally find a good friend and an intelligent cicerone, and who is often the only person through whom he will learn what there is to see, and obtain leave to see it. Entering the little town by a gate over which is the date 1593 and the name of the reigning Doge Pasquale Cicogna, we threaded the uneven and irregular alleys that lead to the church, from whose western bellcot 'mezzo giorno' was being jingled forth by men standing on the roof and striking the clappers against the bells with their hands. The church is not of any antiquity or interest, but possesses a '*pianeta*' or chasuble of cut and embroidered velvet, which, like everything else in the neighbourhood, is said to have been a present from Queen Elizabeth. The style of the design with its cornucopias is not consistent with so early a date, but some small pieces of embroidery which are inserted may have belonged to an older vestment. There is also a silver cross, chiefly of eighteenth century work, but with evangelistic emblems apparently of the twelfth.

Outside the walls is the Church of S. Caterina,

now used as a cemetery chapel, which is believed to occupy the site of a Benedictine abbey suppressed in the year 976[1]. The chancel is a low barrel vaulted structure, possibly part of the Benedictine church, and in the walls of the more modern nave are imbedded some fragments of interlacing bandwork with birds and animals (vid. Plate I. Fig. 3) that belonged to the conventual buildings, and are important as examples of ninth or at the latest tenth century work, supposing the date of the suppression of the abbey to be correctly fixed.

The locanda of Novigrad where we were to lunch was certainly the roughest we encountered in Dalmatia. We entered from the street by a large doorway into a dark rambling place, which had apparently been used as a slaughter-house, and where several men were still seated on the ground busily engaged in scraping the inside of some gory sheep-skins. Across the bloody puddles of the floor we picked our way to a rude ladder staircase which led to rather better quarters above, though even here one side of the room was formed with nothing better than rough planks through which in winter the Bora must make rude entrance. It is however fair to say the dinner exceeded our expectations.

We had some trouble in getting our driver, who was a convivial soul, and was enjoying himself after his fashion lower down the village, to put his horses to and start homewards, and it required all the authority of the Parroco to get him under weigh.

[1] Bianchi, Zara Cristiana, vol. ii. p. 294.

But we had our revenge, for we stopped him at the top of the hill that I might finish my sketch, and consequently we were passed by another carriage, bound like ourselves for Zara. Our driver exclaimed that he felt this as if he had received a deadly wound, and for the rest of the way we had a regular race home until our rival was repassed, and our wounded honour healed.

CHAPTER VI.

SAN MICHELE D' UGLIANO.

ULJAN or Ugliano is a long narrow island opposite Zara, one of those craggy parallel ridges, the crests of partly submerged mountains, that lie often two or three deep with narrow channels between them along the sea coast of northern Dalmatia. Ugliano though some twenty miles in length is for the most part a bare mile in width, and at its widest not three miles from shore to shore. Its lofty backbone is notched and serrated with a succession of peaks rising to the height of from 900 to 1000 feet, one of which is crowned with a castle, the most conspicuous object in the neighbourhood of Zara[1]. The population of the island amounts to 5694, and there are several villages and country houses whither the well-to-do Zaratini resort for their '*villeggiatura*,' which is as regular an institution in Dalmatia as in Italy. To one of these houses we were invited by our kind friend Signor Simeone Salghetti Drioli of Zara, who has a Venetian villa there dating from the eighteenth

---

[1] Monte Grande, the highest peak, is 1000 feet high, and Monte S. Michele, on which the castle is placed, 950 feet.

century[1], with a shady garden and trellised alleys, close to the little port of Oltre directly opposite Zara.

The great object of the visit was the castle of S. Michele, for which we started under a broiling sun with a boatman carrying a basket of grapes and a bottle of water flavoured with aniseed for refreshment by the way. Dalmatia is not a country for pedestrians, and Ugliano certainly can boast nothing like our English country walks. The whole island is under cultivation and entirely enclosed by dry stone walls between which you walk tortuously along the roughest imaginable paths, floundering over boulders of rock and sharp pebbles that cut your boots to pieces.

The distance to the castle was greater than we expected, for the hill on which it stands does not rise from the shore as it seems to do from Zara. Ugliano in fact consists of two long parallel ridges enclosing a valley between them, and the castle is on the farther of the two. From this valley a steep climb of a quarter of an hour brings you to the castle gate, curiously contrived on the landward side—that I mean towards Zara—within a recess between bastions. The door was locked, but my knocking roused a furious barking of dogs within, and brought a wild shaggy peasant who had

---

[1] Farlati speaks of the villas on the island of Ugliano; 'Porro dispersae in aestivos maxime autumnalesque secessus Patritiorum Jadrensium villae frequentissimae sunt, opere eleganti situque peramoeno.'

some trouble to keep his curs in order. Once inside, you rise by a narrow path between walls to the level, or rather unlevel, of the castle-yard. The curtain walls and bastions still surround it, and from the terrace walk on the top of the wall there are fine views of Zara, with the Velebić mountains far away in the background, Nona on an arm of the sea northwards, and the islands of Pago Puntadura and others, while towards the west you look over a series of long narrow ridges with intervening channels to the open Adriatic, beyond which but for an envious haze we ought to have seen the great rock of Ancona, on which stands the ancient church of S. Ciriaco.

Low buildings with lean-to roofs against the outer walls once surrounded the enclosure, but the roofs are now gone. The great square keep stands close to the gate, a mere hollow shell, but still preserving the stone vault at top like the great donjon at Pembroke, and a vault below which is reached by a hole in the floor. In the centre of the castle-yard on a natural table of rock stands a desolate-looking church, dismantled but not ruinous, which is still served once or twice in the year by the village priest from below, when the peasants climb the hill in great numbers. The altar retains its shabby altar-piece, mouldy and stained by damp and sea-air, but all the other fittings are gone. The roof is a plain waggon stone vault, the east end has a plain apse, and there are a few bits of Venetian Gothic detail.

The church belonged to a Benedictine abbey which was founded on this inhospitable spot in the tenth or eleventh century. The original castle was no doubt that built opposite Zara by Rainieri Dandolo, son of the Doge Enrico Dandolo, in 1203, after the crusaders had sailed from Zara, in order to check what the Venetians called the piracies of the expatriated Zaratini. The Zaratini, aided by the gold of the archbishop of Spalato, subsidised ten galleys of Gaieta which happened to be in Dalmatia, and with their help took and destroyed the castle, and put the Venetian garrison to the sword[1]. It is uncertain when the fortress was rebuilt, but a castle certainly existed here in 1346 when the Venetians took it[2] during their siege of Zara, and garrisoned it with a captain and 100 Venetian soldiers, who were afterwards reduced to 50. In 1350 the Venetians dismantled the castle and destroyed the church. It is probable that the offence given to the abbot of S. Michele by the demolition of his church, and the non-fulfilment by the Venetians of their promise to build him another in the plain, was the cause of his betrayal of Zara to the Hungarians in 1357, if the story of his treachery is true[3]. Under the Hungarians, between 1366 and 1373, the castle was restored and the church rebuilt, no doubt in the form in which we now see it. The abbey came to an end between 1453 and 1468. Dominicans were

---

[1] Thom. Archid. c. xxv.
[2] Obsid. Iadrens. l. ii. c. xvii.
[3] Vid. sup. General History, p. 112.

established there in 1570, and the convent was finally suppressed in 1858[1].

As we descended the rocky path to Oltre our ears were greeted by the piping of a strange musical instrument, and on turning a corner we came on a scene that took one back to the shepherds of the Eclogues,—a herdsman followed by his flock, and piping to them on a double flute. The 'fistula' however—it still keeps its classic name—is not divided into two distinct pipes as we see it on ancient gems, and as Raphael has drawn it in the cartoon of Paul and Barnabas at Lystra, but is carved out of a single piece of wood, solid at the double mouthpiece and forked below[2]. The music of which it is capable consists of sustained passages in a minor key with many roulades and turns, and the effect of the simple concords of two notes, when the performer is as skilful as our Meliboeus, is pretty and plaintive.

Not less Virgilian—not to say Adamitic, as our host pronounced them—are the ploughs of Dalmatia (Fig. 17). They are of two kinds, 'the *oralo*,' for use as a labourer expressed it on *rocks* and stony places, for in Dalmatia they talk of rock much as in England we talk of a clay-soil, and the '*plugo*' for better and deeper soil. The former is nothing but two pieces of wood fixed at an angle with an iron

[1] Vid. Article in Annuario Dalmatico, 1884, by Prof. Benevenia, '*Il monte di S. Michele d' Ugliano.*'

[2] Mr. Arthur Evans gives an illustration of one of these double pipes, '*Through Bosnia,*' &c., p. 22.

point to one of them; the latter is somewhat more elaborate, and has an iron coulter and a wooden mould board. The steel share of the latter costs five, and the whole plugo ten or twelve florins; it lasts about three years. Of these two Illyric names the first

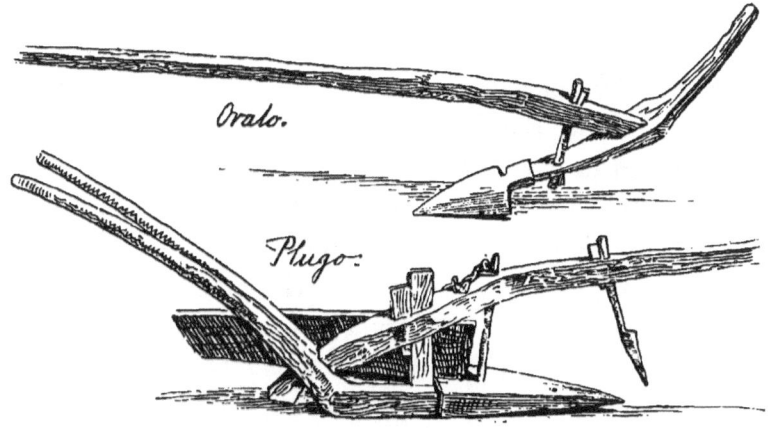

Fig. 17.

seems akin to the Latin word, and the second is curiously like our own. The peasants say these rude implements suit their rocky soil best, and it is quite possible that a less primitive article would not stand the rough shock of the stones of Dalmatia so well.

CHAPTER VII.

Nona. History.

Nona, in Illyric Nin, the Aenona civitas of Pliny[1], and a place of consequence anciently, whence came, according to tradition, the handsome Roman arch which now forms the inner face of the sea-gate at Zara, was less fortunate than the other maritime towns of Dalmatia, and after it had once fallen into the hands of the Croat immigrants it never again recovered its position as a Latin city.

Constantine Porphyrogenitus in the tenth century mentions Νόνα as one of the towns inhabited by the Christianized Croats. It was the chief town of a zupy, the seat of one of the eleven Croatian zupans, and occasionally the residence of the Croatian king. Peter Cresimir, king of Dalmatia and Croatia, dates an edict in 1069, 'in nostro Nonensi Cenaculo residens una cum nostris Jupanis, comitibus, atque Banis, Capellanis etiam nostrae regalis aulae[2].' By this king part of the island of Pago[3] was attached to the see of Nona, whose bishops in consequence of privileges granted by Mucimir in the ninth century

---

[1] Plin. Nat. Hist. l. iii. c. xxi.
[2] Cited by Lucio, de Regn. Dalm. et Croat. ii. viii. p. 77.
[3] Farlati, vol. i. part ii. c. vii, also Lucio.

had at that time all Croatia for their diocese, and who in the fourteenth century enjoyed the prerogative of appointing the zupan[1]. It was to Nona as to a Croatian town that the fugitive Zaratini fled for security on the second capture of their city by the Venetians in 1243, and the names of eleven citizens of Nona attached to a treaty with Arbe in 1284 are all thoroughly Slavonic. From the document in question the people of Nona seem to have fallen into the piratical habits common to the maritime Slavs. Marco Michaeli Count of Arbe had hanged one Dobrissa a pirate of Nona, and in reprisal the men of Nona had captured a ship of Arbe and carried it to Nona; whereupon the count of Arbe had invaded their territory, and one Cernote an Arbesan noble had been slain. The feud was appeased by the mediation of the Venetians; Dobrissa was pronounced properly hanged, and Cernote killed in fair fight; the men of Nona were to pay for the ship they had taken, and the Arbesani for the damage they had done on the territory of Nona, and no further question was to be raised by either side. It is interesting to notice that while the names of those who signed the treaty on behalf of Nona are Slavonic, those of the Arbesan signatories are nearly all Italian[2].

In 1327 Nona, like Traü and Sebenico, was driven by the tyranny of the counts of Bribir to throw herself on the protection of Venice, preserving like those

[1] Luc. vi. 1, p. 271.
[2] For this treaty see Lucio, iv. ix. p. 184.

towns her ancient constitution and privileges. The Venetians garrisoned the place, and were besieged there by the Hungarian Ban on his way to attack Zara in 1357. The Venetians in vain endeavoured to raise the siege, and after the inhabitants had been reduced to eat their horses they were obliged to surrender to the Hungarians. Hither in June 1387 came Queen Maria, the daughter of Lewis and bride of Sigismond, on her release from captivity at Novigrad, and after a few days she sailed hence in the Venetian galleys for Segna, on her way to join her bridegroom.

In 1389 Nona was taken by Tvartko I, king of Bosnia, and about 1420 it passed, like the rest of Dalmatia, into the hands of the Venetians. It was abandoned and partly destroyed by them in 1571, and again in 1646, to prevent its falling into the hands of the Turks. On the latter occasion the town was burned, by the order of the Senate, after the departure of the count and the bishop, and since that day it has never recovered its former importance.

The excursion to Nona is the easiest and perhaps the most interesting that can be made from Zara. Nona is the first town within the limits of Dalmatia whose history connects it almost exclusively with Slavonic as distinct from Italian influences. Except for a short time in the fourteenth century it was a Croatian town from the eighth to the fifteenth century, and when at last it fell under the direct government of Venice it was hurriedly abandoned and burned. Here then I hoped to see what the Slavs of Dalmatia could produce in the way of architecture when left to themselves, and it must be confessed that they have no very great triumphs to record, although from an antiquarian point of view their work is not without interest. The oldest buildings remaining there are based on Byzantine art rather than that of western Europe, although they are so plain and of such humble dimensions that they scarcely amount to works of art at all. To this class belong the domed churches of S. Nicolò and S. Croce: but even the later buildings still cling to the round arch, the shallow tympanum, and the narrow windows of Byzantine architecture, although they shew in one instance perhaps a trace of Hungarian influence, and one church has the singularity of a square end, like our English chancels. Unfortunately so few of the buildings remain in anything like a perfect state that less is to be learned from them than a first view seems to promise.

Zara being on a peninsula there is but one way out, and for some distance our road followed that by which we had gone to Novigrad. On leaving this and turning northwards we traversed a high down-like country, stony and bare except for the short scrubby bushes that were dotted over it, and commanding lovely views of the sea on one side and the Velebić mountains on the other. A drive of an hour and a half brought us within sight of Nona, situated low down to our right, on the margin of what appeared to be an inland lake but was really an arm of the sea, connected, though invisibly to us, by intricate channels with the open sea on our left.

But before reaching Nona we stayed to examine a strange-looking ruin that crowned a lofty barrow, evidently of artificial formation, which may perhaps mark the sepulchre of some Croat chieftain. The ruin is that of a small cruciform church dedicated to St. Nicholas, but it has the air rather of a fortress than of an ecclesiastical building, and the wide breaches that now gape in its walls may perhaps be wounds received when it was on some occasion turned to military uses. In plan (vid. Plate XI) it is a Greek cross, all four arms being equal in length, but the choir and transepts are apsidal and covered with semidomes, while the nave is square in plan, though it too is roofed with a semidome, carried on the conch-shaped squinches in the angles of the square which abound in these early Dalmatian churches. The central space is covered by a dome, which however has transverse ribs laid on its under side, springing from fragments of classic moulding built in to serve as consoles. The west door, which is only 5 ft. $8\frac{1}{4}$ in. high, has a square lintel under a semicircular arch, with a slightly sunk tympanum, and with the head jambs and sill curiously joggled together, in a manner not uncommon in the early work of this district (vid. Plate XI). Externally the dome is concealed by an octagonal tower, battlemented at top, which it is difficult to believe not

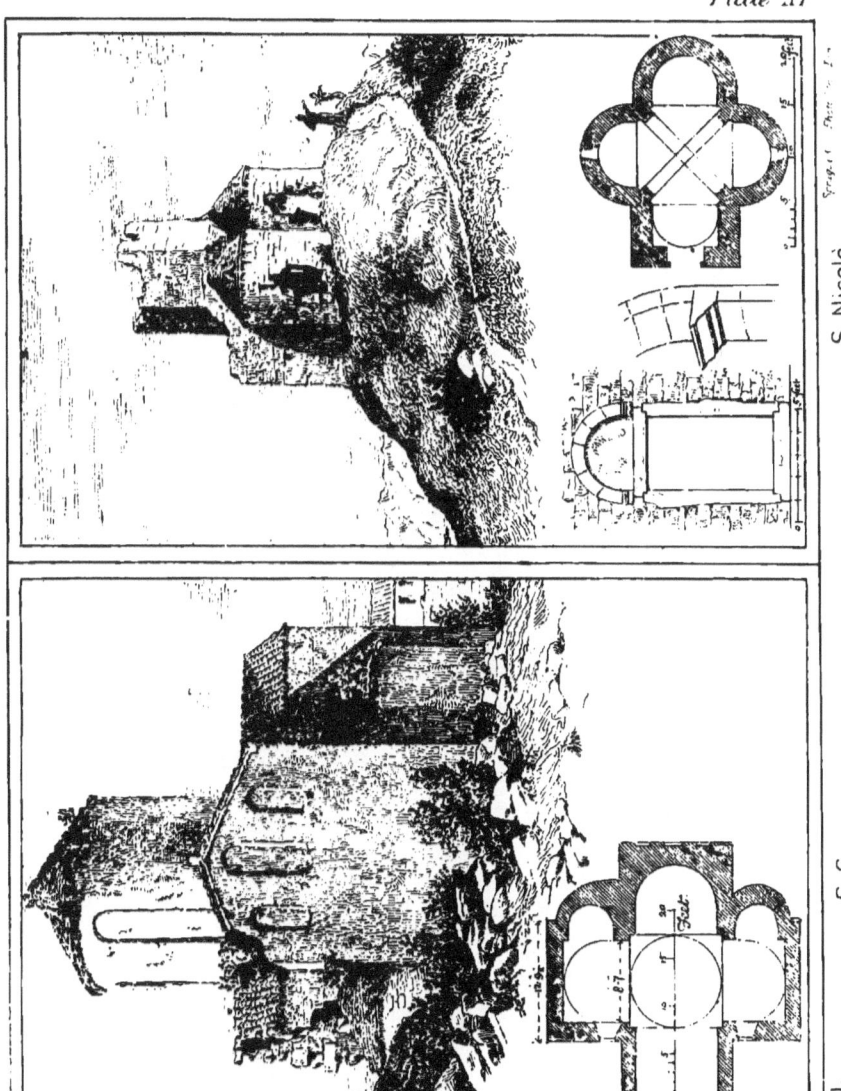

to have been intended for defence. The dimensions of the building are strangely minute; the span of each arm is seven feet, the nave is four feet five inches long, and the total internal length only nineteen feet six inches. Fragments of antique classic work, moulded and fluted, occur in the walls, and on the floor lies a cylindrical stone hollowed on the top, which might be part of a column but that it tapers too abruptly. There is so little to fix the date of the building that it might be attributed with almost equal probability to any time from the ninth to the twelfth century; but the cross-ribs that underlie the dome seem to me to point rather to the later than the earlier part of that extended period.

From S. Nicolò it is less than a mile to Nona, which we found surrounded by shallow water and marshy pools amply sufficient to account for the feverish reputation it enjoys. A more desolate and deplorable looking place never represented the fallen greatness of an ancient Roman city. The town walls and gates are ruined and dilapidated and in places quite broken down, and they reflect themselves sadly in the unwholesome pools that wash their base. The glimpses of the interior which these gaps afford reveal more ruins than houses, and the ravens that croaked dismally over our heads as we approached seemed to read a commentary on the picture of misery and decay that lay before us. Crossing the water by a causeway and entering the town we found ourselves in an irregular straggling street with scattered houses and many ruins; few of the inhabitants were visible, and most of those whom we saw had that 'faccia smorta,' that deathly complexion and enfeebled frame that tells of malaria. In the centre of the town we drew up in front of 'the shop,' where as in an English village everything from clothing to food, candles, and soap, may be had within the limits of a choice, somewhat narrow perhaps, but wide enough for the modest demands of the villager. What little activity exists at Nona is centred in this establishment, and it is the only place where the few strangers who come here can obtain any accommodation, for there is no inn or caffè even of the humblest kind. Here we left our wraps and other encumbrances, and set out on our round of exploration under the guidance of the courteous Parroco, being anxious to lose no time nor to run any risk of delaying our departure till the dangerous evening mists arose charged with their fatal malaria [1].

The Duomo. Of the sixteen churches which Nona is said to have once possessed seven still exist entire or in ruins, though only one is in a condition for use. This is the Duomo, dedicated to S. Anselmo, the cathedral church of Nona during the middle ages and until the series of bishops came to an end in 1804. The actual fabric though on old foundations dates only from the last century and is of no interest. Adjoining and opening from it is another and older

[1] Nona was noted for its unhealthiness during the middle ages. Farlati mentions that the bishop was allowed to live in Zara during the unwholesome season. Illyr. Sacr. tom. iv. p. 204.

church dedicated to S. Ambrogio. The nave of this is square and perfectly plain, the chancel is cross-vaulted and has on the keystone the arms of Bishop DIPHNICA, whose tombstone stands against the wall: obiit MDXXX. The dedication of this church is now changed from S. Ambrogio to the Madonna, to commemorate a local legend resembling that of la Salette.

The treasury of the duomo, which consists of a case over the high altar, contains many objects of considerable interest, of which I noted the following:

(1) Two silver gilt cases containing the feet of S. Anselmo, a saint whom legend reports to have been one of the seventy disciples of Christ, and the first bishop of Nona.

(2) Two coffanetti of silver gilt containing the heads of S. Anselmo and his sister S. Marcella. On the sides are figures under trefoiled arches supported by twisted columns, above which is a slightly embossed band representing a chase of stags and hares, with a huntsman with his horn, &c. Here, as in the case of similar subjects which occur in sculpture at Traü, it is to be observed that stags are unknown in Dalmatia, from which it has been inferred that the artist was a foreigner, possibly, as at Zara, a Milanese. This hunting subject is to be found on both coffanetti, and on the lid of both are the evangelistic emblems embossed from the same matrices. The style is that of the fifteenth century, or at the earliest of the end of the fourteenth.

(3) A pretty little cross standing on a plaque on which are the remains of a fringe of bushes, and

statuettes of the Virgin, St. John, and St. Mary Magdalen. The base is very graceful.

(4) A cross over the altar inscribed in Lombardic letters STEFANVS FECIT. The crucifixion in front, St. Martin as a bishop on the back.

(5) A chalice given by Bishop Diphnica (died 1530), like one I afterwards drew at Curzola.

All the saints revered at Nona, said the Parroco with modest pride, are of the first century.

Behind the duomo lies an antique Roman capital, supposed to have belonged to the church and convent of the nuns of S. Marcella, destroyed by the Turks about 1500.

In front of 'the shop' stands a row of capitals, also attributed to this church, which, to judge from their dimensions and style, must have been a building of stately proportions and good architecture[1]. They seem to belong to the twelfth or thirteenth century at the latest. The palaces of the bishop and the Venetian count are in ruins, and the lion of S. Mark stands degraded on the ground. A large stone, which once formed the lintel over the door of the count's palace, bears on the dexter end the initials HE · M and the date April, 1511, and at the sinister end IO · M · M Janūī 1514; an arm outstretched from either side, and hands clasped in the middle open a wide field for conjecture as to the happy incident intended to be commemorated. The scutcheon seems to be that of the Venetian family of Molino.

[1] Vid. Plate I. Fig. 4.

S. Croce. From the modern duomo we went to the ancient and half-ruined church of S. Croce, the cathedral in Byzantine times (Plate XI). This, like S. Nicolò, is of the tiniest dimensions, with a nave eight feet seven inches wide and a total interior length of twenty-five feet: probably as small a cathedral as any in Christendom. The plan forms a Greek cross with all the arms externally square, but the eastern arm is round internally, and the rest are brought to a semicircular plan above by conchiform squinches as at S. Barbara Traü, and S. Nicolò here, to enable them to be covered by semidomes. Each transept has an apse applied to the east side which is vaulted and roofed in the same solid masonry, like our Pembrokeshire churches at Gumfreston and elsewhere, the slates being bedded on the back of the vault. The chancel is ornamented with three blank arches on the outside, and was formerly lighted by a little window in the east wall. The crossing has squinches in the angles of the square, which carry a conical dome constructed in the rudest way, the plan at the springing being by no means a true circle. The external casing of the dome is carried up as a tower which is only roughly cylindrical, being little better than a square with rounded angles; and it is ornamented with blank arches like the apse, and crowned by a low pyramidal roof.

The church stands north and south, the chancel being towards the south; and the quasi west end has a gable surmounted by a bellcot above three blank windows with a doorway below them.

The most interesting feature of the building is this doorway, a square-headed opening, with a lintel of a single stone which projects with a bevelled face like the side of a sarcophagus. This lintel is richly carved with interlacing knots and scrolls of a Byzantine character, from the design of which Eitelberger infers that the building dates from the ninth century (Plate I. Fig. 2). But the great interest of the doorway consists in the inscription deeply incised in irregular lettering on the soffit of the lintel, in which may be made out the name of the zupan Godeslav. Eitelberger, who gives the inscription after Camesina[1], observes that the letters are Latin, and not Glagolitic nor Cyrillic, and that the language also appears to be Latin, but he does not venture on an interpretation. I measured and sketched this interesting little church, which, like the other outside the town, is valuable as an example of genuine Slavonic architecture. The only details inside are a rude impost at the springing of the arch, and a roughly-formed stoup for holy water.

S. ANTONIO is another ruined church, with a short quadrangular nave and apse at the east end, properly orientated.

THE CHURCH OF S. AMBROGIO (Fig. 18) once belonged to Benedictine monks. It is also in ruins, and about, they said, to be pulled down by leave of the government, who have sold the materials for thirty florins to the peasants of Oltre on the island

---

[1] Eitelberger, Dalmatien, p. 169. His illustration, which I have copied, is apparently taken from Camesina.

of Ugliano, to be used in building a new church there. This is a very great pity, for the church is an ex-

Fig. 18.

tremely interesting building, and though partly roofless, is in other respects quite perfect. The plan consists of a nave and chancel, lighted by small single lights, round-headed and splayed equally inside and out[1], the lights which are mere slits of a few inches wide being in the middle of the wall (Fig. 19).

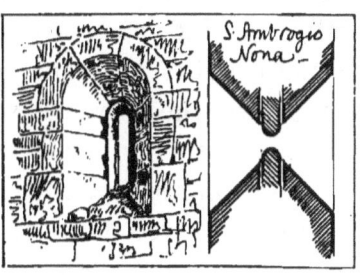

Fig. 19.

The west door is round-headed and has a very singular cross-shaped window above it. The chancel opens to the nave with a semicircular arch devoid of

[1] Compare Traü.

any moulding or impost, and ends, English fashion, with a *square* end. The choir retains its barrel vault which is very slightly pointed in section, and the nave, which is now open to the sky, has had a round barrel vault strengthened with transverse flat ribs springing from flat wall piers with plain imposts. In the east wall, now ruined, are traces of a group of two or perhaps three lancets like those in the side walls. The exterior of this square end, when perfect, with its gable and triplet of narrow windows, must have had the look of a Norman church in some Sussex village. The church dates probably from the thirteenth century. The Benedictines departed in 1440, but the '*abbazia commendataria*' remained till the time of Napoleon.

Close behind this church, which I hope may yet be saved by the intervention of the Conservator at Zara, who I found had not heard of its intended destruction[1], is one of the old gates of the Venetian walls, opening landwards to a causeway across the dismal marshes that hem in the town. St. Mark's lion guards the entrance, which has been flanked by two bastions, only one of which remains.

S. MICHELE stands on the site of the Roman arena, where the Parroco has dug and found walls, columns, and seats. The church has a nave once roofed with wood but now open to the sky, a chancel with a

---

[1] Our visit to Nona was in 1884. On enquiry at Zara in 1885, I was glad to find the government had ordered the contract for the destruction of the church to be rescinded on the representation of the Conservator.

pointed barrel vault, and small side windows splayed inside and outside. Those in the side walls are round-headed, that in the east wall by a strange freak is triangular-headed. There are plain square doors, that to the west with an arched tympanum slightly sunk, and jambs archivolt and lintel flush with the wall face.

Of Roman Ænona scarcely any traces remain above ground. I have mentioned one antique capital lying in the street, and there are a few inscriptions built into the walls of a shabby cottage, but I saw no other remains of classical times. Eitelberger[1] says that numerous inscriptions have been found at Nona which may now be seen at Udine; but at Nona one is told that what were taken away were not inscriptions but statues; and Fortis[2], writing in the last century, mentions that he saw at the house of Dr. Antonio Danieli, a physician who entertained him at Zara, four valuable colossal statues of marble which his host had brought at his own expense from the ruins of Nona[3].

Our party was joined by an extremely lively young gentleman, secretary to the 'Comune,' a Ragusan by birth, but settled here long enough to have become a martyr to the ague. But though, as he said, a

[1] P. 169.
[2] Viaggio in Dalmazia.
[3] Mons. Bianchi, Zara Cristiana, ii. p. 425, gives a catalogue of the marbles in the Danieli collection, which were sold in 1840 by Dott. Casimiro de Pellegrini Danieli to Count Cernazai of Udine. In this collection of 300 pieces were included some found at or near Zara.

constant sufferer from fever, his spirits had suffered no depression ; a merrier party than ours never sat down to hard-boiled eggs and German sausage, and if fever can be kept away by laughter we certainly ran no risk of catching it.

CHAPTER VIII.

Vrana.

History of Vrana. S. Cassiano. Torrette. Castle and Lake of Vrana. Turkish Han. Ali-beg. Luciano di Laurana. Podgrajc the ancient Assesia.

THE castle of Vrana plays a large part in Dalmatian history. There was originally a Benedictine abbey of S. Gregorio on its site, which was granted to the Apostolic See in the time of Gregory VII. by Zuonimir king of Croatia, together with all its treasures, church plate, gospels in bindings of silver, and other goods and chattels, as a 'hospitium' for the Papal legates[1]. How Vrana returned to the possession of the king does not appear from any authority to which I have had access; but in 1138 it was granted by Bela II, 'the blind,' to the Knights Templar, who were subject to the jurisdiction of the Grand Master of Hungary. The Templars built the castle, an oblong court protected by a ditch, which was afterwards increased by the addition of a second parallelogram, and within the walls was enclosed the ancient monastery of their

[1] The text of the deed of gift is given by Lucio. de Regn. ii. x. p. 85–86; the date of it is 1076.

predecessors. Lampridio, archbishop of Zara in 1163, claimed jurisdiction over them on the ground that the convent of S. Gregorio had been subject to the see of Belgrad, but the Templars maintained that they were independent of any bishop but the supreme pontiff; and Alexander III, to whom the dispute was referred, decided in favour of the Templars in 1168. The Templars of Dalmatia were a powerful body, and their possessions were extensive, but they shared the downfall of their order in 1311, when it was suppressed by the Council of Vienne. Here, as elsewhere, they were deprived of their property, and their order was proscribed; and Vrana was given to the Knights Hospitaller of St. John, in whose ranks many of the Templar knights re-enlisted. The most famous of the Hospitaller priors of Vrana were the Counts of Palisna, who played a prominent part in the rebellion of the Croats against Hungary after the death of Lewis. Giovanni or Gianco Palisna, prior of Vrana, was one leader of the conspiracy which invited Charles III. of Naples to dispute the crown of Hungary with Maria. In 1383 Vrana was recovered by the supporters of the Queen, and on Nov. 4 of that year Maria and her mother Elizabeth visited the castle in person. After the murder of Charles III. at Buda in 1386, it was Palisna in concert with the Ban Horvad, who captured the queens and conveyed them to Novigrad where Elizabeth was murdered, and Maria confined till her captor was compelled by the

Venetians to release her in 1387[1]. Threatened by Sigismund, and besieged in his castle of Vrana, Palisna invited Tvartko king of Bosnia to his assistance; the siege of Vrana was raised in 1389, and the besiegers chased to the walls of Zara, and in the year 1391 the army of Sigismund was repulsed before Knin by the forces of Bosnia, under the command of Palisna. In the following year Palisna died, and Tvartko only survived him a month, his death dissolving the kingdom which he had established over the whole of Dalmatia, except Zara and Ragusa. In 1392 the priorate of Vrana was finally suppressed by Vuk Vucich Ban of Bosnia, who seized the last prior and threw him into prison.

Vrana was one of the places which Ladislaus of Naples sold to the Venetians in 1409[2]; they retained it till 1538, when it was surrendered to the Turks after the fall of Clissa, and was left in Turkish possession by the peace of 1540. Under the Turks the place became very prosperous, and the large Han or Khan, still standing close by the castle, was built by them for the accommodation of caravans of traders from the interior to the coast. In the seventeenth century Ali-beg, the Sangiac of Licca, made his residence at Vrana, and like a true Oriental adorned the place with beautiful gardens irrigated with elaborate water-

---

[1] Vid. sup., History, Chapter i. p. 126-129, and Chapt. v. p. 325.
[2] 'Nec non terram Lauranae cum fortalicio et castro ipsius.' Cited by Lucio, v. v. p. 263.

works, of which the ruins might still be seen at the time of Fortis's visit, ninety years ago[1]. But Ali-beg was not left to enjoy his gardens in peace: he was attacked and defeated by Pisani in January 1647, and later in the same year was besieged by the same officer with 5000 men in the fortress of Zemonico. Ali-beg made a desperate resistance, but was compelled to capitulate, the conditions of his surrender being that he should submit to a month's detention at Zara and then be set at liberty. But the treachery of some Turks who had remained hidden in the fortress was considered by the Venetians a breach of this engagement, and Ali-beg instead of being restored to liberty was sent to Brescia, where he died.

The Venetians burned the *borgata* of 600 houses which surrounded the castle, and dismantled the castle itself, in order to avoid the necessity of placing and maintaining a garrison there, and in consequence they were obliged to leave it in the possession of the Turks at the peace of 1669, which only confirmed them in their possession of such places as they had occupied by a garrison. Vrana, however, never played any part again in the wars of the Turks and Venetians, and on the conclusion of the peace of Carlovitz was left in

---

[1] Fortis says:—'The gardens of Hali-Beg are reduced to heaps of rubbish; and the waters that were formerly conducted by art, to adorn and refresh them, now run in disorderly streams mixing with many others which a hundred years ago were also formed into artificial channels and conveyed into the lake.'

the possession of the Republic. It is said that the title of Beg of Vrana still remains among the Turks in the same family which last held it, and that of Prior Auraniae among the titles of nobility at the court of Hungary[1]. In 1752 Vrana was granted as a feud of the Republic to the ancestors of Count Borelli of Zara, the present owner.

The distance from Zara to Vrana is about twenty-five English miles, over bad roads, except for part of the way where there is no road at all. There is no accommodation to be had at Vrana, nor in the neighbourhood, and the only way in which we could visit it was by going and returning the same day. This we managed by sending on a pair of horses the day before to S. Filippo, so as to have fresh beasts to take us over the worst part of the way.

We started between five and six in the morning with a pair of horses, and soon turned out of the main road, which is very good, into a country road that skirts the shore and often runs close to the water's edge. The country was low and undulating, the soil as usual rocky, but well clothed with vegetation. Oliveyards and vineyards alternated with districts of woodland and a thick undergrowth of myrtles, junipers, and dwarf elders; but the woods in Dalmatia are badly managed and cut too

---

[1] Mons. Bianchi, Zara Cristiana, vol. ii. p. 366, says that the last possessor of the title of Prior of Vrana was Mons. Franc. Kralj, president of the chapter of Agram, who left 200 florins to the church at Vrana.

often, so that it is rare to see anything that can be called timber.

Passing Borgo Erizzo, a colony of Albanians, who are said to be the most industrious and meritorious peasants in the district of Zara, we reached Bibigne, and then S. Cassiano, where on a rock in the little bay round which the village is built stands the ruin of the summer retreat built for himself by Archbishop Valaresso, when his jealous relatives prevented him from spending his money on building a campanile for the duomo of Zara[1]. It is a square castellated building standing in the water and totally dismantled: as there was not a boat immediately available we did not stay to visit it, and indeed there seemed little to interest us had we done so.

At the end of four hours we reached Torrette, a little walled village with one old gate and two of its angle bastions still perfect. Torrette was often in danger from the Turks in the seventeenth century and the inhabitants of the neighbourhood were glad to shelter themselves in its narrow and crowded alleys. Now that they have no occasion for this confinement they have moved their quarters into the open country, and the village is full of deserted houses which are falling into ruin. The house of Signor Santini, with whom we were to dine on our return from Vrana, has some traces of Venetian architecture, and commands a lovely

---

[1] See above, p. 281.

view of the Canale di Zara with the outlying islands of Pasman and Ugliano.

At S. Filippo, where we changed horses, we left the sea-shore, and struck inland by a mere mule track across an open down of rock covered with a shrubby undergrowth of myrtle and juniper, and on reaching the top of the ridge the view of the lake of Vrana burst upon us backed up by mountains of considerable elevation. The lake is eight miles long and two miles wide, and is the largest in Dalmatia; its colour is green, contrasting strongly with the deep ultramarine of the sea, which from our standpoint was visible at the same time. Descending to the valley we found a somewhat better road, which took us to Vrana on the farther shore by a wide sweep round the head of the lake, which ends in an extensive reedy swamp over which the road passes by a causeway. Beyond are extensive 'prati,'—a rare sight in Dalmatia,—where much hay is made; but in winter and spring the lake rises and lays a great part of the plain under water. The water is brackish, though not so much so but that the people of Vrana drink it for want of better, but the saltness seems to prove the existence of some subterranean communication with the sea. That the lake is not above the sea level is apparent from the failure of an attempt to drain it by a canal cut to the sound, which had the effect of letting the sea into the lake and making matters worse[1]; and if there is

[1] Paton, Highlands and Islands of the Adriatic, vol. ii. p. 95.

a subterranean communication it would be useless to attempt to drain it by pumping engines as has been suggested. The fishing is said to be good, but we saw no boats except coracles, such as may have been used by the primitive Illyrians, and are still to be seen on our own Welsh rivers.

An hour and a-half after leaving S. Filippo we reached the village of Vrana, which is situated on rising ground at the northern end of the lake.

Fig. 20.

The castle (Fig. 20) is a stupendous heap of ruins covering a very large extent of ground on the summit of a natural elevation. It was a very regular building, consisting of two rectangular courts divided by a central wall, and surrounded by a deep fosse, excavated for the most part in the solid rock. Notwithstanding the enormous strength of the masonry the whole now lies in utter ruin, and never was an ancient castle more thoroughly 'slighted.' In one corner of the first courtyard is pointed out the site and a few remains of the conventual church of S. Gregorio, but one looks in vain for any traces of the great hall, on whose walls were hung the knightly shields and cuirasses of the brotherhood, whose four windows recorded in their richly storied panes the feats of the order, and within which was concerted the conspiracy for overthrowing the two queens and placing Carlo of Durazzo on the throne of Hungary[1]. The outer courtyard has but little left of its girdle of walls and towers, which lie in confused heaps of masonry, thrown about in all directions by the gunpowder of the Venetian engineers. The inner court is more perfect; it seems to have been reached only through the other, and only by one small doorway in the party wall, beside which is an embrasure splayed inwards, and with a round hole outwards as if for a cannon. This is about the only piece of wrought masonry remaining in the building, which has long served the Morlacchi of the neighbourhood for a quarry. The only building within the enclosure of which any considerable part remains perfect is a tower, which may have been the keep, though its dimensions are but small, the interior measuring only nine feet six inches by nine feet on the ground floor within the walls, which are five feet six inches thick. The walls of this tower are riddled in the inside with pigeon-holes like those of our Pembrokeshire churches, perhaps for the same purpose of

[1] Bianchi, Zara Cristiana. Vid. sup. History, p. 125.

affording provision in case of extremity. There is a well in the interior of this courtyard which is now choked up.

Close by the castle is the Turkish Han or caravanserai, now the farmyard of Count Borelli. It is a large square-walled enclosure with entrances on two opposite sides under towers. The entrance archways are pointed, and have an unmistakeably oriental look about them, as have also the few other architectural features the building possesses. The passages through the towers have vaulted ceilings with pointed arches, but the farther tower of the two is much ruined, and so are most of the buildings surrounding the courtyard, a small two-storied building on one side being all that seems habitable. The exterior wall contains many fragments of antique buildings, and is constructed in the oddest and most inartificial way, with stones set upright as slabs, and without any regular coursing, as bad a piece of walling as was ever put together, shewing that the Turkish builders were but poor craftsmen.

Vrana is now a collection of scattered cottages distributed about the neighbouring hills, with here and there a little fort or watch-tower, once an outpost of the great castle. The population amounts to something over 300 at the present day, but round the castle may still be seen the foundations of the houses and streets of a considerable town, which was destroyed during the wars of the Turks and Venetians. Vrana was the birthplace of Luciano Laurana, the architect of the palace at Urbino, who first saw the light here in 1420. The fact that there is no place in Dalmatia now going by the name Laurana, and that there is a place on the eastern coast of Istria near Fiume called Lovrana, has led Gaye and others to make Luciano an Istrian of the latter place. Against this there is in favour of his Dalmatian origin the fact that he is described in one document as '*egregius vir Lucianus . . . q. Martini de Jadia Provinciae Dalmatiae architectus*,' and in another as '*Magister Lucianus Martini de Lauranna architector*.' Jadia can hardly be anything but Jadera or Zara, within the territory of which place Vrana is situated, while Lovrana is far distant across the Quarnero, and not in Dalmatia at all. Laurana is known also to have been an old form of the name Vrana; it occurs in the deed of sale by Ladislaus of Naples of his rights in Dalmatia to the Venetians in 1409, where there is no room to doubt that the Laurana in question is the Vrana of which Ladislaus had shortly before become possessed[1]; and Farlati quotes a passage from the 'Topographus Magni Regni Hungariae,' which seems to dispose of any doubt that may remain on this subject : '*Urana alias Aurana sive Laurana celebris in primis est a Rhodiorum equitum statione.*'

[1] Vid. Lucio de Regno, l. v. c. iv. p. 260, '*Vranam* obsedit, deditioneque recepit;' Ib. c. v. p. 263, 'the king sells,' Civitatem Iadrae . . . nec non terram *Lauranae* cum fortalicio et castro ipsius.' These passages, and also that from Farlati, cited in the text (Illyr. Sacr. Proleg. ii. v. § iv.), are not noticed by Prof. Brunelli in his essay on the subject in the Annuario Dalmatico for 1884—q.v.

Luciano Laurana studied his art probably at Venice, but found employment at Naples, where he is said to have built the palace of Poggio reale, which is now destroyed, though the dates present some difficulty. Baldi[1] says that his employment at Urbino was due to the recommendation of the King of Naples. Duke Federigo da Montefeltro *'having made enquiry of many princes in order to obtain architects able to give him satisfaction, among many others one was sent to him by the kings of Naples named Luciano, born at Laurana, a place of Sclavonia.'* Baldi says that Luciano was a good draughtsman and painted skilfully, as may be *'seen from certain little pictures in which certain scenes are drawn in perspective and coloured, about which there is no doubt that they are his, he having written his name on them, and other things, in the Sclavonic language and character.'*

The patent of Federigo of Montefeltro, Count of Urbino and Castel Durante, and Captain General of the League, is dated from Pavia, June 10, 1468. It begins by reciting the honour and commendation due to those who excel in architecture, and goes on to say that *'having searched everywhere, and especially in Tuscany, where is the fountain of architects, and not having found a man truly intelligent and well skilled in that craft,'* the Count had finally selected Messer Lutiano to build his new palace. This is a high tribute to the reputation enjoyed

---

[1] Descrizione del palazzo ducale d' Urbino. Venezia, 1590.

by this Dalmatian master among contemporary artists[1].

The greater part of the exquisite palace at Urbino must be assigned to Baccio Pintelli, who succeeded to the post of architect after the death of Luciano, which occurred at Pesaro probably in the year 1481. But we may still see the hand of the original architect in the earlier parts of the building, such as the windows of two lights towards the street leading upward from the duomo, which are easily distinguishable from the later work of Baccio in the Cortile[2]. The name of Luciano is preserved by Giovanni Santi, the father of Raffaelle, in his eulogistic poem on the great Federigo his patron.

> 'E l' architetto a tutti gli altri sopra
> Fu Lucian Lauranna, huomo excellente
>   Che il nome vive, benchè morte el cuopra.
>   Qual cum l' ingegno altissimo e possente
> Guidava l' opra col parer del Conte,
>   Che a ciò il parer aveva alto e lucente
> Quant' altro Signor mai e le voglie pronte.'
> Canto lvi.

A mile from the castle is Podgraje, the ancient Asseria or Assesia, with Roman remains, which we

---

[1] The whole patent will be found in Pungileoni, Vita, &c. di Bramante, p. 63, ed. 1836. It was first published by this writer. The original is in the Archivio di Urbino unito all' Archivio Mediceo, Divis. B. fila. viii. It was republished by Gaye, Carteggio inedito d' artisti dei Secoli xiv–xvi.

[2] For further particulars relating to this subject see the article by Prof. Brunelli in the Annuario quoted above; Dennistoun's Dukes of Umbria, vol. i; and the 'Palast von Urbino,' by Fried. Arnold, Leipzig. Also Gaye's Carteggio, &c. &c., vol. i. p. 214, &c.

were unable to visit. They are described by Fortis, who gives a plan of the walls and gates. He says that the walls vary in thickness from eight to eleven feet, that they are faced with stones some of which are ten feet long, and that in places they are thirty feet high. One of the gates retained at the time of his visit part of its arch, and one of the bastions was polygonal in plan, with a point to the front like modern fortifications. Bastions of the same kind are to be seen in the Roman walls of Salona.

In the same neighbourhood Mr. Paton[1] visited a natural grotto with the figure of a recumbent water nymph cut in the rock, of which we heard nothing at the time of our visit. There was no one at Vrana to help us in our researches. . Visitors are extremely rare, and the antiquities of the place have received very little attention. The Croat peasant who acted as our guide was much interested in our visit, and made many enquiries about us of the Dalmatian gentleman who had accompanied us from Zara. 'These signori are English?' 'Yes.' 'From what part of England?' 'London.' 'They come here then from the largest city in the world to see our things, and yet our own people never think of coming to look at them.'

We returned to Torrette in time to enjoy the truly Dalmatian hospitality of Signor Santini, and to see his famous grey thoroughbred horse, the pride of the neighbourhood. And when it was time to start and our poor tired jades were brought round, the gallant

[1] Highlands and Islands of the Adriatic, vol. ii. p. 99.

grey was put to, and Signor Santini and I flew a few miles along the road before we turned to rejoin our equipage and say farewell. I heard afterwards that I had had an escape, for that the grey horse had caused Signor Santini many an upset. We reached Zara again about eight o'clock in the evening.

CHAPTER IX.

SEBENICO.

History. The Duomo. The Sacristy. Other Churches. Giorgio Orsini. Scardona. Falls of the Kerka.

ALTHOUGH the Sebenzani in their public inscriptions latinize the name of their city into Sicum, and their own into Sigenses, Sebenico has no claim to represent the ancient Roman colony of Sicum where Claudius settled his veterans[1]. Sicum is placed by Pliny between Tragurium and Salona, and stood probably near Castel Vitturi, on the Riviera dei Castelli, where a place named Siclis is mentioned in the Peutinger table. Sebenico has in fact no pretensions to antiquity; it was unknown to Porphyrogenitus, and first makes it appearance in history as a Croatian and not a Dalmatian town. Giustiniani, a writer who preceded Lucio[2], says it was founded by bandits or *euscocchi*, who at first from a fort on the hill watched the sea for ships which they attacked and plundered, and afterwards formed a

---

[1] 'Tragurium civium Romanorum marmore notum; Sicum in quem locum Divus Claudius veteranos misit. Salona colonia,' &c. Plin. iii. xxii. Farlati says, 'errant vel maxime qui Sicum inter ac Sibenicum nihil interesse existimant.' Part ii. Proleg. c. v. § iii. Vid. Sir J. Wilkinson, vol. i. p. 76.

[2] Quoted by Fortis, Viagg. in Dalm.

colony on the shore which they surrounded with a palisade or 'sibue,' whence came the name Sebenico. Whatever its origin may have been, Sebenico was a favourite place with the kings of Croatia, many of whose acts are dated 'apud castrum Sibenici,' and it was visited by Coloman in 1105, after the Hungarian conquest of Dalmatia. In 1117[1] the 'impregnable' town of Sebenico was taken and destroyed by Ordelafo Faliero, together with the other Croatian towns of Belgrad Nona and Novigrad. Sebenico was however but a small place[2] till 1127, when the Croatian city of Belgrad (Zara Vecchia) was destroyed by the Doge Domenico Michieli, the bishop and clergy were removed to Scardona, and the bulk of the population took refuge at Sebenico, which from that time rapidly advanced in importance. In 1167 Stephen III raised it to the rank of a free city conferring on it a charter and privileges similar to those enjoyed by the old Dalmatian cities of Traü and Spalato, and from that time forward Sebenico must be reckoned as within the Dalmatian pale, though a Croatian town by descent and tradition[3]. Lucio says the Sebenzani were some time in learning to wear their new privileges easily; accustomed for so long to be governed despotically, they accommodated themselves with difficulty to the Dalmatian laws; they had counts appointed for life, and not for

---

[1] 'Inexpugnabile castrum Sebenici obtinuit et diruit.' Dandolo, lib. ix. c. xi. pars 21.
[2] 'Parvi circuitus oppidum.' Luc. iii. vii. p. 125.
[3] Luc. iii. vii. p. 127.

a short term like the other cities, who were with difficulty restrained from their old habits of piracy, and they were more exposed than the other cities to the arbitrary interference of the Ban[1]. Gradually however the Sebenzani became Latinized, and in later ages the city was described by Fortis as next to Zara the best built in Dalmatia, and inhabited by the greatest number of noble families, 'as far removed from the barbarous manners of ancient pirates as their houses are unlike the former cottages or *sibice*;' and the same writer tells us that 'in the sixteenth century the arts and sciences flourished in this city more than in any other of Dalmatia[2]'.

Like her neighbours Sebenico passed under the rule of Manuel in 1171–80, and an accusation of piracy made against the Sebenzani while under the imperial government may perhaps be explained by political reasons. Alexander III writes from the Rialto to complain that Nestros and Porlat, two counts of Sebenico, had robbed his envoy the sub-deacon Raimondo on his way back from the King of Naples, and had taken from him everything excepting sixty marks, including the letters he was bearing from the King to the Pope, which latter theft Lucio thinks may have been made at the instigation of Manuel or his officers.

During the confusion that succeeded the Tartar

[1] Luc. vi. ii. p. 275.
[2] Vid. above Chap. i. p. 177 for a list of the illustrious natives of Sebenico.

invasion and retreat, Sebenico, like Traŭ and Spalato, was for a short time independent, but unfortunately, like them, she used her liberty for a cloak of contention and plunged into a quarrel with the Traŭrini. The independence of Sebenico was soon overshadowed by the rising power of the counts of Bribir, but while the Sebenzani had been occupied in their dissensions with Traŭ, the people of Zara had taken the opportunity to filch from them their islands of Mortér Zuri and Arte.

In 1298 Sebenico, which had been till then in the diocese of Traŭ, was raised to the dignity of a see, by the influence of Gregory count of Bribir and Maria queen of Naples with the Pope Boniface VIII, '*in vanum reclamantibus Traguriensibus*[1].' The first bishop was Martino, a Franciscan of Arbe[2].

In 1322 the tyranny of the counts of Bribir drove the people of Sebenico and Traŭ, who had hitherto been at variance, to ally themselves together, and invoke the aid of the Venetians. With their help Mladin of Bribir was defeated; and while the Traŭrini attacked one of his piratical strongholds at Almissa the Sebenzani did the same at Scardona, burning and spoiling the town and carrying off the boats to Sebenico. The Venetians sent Dardi Bembo as count to Sebenico; and under the wise government of the Republic the civil feuds and factions, which it

[1] Luc., p. 202.
[2] Galvani, Il rè d' armi di Sebenico. Two bishops had been previously elected by the people, but did not obtain the papal confirmation: Paolo Erizio, a Venetian, in 1274, and Leonardo Faletro or Falieri in 1287. Gams mentions a Stefano in 1253.

had been the policy of the counts of Bribir to encourage, were composed. The Venetians restored the islands of Mortér Zuri and Arte to the Sebenzani in 1324, giving thereby mortal offence to the Zaratini, who often tried to recover these islands, and in the end revenged themselves by their fourth and last revolt from Venice in 1345.

On the second invasion of Dalmatia and siege of Zara by the Hungarians, the people of Sebenico, seeing their territory ravaged, and disgusted with the insolence of the Venetian mercenary soldiery, sent envoys to the Ban who was then besieging Nona, and made their submission to Lewis of Hungary. Their allegiance was accepted, Andrea Giustiniani the Venetian count was expelled, and by the treaty of Zara in 1358 the right of Lewis to the whole of Dalmatia was formally recognised.

In the succeeding war of Chioggia Sebenico was taken and burned by the Venetian admiral Vittore Pisani in 1378, and a Venetian garrison was introduced, but Hungarian authority was restored by the peace of Turin in 1381.

During the troublous times that followed the death of Lewis in 1382 Sebenico, like the rest of Dalmatia, owned in turn the authority of Maria, Tvartko, Sigismund, Ladislaus, and Sigismund again. In 1410 the city was torn by civil dissensions between the popular party who were for Hungary, and the nobles who were for Venice. The popular party expelled the nobles, who established themselves in a fort at the mouth of the harbour and endeavoured to force their way back again. Sigismund interfered, punished the leaders of the popular party with death, and restored the 'fuorusciti;' but this and the construction of a castle to overawe the town alarmed the people and disgusted them with Hungarian rule, and on Oct. 30, 1412 they surrendered the city to the Venetians under certain conditions, of which the following are the most important :—

§ I. The rights and privileges which the city had enjoyed under the kings of Hungary were to be confirmed.

§ IV. The count was to be a Venetian noble, and the Sebenzani were not to be called upon to pay him more than 700 ducats for his salary.

§ VI. The obnoxious castle was to be destroyed, and no other to be built in the city or district.

§ IX. Scardona was to be subject to Sebenico.

§ XII. Sebenico was to retain as part of her territory all the islands she had held under Lewis[1].

Sebenico was fortified by the Venetians against the Turks, and under Venetian government she advanced rapidly in wealth and consequence. The principal event in her after-history is the invasion of Dalmatia by the Turks under Tekely pasha of Bosnia in 1647, when the place was besieged by the pasha and successfully defended by Degenfelt, who repulsed the enemy with a heavy loss of 4000 killed, besides 5000 who had been struck down by disease.

In 1809 a French commission sat at Sebenico to try, imprison, or shoot those Dalmatians who had

[1] Luc. v. c. xv. p. 264–7.

been guilty of bringing back the Austrians at the beginning of that year, and the fort S. Nicolò at the harbour mouth was crowded with political prisoners.

At the present day Sebenico is one of those towns where party feelings run highest between the Latin and the Slav, and disturbances and crimes of violence frequently occur on these grounds of difference. Sebenico is gradually losing the reputation for politeness and high culture by which it was distinguished in the days of Fortis, and seems likely to become once more a Croatian city.

The course of the steamers from Zara to Sebenico lies within the channel formed by the long narrow islands of Ugliano Pasman and Incoronata. Zara on its low flat peninsula shone brightly in the sun behind us as we steamed down the Canale di Pasman, which was as smooth as a mill pond, effectually protected from the movements of the open Adriatic by a double line of natural breakwaters. The country became wilder and more barren, and the hills approached gradually nearer the shore, but they never attained any great elevation, and were only remarkable for their regular pyramidal or tent-like shape. Passing the little villages of Bibigne S. Cassiano Torette and S. Filippo we arrived off Zara Vecchia, a large village on the site of the old Croatian city of Belgrad. At Belgrad, or Bielo-grad, the white city, Coloman celebrated his marriage with the Norman princess Busita in 1097, and in

1102 he came here to receive the crown of Dalmatia and Croatia. Destroyed by the Venetians in 1127[1] its ruins afforded shelter to the homeless Zaratini after the fall of Zara in 1202, and when they were allowed to return in 1205 and build a new Zara their temporary home at Belgrad received the name of Zara Vecchia, which it still retains[2].

The only other place at which the steamer touches on its way to Sebenico is the island of Mortér, the largest of the group which belonged to the territory of Sebenico. It has a population at the present day of 7000, of whom 1300 inhabit the village of Stretto, situated where the island so nearly touches the mainland that the channel is spanned by a moveable bridge. Fortis describes the inhabitants of Mortér ninety years ago as 'a worthless people;' and says that '*in every piratical boat of those parts there is at least one of that island who serves the robbers as pilot through all the passes, and as a guide to the most unfrequented creeks and hiding places.*' Since the disappearance of piracy the good seamanship of the people of Mortér has no doubt found a more legitimate field for its display. Beyond Mortér lie the islands of Zuri Capri Provicchio and Zlarin with many more of smaller note. Zuri Provicchio and Zlarin were all inhabited by Romans, and remains of ancient buildings are to be seen there[3]. At Zlarin in the sixteenth century a sepulchral marble was

---

[1] Vid. supra, History, pp. 42 and 46.
[2] Luc. de Regn., l. iv. c. ii.
[3] Palladius Fuscus, also Fortis.

dug up with the name of Pansiana, queen of some kingdom hitherto not identified[1]. Zlarin is now famous for its coral and sponge fisheries. The coral is gathered by an ingenious dredge which is towed behind the vessels, with a heavy swinging weight to break the coral off, and a bag net which follows and catches it.

Sebenico is not visible from the sea, though the hill fort that commands the town appears above the

Fig. 21.

low grey hills that fringe the shore. Leaving the open sea the steamer turns suddenly into a narrow tortuous channel, and emerges no less suddenly into a splendid inland haven to which there is only this one approach. On the further side is the city (Fig. 21), an imposing mass of picturesque old houses piled up the mountain side, with the great white-domed cathedral in the middle, the massive towers of the castle of S. Anna in the highest point of the

[1] Fortis.

town, and two other old forts weathered to a rich mellow brown colour crowning the barren summits of two loftier hills in the background[1]. The quays were crowded with men and women in their becoming national costume, and the port filled with gaily painted coasters with huge lateen sails, laden with wine casks, or crammed with peasants from Zlarin and the other islands returning from market. There is no place on the coast more inviting to a painter's pencil than Sebenico.

The interior of the city is not less picturesque than the outside. Its little piazzas and its steep and winding alleys,—they can hardly be called streets,—abound in handsome doorways and windows of Venetian Gothic or of the early renaissance. Everything here is Venetian; not a single architectural feature that meets the eye can be referred to a date prior to the final Venetian acquisition of the town in 1412. There are numerous doorways with a straight lintel under a pointed tympanum enclosed by the Venetian billet moulding and charged with well designed heraldry and flowing mantling. Heraldry indeed was rather the fashion at Sebenico; there is perhaps no town in Dalmatia from which a larger collection of escutcheons can be made, and Sebenico is fortunate in having among her citizens a gentleman whose industry and acquirements as an antiquary have been turned to good account in

---

[1] The highest fort is that of S. Giovanni: the next is Forte Barone, named after Baron Degenfelt, the gallant defender of Sebenico in 1647. It is now abandoned and ruined.

illustrating the history of his native city by the heraldic bearings on the public and private buildings, most of which he has succeeded in assigning to their proper families[1].

Through a labyrinth of narrow streets we reached the Piazza del duomo, which though small compared with the piazzas of most Italian towns, is not inferior to many of them in architectural interest. On the left is the cathedral, and on the right, built against the steep hill side, and overtopped by the buildings on the ascent behind, is the old loggia, a long arcaded building of two stories, now turned into a caffè below and a casino or club room and reading room above. It is dated 1552 and is a structure of some stateliness. But the duomo opposite (vid. Plate XII), is worthy to rank with any Italian work of its date and class that I know, and though there are churches as beautiful on the other side of the Adriatic, it would be difficult to match it in singularity of construction. Indeed not only Italy but Europe may be challenged to show another church of this size in which neither timber nor brick is employed, everything being constructed of good squared stone, marble, and metal. In England we have a few rude churches in Pembrokeshire, the chapel at Abbots-

[1] Il rè d'armi di Sebenico, by Dr. F. A. Galvani, I. R. Notary of Sebenico, published at Venice, 1884, contains illustrations of several hundred escutcheons from the buildings of that city, with historical notes of their respective families, and the members of those families who held any office at Sebenico. Dr. Galvani's promised History of Sebenico will be a welcome addition to the literature of Dalmatia.

The Duomo.

bury, and the little fourteenth century treasury at Merton College, in which the vault and roof are united in one solid structure of masonry, and in Ireland we have the chapel of S. Cormac at Cashel similarly constructed, but nearly all of these are on a diminutive scale. At Sebenico, however, the whole of a great cruciform church is covered by a waggon roof of stone, the underside of which forms the ceiling, the stone covering being visible both internally and externally, without the outside roof of timber and tiles or lead which exists in ordinary cathedrals above the stone-vaulted ceiling. The effect both within and without of these simple waggon vaults over nave choir and transepts, interrupted only by a dome at the crossing, is very simple and imposing, and the design is not less successful architecturally than it is original.

The architectural history of the duomo may be read with tolerable exactitude from the stones themselves. It is evidently the work of two architects and two periods, and in the interval which divides them occurred the great artistic revolution of the renaissance, so that while the earlier work is in regular Italian Gothic, the later work is in a style resembling that which we connect with the name of Pietro Lombardo and his sons and pupils. The evidence of the building itself is confirmed by documentary proof, and with the help of the latter there is no building in Dalmatia whose history can be written with so much certainty as this; the architecture speaks for itself, and the chain of documentary evidence when tested by that of the architecture is clear and complete.

In the year 1402 a committee was appointed, consisting of the count, the bishop Bogdano Pulsich, and certain nobles, to consider the question of enlarging the old cathedral of S. Giacomo, which was too small and otherwise unworthy of the growing importance of the city[1]. A tax was laid on the vineyards, and an impost of one-tenth on the wine produced within the territory, and nothing more was done for twenty-six years, during which funds were accumulating. In 1412 the city became part of the Venetian territory, and on April 23, 1428, when matters seemed ripe for beginning the new cathedral, Francesco Michieli being the Count of the city and territory, it was resolved by the Comune that the new cathedral should be built on a different site higher up in the city, where the church of S. Giovanni now stands. Nothing was done however to put this resolution into effect, and on June 4, 1430 it was rescinded by a new one, which left the choice of the site to the bishop Bogdano, the count Moisè Grimani, his 'curia,' and ten nobles of the city, by whom it was decided that the new cathedral should occupy the site of the old one ; '*quod ecclesia Cathedralis*

---

[1] 'Propositum fuit in dicto generali concilio per praefatum dom. Comitem et suam curiam si videretur dicto concilio pro augmentatione et fabrica eccl^e. Cathedralis Sti. Jacobi dictae civitatis Sebenici . . . ac pro amplianda et crescenda et augmentanda dicta ecclesia quae ad praesens non est sufficiens in tanta civitate propter parvitatem et incongruitatem suam,' &c. &c. Atto of 1402 in the Libro Rosso del Comune.

communis Sebenici fundari et aedifichari debeat in platea communis juxta episcopatum in loco ubi ad praesens est ecclesia Cathedralis[1].'

The new cathedral was begun at once and well advanced during the countship of Moisè Grimani, 1430–32, whose arms appear on the north angle pier of the west front. The architect to whom it was entrusted has long met with unmerited oblivion, and Dr. Galvani is entitled to the credit of having discovered his name and restored it to fame. In the 'Atti' of the notaries of Sebenico in 1435 and 1436 he has found the name of Messer Antonio, son of Pietro Paolo, a Venetian, master of the works, that is Architect, of the church of S. Giacomo of Sebenico, to whom the design of the earlier part of the building must therefore be attributed[2]. His work includes

---

[1] Cod. Suppl. N. 541, nella bibblioteca di Corte in Vienna e Coletti Cod. iv. 715. (Galvani, Il rè d' armi, i. 32.)

[2] 'Ibique Ser Zacharias q . . . de Sibenico dedit vendidit tradidit et transtulerit magistro Antonio q. Petri Paoli lapicida (*sic*) di Venetia nunc habitator (*sic*) Sibenici et magistro Sancti Jacobi de Sibenico ibi praesenti et per se,' &c. &c.

Mai 10, 1435. 'Atto del notajo Michele, q. Giovanni, Ibique magister Antonius q. Petri Paoli de Venetia lapicida habitator Sibenici et magister fabrice ecclesie Sancti Jacobi de Sibenico dedit vendidit,' &c. &c.

Oct. 1436. 'Atto del notajo Giacomo Vuksich.' I am indebted to the kindness of Sign. Dr. Galvani for these and other extracts from the Atti, and the Libro Rosso, which was in his custody when I was last at Sebenico in 1885.

The author of some interesting articles on this church in the *Blätter des christlichen Kunstvereines der Diöcese Seckau*, 1886, conjectures that Antonio is the son of Pietro Paolo delle Massegne, the architect of the choir screen of St. Mark's at Venice, which in many details resembles the work of Antonio at Sebenico.

the whole of the lower story of the nave and its side aisles; that is to say, the pillars and arches of the nave as high as the foliaged cornice above them, with the two western piers of the four on which the central lantern and cupola rests; also the exterior walls of the aisles as high as the top of the cornice of intersecting arches (vid. Plate XIII); also the rib and panel vaults of the aisles, the great west and north

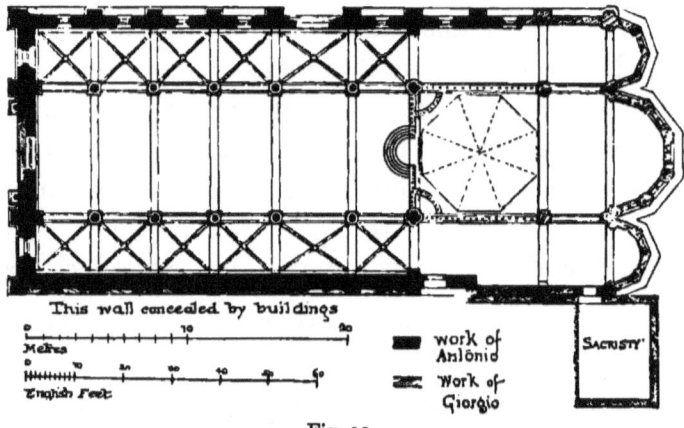

Fig. 22.

doorways, and the north exterior wall of the transept as high as the aforesaid cornice of the aisle, which is continued at the same level across the transept. The upper part of the aisle and transept walls above this cornice is the work of another and later hand.

In the ground-plan, Fig. 22 [1], I have attempted to distinguish the work of Antonio from that of his successors.

[1] Adapted from that by Prof. Grausz in the *Blätter*, &c.

The central crossing and choir were thus left for the present unattempted, it is difficult to say why, unless the old cathedral occupied that part of the site, and was left standing until the nave should be finished and occupied, when, without interruption of the church services, the old building might be removed to make way for the new choir and transepts. It seems certain that in some way or other the old church *was* preserved during the building of the new, for there are acts dated '*nel coro*' during this period.

The architecture of Messer Antonio di Pietro Paolo is of excellent Italian Gothic, with more of the merits and fewer of the faults of that much-abused style than most examples of it. The exterior (vid. Plate XIII) is divided into bays by square buttress piers, which were to have been crowned no doubt by little tabernacles containing statues, like those between the great ogee gables of St. Mark's at Venice, or those which actually appear over the flanking statues of the north doorway here. The windows are deeply splayed outside, have a pointed arch with a billet moulding, and are divided by a slender shaft into two narrow lights with simple tracery in the head. Along what was to have been the top of the wall runs a rich cornice of intersecting semicircles springing from little corbels carved into heads, the pointed arches formed by the intersections being trefoil-cusped. At the west end and in the north wall are two magnificent doorways, which are full of excellent detail and deserve careful study. The northern or '*Lion doorway*,' as the people call it from the two lions that guard the entrance, is of very beautiful Italian Gothic (vid. Plate XIII), the leaves that run round it are undercut and pierced behind, and the columns are delicately arabesqued, or else twisted and fluted with rosettes set in the flutings. From the lions' backs rise octagonal shafts with spreading capitals supporting statues of Adam and Eve, above which are little Gothic tabernacles containing each a statue. The figures of our first parents are as usual ill-made, and show that ignorance of the human figure which is apparent whenever a mediaeval sculptor tried his hand at the nude.

Though this doorway is evidently from its style part of Antonio's work it appears from three escutcheons[1] over it that the wall above, though it follows his design, was not finished till about 1454, after he had ceased to be architect. The west end was evidently raised more rapidly than the north wall.

The west doorway is in the same style but still richer than the other. On each side of the opening a column carries a two-storied tabernacle: figures in niches run round the arch and are continued down the jambs, and as a keystone is the figure of our Lord holding an orb in one hand and blessing with the other. The tympanum is glazed. The opening of the doorway is surrounded by a border of very bold Venetian foliage springing from naked figures, and the shafts are twisted and fluted, or else richly arabesqued. By the scutcheon of Count Andrea

[1] Those of Leonardo Venier, Count 1453-4; Urbano Vignaco, Bishop 1454-68; Giorgio Sisgorich, Bishop 1453.

Porta dei leoni.

Loredan, on the buttress adjoining to the south, it appears that this doorway was finished in 1438 or 1439.

The proportions of the nave arcades of the interior (Fig. 22), which are also of Gothic work and by Antonio the Venetian, are singularly pleasing. They have more relation to the arcades of northern Gothic churches than to those of Italian Gothic; for instead of being spread out to the enormous span and finished with the simplicity or rather baldness of such arcades as those of S. Maria at Florence, S. Petronio at Bologna, or S. Antonio at Padua, which reduce the apparent scale of the church by fully one-half, the arcades at Sebenico are so proportioned as to look fully as large as they are, and to give full effect to the length of the nave, and the arches are well moulded and handsomely finished. The spandrils towards the nave are filled with red Verona marble with a gilt ball in the centre of each. All the arches are pointed, and at their springing die against wall piers, segments of an octagon, which rise like vaulting shafts from each column (vid. Fig. 22 A).

The shafts are monoliths, cylindrical without entasis or diminution, resting on Attic bases with angle leaves or 'toes,' and their capitals are massive and simple in outline, and carved with vigorous foliage of a simple Venetian type. The two larger piers that carry the western side of the central cupola are also monoliths of a white stone almost equal to marble; their section is a quatrefoil with the addition of a roll in each hollow, and their capitals are magni-

Fig. 22 A.

ficent examples of the richest kind of Venetian foliage, in which with marvellous art the sculptors of that school contrived to indulge in an almost oriental luxuriance without weakness, and in an almost extravagant wealth of detail without confusion (vid. Plate XIV). These two larger piers, like the rest, are the work of Messer Antonio[1].

To him also must be attributed the interior vaulting of the aisles, which are divided into square bays, except that the arch opposite the north doorway is much wider than the rest—a daring irregularity in so small and so symmetrical a church. The vaulting is quadripartite, the transverse ribs are wide bands with a moulded edge, and the diagonal ribs are cabled. There are also slight wall ribs. The central bosses are well carved; those of the north aisle with rosettes and the heads of a man and a lion; those on the south with the evangelistic emblems, which are very finely designed and executed, and a saint with staff and book, perhaps S. Giacomo, to whom the church is dedicated. One of the arches has at its apex a prettily carved shield bearing a lion rampant, and a helm with the crest of a child holding two little lions' heads with outstretched arms[2].

With this we come to the end of the work of the earlier architect, Messer Antonio di Pietro Paolo, who had charge of the building from its beginning

[1] They prove that a transept was part of the original plan though it was not realized by the original architect.

[2] These arms have not been identified. The altar below was to have been given by the family of Rafcich. Vid. Il rè d' armi, vol. ii. p. 5.

in 1430 or 1431 till the year 1441[1]. In that year, for reasons which are not quite intelligible, the building committee became dissatisfied with their architect and his plans; they complained, without as it seems to us due reason, that there were many errors and defects in the work; that it was not done as they intended; that much of the money spent on ornament had been quite thrown away, and that unless a change were made things would go from bad to worse[2]. To us there seems no fault in the design of Antonio, and no extravagance in his ornamentation; his construction is solid and well put together, and in his sculpture we recognise the touch of a master hand. Messer Antonio, however, was dismissed, and another architect, Messer Giorgio, invited from Venice to continue and complete the cathedral[3].

[1] This appears from the arms of Count Moisè Grimani (1430-2), above mentioned, at the north-west angle, and those of Count Marco Erizzo (1434-36) on one of the buttresses of the north front, and Count Andrea Loredan (1438-39) on the pier to the right or south of the west entrance door.

[2] Ap. 23, 1441. Libro Rosso del Municipio: 'Cum in fabricatione dictae ecclesiae Cathedralis S. Jacobi de Sebenico commissi fuerunt multi errores et defectus praeter omnem intentionem nobilium civium Sibenicensium, et aliorum qui in ejus fabrica porrigunt manus suas adjutores, et facta fuerunt magna expensa pro hornamento et decore ipsius ecclesiae que expensa abjecta fuerunt, quoniam edificia et partimenta ipsius ecclesiae non fuerunt debitis modis composita et fabricata, et justissima res sit . . . errores et defectus quo ad melius fieri poterit reformare, et providere ne in futurum de malo in pejus convertantur quin immo de bono in melius reformentur,' &c. &c.

[3] Monsignor Fosco, the present bishop of Sebenico, has written the history of his cathedral, and has there collected particulars

SEBENICO. Plate XIV

T.G.J.   Capital of north west pier
         supporting the lantern.

Giorgio seems to have been born at Zara. His father, Matteo, was a scion of the ancient and princely Roman house of Orsini; but the branch to which he belonged had sunk in the world, and been reduced to support itself by manual arts inconsistent with the idea of nobility as then understood, and the family name had been allowed to fall into disuse[1]. Giorgio seems to have studied architecture at Venice, where we find him, still a young man, married to Elisabetta da Monte, who brought him as her dowry some house property in that city. After his engagement at Sebenico in 1441 he seems to have made that city his domicile; it was here that he invested his savings in concert with two partners in a grocery business, and in a merchant ship, connected perhaps with the former concern; and here he finally built himself a house and settled down close to the great church on which his fame as an architect principally rests[2].

concerning the life and works of Giorgio Orsini which are very valuable. The original contract between the procurators of the church and certain nobles of Sebenico on the one part, and Giorgio the son of Matteo of Zara on the other, is published by Mons. Fosco in an appendix to the pamphlet on the church of Sebenico by Nicolò Tommaseo, a native of Sebenico, whose name is famous in Italian politics and literature. I shall append the contract to this chapter. It is extremely interesting as illustrative of the position and practice of a mediaeval architect. Vid. p. 416, infra.

[1] His family descent from the Orsini was formally recognised in 1540 in the person of his grandson Giacomo, an advocate.

[2] Vid. an article by Dr. F. A. Galvani in the Annuario Dalmatico, vol. i. 1884, Zara. That Giorgio was not a native of Sebenico is proved by the description of him in several 'Atti' of 1441–1450; e. g. 'Magister Giorgius lapicida quondam Matthaei di Jadra, habitator Venetiarum ad praesens existens Sibenic,' &c. &c.

Giorgio was already more than half a convert to the renaissance, although that movement had hardly begun to make itself felt at Venice. He discarded the style of his predecessor all the more easily, no doubt, because of the discredit that had fallen on his plans, and started at once in the new manner. The task before him was to build the choir, of which the foundations had not been laid, to raise and roof the nave which was only completed to the top of the aisle vaults, and to construct some covering either by a lantern and cupola or otherwise over the crossing.

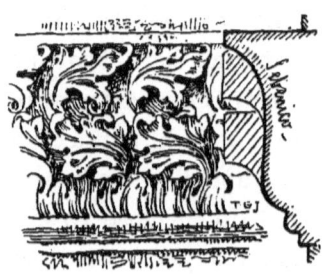

Fig. 23.

Giorgio did not live to accomplish his task; but before entering into the question how far the later part of the building is of his designing it will be well to describe it in its present completed form.

The choir is prolonged with one short bay eastward of the transept and finishes with three apses; on the Gothic cornice of the nave aisles is raised a low wall, which is crowned with a second cornice, from which springs the external roof of the aisle; in the nave the new work starts from the rich foliaged cornice (Fig. 23) which runs above the nave arcades, over which it begins with a roll moulding carved into laurel leaves classic fashion; on this is placed a low triforium gallery of square-topped openings divided by fluted piers, and above this is raised a lofty clerestory wall, pierced with a plain round-arched window in each bay, and crowned with a rich cornice from which the roof springs. The roof itself is the most original part of the design; it consists of a waggon vault of long stones supported by a strong rib at each bay, each course of the vaulting stones being tongued and grooved and accurately fitted together so as to be impervious to weather. This is continued over nave, choir, and transepts, and the gable ends of these four arms instead of being as usual triangular are semicircular, like the roof which generates them. The aisles throughout are covered by quadrant roofs of the same construction, those of the nave aisles being placed above and clear of the early vaults, so as to form a triforium or gallery between the two systems of vaulting. In the centre over the crossing a low square tower is raised till it surpasses the height of the four abutting roofs, when it turns into an octagonal lantern covered by an octagonal cupola which rises to a point, the whole constructed of slabs of stone like the nave vaults, and crowned by a gyrating angel (vid. Plates XII. and XV).

The construction of this central part and of the vaults throughout is wonderfully light, and indeed perilously so. The whole depends, it need hardly be said, on iron ties, for there are no external buttresses to resist the thrust of the vault, nor indeed is it possible to buttress a barrel vault. The architect has gone to the verge of overdaring; his lantern is all window, having two large windows in each face; and the four piers that support the central lantern and cupola are astonishingly slender, being in fact monoliths set end ways of the bed. The daring of the design, however, has been partially justified by the stability of its construction down almost to our own days. Unhappily in 1843 symptoms of danger had appeared, owing perhaps more to the disintegration of the stone of which the building was constructed than to any fault of design. Under the direction of Signor Paolo Bioni, an architect of Sebenico, the whole of the nave vault was taken down and reset, and a good deal of it replaced by new stone, the grooved joints being made good with cement, instead of as heretofore with lead. The cupola also was taken down to the top of the four supporting arches and rebuilt, and one of the columns of the nave arcade with its capital was taken out and replaced by new, the superstructure being meanwhile carried on shoring. The repairs lasted several years and cost 200,000 florins, equal to about £16,000 of our money, and the church was not reopened for service till 1860.

The general effect of the interior is extremely beautiful; I know no other church of its size that creates so profound an impression. The effect is owing in great measure to the simplicity of the plan, the height of the vaults, and the elevation of the choir. The latter occupies the space under the dome, and the shallow transepts which do not pass the line of the aisle walls are floored across

with large slabs of stone to form galleries behind the stalls, one for the organ, the other for the singers. An admirably finished balustrading of twisted shafts and little round arches in white marble forms the front of the galleries, and is continued on each side with a sweep half round the great piers at the entrance of the choir so as to form an ambo to the right and left[1]. Nothing was ever better imagined (vid. Fig. 22 A). The choir itself is curious, the seats and backs being of marble, as if the architect had resolved that no wood should enter into his building even in the shape of furniture.

Giorgio, as I have said, did not live to see his building finished. He assumed the direction of the works in 1441, and it appears from the following inscription on the north-east angle that the foundation of the new choir and apses was laid in 1443:—

TEMPLA TIBI CVRE PRESVL VENERANDE GEORGI
SISGORIDE STIRPIS CLARO DE SANGVINE NATE
VRBS A FANTINO REGITVR PROCOMSVLE DIGNO
PISAVRE PROLIS VENETVM DOMINANTE SENATV
CVM PARS ISTA DOMVS DOMINI PRIMORDIA SVMPSIT
MILLE QVATER CENTVM DOMINI LABENTIBVS ANNIS
QVADRAGINTA TRIBVS MICHAEL DVM PROTEGIT VRBEM
ARMIGER EJVSDEM REGIS QVOQVE JANITOR ALMVS

hoc opus cuuarum fecit magister Georgius Mathaei Dalmaticus.

In the August of that year he contracted with one Zanchetti of Zara for 200 or 210 rough blocks

[1] The date of these ambos and balustrades is 1547.

of marble from Arbe. In the following year he contracted with certain noble families of Sebenico for a series of altars, one to each bay of the nave, with the arms of each donor above his respective altar; but this project was never carried out. In the same year Giorgio was occupied in building the chapel of S. Rainerio at Spalato, now hidden within the military hospital, but his principal attention was given to the great work at Sebenico which was carried on with energy till 1448, when for want of funds it was suspended [1], and it was not resumed till the time of bishop Luca di Tollentich, 1469-91. Giorgio in the meanwhile was occupied busily elsewhere. In 1448 he designed and erected the altar of S. Anastasio in the duomo of Spalato with an Italian Gothic canopy, the conditions being that it should correspond in all respects with the opposite altar and canopy by Bonino di Milano. From 1450 to 1461 he was absent from Sebenico, and we hear of him at Venice, and also at Ancona, where he completed the loggia dei Mercanti between 1451 and 1459, and built the front of S. Francesco della Scala in the same city; also at Recanati, where he was employed on the church of S. Agostino, and at Cittanuova in the Marches, where he began the facade of the church of S. Maria. In 1464 he was again at Sebenico, but was summoned to Ragusa to undertake those works on the Rectorial Palace which we shall have to consider when we reach that building. His

[1] Libro Rosso del Comune, cited Fosco, p. 9.

engagement with the Ragusan signory began in June 1464. In 1466 he was employed by Antonio Palcić Bishop of Ossero on a new palace at Pago, whither that prelate hoped to transfer his see, but the work was not completed. He was engaged also on the front of the cathedral at Pago and on the chapel of S. Nicolò there, and it is thought he may have been the architect of the new cathedral which Bishop Palcić began at Ossero, though I saw nothing in that building that reminded me of his work at Sebenico or Ragusa. He was again at Sebenico in 1467 and 1468, as appears from various documents containing his name, and in 1470 he was honoured by his fellow-citizens with a mission to Rome on matters connected with a charitable bequest of Bishop Vignacco, and he was invested with plenipotentiary powers to act on their behalf at the papal court. His return took place at all events before May 1471, as we find him on the 22nd of that month taking an apprentice for eight years.

His presence indeed had become necessary, for about the same time the works at the Duomo were resumed.

The new bishop Luca de Tollentich set to work in earnest to complete his cathedral and contributed largely from his own purse to the expenses. The work must have been begun again in 1470 or 1471, and it was carried on vigorously until the death of the bishop in 1491.

In 1475 Giorgio died leaving his building incomplete.

If we turn to consider critically the artistic merit of those parts of the design which may with certainty be attributed to Giorgio, it will be found to consist rather in boldness and originality of conception than in any great skill or keen sense of beauty in the elaboration of details. The general effect of the exterior of his building is admirable, but the details are not always commendable. His cornices and mouldings are graceful and refined, and there is a good deal of fancy and caprice in the friezes of little boys grouped in pairs and holding festoons, and in the capitals of birds wreaths and bunches of grapes in the interior of the transept, which are no doubt in great part carved by his own hand, the terms of his contract binding him to work manually not only as a mason but as a sculptor; but on the other hand there is a good deal of sham perspective in niches and panels, which are but dull conceits, and detract from the beauty and purity of the design. In respect of his details Giorgio must yield the palm to his predecessor Messer Antonio, whose hand was much surer, and who though perhaps inferior to Giorgio as an engineer was certainly a better artist. Nothing makes the superiority of Antonio's detail more apparent than the comparison of the magnificent capitals of the two *western* piers of the cupola which are by his hand (vid. Plate XIV.) with the very indifferent capitals of the two *eastern* piers which are by Giorgio.

The most sumptuous part of Giorgio's building

is the little baptistery, occupying a lower story in the southern apse below the raised tribune of the south transept. It is square, and has a column with a capital of good Venetian foliage in each corner, much undercut, on which stand niches of regular Italian Gothic with twisted shafts and semi-octagonal canopies. Each contained, and two still contain, statuettes of prophets: in that to the north-east is Simeon with a scroll bearing the words in Roman letters NUNC DIMITTIS DNE SERVVM TVVM.; in another is David, crowned, and holding an imperfect scroll with the words in Gothic lettering **vox dni super aquas deus** . . . . In each side of the baptistery is a rounded recess or apse covered with a conch, and the spandrils above these conchs are filled with regular Gothic tracery, of which that to the east is pierced to allow light to pass from a window behind. Above this the ceiling is gathered into a circle of Venetian foliage on which rests the flat dome, divided into four segments by ribs from the four angle columns and niches. These segments are filled with angels in a classic style with flowing draperies of good but unequal design. In the centre is a boss, with the figure of the first person of the Trinity holding a scroll bearing the words HIC EST FILIVS MEVS DILECTVS IN QVO MIHI BENE COMPLACVI IPSVM AVDITE, and the dove with outspread wings.

The whole of this tiny chamber is a marvel of richness, but the style is curiously mixed and confused, and the execution of the renaissance ornament is of an inferior quality. The font is of breccia marble carried by three naked boys, well imagined but indifferently executed.

It is not only here that Giorgio seems to have been unable to forget the old Gothic style which was still disputing the ground with its younger rival. In the great windows of the principal apse, though he has divided the width by a fluted column with a renaissance capital, he has not been able to avoid filling the heads with trefoil cusps and Gothic tracery, and it is done so naturally and innocently that it seems quite at home and strikes one with no sense of incongruity (Fig. 24)[1].

Giorgio's credit for great original genius must stand or fall principally by the question whether it was he or his successor who conceived the idea of the mighty stone roofs which make this church differ from all others. When he died in 1475 the church was not ready for the roofs: the nave had not even its clerestory walls built; the choir was hardly raised to the crown of the great apse arch, which bears on its key-stone the arms of Girolamo Pesaro, count 1476–9; and the transept was prob-

---

[1] The writer in the *Blätter des Christlichen Kunstvereines der Diöcese Seckau* argues that Giorgio began at Sebenico as a Gothic architect, and developed into a renaissance architect as he went on. He attributes his conversion to his association with Michelozzo at Ragusa in 1464. If I am right in understanding him to attribute the two Gothic doorways to Giorgio in his Gothic manner I cannot agree with him. We see Giorgio's Gothic work in the Baptistery which was built before he left Sebenico for Ragusa, and find it already mixed with renaissance details, and very unlike the pure Gothic of the doorways.

ably at about the same level, as the arms of Piero Canal, count 1471–3, appear on the key-stone of the exterior blank arch below the springing line of the

Fig. 24.

roof. If then the *opus cuvarum*[1] which Giorgio claims as his work is to be referred to any part of the vaulting, it must be to the domes of the two

---

[1] The writer in the *Blätter Christl. Kunst.*, &c. above quoted understands by 'cuvae' the apses, not the vaults.

small apses which were no doubt finished in his lifetime, that of the large apse which was on the point of completion, and perhaps the waggon vaults over the choir aisles. If these are really Giorgio's they contain the motive of the vaulting of the whole church, which in that case would be of his conception. It is impossible that he should have carried his work as far as he did without having made some plan, and some special preparation for his roofs, and the consistency of the subsequent work in its character and details with that which he left imperfect favours the presumption that he left behind him designs for the completion of the church, perhaps a model such as that which we know he made for the sacristy[1], and that these designs were carried out by his successors.

The high vaults however were not closed till long afterwards: on the outside of the north clerestory of the nave are the arms of Nicolò Navager, count in 1489. The vaults of the choir, nave, and transepts were probably completed before the death of Bishop Luca di Tollentich in 1491, but the semicircular gable of the west front was not closed till 1536, in the time of Bishop Lucio Staffileo and Count Andrea Gritti (1534–7), as appears by an inscription at the west end. The cupola was finished in 1555, and in that year the church was solemnly consecrated, exactly a century and a quarter after the foundation was laid in 1430.

The names of several architects employed on the

[1] See below, page 403, contract for the sacristy.

church after the death of Giorgio have been discovered by the researches of Dr. Galvani and others. On July 1, 1477, a contract was made with Nicolò di Giovanni da Firenze, who bound himself for ten years to devote himself to this work and to undertake none other, except that he was to have leave to go occasionally to Traù and elsewhere when business called him. It is to Nicolò that the construction of the stone roofs is to be attributed, and it is of course an open question whether he is not also entitled to the glory of having invented them, instead of his predecessor Giorgio. We shall hear of Nicolò again when we come to the campanile of Spalato, and the later chapels of the cathedral of Traù [1].

In the year 1517 we find the work in the hands of Bartolommeo q*m* Giacomo da Mestre, who is mentioned in the Atti of Notary Butrisić of Sebenico as 'protomagister fabricae Sancti Jacobi.' He is supposed to have been at Ragusa in 1520, and to have designed the votive church of S. Salvatore, which is confirmed by the fact that at that time the name of another architect appears as the protomagister at Sebenico, and that Bartolommeo reap-

[1] 'Conduxerunt pro prothomagistro fabricae dictae ecclesiae S. Jacobi discretum et prudentem magistrum Nicolaum Johannis Florentinum lapicidam ibi praesentem, stipulantem et se obligantem pro annis decem .... item quod si erit opus ipso magistro Nicolao interdum ire Tragurium vel alibi pro agendis suis per duobus aut tribus diebus teneantur ipse Vicarius procuratores et operarii et successores eorum dare licentiam tempus et commodum ipsi magistro Nicolao pro ipsis diebus,' &c. Libro Rosso del Comune.

pears there in 1523[1]. He is mentioned as late as 1535.

The western gable was finished in 1536 by Giovanni Masticevich of Zara[2].

The church contains the tombs of several bishops. Giorgio Sisgorich (d. 1453) lies in a niche in the west wall to the south of the door, with a modern epitaph, and Lucio Staffileo (d. 1557) to the north of it. On tilted planes, let into the riser of the choir platform on each side of the steps, are the effigies of two more, Luca Spignaroli (d. 1589), to the left, and Domenico Calegari (d. 1722) to the right.

Adjoining the duomo, on the south side of the choir, is the sacristy, a spacious chamber raised on a bold stone barrel vault which springs from the wall of the bishop's palace on one side, and rests on five columns on the other, forming an open loggia from which there is an entrance to the baptistery. The construction is extremely hazardous, and was originally still more so, for there were at first but three columns, and the two others were added for strength at a later date. In spite of this the Sebenzani have an incredible tradition that the sacristy and this open story below were but the beginning of a lofty campanile which it was intended to raise above it. The soffit of the vault is effectively divided into panels by raised fillets,

---

[1] Gelcich, Dello sviluppo civile di Ragusa, p. 77.

[2] *Blätter Christl. Kunst.*, &c. The writer relies throughout on the authority of MSS. of Monsign. Fosco.

and the walls of the sacristy above are decorated with flutings and panellings like the later work in the duomo. For this sacristy is also the work of Giorgio, and the contract with him, dated Mar. 1, 1452, is still in existence. The following extracts are interesting as illustrating the practice of an architect in the fifteenth century. The accuracy with which the dimensions and position of the building are stated seems to show that there were no scale drawings employed, but it appears that something of the nature of a model in clay or plaster was exhibited to give the employers an idea of the effect the building was intended to produce when completed.

'. . . . Itidem dictus magister Giorgius promisit et se obligavit predictis stipulantibus nomine dictae ecclesiae facere unam sacrestiam dictae ecclesiae contiguam baptisterio et episcopatui, super quinque pilastris quorum tria erunt versus praetorium comitatus et duo in muro episcopatus, super quibus pilastris ab utraque parte ponantur bordonalia[1] super quibus fundare debeat archivoltus dictae sacrestiae, quam sacristiam laborare promisit a tribus lateribus, quorum unum erit versus ecclesiam longum pedibus quatuordecim cum dimidio, aliud laterum erit versus palatium comitatus longitudinis pedum viginti unius, et aliud esse debeat versus portam qua exitur ad littus maris et erit longitudinis pedum quatuordecim cum dimidio, et omnia praedicta latera sive facies facere promisit altas a

[1] *Bordonalia* are lintels.

pilastris sursum pedibus viginti quatuor, et pilastra promisit laborare ad similitudinem illorum quae facta sunt, et erunt duorum petiorum[1], et archivoltum promisit laborare de lapidibus quadratis de medio bastone [2], et facies dictae sacrestiae laborare promisit ad suasas[3], bastonos, cunetas[4], et alia laboreria juxta formam de creta factam . . . . per dictum Giorgium, cum portis fenestris et necessariis ornatis juxta ejus conscientiam et magisterium, intelligendo quod idem magister Giorgius non teneatur facere cornisas quae erunt in apicibus murorum dictae sacrestiae.'

Everything corresponds exactly with this specification, and the cornices are not made, but stop abruptly after returning from the main wall of the choir. The contract proceeds :—

'Quam sacrestiam facere et fabricare promisit dictus magister Georgius omnibus suis sumptibus ex lapidibus cavatis sive cavandis ex insula Braze et laborare sive laborare facere perpolite uti decus est et facere conduci et in opere poni expensis ipsius.'

From which it appears that Giorgio had to act as contractor as well as architect. He bound himself further to complete his contract within twenty months, and he was to receive 600 golden ducats for the work. The building, however, as

---

[1] *Petiorum*, sc. pezzi, pieces.

[2] *Mezzo bastoni*, the half round fillets or beads that divide the coffers.

[3] *Suaza* is a Venetian word for a dial or picture frame, probably here a *panel*.

[4] *Cunetae* are flutings.

usual, was not finished to time, and the date of the release given him by his employers is March 16, 1454[1].

Of the other churches in Sebenico there is little to be said. The Franciscan convent was rebuilt between 1322 and 1340, but contains little that can be referred to that date. Two inscriptions in Lombardic lettering of 1361 and 1397, the latter to the mother of a canon of Sebenico, are built into the exterior wall of the church. The west door of the church has an ogee arched tympanum with the remains of a fresco of the Madonna and the infant Saviour between Saints Francis and Clara (?). In the interior the ceiling of unpainted deal, which has turned a rich copper colour, and has paintings in the panels, is not amiss, and the gallery is supported by curious capitals, of which two are like Byzantine work, with interlaced stems and foliage undercut and detached from the ground. They are not really so old as they look at first sight.

The church of S. Giovanni in the centre of the town adjoining the little Piazza dell' Erbe has a picturesque exterior staircase leading to an upper story, and the Greek church, a little lower down the street, has a curious western bell-cot with projecting balconies for the ringers. These and all the other churches of Sebenico not already named are

---

[1] Atti del notajo Carlo Vitale, Mar. 16, 1454. 'Igitur dicti operarii et procuratores confessi fuerint (*sic*) factum et completum fuisse totum opus quod obligatus erat dictus magister Giorgius facere virtute praeallegati instrumenti, Mar. 1, 1452.'

of late work, and there are no traces of any other public buildings of greater antiquity than the sixteenth or seventeenth century.

One building, however, or rather one doorway—for nothing but a doorway remains—must not be left unvisited. In June 1455, Michele Simeonich, a noble of Sebenico, sold to Giorgio Orsini for 200

Fig. 25.

golden ducats 'of good and just weight' a house in the contrada of S. Gregorio, of which the position and boundaries are accurately defined in the act of the notary Manfredo Petrogna[1]. To this spot we were guided by Monsignor Fosco, the bishop and historian of Sebenico, and there sure enough we saw a door-

[1] Vid. Annuario Dalmatico, 1884. Article by Dr. Galvani.

way, on the lintel of which is carved, by the hand no doubt of Giorgio himself, the bear that symbolized his ancestral house of the Orsini, while on each jamb, amid pendent bouquets of flowers, hang the mallet and chisels of his sculptor's art (vid. Fig. 25).

The costume at Sebenico is slightly different from that at Zara. We saw less of the silver ornaments here than there, although we were present on a festa and a Sunday when both lads and lasses come out in their bravest attire. The women wear bodices laced across the front very prettily. Unmarried girls cover the bosom with a white linen front, which on festa days is beautifully clean and stiffly starched, and fastened with gold or silvergilt buttons. When they marry they cover the bosom with a square of crimson velvet, which hides the laced boddice and the white smock, and when they have a great many children they proclaim their maternal achievements to an appreciative public by exchanging the crimson for black. Their petticoats are marvellously plaited in close folds, which however disappear with wear, and their hair is twisted up with a wisp of white cloth plaited into it and wound round the head, over which a white '*panno*' is fastened like a turban with a pendent end behind. This twisting and mixing the hair with a foreign substance seems before they grow old to wrench the hair off their heads, and many of the women are as bald as coots. This curious head-dress is no doubt designed to enable them to carry burdens easily.

The dress of the men is somewhat the same as at Zara, but with less silver and more woollen tassels (Fig. 26). Their physique is splendid; they are not only big and broad-shouldered but as lithe and active as leopards; and the Austrian navy, which is manned by Dalmatians, ought to be a match, so far as the crews go, for any in the world.

Fig. 26.

There are, however, many degrees among these Slavs. Along the roads outside the town and in the town itself we met scores of the wildest and rudest figures imaginable. The Morlacchi were bringing in the crushed grapes and juice of the vintage, and as the vintage is very dirty work we saw them at their worst. They ride singing and shouting on their rough carts drawn by shabby little ponies, sitting among the casks of trodden grape-juice, and they stare at you from under wild shocks of unkempt hair, on which is pressed the universal red bonnet with its black tassel over one ear, though the red is generally faded to a purple or claret colour very attractive to a painter's eye. They wear long floating moustaches and ragged beards, and often cover their shoulders with a coat of goat's skin with the hair on, the hairy side being worn inside in winter and outside in summer. Round their waists are sashes of striped stuff, with a curious, many-folded leather pouch in front containing a wonderful medley of property, together with two or three knives with ornamented handles of bone stained green or spangled with metal, among which often peeps out the butt of an old-fashioned pistol.

The harbour of Sebenico is the estuary of the river Kerka, the ancient Titius, which bursts forth into life a full-grown river from a cavern at the foot of Monte Dinara near Knin, and after falling over a succession of cascades at various points in its brief but lively career, enters the sea by the tortuous channel that admitted us to the land-locked haven of Sebenico.

The last and finest of these cascades is near Scardona, and not more than twelve miles up the river from Sebenico. We made the excursion in a boat with four rowers, starting early and returning late so as to have as many hours as possible at the falls. Our four oarsmen dressed in national costume of blue serge trousers and waistcoats, homespun shirt fastened at the throat with a silver filagree stud, and the never-failing red cap with its black tassel over the right ear, stood and rowed Venetian fashion, pushing like a gondolier, instead of pulling as we do, this being the way of all boatmen in the Adriatic.

At the northern end of the harbour the hills gradually close in till the sea becomes a river: but this river is unlike those of less sterile regions; it has no flat alluvial banks and meadows, but simply fills the hollows of the barren hills on either side, and consequently it has no regular uniform channel but resembles rather a succession of lakes or basins connected by narrower reaches. The haven of Sebenico is but one of this series, and belongs more to the river than to the sea, the water being so slightly salt that in winter it is not unfrequently frozen over.

For an hour and a half we wound our way between bluffs of the barest rock which descended with abrupt slopes into the water. The cliffs were of a whitish yellow colour, deepening sometimes to a full orange, and the water, of a turbid greenish yellow, seemed only another shade of the same colour. Here and there was the miserable hovel of a shepherd, which almost escaped observation but for the square black spot in the landscape formed by the hole that served it for a window. This was the refuge of the herdsman and thirty or forty lean sheep or goats, which he pastured by day and drove indoors at night; but the pasturage is miserable enough, and it is a saying of the Dalmatians that their sheep feed on stones. After an hour and a half the river expanded into a large sheet of water, the lake of Prokljan, which we were warned would be the end of our journey if a Bora were blowing, as the rowers would not be able to get across in the face of it. Luckily for us Boreas was safely bagged up, and we got across without trouble, though on our return there was a strong scirocco blowing, which made the work rather heavy. The comparatively level shores of this lake are well clothed with vines and olives, and no less than three little hamlets reflect themselves in the water.

After leaving the lake, however, the river resumes its old character, and runs between barren white cliffs till a sudden sweep reveals a wider basin, and in the gorge of a valley that descends from the left is the little town of Scardona, with the ruins of an old castle on a crag above it. The situation is pretty enough, and in the midst of a dry stony desert it is a surprise to hear that the air is pestilential and the people victimized by ague and fever. The sight of the landlord's face at the little inn where we ordered dinner to be ready on our return spoke volumes as to the malarious climate, and as we wandered about the narrow streets we saw everywhere the same deathly complexion and the same dull sunken eye and emaciated form. The malaria arises from a marsh behind the town formed by the stagnant water of a little tributary of the Kerka, and the partial success of an attempt to drain it and convert it into orchards and gardens has had a good effect in diminishing the prevalence of fever, though the evil is not yet extirpated.

Although there is nothing now to be seen at Scardona it was once a place of consequence. Pliny[1] mentions it as the capital or 'conventus' of Japidia and Liburnia, maritime Illyricum being divided into three conventus, of which those of Salona and Narona were the remaining two. After the great Slav irruption in the seventh century Scardona ceased to be a Latin town, and is mentioned by Porphyrogenitus as one of the towns of the 'baptized Croats[2].' It remained a Croatian town through the middle ages, and in 1127, on the destruction of Belgrad by the Venetians, it became the seat of a bishopric which survived till 1830, when the diocese was united to that of Sebenico. In 1322 Scardona was sacked and burned by the Sebenzani on account of the piratical habits of its inhabitants, which were encouraged by Mladin Count of Bribir. In 1411 it fell into the power of the Venetians, and was by them made subject to Sebenico when that city sub-

---

[1] Plin. iii. xxi. 'Conventum Scardonitarum petunt Iapides et Liburnorum civitates xiv, e quibus Lacinienses, Stulpinos, Burnistas, Albonenses nominare non pigeat.'

[2] Vid. sup., History, p. 17.

mitted to them. Scardona, however, with the other places of the interior, was secured to the Hungarians by the treaty of Prague in 1437, when Venice was confirmed in the possession of the maritime cities. Pressed by the Turks and abandoned by the Hungarians, the Croats offered the city to the Venetians in 1522; but the Republic was unable to undertake its defence, and the inhabitants fled to Sebenico, leaving their city to be occupied by the enemy. In 1537 the Venetians recovered it from the Turks, but afterwards abandoned it, destroying the fortifications before their departure. The Turks were again driven out by Foscolo in 1647, but Scardona was not finally recovered till 1683, and the Venetians were finally secured in their possession by the peace of Carlovitz in 1699. In 1809 Scardona was condemned by the French to be destroyed for having sided with the Austrians, but it was spared on the intervention of Marmont, and allowed to purchase its safety by a penalty of 24,000 ducats.

After such a disastrous history it would be vain to expect any architectural remains at Scardona. It is now a village of 900 inhabitants, and has its industries, among which that of producing silk is important, and a few years ago it was the place chosen for a general Industrial Exhibition of Dalmatian arts and manufactures.

Embarking afresh, we ascended the river for about three-quarters of an hour through a gorge of the mountains if possible still more sterile and white than any we had seen. And lastly, at the end of a long straight avenue of rock, there appeared the loveliest vision imaginable of silver falls set in rich green foliage, and reflected perfectly in the still water. At that distance we could neither hear the roar nor see the movement of the water, which seemed fixed and silent, caught as it were in the act of falling, a picture rather than a reality.

The falls are on a really magnificent scale, reaching in various interrupted cascades all across the valley. The damp mist they throw up has encouraged a luxuriant vegetation, and the whole is embosomed in rich copses, through which there peeps in every direction the silver of numerous smaller cascades leaping down to join the main stream below. The river does not pour over the ledge in one unbroken sheet as at Niagara, but in several independent cascades of various widths, the largest of which cannot be much less than 200 or 250 feet across. The total height of the falls, which are broken into several steps divided by stretches of glassy rapids, is said to be 170 feet. The upper fall is magnificent, formed by two streams falling together at an angle and uniting as they fall, but the lowest fall is perhaps the finest of all, thundering down into a great basin and throwing up clouds of spray, in which we saw a rainbow.

About an hour and a half above the falls is the lake of Vissovaz with a Franciscan convent on an island, and another hour beyond that brings one to the fall of Roncislap, which we were unable to visit. Beyond that again is the Greek convent of S. Arcangelo which we visited subsequently from Knin and Kistagne, and near which are the ruins of the Roman city of Burnum. Higher up, the Kerka washes the impregnable rock of Knin; and seven miles beyond, it issues from its cavern in Monte Dinara, after a subterranean course which we will not attempt to trace.

Returning to Scardona we found a tough repast awaiting us, but even hunger failed to render palatable the wooden fowl whose innocent life had been cut short during our absence at the falls, nor could we make anything of the black beans girkins and garlic in vinegar which a Dalmatian gentleman, our companion, devoured as if they had been potatoes.

As we rowed home in the dusk we induced our Croat boatmen, who were young and shy, to sing to us. Their songs were strange wild melodies in short snatches and a minor key, all pitched very high, but they were not unmusical, and made me not for the first time regret my ignorance of the language.

There is a small village at the falls consisting chiefly of mills worked by water power, which have always been reckoned a valuable possession by the Sebenzani, and form an article in many of their treaties and charters of privileges. They are now turned to excellent account in working a large pumping engine, which raises the fresh water of the river and sends it all the way to Sebenico, thus supplying what an old writer says was the only thing wanting at Sebenico, namely fresh water[1]. The city is now entirely supplied from this source.

[1] *Palladius Fuscus*, A.D. 1540. 'Habent Sibenicenzes arva vinetaque et obliveta feracissima neque ulla re ex iis quas usus postulat nisi aqua dulci indigent. Cujus penuria aestivo praesertim tempore adeo laborant ut aliunde advecta publice vendatur.'

APPENDIX.

Contract with Giorgio Orsini for his services as architect of the cathedral of Sebenico, A.D. 1441. From Monsign. Fosco, as above, vid. p. 98 note.

Die xxii dicti mensis (an. 1441, indictione quarta) actum Sibenici in platea Comunis. Ad bancum ante Cancellariam Comunis coram praefato spectabili et honorabili Jacopo Donato, g. D. comiti et Capitaneo Sibenici et sua Curia; et coram probo Jacobo Nicolini examinatoris Comunis; praesentibus probo Civitaneo Perisicich nobili sibenicensi, et probo Lutiano de Cega de Tragurio habitantibus Sibenici testibus habitis, etc.

Ibique cum licentia, voluntate et consensu Reverendissimi in Christo Patris et D.D. Georgi Sisgorich Dei et Apostolicae Sedis gratia Episcopi Sibenicensis et praefati spectabilis g. D. Comitis et Capitanei Sibenici et ejus Curiae venerabilis vir dominus presbyter Jacobus Zilienich Canonicus Sibenici et probus Michael quondam probi Civitani nobilis Sibenici, tanquam procuratores et procuratorio nomine Ecclesiae Cathedralis et fabricae S. Jacobi de Sibenico per se et successores suos ac nobiles viri probus Radichius Sisgorich Joannes Tobolonich Marcus Dobroevich Simon Dunnich et Saracenus Nicolai cives Sibenici electi et deputati per generale Consilium Nobilium Civium Sibenici ad infrascripta et etiam alia facienda et contrahenda ut apparet parte capita in dicto

Concilio die 23 Mensis Aprilis proxime practeriti etiam nomine et vice fabricae et Ecclesiae predictae ex una parte et providus vir magister Georgius lapicida quondam Mathaei de Jadra habitator Venetiarum ad praesens existens Sibenici ex alia.

In Dei nomine et gloriosae Virginis Mariae et beati Jacobi Apostoli tales conventiones et talia pacta invicem fecerunt et contraxerunt. Quia dictus Magister Georgius promisit et solemniter se obligavit praedictis procuratoribus et nobilibus deputatis nominibus quibus supra stipulantibus venire ad standum et habitandum in Sibenico per totum mensem Augusti proxime futuri pro sex annis continuis incepturis die quo recedet ex Venetiis modo nuper quando ibit Venetias pro sua familia reversurus Sibenicum de quo die sui recessus stabitur simplici verbo ipsius Magistri Georgii. Et cum fuerit Sibenici promisit superesse pro prothomagistro fabricae Ecclesiae Cathedralis praedictae S. Jacobi de Sibenico et in dicta fabrica toto dicto tempore annorum sex facere sollicitare et procurare laborare et laborari facere aliis laboratoribus, omnia et singula laboreria et haedificia necessaria ad ornamentum et fabricam ipsius Ecclesiae et laborare de sua manu tam in fabricando quam in sculpendo ad laudem cujuslibet boni sculptoris et magistri artis lapicidae.

Item promisit ire ad quascumque petrarias in quocumque habili loco positas quotiescumque fuerit opportunum pro dicta fabrica et ibi superesse et facere fieri cum bona diligentia omnia ea quae fuerint necessaria in foditione et conductione lapidum pro dicta fabrica non tam puntando neque scindendo lapides in petraria neque onerando aut exonerando sed faciendo ordinando et laborando alia laboreria utilia et necessaria pro dicta fabrica.

Item promisit quod toto dicto tempore sex annorum non accipiet aliquod aliud laborerium per eum laborandum tam de die quam de nocte sine licentia praedictorum procuratorum et nobilium sive majoris partis eorum.

Item promisit superesse pro prothomagistro et superstante omnibus aliis laboreriis haedificiis magistris operariis et manoalibus dictae Ecclesiae et fabricae et eis dare modum ordinem et mensuras circa laboreria dictae fabricae et eos appuntare in omnibus et singulis eorum defectibus.

Item promisit et pacto convenit quod quandocumque constiterit et apparebit legittime procuratoribus praedictis et nobilibus deputatis ipsum Magistrum Georgium non facere suum debitum circa omnia et singula praedicta quod liceat eis et possint licentiare ipsum Magistrum Georgium ante terminum praedictorum sex annorum ad libitum eorumque voluntatem cum consensu Reverendissimi Episcopi et spectabilis Domini Comitis Sibenici qui pro eo tempore fuerint.

Quae omnia et singula superscripta promisit et ad ea se obligavit dictus Magister Georgius quia versa vice praedicti procuratores et nobiles deputati nominibus quibus supra cum consensu et voluntate ut supra solemniter promiserunt praedicto Magistro praesenti pro se et suis haeredibus et successoribus dare et solvere eidem pro ejus salario mercede et manifactura de denariis Ecclesiae et fabricae praedictae anno singulo ducatos centum quindecim aureos boni et justi ponderis venetos faciendo eidem Magistro Georgio omni mense pagam suam pro rata usque ad complementum dicti termini annorum sex. Et eidem dare habitationem habilem et condecentem in Sibenico pro toto dicto tempore. Et solvere eidem nabulum pro veniendo Sibenicum ejus familia rebus et masseritiis suis . . . .

The contract was renewed for ten years on Sept. 1, 1446, with an addition of five golden ducats to Giorgio's salary. The building however came to a stand, as we have seen, in 1448, and stood still until 1470.

www.ingramcontent.com/pod-product-compliance
Lightning Source LLC
Chambersburg PA
CBHW051857300426
44117CB00006B/431